David C. Parker
Manuscripts, Texts, Theology

Arbeiten zur
Neutestamentlichen Textforschung

Herausgegeben im Auftrag des
Instituts für Neutestamentliche Textforschung der Westfälischen
Wilhelms-Universität Münster/Westfalen

von David C. Parker und Holger Strutwolf

Band 40

Walter de Gruyter · Berlin · New York

David C. Parker

Manuscripts, Texts, Theology

Collected Papers 1977–2007

Walter de Gruyter · Berlin · New York

∞ Printed on acid-free paper which falls within the guidelines
of the ANSI to ensure permanence and durability.

ISBN 978-3-11-048790-9
ISSN 0570-5509

Library of Congress Cataloging-in-Publication Data

A CIP catalogue record for this book is available from the Library of Congress.

Bibliographic information published by the Deutsche Nationalbibliothek

The Deutsche Nationalbibliothek lists this publication in the Deutsche Nationalbibliografie;
detailed bibliographic data are available in the Internet at http://dnb.d-nb.de.

© Copyright 2009 by Walter de Gruyter GmbH & Co. KG, D-10785 Berlin

All rights reserved, including those of translation into foreign languages. No part of this book
may be reproduced in any form or by any means, electronic or mechanical, including photocopy,
recording, or any information storage and retrieval system, without permission in writing from
the publisher.

Cover design: Christopher Schneider, Laufen

Printed in Germany

Contents

Places of Original Publication VII
Abbreviations and Commonly Cited Works IX

Introduction 1

I. Manuscripts

1. A Dictation Theory of Codex Bezae 5
2. A Copy of the Codex Mediolanensis 19
3. Unequally Yoked: the Present State of the Codex Bobbiensis .. 25
4. The Majuscule Manuscripts of the New Testament 33
5. Was Matthew Written Before 50 CE? The Magdalen Papyrus
   of Matthew 55
6. Codex Bezae and other Greek New Testament Manuscripts
   in Cambridge University Library 65
7. A New Oxyrhynchus Papyrus of Revelation:
   P115 (P. Oxy. 4499) 73
8. Some New Manuscripts of the Greek New Testament
   in Boston and Cambridge (with M.B. Morrill) 93
9. Codex Bezae: The Manuscript as Past, Present and Future ... 103
10. The Date of Codex Zacynthius (Ξ): A New Proposal 113
11. Manuscripts of John's Gospel with *Hermeneiai* 121
12. Greek Gospel Manuscripts in Bucharest and Sofia 139

II. Textual Criticism

13. The Development of Textual Criticism since B.H. Streeter 151
14. The Translation of ΟΥΝ in the Old Latin Gospels 167
15. *The Principles and Practice of New Testament Textual Criticism*:
    Collected Essays of G.D. Kilpatrick. A Review 197

16. The Development of the Critical Text of the Epistle of James. From Lachmann to the *Editio Critica Maior* 203
17. A Comparison between the *Text und Textwert* and the Claremont Profile Method Analyses of Manuscripts in the Gospel of Luke 217
18. The Quest of the Critical Edition 253

III. Textual Criticism and Theology

19. Scripture is Tradition 265
20. The Early Tradition of Jesus' Sayings on Divorce 273
21. Through a Screen Darkly: Digital Texts and the New Testament 287
22. Jesus in Textual Criticism 305
23. *Et Incarnatus Est* 311
24. Textual Criticism and Theology 323
25. Calvin's Biblical Text 335

Indexes

Index of Manuscripts 355
Index of Biblical Citations 360
Index of Names and Subjects 370

Places of Original Publication

1. *Journal for the Study of the New Testament* 15 (1982), 97–112.
2. *Journal of Theological Studies* 41 (1990), 537–41.
3. *Journal of Theological Studies* 42 (1991), 581–8.
4. *The Text of the New Testament in Contemporary Research. Essays on the Status Quaestionis* (Festschrift for B.M. Metzger), ed. B.D. Ehrman and M.W. Holmes, Grand Rapids, Eerdmans 1995, 22–42.
5. *The Expository Times* 107 (November, 1995), 40–3.
6. *Cambridge University Library. The Great Collections*, ed. P. Fox, Cambridge, University Press 1998, 33–43.
7. *New Testament Studies* 46 (2000), 159–74.
8. *Harvard Theological Review* 95 (2002), 237–44.
9. *The Bible as Book. The Transmission of the Greek Text*, ed. S. McKendrick and O. O'Sullivan, London and New Castle DE, 2003, 43–50. [Reproduced by kind permission of the British Library and Oak Knoll Press]
10. *Journal of Theological Studies* 55 (2004), 117–22, 30–31.
11. *Transmission and Reception: New Testament Text-critical and Exegetical Studies*, ed. J.W. Childers, (TS 4), Piscataway, Gorgias Press 2006, 48-68.
12. *Bulletin of the John Rylands University Library* 85 (2003), 3–12.
13. *New Testament Studies* 24 (1977), 149–62.
14. *New Testament Studies* 31 (1985), 252–76.
15. *Journal of Theological Studies* 43 (1992), 210–14.
16. *New Testament Textual Criticism and Exegesis. Festschrift J. Delobel*, ed. A. Denaux (BETL 161), Leuven, Peeters Press 2002, 317–30.
17. *New Testament Studies* 49 (2003), 108–38.

18. *Variants* 1 (2002), 33–42.

19. *Theology* 94 (1991), 11–17.

20. *Theology* 96 (1993), 372–83.

21. *Journal for the Study of the New Testament* 25 (2003), 395–411.

22. *Jesus in History, Thought, and Culture. An Encyclopaedia*, ed. J.L. Houlden, 2 vols., Santa Barbara, Denver and Oxford, ABC-CLIO 2003, Vol. 2, 836–41.

23. *Scottish Journal of Theology* 54 (2001), 330–43.

24. *The Expository Times* 118 (2007), 583–9.

25. I. Calvini *Commentarius in Epistolam Pauli ad Romanos* (Ioannis Calvini Opera Omnia denuo recognita et adnotatione critica instructa notique illustrata, Series II Opera exegetica Veteris et Novi Testamenti), ed. T.H.L. Parker and D.C. Parker, Geneva, Librairie Droz 1999, XXXII–LI.

Abbreviations and Commonly Cited Works

Aland and Aland, *Text*[1]	B. and K. Aland, *The Text of the New Testament. An Introduction to the Critical Editions and to the Theory and Practice of Modern Textual Criticism*, trans. E.F. Rhodes, Grand Rapids and Leiden, 1987
Aland and Aland, *Text*[2]	B. and K. Aland, *The Text of the New Testament. An Introduction to the Critical Editions and to the Theory and Practice of Modern Textual Criticism*, trans. E.F. Rhodes, 2nd ed., Grand Rapids and Leiden, 1989
AnBib	*Analecta biblica*
ANRW	Aufstieg und Niedergang der römischen Welt
ANTT	Arbeiten zur neutestamentlichen Textforschung
ANTT 5	K. Aland (ed.), *Die Älten Übersetzungen des Neuen Testaments, die Kirchenväterzitate und Lektionare*, Arbeiten zur neutestamentlichen Textforschung 5, Berlin and New York, 1972
APF	*Archiv für Papyrusforschung*
BBC	*Bulletin of the Bezan Club*
BETL	Bibliotheca ephemeridum theologicarum lovaniensium, Leuven
BJRL	*Bulletin of the John Rylands Library*
Cavallo, *Ricerche*	G. Cavallo, *Ricerche sulla maiuscola biblica*, Studi e testi di papirologia 2, Florence, 1967
Cavallo and Maehler, *Greek Bookhands*	G. Cavallo and H. Maehler, *Greek Bookhands of the Early Byzantine Period A.D. 300–800*, University of London Institute of Classical Studies Bulletin Supplement 47, London, 1987
CHB	Cambridge History of the Bible

Editio Critica Maior	B. Aland, K. Aland, G. Mink, K. Wachtel (eds.), *Novum Testamentum Graecum Editio Critica Maior*. IV *Die Katholischen Briefe*, Stuttgart, 1997–
Ehrman and Holmes, *Contemporary Research*	B.D. Ehrman and M.W. Holmes (eds.), *The Text of the New Testament in Contemporary Research. Essays on the* Status Quaestionis. *A Volume in Honor of Bruce M. Metzger* (SD 46), Grand Rapids, 1995
GLB	Aus der Geschichte der lateinischen Bibel, Freiburg
HTR	*Harvard Theological Review*
JBL	*Journal of Biblical Literature*
JSNT	*Journal for the Study of the New Testament*
JTS	*Journal of Theological Studies*
Jülicher, *Itala*	A. Jülicher (ed.), revd. W. Matzkow† and K. Aland, *Itala. Das Neue Testament in altlateinischer Überlieferung nach den Handschriften*, 1. *Matthäusevangelium*, Berlin and New York, 2nd ed., 1972; 2. *Marcusevangelium*, Berlin, 2nd ed., 1970; 3. *Lucasevangelium*, 2nd ed., Berlin and New York, 1976; 4. *Johannesevangelium*, Berlin, 1963
Legg, *Mark*	S.C.E. Legg, *Nouum Testamentum Graece secundum textum Westcotto-Hortianum. Euangelium secundum Marcum*, Oxford, 1935
Legg, *Matthew*	S.C.E. Legg, *Nouum Testamentum Graece secundum textum Westcotto-Hortianum. Euangelium secundum Matthaeum*, Oxford, 1940
Liste	K. Aland, *Kurzgefasste Liste der griechischen Handschriften des Neuen Testaments*, ANTT 1, 2nd ed., Berlin, 1994
Liste[1]	K. Aland, *Kurzgefaßte Liste der griechischen Handschriften des Neuen Testaments*, ANTT 1, Berlin, 1963
Lowe, *Codices Latini Antiquiores*	E.A. Lowe, *Codices Latini Antiquiores. A Palaeographical Guide to Latin Manuscripts Prior*

Abbreviations and Commonly Cited Works XI

	to the Ninth Century, 11 vols. + supplement, Oxford, 1934–71
Martini, *Il problema del codice B*	C.M. Martini, *Il problema della recensionalità del codice B alla luce del papiro Bodmer XIV*, AnBib 26, 1966
Metzger, *Text of the New Testament*[2]	
	B.M. Metzger, *The Text of the New Testament: Its Transmission, Corruption, and Restoration*, 2nd ed., Oxford, 1968
Metzger, *Text of the New Testament*[3]	
	B.M. Metzger, *The Text of the New Testament: Its Transmission, Corruption, and Restoration*, 3rd ed., New York and Oxford, 1992
Metzger, *Textual Commentary*[1]	B.M. Metzger, *A Textual Commentary on the Greek New Testament: A Companion Volume to the United Bible Societies' Greek New Testament (third edition)*, London and New York, 1971
Metzger, *Textual Commentary*[2]	B.M. Metzger, *A Textual Commentary on the Greek New Testament: A Companion Volume to the United Bible Societies' Greek New Testament (fourth rev. edition)*, 2nd ed., Stuttgart and New York, 1994
Metzger, *Early Versions*	B.M. Metzger, *The Early Versions of the New Testament*, Oxford, 1977
Milne and Skeat, *Scribes and Correctors of the Codex Sinaiticus*	
	H.J.M. Milne and T.C. Skeat, *Scribes and Correctors of the Codex Sinaiticus, including contributions by Douglas Cockerell*, London, 1938
Münster *Bericht*	*Bericht der Hermann Kunst-Stiftung zur Förderung der neutestamentlichen Textforschung*, Münster
Nestle-Aland[26]	*Nestle-Aland. Novum Testamentum Graece* ... ed. K. Aland, M. Black, C.M. Martini, B.M. Metzger, A. Wikgren, Deutsche Bibelgesellschaft Stuttgart, 1979, 9th printing 1987
Nestle-Aland[27]	*Nestle-Aland. Novum Testamentum Graece*, ed. B. and K. Aland, J. Karavidopoulos, C.M. Martini, B.M. Metzger, 27th ed., 8th (revised) impression, Stuttgart, 2001

NovT	*Novum Testamentum*
NovT Suppl	Supplements to Novum Testamentum
NTS	*New Testament Studies*
NTTS	New Testament Tools and Studies
Parker, *Codex Bezae*	D.C. Parker, *Codex Bezae. An Early Christian Manuscript and its Text*, Cambridge, 1992
Parker, *The Living Text of the Gospels*	
	D.C. Parker, *The Living Text of the Gospels*, Cambridge, 1997
Parker and Amphoux, *Codex Bezae*	
	D.C. Parker and C.-B. Amphoux (eds.), *Codex Bezae. Studies from the Lunel Colloquium June 1994*, New Testament Tools and Studies 22, Leiden, 1996.
PBA	*Proceedings of the British Academy*
SD	Studies and Documents
SJT	*Scottish Journal of Theology*
SNTSMS	Society for New Testament Studies Monograph Series
TU	Texte und Untersuchungen
UBS[1, 2, 3 or 4]	*The Greek New Testament*, ed. K. Aland, M. Black, C.M. Martini, B.M. Metzger, and A. Wikgren (1st ed. 1966, 2nd ed. 1968, 3rd ed. 1975, 4th ed. 1983)
Westcott and Hort	B.F. Westcott and F.J.A. Hort, *The New Testament in the Original Greek*, 2 vols., London, 1881
ZNW	*Zeitschrift für neutestamentliche Wissenschaft*
Zuntz, *The Text of the Epistles*	G. Zuntz, *The Text of the Epistles. A Disquisition upon the Corpus Paulinum* (The Schweich Lectures of the British Academy 1946), London, 1953

Introduction

Thirty years after my first published article seemed a good time to publish a collection of them. In doing so, I do not have a lot to say by way of either preamble or discussion.

I have edited very lightly, seeking standardisation in presentational matters such as always using footnotes even when the original article had endnotes. Footnote styles have been standardised. The original page numeration is given in the margin. Obvious errors are corrected. Sometimes the style of an article was quite heavily revised by an editor. Some such revisions I have adopted, others I dislike, while sometimes I have adopted a fresh wording, so these versions are not necessarily identical with their originals. Only nothing of substance has been changed.

The collection is divided into three sections, and the articles within each are in chronological order. These sections reflect three broad areas: studies of Greek and Latin manuscripts, textual criticism, and the contribution of philology to theology.

I have occasionally added brief notes at the end of articles. They offer some information about the contribution, where I think it useful to make it more intelligible to the reader. Sometimes I have corrected a matter on which I now know I was inadequately informed, sometimes I have commented on things with which I no longer agree. But often I have left the article to stand with no further comment.

David Parker
Institute for Textual Criticism and Electronic Editing
University of Birmingham
May 2008

I. MANUSCRIPTS

1 A Dictation Theory of Codex Bezae

In an article in the sixth number of this periodical, Professor Sheldon MacKenzie analysed a number of 'phonological errors' in the Latin column of the Bezan text of Acts. He concluded that this column, 'as we have it today, originated in a center where the scribe wrote under the guidance of a dictator... These errors are older than the fuller readings and are unaffected by them'.[1] It is not possible to agree with this conclusion. In explaining why not, I shall first discuss his main argument by studying the examples he gives, and then offering some further views. Next I shall turn to his opinion about the fuller readings, and finally look briefly at the relevance of what he has written to the study of the Greek text of the manuscript.

Professor MacKenzie states that there are in Codex Bezae errors which are the result of a scribe writing a word according to the pronunciation current in his day, and that such pronunciation was that of a dictator, not of the scribe as he repeated the word to himself while writing.

In all, he gives sixty-nine examples of such errors. Many more could be found. In the majority of these examples, however, it can be shown that the cause of error was not the mishearing of a word. There are five categories into which they may be divided.

1. Errors that do not exist.
2. Errors of such frequency in Latin manuscripts that they prove nothing.
3. Errors of paraplepsis and assimilation to the context.
4. The writing of one word for another.
5. Errors not to be explained in any of these four ways.

In discussing each reading, I will give the biblical reference, the folio and line numbers in the manuscript (for easy consultation of the facsimile or the codex), the error, and the page number in Professor MacKenzie's article. Readings of D/d are in uncial.

[98]

---

1 'The Latin Column in Codex Bezae', *JSNT* 6 (1980), 58–76, 60.

1. There are two places where I am not convinced that an error exists.

17.19 F 489, l. 5: COGITANTES for *rogitantes* (p. 68).
The emendation was suggested by J.R. Harris.[2] Although the rendering of πυνθάνομαι by *cogito* is not attested elsewhere in the codex, or in either Jülicher's *Itala* or Wordsworth and White's *Actus Apostolorum*, I would prefer a slight discrepancy between the Greek and Latin to the unusual word *rogito*.[3] As a matter of fact, d elsewhere always translates πυνθάνομαι by *interrogo*.

20.23 F 502, l. 4: MI for *mihi* (p. 71).
Under the influence of the Greek μένω, *maneo* takes the dative (in another use of the word) at Acts 5.4. Unfortunately the only comparable use of the verb in the codex is at Ac 20.5, where EMENON AYTON is translated as EXPECTABANT NOS. But a comparison with the way in which *adoro* can take either accusative or dative, under the influence of προσκυνέω will show that the dative is by no means impossible here. Although MIHI appears everywhere else in d, MI is not out of the question. It is used, equally out of the blue, by the Vulgate manuscript V at Mt 26.15.

Reflection on the following three categories will be aided by James Willis, *Latin Textual Criticism*,[4] especially by Part II. This author is concerned with the restoration of the text, and not with questions of book production, and his manuscripts are much later than ours. But he is discussing errors of a similar type, in manuscripts which, just because of their date, were quite certainly copied without a dictator.

2. The next class of error is one of so-called spelling mistakes, which are all to a greater or lesser extent widespread in Latin manuscripts. They were perhaps unimportant to all but the more punctilious scribes. I include here those readings listed by Professor MacKenzie, which are either regular in Codex Bezae, or that I have noted in other manuscripts. The comparison of the manuscript which we are discussing with, for example, one copied in Spain in the ninth century, is of value because there is no close connection between them; that is, an agreement between them will have no particular significance for either.

The widely read will without doubt be able to add many examples that they have noted, to the few that are given here.

---

2   *A Study of Codex Bezae*, Texts and Studies 2.1, 1891, 79.
3   *Vide* Lewis and Short, *A Latin Dictionary*.
4   Illinois, 1972.

1.14   F 417, l. 29: PERSEBERANTES (p. 69).
3.8   F 425, l. 10: VASES for *bases* (p. 69).
This confusion is remarkably widespread,[5] and instances in d alone make a long list.

1.22   F 418, l. 29: USQUAE (p. 72).
USQUAE occurs also at Mt 11.23; 23.35; Lk 11.50, 51; Acts 13.6, 31, 47; 20.4, 11. USQUE is written sixty-seven times. The variant is common enough to be an alternative spelling.

2.19   F 421, l. 11: SUSUM (p. 69).
The word only comes again at Jn 11.41: SUSUM d l p r¹ E: *sursum* ff² Vg^cet. Note also that *desursum* is *desusum* at its two appearances: at Lk 1.3 only d has the word; at Jn 3.31 it is read with b e l q r¹ E (E repeats *desusum* later in the verse).

3.7   F 425, l. 7: ADPRAEHENSUM (p. 72).
This reading is shared with five Vulgate Manuscripts; C F G Θ render *adpraehensa,* and U *appraehensa*. ADPRE- occurs only five times in d (three of these in Acts); ADPRAE- is used twenty-six times (seven in Acts). The latter thus has a claim to be the standard spelling.

4.6   F 428, l. 2: QUODQUOD for *quotquot* (p. 64).
C F* I S T have the same reading here. Consistency on this word certainly does not exist in d, and might be hard to find in any manuscript

4.11   F 428, l. 21: CAPUD (p. 65).
16.12 F 482, l. 22: CAPUD (p. 65).
The same error occurs elsewhere in the codex: Mt 27.39; Jn 20.7 (with e W Y Δ), 12 (with e B Δ O T W Y); Mk 6.28 (with E L R Y; e is lacking).

5.9   F 432, l. 11: TEPTARE for *temptare* (p. 63).

d also has Mt 19.3 TEPTANTES, and 22.18 TEPTATIS. In Wordsworth and White may be found:
    Lk   4.12: *teptabis* K
              10.25: *teptans* K
              11.16: *teptans* R

10.43 F 459, l. 10: PERIBENT for *perhibent* (p. 61).
The reading is shared with the Vulgate Manuscripts C R T.

11.5   F 460, l. 17: QUODAM for *quoddam* (p. 66).

---

5   Willis, *op. cit.*, 58.

18.23   F 493, l. 24: QUODAM (p. 66).
Note the following other readings:
   Mt 13.23: QUODAM for *quoddam*.
   Lk 10.38: QUODDAM with all Latin manuscripts except a e.
   Ac 10.11: QUODAM with I S.
      11.5: QUODAM with I.
      18.23: QUODAM.

13.19   F 468, l. 32: SEPTE for *septem* (p. 63).
The error occurs also at Mt 16.10; Mk 8.5. I have noted it at Acts 20.6 in C.

21.18   F 506, l. 1: PRAESBYTERI (p. 72).
PRES- comes twelve times in d (ten are in Acts). PRAES- comes four times (thrice in Acts), The same error is made in the Vulgate (where the word is much rarer), at Ac 14.23 (B F Θ K V) and 15.2 (B F G Θ K V). This, USQUAE and ADPRAEHENSUM are just three examples of a common confusion. Codex Cavensis consistently writes *senior* (used by the Vulgate instead of *presbyter*) as *saenior* (I have noted Lk 20.1; Jn 8.9; Acts 11.30; 15.4, 22; 16.4). Aecclesia for *ecclesia* is very widespread in the Vulgate, as just one other example.

3. The third group of readings is the largest one. It consists of those errors caused by the context, when a word, syllable or ending caught the scribe's eye, or stuck in his mind, and made him mistake the word that he was writing. Some of these errors are those correctly to be described as perseveration or anticipation.[6] These examples provide the most concrete evidence for visual copying to be gained from such errors; I will return to this point, which some would dispute, later.

[101]   1.11   F417, l. 11: QUI for *quid* (p. 66).
The reading is shared with t. It may be explained by QUI in line 10, or else the scribes may have mistaken the construction.

2.6   F419, l. 31: QUIAUDIEBIANT (p. 73).
This is an error of haplography, the omission of an *a*. Professor MacKenzie makes the suggestion that the Greek has been corrected to the Latin. If that were the case, one wonders why the Greek did not become οἳ ἤκουον, or ἀκούσαντες or ὅτι ἤκουον. The Greek may be a variant reading, but it does not agree with the Latin.

---

6   Willis, *op. cit.*, 92–7, 98f.

2.15   F420, l. 32: HEBRII for *ebrii* (p. 62).
The previous word is HII (with B C D I O R S T W), as Professor MacKenzie notes. The source of error is either in this or, possibly, in the scribe having at the back of his mind the knowledge that the apostles were Hebrews.

3.24   F 427, l. 6: OMNIS for *omnes* (p. 70f).
OMNIS is written in line 4. IS in DISPERIBIT is directly above in line 5.

4.15   F 428, l. 33: HABIRE for *abire* (p. 61).
HABEBANT in line 32 explains the mistake.

5.5   F 431, l. 31: AUDIES for *audiens* (p. 66f).
ES in line 30 stands immediately above the error. It should, however, be added that at Mt 25.11 we have DICETES for *dicentes* (here the scribe was preoccupied with getting his letters into a little space), and at Lk 12.16 DICES for *dicens*, where there is no obvious reason for the error.

5.13   F 432, l. 28: POPULOS for *populus* (p. 73).
The preceding word is EOS. This error is shared with t G.

5.17   F 433, l. 11: AEPULATIONEM for *aemu-* (p. 64).
One may point to INPLETI SUNT standing before it, and to ΕΠΛΗCΘΗCAN in the Greek.

5.24   F 434, l. 3: PONTEFICES for *ponti-* (p. 71).
TEMPLI earlier in the same line could conceivably have caused the error. But, given the mistakes PONTEFEX at 4.6 (p. 71) and PONTEFIX at 5.27, one may conclude that the scribe was not very good at spelling this word.

5.36   F 435, l. 13: QUAGRIGENTORUM (p. 66).
Experiment will show the reader that this is not an easy word to speak aloud and to write down at the same time; the scribe's pen ran ahead of his ear.

5.38   F 435, l. 27: HOPUS (p. 61).
The following word is HOC (and note HOMINIBUS in line 26). But the confusion of aspiration in the manuscripts is very common – Codex Cavensis makes the same mistake here, and seems in general to add an *h* if in doubt (e.g. *husque* consistently). This error is comparatively rare in d.

[102]

7.10   F 439, l. 16: REGAE for *rege* (p. 72).
The next word is AEGYPTI. But see Professor MacKenzie's footnote,[7] and what has already been noted about PRAESBYTERI etc.

10.9   F 455, l. 19: HORABIT for *orabit* (p. 61).
HORA in the same line explains this.

11.11   F 461, l. 3: ERANT for *eramus* (p. 62).
The text should read ERAMUS for the Greek HMEN (with P[74] ℵ A B D[Gr] it[a r]), and not the *eram* suggested by Professor MacKenzie, which would be a translation of the corrupt ἤμην of the TR. It is probable that the TRES VIRI/ SUPERVENERUNT in lines 1–2 confused the scribe as to person.

11.22   F 462, l. 12: BARNABANT (p. 62f).
I doubt if, in this manuscript tradition, the word here ever had the ending -*am*. BARNABAM comes at 13.50; 15.12; but BARNABAN at 13.2, 7, 43; 14.12, 20; 15.36. It is more likely that the previous word, MISERUNT, has influenced BARNABAN.

12.16   F 465, l. 15: EUNT for *eum* (p. 63).
The previous word is VIDERUNT, the next but one OBSTUPUERUNT.

13.8   F 467, l. 22: PROCONSOLEM (p. 73).

19.38   F 499, l. 7: PROCONSOLES (p. 73).

The first two *o*'s in the word may have caused the error. PROCONSOL comes at 18.12. The analogy with *pontefex* is interesting, and suggests a trait in the copyist rather than a phonological mistake. Since *proconsul* is only twice spelt correctly (13.7, 12), the reader may prefer to consider this mistake to be an acceptable spelling for the age, or else the word to be another one of which the scribe was unsure.

13.10   F 467, l.28: INIMICAE for *inimice* (p. 72).
IUSTITIAE later in the line caused this. Note how at the end of line 27 DIABOLE stands for *diaboli*, in anticipation of *inimice*. In the Vulgate manuscripts O S, on the other hand, we have *inimici* by perseveration of *diaboli*.

13.42   F 471, l. 20: PROGREGIENTIBUS (p. 66)
Like QUADRIGENTORUM, this is a word to stumble over. The scribe has persevered with the guttural.

---

7   N. 37, 72, quoting R.C. Stone, *The Language of the Latin Text of Codex Bezae*, Illinois, 1946, 18.

15. 17   F 478, l. 21: ET EXQUIRAM for *ut exquirant* (p. 63).
The cause of this error is the preceding list of future first person singulars in lines 17–20: CONVERTAR ... AEDIFICABO ... AEDIFICABO ... ERIGAM. *ut exquirant* became ET EXQUIRAM by perseveration. The slip was made easier by the fact that *exquiram* is the first person singular of both the tenses involved.

16.19   F483, l. 24: ISPES (p. 72, n. 40).
Could VIDISSENT, directly above in line 23, be the cause?

16.20   F 483, l. 30: PERTURBAM for *perturbant* (p. 63).
The following words are NOSTRAM CIVITATEM.

17.11   F 487, l. 31: EXANIMANTES for *examin-* (p. 68).
ANIMATIONE stands in line 30.

19.8   F 495, l. 11: TRENS (p. 67).
The following word is MENSES. Note also PERSUADENS in line 12.

19.37   F 499, l. 1: HOC for *huc* (p. 74).   [104]
The two preceding words are VIROS ISTOS. The similarity of pronunciation that is noted would have made this slip an easy one.

21.21   F 506, l. 10: DOCENS for *doces* (p. 67).
doces is read by e Aug, *doceas* by the Vulgate. The previous word is ABSCENSIONEM; it may be noted that DICENS is omitted at the end of line 11 (as is ΛΕΓΩΝ in the Greek). It probably stood in the exemplar and contributed to this error. There is also GENTIBUS in line 11. If it is accepted that *doces* was the reading in the exemplar, then this error is the reverse of that at 5.5.

4. In the fourth group of readings, one word has been substituted for another, or at least the form of one word has influenced that of another. This is a trick of the mind possible after either hearing or reading a word.[8]

2.46   F 424, l. 13: CAPIEBANT for *carpebant* (p. 69).
At first I was unconvinced that CAPIEBANT was in error for *carpebant*. But I grant it, as an error of this type.

---

8   Willis, *op. cit.*, 74–86.

4.3   F 427, l. 25: ADSERTIONEM for *adservationem* (p. 70).
The omission of a syllable was an easy mistake. Professor MacKenzie does not claim this as a dictation error. In fact the only attestation for *adservatio* mentioned by Souter[9] is here and at 5.18 in d, the two places where ΤΗΡΗΣΙΣ occurs.

7.20   F 440, l. 15: ELIGANS for *elegans* (p. 71).

7.32   F 441, l. 25: AUDIEBAT for *audebat* (p. 73).

7.46   F 443, l. 19: REFERIT for *reperit* (p. 64).

10.34   F 458, l. 11: EXPEDIOR for *experior* (p. 68).
Experior occurs nowhere else in d, while *expedio* is to be found correctly in eight places; it was a rather more familiar word.

11. 23   F 462, l. 16: ADORABANTUR for *adhortabatur* (p. 61).
Adhortor never does come in d, having been foiled here, while *adoro* is used twenty-nine times in all. Compare Cicero, *Arch.* II. 28.

12.6   F 463, l. 30: PRODOCERE for *producere* (p. 73).

19.19   F 496, l. 29: DOCENTA for *ducenta* (p. 74).

15.12   F 478, l. 4: DESPONENTES for *despondentes* (p. 66). A half-adopted recollection of *dispono*.

15.29   F 480, l. 3: CONVERSANTES for *conservantes* (p. 70).
s.m. corrected to *convertantes*, a common word in Acts, but one used to translate στρέφω and its compounds, with two exceptions.[10] The other two appearances of *conservo* (Lk 2.19 for συντηρέω and 2.51 for διατηρέω) make it clear that it is the right reading here.[11]

17.12   F 488, l. 4: PLERES for *plures* (p. 71), or *pleri*.
This is the only place in d where ἱκανός is translated by *pleres/plures*. It is also conceivable therefore that *pleri* has become *pleres*, partly by confusion with *plures*, partly because of the -EC endings in the Greek. There is no means of ascertaining by comparison which is the more probable.

5. The fact that we are now left with only fourteen of the examples that he gives, does not destroy Professor MacKenzie's theory. One clear example,

---

9   *A Glossary of Later Latin to 600 A.D.*, Oxford, 1949.
10 The exceptions are Jn 11.38 (IRA CONVERSUS for ENBPEIMΩMENOC) and Acts12.11 (for ΓENOMENOC).
11 Compare the confusion of *versantur* and *servantur* in the printed text of Macrobius (Willis, *op. cit.*, 81f).

which could be explained in no other way, would suffice for him. But, if we here list the remaining fourteen, the reader will be able to decide for himself whether such a decisive proof is to be found among them.

Aspirate *h:*	21.20 F 506, l. 8: HEMULATORES (and note HEMULATI at 7.9) (p. 62).
m in words containing *p*:	17.5 F 487, l. 5. ADSUPTIS for *adsumptis* (p. 63).
Substitution of *p* for *m*:	13.34 F 470, l. 25 PORTUIS (p. 64).
The consonant *t* (p. 65):	7.54 F 444, l. 9 DENDIBUS.
	20.23 F 502, l. 4 MANEN.
The consonant *n* (p. 67):	2.40 F 423, l. 27 HANC for *hac*.
	7.15 F 439, l. 33 DEFUCTUS for *defunctus*.
	14.19 F 475, l. 12 ISTIGASSET.
	18.22 F 493, l. 22 ASCEDISSET.
The consonant *r*:	16.6 F 482, l. 1 PHYGIAM (p. 69).
i for *e*:	2.4 F 419 l. 24 COIPERUNT (p. 70).
e for *i*:	4.6 F 427, l. 33 PONTEFEX (p. 71). Cf. p. 101 [9] above.
Other errors with *i*:	3.16 F 426, l. 13 CONSOLDAVIT (p. 73).
	4.17 F 429, l. 7 SERPIAT (p. 72f).

These remaining examples are of two types. All but four are shown by reference to Stone[12] to be frequent in Late Latin. That they may be words written as they were pronounced at the time, nobody will be in a hurry to deny. But that they are to be ascribed to the quasi-romantic accent of a dictator remains to be proved. Once R.C. Stone has been consulted, we are left with the words PORTUIS, PHYGIAM, COIPERUNT, and CONSOLDAVIT. These cannot be used to prove any theory. They serve only to remind us that scribes periodically made silly and unreasonable mistakes.

Now that the examples have been studied, it is necessary to enquire what we have learned.

The examples do not give any proof of a stage of dictation in the tradition behind Codex Bezae. This negative conclusion is of little value unless we can establish with confidence that there is evidence for visual copying. But in fact we cannot use these examples at all in making statements about the tradition of the manuscript's ancestors. There are two reasons why these errors must be, for the most part, by the scribe of the codex itself, or by an immediate predecessor.

First, it is improbable that most of these accidental slips would last long in a tradition, certainly in such numbers: they would be either easily

---

12 *Op. cit.*, especially 17–23.

corrected, or falsely emended. We cannot expect a group of them to be perfectly preserved, as it were fossilised, through a succession of copyings.

Second, a great many of these errors were corrected by the hand called *G*. He confined himself chiefly to correcting the errors – and generally the more obvious ones – of the scribe. This may be seen by looking at almost any page of the first Gospel. In Acts, he corrected in Ff 416–428. Eighteen of Professor MacKenzie's examples appear on these pages, and ten of them were corrected by *G*:

1.11:	QUI to QUID.
1.14:	PERSEBERANTES to PERSEVERANTES.
1.22:	USQUAE to USQUE.
2.4 :	COIPERUNT to COEPERUNT.
2.15:	HII to HI.
2.40:	HANC to HAC.
3.8 :	VASES to BASES.
4.3 :	ADSERTIONEM to ADSERVATIONEM.
4.6 :	PONTEFEX to PONTIFEX.
4.15:	HABIRE to ABIRE.

He failed to correct:

2.6 :	QUIAUDIEBANT (this was emended by the hand called *K*).
2.19:	SUSUM.
2.46:	CAPIEBANT.
3.7 :	ADPRAEHENSUM.
3.16:	CONSOLDAVIT.
3.24:	OMNIS.
4.6 :	QUODQUOD.
4.11:	CAPUD.

Of these eight, three at any rate 'looked right' as words (2.6, 46; 3.24), and four were spelling errors that he may have regarded as acceptable. The remaining one (3.16) is a testimony to his imperfection as a corrector.

For these two reasons it must be stated that at least the majority of the errors that we are discussing were made by the scribe of Codex Bezae, and cannot be referred to an earlier period in the history of the text. The only singular errors which are demonstrably older than the existing manuscript, it may be laid down as a general rule, are those in which the corruption can be shown to have more than one stage, and those in which one column has influenced the other; those errors which make sense of some kind can be of any age.

It would be easy to proceed to the conclusion that the manuscript was copied visually. But, as I have said, we have only reached the stage of saying that there is no evidence for copying by dictation. Can it definitely be said that Codex Bezae was copied visually? The influence of the context on the scribe is evidence in favour of it. To substantiate this would need a wider canvas, one on which the entire method by which Codex Bezae was produced would have to be described. I will here restrict myself to more general observations.

[108]

Dr C.H. Roberts, writing in *The Cambridge History of the Bible*,[13] considers the use of dictation in the earliest church to have been improbable, first because in Judaism the practice was forbidden, second because the variety of hands in the earliest Christian papyri indicates that there were no central *scriptoria*. It is, he writes, to the work of Origen and the Alexandrian Catechetical School that the introduction of specialised book production in the church is due. One could add that, when the uncertainty of the times is considered, it may be supposed to have been only after the accession of Constantine that such ventures became a permanent feature of Christianity, Even then, there is no reason for believing the use of dictation to have been widespread. Codex Bezae, with its 'provincial look',[14] and with no regular *diorthotes*, is more likely to have been produced to meet the need of a local congregation than as a commercial production. This is to assume that a dictator was used only for the production of more than one volume at a time. Commercially, this must surely have been the case. But it would be arbitrary to say that collaboration between dictator and copyist never occurred in the production of unique books. Indeed, T.C. Skeat gave an interesting example of such a partnership.[15] But it may be significant that this collaboration was in the collation of one manuscript with another, not in the production of a new one.[16]

The circumstances surrounding the creation of Codex Bezae, then, are also favourable to the belief that it was copied visually. Skeat considered such evidence to be important in determining by which means a manuscript was produced, and he isolated two other factors that might indicate the use of a dictator. The more certain of these was the existence of errors that may be ascribed to a lack of liaison between dictator and scribe. Perhaps the best example of what he means is the

---

13 CHB, Vol. 1, Chapter 4, 49f, 65.
14 Lowe, *Codices Latini Antiquores*, Part 2, London, 1972, Entry 140.
15 'The Use of Dictation in Ancient Book-Production', PBA 42 (1956), 179–208.
16 Criticism of the theory that dictation was common is most clearly expressed by A. Dain, *Les Manuscrits*, 3rd edition, Paris, 1975, 20–2.

Η Ϲ Η ⊢ of the Sinaiticus at 1 Macc 5.20, where the dictator may have been unable to read the exemplar, and therefore rashly said ἢ ἐξ ἢ τρισχίλιοι.¹⁷ His second criterion was the existence of a large number of singular errors. But since most of these errors will be of a neutral kind, they may equally be ascribed to a bad copyist. Although Professor E.G. Turner mentions the ambiguity of the evidence of the manuscripts,¹⁸ I must confess to be somewhat sceptical towards the conclusion that all errors of parablepsis are equally attributable to either manner of copying. Errors of pronunciation are more certainly ambiguous; the statement that a copyist always repeated aloud his text has not been challenged.¹⁹

Until evidence can be produced that shows unambiguously that a dictator was used, it must be allowed that Codex Bezae was copied visually. In the light of what has been said here, it is very improbable that such evidence is there to be found.

Since the errors in question are the work of the scribe of d, then Professor MacKenzie's statement that the longer readings are free from them might be extremely hard to explain. The fact might be a matter of chance, since sixty-nine errors in ninety-two pages is not very many. But actually the longer readings are not free from errors of this kind. I will prove this point, about which there is no doubt, in a wholly arbitrary way.

If one goes through Clark's edition of the Greek text of Acts, in which the longer readings are conveniently given in heavy type, referring to the Latin on each occasion, the following typical errors appear in chapters 1–6.

1.5	F 416,	1.22:	PENTECOSTEN.
2.30	F 422,	1.22:	SECUNDUM CARNE.
5.15	F 433,	1.1:	LIVERABANTUR.
		1.2:	AB OMNEM VALITUDINEM.
5.18		1.14:	ABIERUNT UNUSQUISQUE IN DOMICILIA.
6.1	F 436,	1.16:	HAEBREORUM (cp. line 13, AEBRAEOS).

---

17 Milne and Skeat, *Scribes and Correctors of the Codex Sinaiticus*, 55–9.
18 *Greek Manuscripts of the Ancient World*, Oxford, 1971, 19f.
19 B.M.W. Knox, 'Silent Reading in Antiquity', *Greek, Roman and Byzantine Studies* 9 (1968), 421–35, criticises only the idea that people always spoke the text out loud when reading a book to themselves.

If one also looks at the examples of longer readings discussed by Clark, in his Introduction, pp. xlv–xlix, the following errors may be noted.

12.10   F 464, 1.23:   GRADOS for *gradus*.
14.2   F 473, 1.10:   COMFESTIM. This may be found too at Mk 9.15.
18.26–7 F 494, 1.7:   AEPHESUM. EPH- is written everywhere else.

It is clear, from these errors alone, that the longer readings do not possess a purity lacking in the rest of the text.

[110]

I turn finally to Professor MacKenzie's comparison of the Greek and Latin columns. There is absolutely no reason why most of the errors of this type should have affected the Greek text. For one thing, many of them do not change the sense, being spelling mistakes. For another, they were made by the scribe of the Codex Bezae, and therefore could not affect the Greek, which was copied first. Professor MacKenzie's study has no light to throw on the Greek text. But there are some questions concerning it which arise out of our discussion.

First, it is not enough to make a statement concerning the transmission of a bilingual text, having examined only one column. For instance, does Professor MacKenzie consider there to have been a stage of copying by dictation in the Greek text also? I do not wish to give evidence for the visual copying of the Greek column here; until I do so, my statements regarding the copying of D/d can only be provisional.

Second, the question as to whether the Latin text has influenced the Greek is a far more open one than has been assumed since the days of J. R. Harris. It would be out of place here to discuss this matter in detail. But I will make a statement and a suggestion.

The statement is, that the claim of Latin influence on the Greek cannot be substantiated on its own. It must be shown how this fits into the whole history of the manuscript's tradition. An explanation for the influence needs to be given which is more precise than that of 'uncontrolled texts' and the like.

My suggestion concerns the place of Codex Bezae in the history of the text which it transmits. One may enquire whether, in the event of a manuscript being copied from it, the mistakes made by the scribe in the Latin column would have affected the Greek; whether the reading AUDIEBAT at Acts 7.32 would have made the Greek into ἤκουε, or at 15.17 ΟΠΩΣ ΑΝ ΕΚΖΗΤΗΣΩΣΙΝ could have become καὶ ἐκζητήσω because of ET EXQUIRAM. I suggest that these errors would not have affected the Greek Text, not only because of the priority of the Greek text, but also because Codex Bezae stands at the end of a bilingual tradition. So few of its correctors ever troubled to correct both texts at once that even within the history of this one manuscript, the two texts have drifted somewhat apart. It is generally assumed that the discrepancies between the Greek and the Latin are relics from their once separate existences. The question needs to be asked, whether they do not reflect the disintegration of a harmonious bilingual tradition.

In conclusion, we must reject the several theories put forward by Professor MacKenzie, and instead make these three statements.

1. Assimilation to the context is an important habit of the scribe of Codex Bezae.
2. Many errors in spelling are so widespread that the relevance of phonetical theories for the study of Codex Bezae is far less than has been suggested.[20] To write of a reading in d without referring at the very least to Wordsworth and White is pointless and almost certainly misleading. It is a pity that Jülicher's *Itala* contains hardly any information on the spelling adopted in the various manuscripts.
3. It is to be concluded, as far as is possible from a study of the Latin text in isolation from the Greek, that the scribe of Codex Bezae copied from the exemplar visually, without the help of a dictator.

Note

This was my first publication on Codex Bezae. The case seems to be solid still. The only comment to be added is to repudiate the observation that 'This is to assume that a dictator was used only for the production of more than one volume at a time. Commercially, this must surely have been the case'. I seem to have accepted the idea of a roomful of scribes writing at the same time to dictation. For the many difficulties with such an idea, see my *Introduction to the New Testament Manuscripts and Their Texts*, Cambridge, 2008, 154–7.

---

20 See B. Fischer, 'Das Neue Testament in lateinischer Sprache', in ANTT 5, 41, n. 131.

2 A Copy of the Codex Mediolanensis

The Vulgate Gospel manuscript Codex Mediolanensis (Milan, Biblioteca Ambrosiana C. 39.inf., given the letter M in editions of the Vulgate) was copied in North Italy in the second half of the sixth century. It has probably never travelled very far from its original home, and has been in the Ambrosiana since 1605. Besides several restored leaves, it contains in the middle of Quire 39 a gathering of eight leaves (278–285) written in tenth-century minuscule, containing Jn 13.1–18.36. These pages are not, as Lowe writes (*CLA* 3.313)[1] a restoration of the original codex – which has the passage complete – but a copy of it. As far as I am aware, nobody has yet paid these leaves any particular attention. After a brief description, I shall provide evidence for my opinion, and a complete collation of the text.

The size of the page is that of the main codex (160 x 260), whilst the written area is 100 x 200. It has double bounding lines, with each sheet probably ruled separately. Ruling is on the hair side, and the outer surface of each gathering is hair. Prickings are in the outer margin. There are twenty-five lines to the page, the lines rather irregular in length, but with the right margin always between the two bounding lines. It is not written *per cola et commata*, but a medial point is used to mark these divisions. Sections begin with an enlarged initial letter. There are no running titles. There is some variation in the letter forms of the script: for example, *y* is found with and without a long descender; *m* is sometimes round and sometimes angular; initial *A* is in at least four shapes, of which one is a rustic capital and two have their only parallels in the Codex Mediolanensis itself.

The evidence that it is a copy of the codex with which it is bound is of several kinds.

First, palaeographical, is the way in which initial *A* in the later text sometimes imitates the extremely distinctive triangular bow of the older hand.

Then there is the fact that the point at which the later text breaks off is marked by a cross in the right-hand margin of the older one. Several corrections to the older text may even be by the later copyist: the

---

1   Lowe, *Codices Latini Antiquiores* 3, *Italy: Ancora–Novara*, 13.

alteration of *e* to *ae* at 13.17, 33; 16.2. This I have called M² (M¹ is close in time to the original hand).

Thirdly there is the textual evidence. Of one kind is the fact that at 18.11, *vaginam* comes at the end of a line in M and was therefore written with the final *m* as a horizontal stroke that was either very faint or actually omitted (the ink has flaked here); the more recent text reads *vagina*.

A collation of the two texts with the Stuttgart Vulgate[2] reveals that they share four readings for which there is no other support in Jülicher,[3] Wordsworth and White[4] or the Stuttgart Vulgate:

> 13.16. OM *suo* (+ *suo* M$^{abs.\ s.m.}$)
> 14.30. *multa*] *ultra*
> 17.17. + *pater* ad inc.
> 18.19. *iesum*] $\overline{ihu}$ ($\overline{ihu}$ M^{abs})

In the following readings, their shared reading enjoys little other support:

> 13.38. *amen* semel c. e
> 14.3. *ut*] *et* c. D T a
>   13. *filio*] *filium* c. q
>   30. *huius mundi* c. D G T ff²
> 15.4. *palmes*] *palmis* c. P G S
>   6. *palmes*] *palmis* c. G O X
>   13. *quis ponat*] *ponat quis* c. G Θ
> 16.2. *praestare*] *prestare* c. ℲF C D F
> 17.12 *impleatur*] *adimpleatur* c. r¹
> 18.3 *pontificibus*] *principibus* c. D*
>   18 *calefiebant*] *calefaciebant* c. D R X aur c f
>   28 *a Caiapha*] *ad Caiapha* (*Caÿpha* M^{abs}); *ad Caipha* H* O* f.

In all, they share forty-four readings against the Stuttgart text. The remaining twenty-eight are:

> 13.8. *habebis*; 14. *pedes vestros*; 26. *cui respondet*; 32. *clarificabit*¹; 37. *te sequi*; 14.7. *cognoscetis*; 15.4. *palmis*; 13. *hanc*; 16. *afferatis*; 16.11. *huius mundi*; 13. *loquitur*; *annuntiabit*; 14. *annuntiabit*; 15. *accipiet*; *annuntiabit*; 25. *annuntiabo*;

---

2 *Biblia Sacra iuxta Vulgatam Versionem*, ed. R. Weber, Stuttgart, 1969. I have used the 1969 edition, because that was the copy available in the Ambrosian Library.
3 Jülicher, *Itala*, 4. *Johannesevangelium*.
4 *Nouum Testamentum Domini nostri Iesu Christi Latine*, ed. J. Wordsworth and H.J. White, Vol. 1, Oxford, 1898. I should note that there is a difference between their citations of M and mine. Their evidence was drawn from a collation made by Fortunato Villa, a scrittore of the Ambrosiana before 1884, and then a dottore from 1884 till his death in October 1888. At 17.25 he did not notice that M originally included *et*¹. I am greatly indebted to Don Cesare Pasini of the Ambrosiana for his help in checking several readings against my notes, including this one.

27. *amatis; creditis*; 32. *dispargimini;* 33. *habebitis;* 17.3. *deum verum;* 11. *hi;* 22. *illis;* 23. + *et;* 25. *hi;* 18.2. OM *ipsum;* 19. OM *suis;* 29. *affertis*

The number of places where a distinctive reading of M is not followed by the later text is quite small. In these readings, M reads a different text from that of the Stuttgart edition, while the copy follows the majority text (the Stuttgart reading in every case except 18.24). [539]

    13.17. *hec* M* W; *hęc* M²; *haec* M^{abs}
        33. *athuc* M F S X²; *adhuc* M^{abs}
    15.10 *pracepta* M*; *praecepta* M¹; p̄cepta M^{abs}
    16.14. *clarificavit* M M̄ O X; *clarificabit* M^{abs}
        29. OM *ei* M* G; *ei* M¹ M^{abs}
    17.1. *ut et* M Ƀ ^C Θ; *ut* M^{abs}
        3. *vitam aeternam* M* H; *vita aeterna* M³ M^{abs}
        9. *qos* M*; *quos* M^{s.m.} M^{abs}
        16. OM *et* M F* H R X*; *et* M^{abs}
        19. OM *ego* M D b c e q [r¹]; *ego* M^{abs}
    18.24. *Caiapham* M; *caẏphan* M^{abs}
        31. *palatus* M; *pilatus* M^{abs}

It will be seen that the later text is generally either following a corrector, or emending an error. Only at 17.1, 16 and 19 is there a more significant difference.

These are not all the places where the two copies differ. There are some readings in which M^{abs} has got its reading from elsewhere. Including orthographical changes, these are:

    13.33. *quaeretis* M] *quaeritis* M^{abs}
    14.9 *vidit* bis M] *videt* bis M^{abs} B(?)
        10. *credis* M] *creditis* M^{abs}
        14. *me* M] OM M^{abs}
        23. *mansiones* M] *mansionem* M^{abs}
    15.7. *petetis* M] *petieritis* M^{abs}
        15. *facit* M] *faciat* M^{abs}
        25. *me habuerunt* M] *hab. me* M^{abs}
        27. *perhibetis* M] *perhibebitis* M^{abs}
    16.9 *credunt* M] *crediderunt* M^{abs}
        18. *loquitur* M] *loquatur* M^{abs}
        22. *tollit* M] *tollet* M^{abs}
    17.3 *est* M] OM M^{abs}*; *est* M^{abs s.m.}
        25. *et¹* M*] OM M^{s.m.} M^{abs}
        11. *vagina*[¯] M] *vagina* M^{abs}
        21. *hi* M] *hii* M^{abs}
        31. *ei* M] OM M^{abs}

This more extensive list (eighteen readings) shows the later text to contain many of the typical lapses of Vulgate copyists of the Fourth Gospel, particularly confusions of verbal endings. The scribe seems also to have been rather inaccurate, and regularly to have allowed his memory to replace his exemplar.

From the full collation, we can see how the scribe changed his exemplar's spelling. And we can see that he marked and corrected the exemplar (though not extensively, and not at every place where he did not follow it). At 16.2 he seems to have corrected the *prestare* of M to *praestare*, only to write it himself as *prestare*.

The interest of this gathering lies in the way that it provides us a glimpse of a tenth-century scribe at work. It encourages us in the task of distinguishing valuable materials in less ancient manuscripts.

Why was it written? It seems to be a quire complete in itself. Two possibilities spring to mind. One is that it is an exercise, a trial copying by a novice. The variation in certain letter forms – and the influence of the exemplar's hand – might substantiate this. The other possibility is that it was to reduce the over use of an old and valued manuscript. Was M used liturgically at a particular time in the year? Some of the leaves that have been copied may be rather more worn than those elsewhere, but then some of them are in perfectly good condition. The presence of the lectionary formula at the beginning of the copy may support this theory.

Collation of M^{abs} with the Stuttgart Vulgate

John Chapter 13
Inc. (in uncials): *hec lec̄ legenda ē in cena dn̄i ad collationem*

v.1 *paschae*] *pasche*; 2. *Scariotis*] *Scariothis*; 5. *coepit*] *cępit*; 8. *habes*] *habebis*; 14. *vestros pedes*] *pedes vestros*; 16. *suo*] OM (added in margin by M^{abs s.m.}); 26. *respondit*] *cui respondit*; *intinxisset*] *intincxisset*; *scariotis*] *scariothis*; 27. *satanas*] *sathanas*; 32. *clarificabit*] *clarificavit*; 33. *quaeretis*] *quaeritis*; 37. *sequi te*] *te sequi*; 38. *amen amen*] *amen*

Chapter 14
2. *multae*] *multe*; there is an erasure, almost a whole line long, after *vobis locum*; 3. *ut*] *et*; 7. *cognoscitis*] *cognoscetis*; 9. *vidit* bis] *videt* bis; 10. *credis*] *creditis*; 13. *filio*] *filium*; 14. *me*] OM; 16. *paracletum*] *paraclitum*; 18. *orfanos*] *orphanos*; 22. *scariotis*] *scariothis*; 23. *diliget*] *diligit*; *mansiones*] *mansionem*; 26. *paracletus*] *paraclitus*; 30. *multa*] *ultra*; *mundi huius*] *huius mundi*; 31. (ends on a line ending) in the right-hand margin is *fin̄* followed by a cross.

Chapter 15

2. *adferat*] *afferat*; 4. *palmes*] *palmis*; 6. *palmes*] *palmis*; 7. *petetis*] *petieritis*; 10. *praecepta²*] *precepta*; 13. *hac*] *hanc* p.m. *(n* eras. p.m. or s.m.*)*; *quis ponat*] *ponat quis*; 15. *facit*] *faciat*; 16. *adferatis*] *afferatis*; 25. *me habuerunt*] *hab. me*; 26. *paracletus*] *paraclitus*; 27. *perhibetis*] *perhibebitis*

Chapter 16

2. *praestare*] *prestare*; 7. *paracletus*] *paraclitus*; 9. *credunt*] *crediderunt*; 11. *mundi huius*] *huius mundi*; 13. *loquetur*] *loquitur*; *adnuntiabit*] *annuntiabit*; 14. *ille*] *illae*; *adnuntiabit*] *annuntiabit*; 15. *accipit*] *accipiet*; *adnuntiabit*] *annuntiabit*; 18. *loquitur*] *loquatur*; 19. *quaeritis*] *queritis* ; 22. *gaudebit*] *videbit* then *gaudebit*; *tollit*] *tollet*; 25. *adnuntiabo*] *annuntiabo* ; 27. *amastis*] *amatis*; *credidistis*] *creditis*; 30. *nunc*] *nun* then *nunc*; 32. *dispergamini*] *dispargamini*; 33. *habetis*] *habebitis*

[541]

Chapter 17

3. *est*] OM p.m; *verum deum*] *deum verum*; 11. *hii*] *hi*; 12. *impleatur*] *adimpleatur*; 17 ad inc.] + *pater*; 22. *eis*] *illis*; 23. *consummati*] *consumati*; *sicut*] + *et*; 25. *et¹*] OM; *hii*] *hi*

Chapter 18

1. *hortus*] *ortus*; 2. *ipsum*] OM; 3. *pontificibus*] *principibus*; *pharisaeis*] *phariseis*; 11. *vaginam*] *vagina*; 13. *caiaphae*] *caiphae*; 14. *caiaphas*] *caiphas*; 18. *calefiebant*] *calefaciebant*; 19. *iesum*] *ihu*; *suis*] OM; 20. *iudaei*] *iudei*; *nihil*] *nichil*; 24. *caiaphan*] *caÿphan*; 28. *a*] *ad*; 29. *accusationem*] *accusacionem*; *adfertis*] *affertis*; 31. *eum²*] a letter with a supralinear stroke written after it, later erased; *ei*] OM

3 Unequally Yoked: the Present State of the Codex Bobbiensis

The Old Latin Gospel manuscript Codex Bobbiensis (k, Turin, Biblioteca Nazionale G. VII. 15),[1] is now kept unbound, with each bifolium stretched and mounted in its own cardboard frame. It has been kept like this since its restoration after the disastrous fire which swept through the Biblioteca Torinese in 1904.[2] Each bifolium is separated into two, at the fold. Plate 15 of Cipolla's *Codici Bobbiesi*[3] seems to show folios 4b–5 bound as the centre of a gathering with

---

1   The manuscript was first critically used by Lachmann, *Novum Testamentum Graece et Latine*, Vol. 1, Berlin, 1842, xvff, and first edited by F.F. Fleck, *Wissenschaftliche Reise*, 1837, Vol. 2, Part 3. This was followed (much more accurately) by Tischendorf, to whom we owe the designation 'k': 'Rechenschaft über meine handschriftlichen Studien auf meiner wissenschaftlichen Reise von 1840 bis 1844', *Jahrbücher der Literatur* 120 (1847), 36–56, 43–56; 121 (1848), 50–72; 123 (1848), 40–6; 124 (1848), 1–8; 126 (1849), 1–76. This was succeeded by J. Wordsworth, W. Sanday and H.J. White, *Portions of the Gospels according to St. Mark and St. Matthew from the Bobbio MS. (k), . . . together with other fragments of the Gospels from six MSS. in the libraries of St. Gall, Coire, Milan and Berne* . . . (Old Latin Biblical Texts 2), London, 1886. This is henceforth cited as Wordsworth. Corrections to this may be found in C.H. Turner, 'A Re-collation of Codex k of the Old Latin Gospels (Turin G. VII. 15)', *JTS* 5 (1904), 88–100; and F.C. Burkitt, 'Further Notes on Codex k', *ibid.*, 100–7. A facsimile edition was overseen by C. Cipolla, *Il Codice evangelico k della Biblioteca universitaria nazionale di Torino riprodotto in Fac-simile* (Raccolta di codici riprodotti in fac-simile a cura della regia accademia delle scienze di Torino), Turin, 1913. Transcriptions of the manuscripts may also be found in H. von Soden, *Das lateinische Neue Testament in Afrika zur Zeit Cyprians* (TU 33), Leipzig, 1909, 367–98, 429–49, and in Jülicher, *Itala*, 1. *Matthäusevangelium* and 2. *Marcusevangelium*. For a brief account of studies of the manuscript, see A.H.A. Bakker, *A Study of Codex Evang. Bobbiensis (k)*, Part One, Amsterdam, 1933, 5–7. An important and cogent discussion establishing the African origin of the manuscript may be found in Lowe, *Codices Latini Antiquiores*, Supplement, vii-x, Plates I-VII.

2   See von Soden, *op. cit.*, 107. The footnote cites the Inventario dei codici superstiti greci e latini antichi della Biblioteca Nazionale di Torino in the *Rivista di Filologia ed Istruzione classica* 1904, 443: 'conservato, non senza danni, disciolto in fogli'. An effect of the fire is that the parchment shows as discoloured in the facsimile edition. As a result, identification of hair and flesh sides is precarious. The manuscript had already suffered much from damp (Wordsworth, *op. cit.*, ix).

3   C. Cipolla, *Collezione paleografica bobbiese*, Vol. 1. *Codici bobbiesi della biblioteca nazionale universitaria di Torino*, 2 vols.: text and plates, Milan, 1907.

thread visible. But elsewhere Cipolla throws this into doubt.[4] Certainly the manuscript was bound when Tischendorf saw it, for he refers to a 'Versehen des Buchbinders' in the ordering of the sheets.[5] And this may still have been the case in 1886.[6] But the leaves must have been separated at the spine by this time, for Tischendorf to make the claim about the order of the sheets that is discussed below.

The card mounts all have a folio number between 1 and 96, and a quire number between 1 and 12. The folio numbers match those written on the top right-hand corner of the recto of each sheet. These are probably of the eighteenth century. When I examined the manuscript in May 1989, I was initially struck by the fact that the left and right pages sometimes looked unevenly worn, or at a glance did not seem to be an obvious pairing. I was hampered in my investigations by the fact that I was only allowed to look at four bifolia at a time. This made it hard to examine the make-up of the manuscript properly. But it became clear, and subsequent investigation confirms it, that the pairs of half leaves have, for part of the manuscript, been wrongly mounted, so that what are presented as pairs forming a single sheet are actually the halves of two separate sheets. It should be said that the present arrangement does not, in current opinion at the library, intend to have any claim to codicological pretensions.

This wrong pairing may not appear to be a matter of great moment, but it has had its effect on palaeographical enquiry. Thus, for example, Lowe in his description of the manuscript:

> Ruling on the hair side, several leaves at a time after folding, an Insular practice and otherwise unknown in MSS. of such antiquity ... gatherings irregular, but mostly of eights, with hair-side outside.[7]

Moreover, the present arrangement would lead one to suppose that the quire signatures were written on the verso of the first sheet of each gathering – a most extraordinary practice were it authentic.

---

4   'Nel 1907 quando riprodussi i fogli 4v–5r, 41v–42v [scil. 42r] dati nelle tav. XIV e XV de *I Codici Bobbiesi* i fogli erano già divisi e quasi terminato n'era ormai il restauro' (*Il Codice evangelico* k, 12).
5   *Jahrbücher der Literatur* 120 (1847), 47, n. 1.
6   One could so interpret the statement that 'The form of the volume is a middle-sized quarto', Wordsworth, *op. cit.*, ix. On p. x, Wordsworth notes that the quire signature on F48v is taken off by damp on the opposite page, F49r. Since there is a leaf missing in between, this must have happened in at least comparatively recent times, and it may be suggested that the manuscript must have been bound for it to have happened.
7   Lowe, *Codices Latini Antiquiores*, Part 4 *Italy: Perugia-Verona*, Entry 465 (p. 18).

The present numberings on the card mounts give the following gatherings:
I: 1–8
II: 9–16
III: 17–24
IV: 25–32
V: 33–40
VI: 41–48
VII: 49–54
VIII: 55–62
IX: 63–72
X: 73–78
XI: 79–86
XII: 87–96

According to this reconstruction, there were two quinions, eight quaternions, and two ternions.

These pairings and gatherings cannot all be original since they do not take account of the lacunae between folios 48 and 49, and between folios 94 and 95. The first gap (between Mt 3.10 and 4.2) amounts to one leaf (there are an average of something like 330 letters to a page; the missing passage comes to 694 letters in the top line of Jülicher).[8] The second, Mt 14.17–15.20, was of four leaves (the number of letters for the passage in the Codex Palatinus [Old Latin manuscript e] comes to 2718, and 330 letters for a page of k adds up to 2640). Thus it is possible that up to folio 48 the pairings of leaves and the gatherings could be right. From there on it is impossible.

Tischendorf[9] believed the leaf numbered 1 to belong in fact directly after Leaf 96, and to contain Mt 15.37–16.1, 5–7, writing 'Das erste Blatt im Ms. ist dem Inhalte nach das letzte; durch ein Versehen des Buchbinders ist es zum ersten geworden'.[10] If this were so, then the pairing of leaves up to Folio 48 *could* not be right. The question is whether Folio 1 contains Mk 8.8–11, 14–16, or the parallel passage in Matthew. It is a confusing coincidence that the extant portion of the manuscript begins and ends in the middle of the same passage from each Gospel. Against Tischendorf's theory is the fact that F96ᵛ ends with *discentibus* (Mt 15.36), so that οι δε μαθηται τοις οχλοις. και

[583]

---

8   *Ibid.*, Vol. 1.
9   Following Fleck, according to Wordsworth, *op. cit.*, xi.
10 *Jahrbücher der Literatur* 120 (1847), 47, n. 1.

εφαγον παντες και would be missing from the Latin text. Altogether, the text of the leaf seems to be closer to that of Mark.[11]

The only firm evidence for the original gatherings is the traces of signatures. These are found in the bottom right-hand corner of folios 48v, 55v, and 79v. Since the normal position for quire signatures in Latin manuscripts of the period is the bottom right-hand corner of the last verso of the gathering, and since the position of the signature on the page is normal, we are justified in assuming that the position in the gathering is also normal. The missing leaf between folios 48 and 49 and those up to 55 comprise a quaternion, with the hair side outwards. Going on ahead, there are 24 leaves before the next signature on folio 79v. This is most probably a set of three quaternions. Wordsworth found the X of XL on F63v, which confirms this.[12] What remains of the codex consists probably of another quaternion (80–87), seven of the eight leaves of another (88–94), and the centre sheet of yet another (95–96).

If we work back from folio 41, then another quaternion will consist in folios 33–40. It seems probable that the preceding 32 leaves make up four quaternions. Leaves 17–24 are a gathering in which the third sheet from the bottom of the pile was placed hair down instead of flesh down, so that the second and third, and fifth and sixth openings do not match. That is, the scribe forgot to lay them with alternate sides facing up before he folded them.[13] There seem to be no reasons why the first sixteen extant sheets should not comprise two quaternions.

Let us return to the quire signatures. Cipolla read the one on folio 48v as the remnants of XXXV. However, XLII is fairly clear on folio 79v. This makes 48v the end of Quaternion XXXVIII, so that it is likely that the three final numerals are lost (the V is right up against the present edge of the leaf). 55v will then be the end of XXXIX. We can therefore reconstruct the original size and contents of the manuscript. Mark 1–7 will have taken up thirty-two leaves, preceded by John and Luke with

---

11 In his eighth edition, Tischendorf continued to treat the leaf as Matthew not Mark. There is a discrepancy here with C.R. Gregory's *Prolegomena*, where it is described as Mk 8.8-11, 14–16 (960). No subsequent editions which I have checked follow Tischendorf. Wordsworth writes that he had been assured by Rossi that *CATA. MARC.* could be read at the top of F1r (*op. cit.*, xi).

12 *Op. cit.*, x.

13 It would be wrong to conclude from this that the scribe was incompetent. Burkitt showed how certain irregularities of spelling 'agree with those in the best MSS of Plautus' (*art. cit.*, 106). He concluded that 'the scribe was a professional copier of books, perhaps a heathen or only a recent convert' (*ibid.*, 107).

224.[14] The original length of Mark 8 to Matthew 15 was 101, and we can add fifty-eight for the rest of Matthew. This gives us a total of 415 leaves, one leaf short of fifty-two quaternions.[15]

From the evidence we have gathered, the quaternions should be as follows:

XXXIII: 1–8
XXXIV: 9–16
XXXV: 17–24
XXXVI: 25–32
XXXVII: 33–40
XXXVIII: 41–48
XXXIX: 49–55
XL: 56–63
XLI: 64–71
XLII: 72–79
XLIII: 80–87
XLIV: 88–94
XLV: 95–96

The first five gatherings are identical with those into which the manuscript is grouped in its present state. From there on, however, both the groupings into gatherings and the pairing of leaves in the cardboard mounts is wrong. In the accompanying figures, on the left is shown the present arrangement into pairs of the leaves, and the resultant make-up of the gatherings. On the right, in bolder lines, is the correct pairing of the leaves and resultant quaternions.

A question still to be addressed is whether the outer faces of the gatherings are hair or flesh. My original notes are incomplete on the point, since I only became fully aware of the problem afterwards. They do not always coincide fully with the evidence of the facsimile, and it may be that I was confused into error by the discoloration of the leaves.

---

14 This is an unusual order of the Gospels. It was once believed to be found in X (033) (see Wordsworth, *ibid.*, citing Gregory's *Prolegomena* to Tischendorf, Leipzig, 1884, 397f). But see T. Zahn, *Geschichte des neutestamentlichen Kanons*, Vol. 2, Erlangen and Leipzig, 1890, 370, n. 1. The minuscule manuscript 90 has the order John–Luke–Matthew–Mark (according to Zahn, 371, n. 3), or John–Matthew–Luke–Mark (according to B.M. Metzger, *The Canon of the New Testament, Its Origin, Development, and Significance*, Oxford, 1987, 296f). This is a sixteenth-century copy of a late thirteenth-century manuscript. The latter sequence is also followed by 19 (twelfth century), and by a few other authorities (see Metzger, 297). There are thus known orders in which John is placed first, but none beginning with Luke. The overwhelming weight or probability is in favour of our manuscript originally having contained John and Luke before the extant portions.

15 Compare Cipolla, *Il Codice evangelico* k, 7. See also Wordsworth, *op. cit.*, xii.

Since the colour is no guide, one has to rely on the fact that the hair side will have absorbed and retained the ink better than the oilier flesh side. Since my visit, and subsequent study of the facsimile, I have received the opinion of Dr Edmondo Lupieri, of the University of Turin, who very generously gave his time to examine the manuscript for me, with the assistance of two members of the library staff. His findings are contained in a letter to me of 29 July 1990. These findings allow me to make full sense of my notes, and establish the main points. It appears that, with one exception, the gatherings all have the flesh on the outside. The exception is Quaternion XLI, which certainly has hair on the outside. Gathering XXXIX is a problem, for the first half of the outer sheet is missing. F55^r looks from the facsimile like a hair side, for follicles are showing in the bottom outside corner. This would make F55^v, the outside of the gathering, a flesh. Dr Lupieri confirms this. We have a similar problem with Quaternion XLIV, of which we only have the first half of the outer sheet. This also is *probably* flesh outwards. Due to the state of the manuscript Dr Lupieri was unable to determine with certainty which side was outward in Quaternion XXXIII, but it is probably flesh.

To return to the original questions, the following points may be drawn from this discussion.

1. The extant portion of the codex consists solely of quaternions; there are no irregularities in the number of leaves to a gathering.[16]

2. The quire signatures were on the bottom right-hand corner of the last page of the gathering.

3. The scribe was occasionally rather careless in ensuring that facing pages were matching hair or flesh.

4. Lowe's claim that ruling was 'on the hair side, several leaves at a time after folding'[17] is in doubt. Earlier, he had stated that the manuscript is ruled sometimes on the hair, sometimes on the flesh side.[18] This is borne out by Dr Lupieri, who writes that there seems to be no fixed rule. For example, in Quaternion XXXV there is ruling on

---

16 Wordsworth stated that the codex is composed of quaternions, and gives the evidence on pp. x–xi. I had deliberately set out my theories before consulting any other writer, so my conclusions are quite independent. Sanday is followed by P. McGurk, *Latin Gospel Books from A.D. 400 to A.D. 800* (Les Publications de Scriptorium 5), Paris, Brusselles, Anvers and Amsterdam, 1961, entry 106 (92), where his entry includes the statement 'quires of quaternions'.

17 See above, p. 26.

18 'More Facts about our Oldest Latin Manuscripts', *The Classical Quarterly* 22 (1928), 43–62, reprinted in *Palaeographical Papers*, ed. L. Bieler, Oxford, 1972, Vol. 1, 251–76, esp. 253.

F17r, which is a flesh side, while in Quaternion XXXIII it is found on F3v and F4r, both of which are hair sides. Dr Lupieri suggests that it seems that the scribe prepared two or three sheets together. It looks as if at least the vertical rulings of Quaternion XXXV were made after the sheets had been folded, several at a time, and this seems to be the case with the horizontal rulings of Quaternion XLIV. Altogether, his examination encourages us to accept Lowe's earlier description as more accurate.

5. The manuscript should be rebound correctly (the mounts are wearing out in any case). At the same time, the sheets should be renumbered to take account of the missing leaves. 1–48 should become 257–304, 49–94 become 306–51, 95–6 become 356–7. Or, if the first 256 sheets are not counted, the gaps between our extant sheets should be indicated, giving a sequence 1–48, 50–95, 100–1.

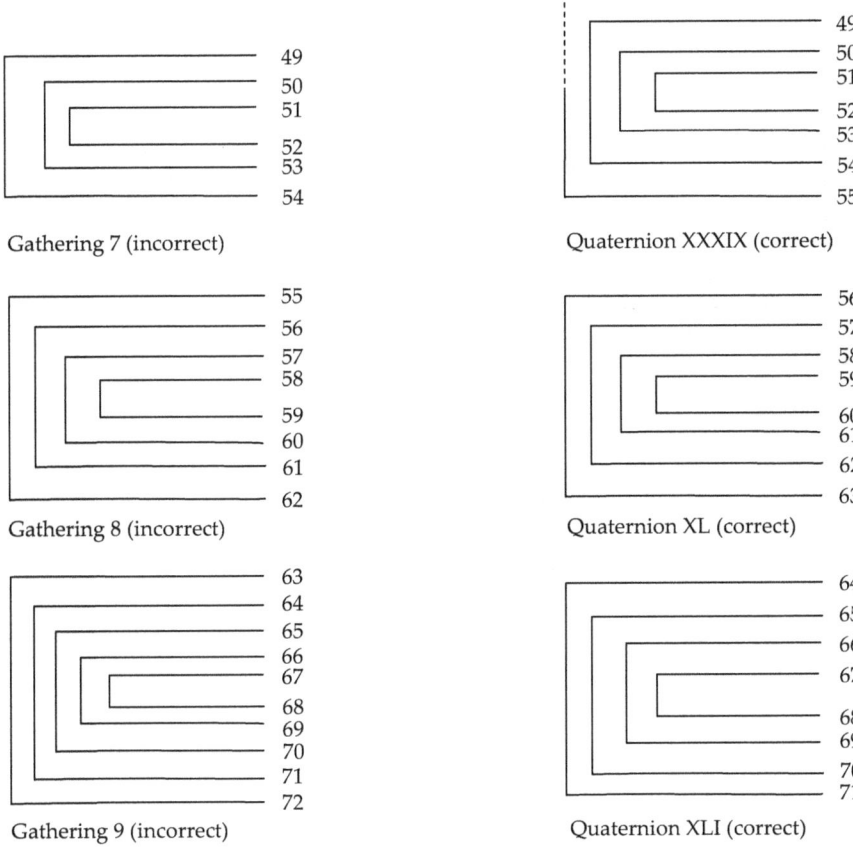

Unequally Yoked: the Present State of the Codex Bobbiensis

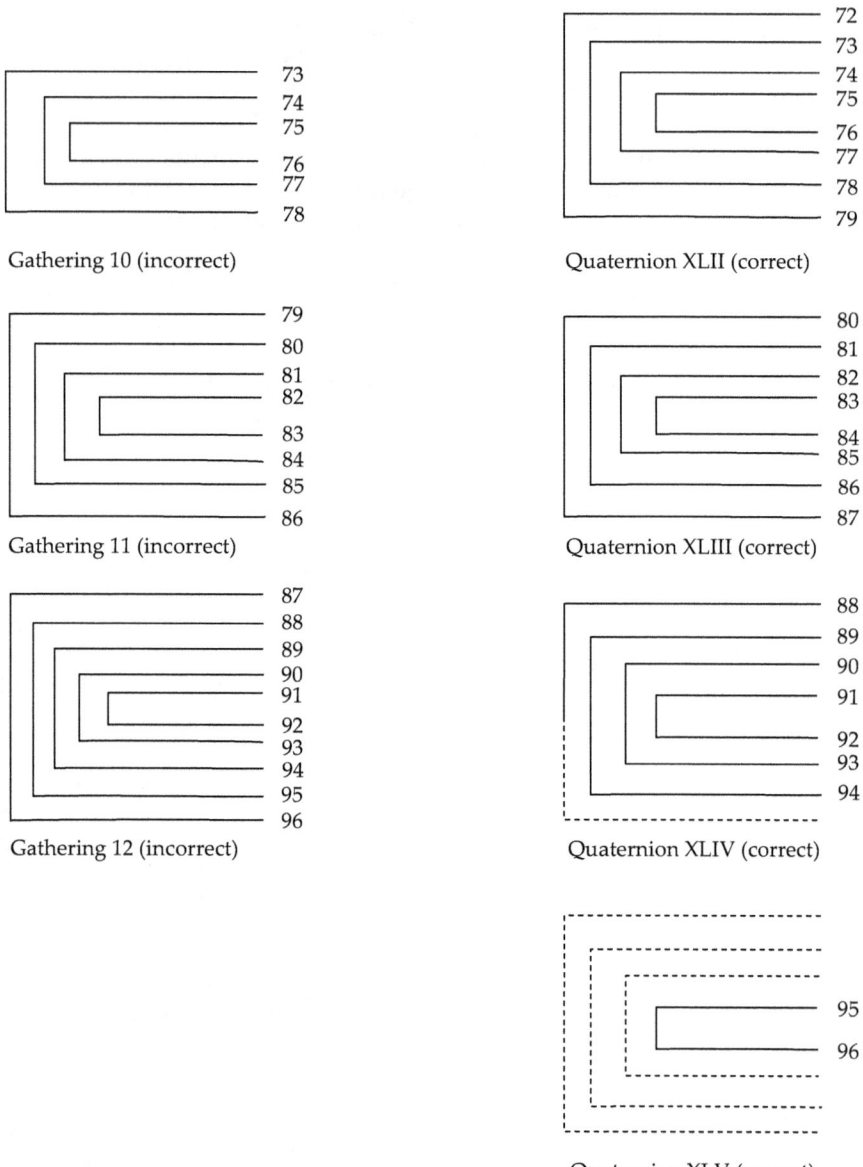

4 The Majuscule Manuscripts of the New Testament

1. Description and Nomenclature

It has long been habitual to describe this class of manuscripts as uncials. The word's use has its origin in Mabillon's interpretation of Jerome's phrase about manuscripts written *uncialibus litteris*.[1] Whatever the original meaning, a consensus has emerged that the name should only be applied to a particular kind of Latin majuscule.[2] The word majuscule should be used to designate the class of Greek hands of which we write. It means 'of a fair size', as opposed to minuscule, 'rather small'. To attempt a definition of a hand given this name: a formal book hand of a fair size in which almost all of the letters are written between two notional lines.

With regard to the class of manuscript of the Greek New Testament with which we are concerned, there are three criteria which a manuscript must satisfy if it is to be included: script, material and contents. Majuscule in script, parchment as to material, and with a continuous text rather than lections (though the lections may be marked, in the margin or even in the text). If a manuscript in a majuscule hand is written on papyrus, then it is classified among the papyri; if it is a lectionary as to contents, then it should be classified among the lectionaries. There are about 270 lectionaries written in majuscule.

Because of these three criteria, it could be argued that the designation 'uncial' refers not to the script so much as to the whole character of the book in question. This usage is so common as to be almost universal. Nevertheless, it is palaeographically inexact, and we must learn to do without it. The term 'majuscule' will be employed throughout the present study.

On the question of contents, it should be noted that a significant number of our manuscripts are bilingual. I believe there to be eleven

---

[1] Prologus in Libro Iob, *Biblia Sacra*, 1.732. For a recent explanation, see P. Mayvaert, '"Uncial letters": Jerome's Meaning of the Term', *JTS* 34 (1983), 185–8.
[2] See Cavallo and Maehler, *Greek Bookhands*, v.

Graeco-Latin, twenty-one Graeco-Coptic, and two Graeco-Arabic majuscule bilinguals.³

The script and material of our manuscripts form a group reflecting various social, political, economic and religious factors. Apart from our five oldest examples, they all come within a period delimited by two events. The first was the Peace of Constantine, and the innovation was a change from a preponderance of papyrus manuscripts to a preference for parchment, with a general adoption of biblical majuscule as the most common script. The demise of the majuscules coincides with an explosion in the production of written books in the tenth century that made it necessary to produce more books from the same parchment supply. The innovation here was the transition to minuscule scripts.

2. The Majuscules in History and Scholarship

With the transition to minuscule, the majuscule manuscripts passed out of use. What happened to them? Professor Metzger draws our attention to the fact that 'Instances of a known copy of another manuscript are exceedingly rare, which suggests that only a very small percentage of manuscripts have survived'.⁴ Weitzman has produced a statistical model suggesting that '10 per cent of all books now lost were still extant in A.D. 900'.⁵ With New Testament manuscripts produced in late antiquity, the proportion is likely to have been far higher. This challenges our belief that the greater part of manuscript loss happened in antiquity. Could it be that, just as the Colosseum and Hadrian's Wall survived the depradations of earlier barbarians, only to succumb in modern times, the one to the aspirations of Renaissance popes, the other to the indifference of Victorian farmers, so our ancient manuscripts may have survived a millennium, only to perish within sight of land? Codex Sinaiticus may still have been complete in the seventeenth-eighteenth century. A glance at the history of the palimpsests reinforces the idea.

---

3   A list of all bilinguals is given in Parker, *Codex Bezae*, 60–61. To my list of Graeco-Coptic manuscripts should be added 0114 + *l*964a + *l*1353b, 0276 + *l*962 + *l*1353a, 0298 and 0299 (I am indebted to James Mitter for this information). Another list is provided in B.M. Metzger, *Manuscripts of the Greek Bible: An Introduction to Greek Palaeography*, New York and Oxford, 1981, 56.
4   Metzger, *Manuscripts*, 54.
5   M.P. Weitzman, 'The Evolution of Manuscript Traditions', *Journal of the Royal Statistical Society* A 150, Part 4 (1987), 287–308.

There are fifty-seven majuscule palimpsests, and a further fifty-one (or possibly fifty-two) majuscule lectionary palimpsests.[6] The definition of palimpsest often includes pieces used to strengthen binding.[7] Those manuscripts on which it has been possible to gather information were rewritten in the following centuries (precise year in brackets; the phrase 'lower script' refers to the older text of a palimpsest, 'upper script' to the newer ones[s]):[8]

[24]

VIII	024 026 0208 (first half)
VIII–IX	027
IX	068 0250
IX–X	0240
IX–XI	0197
X	035 (or later) 065 066 067 078 079 088 096 097 0120 0245 (983) 0257
XI	094 0132 0247
XI–XII	0130
XII	04 0103? 0104? 0248 0249
XIII	025 040 0134 0233 (1247)
XIV	098 0116 0209
XV	0133 (1431) 0135 0161 0269 0271 0272 0273 0297
XVI	
XVII	048 (1696–9)

---

6 The majuscule group is conveniently listed by Metzger, *Text of the New Testament*[3], 12, n. 1. Since 0250 (the last in his list), are to be added 0254, 0257, 0269, 0271, 0272, 0273 and 0297. 0114, not shown to be a palimpsest in *Liste*[1] or *Liste*, should also be added. In his list, 0196 and 0229 are the upper scripts. For the rest, our majuscules are the primary writing. The uncertainty with regard to the number of lectionary examples is due to the state of the lower writing in the fourteenth century *l*2008: the note in K. Aland, 'Die griechischen Handschriften des Neuen Testaments. Ergänzungen zur "Kurzgefaßten Liste" (Fortsetzungsliste VII)', *Materialen zur Neutestamentlichen Handschriftenkunde*, ANTT 3; Berlin, 1969, 1-53 [henceforth cited as Supplement to the *Liste*])) 30 reads 'untere Schrift kaum U-l'. It is included in the list below.

7 See, for example, the description of *l*1836 in R. Devreesse, ed., *Bibliothèque Nationale. Département des mss. Catalogue des mss grecs. II. Le fonds Coislin*, Paris, 1945.

8 Some are beyond our reach: the whereabouts of 062, 072, 0144, 0158, 0159 and 0254 are not known. They were a group seen by Tischendorf in Damascus: see W.H.P. Hatch, 'An Uncial Fragment of the Gospels', *HTR* 23 (1930), 149–52 (his article is mainly about 0196). Hatch could only find 0144 when he visited Damascus in 1929. His assertion that the other manuscripts were removed to Germany in 1918 is robustly dismissed as gossip by E. von Dobschütz, 'Zur Liste der NTlichen Handschriften', *ZNW* 32 (1933), 191. 093 is one of the Cambridge Cairo Geniza fragments; it is not possible to date the upper hand (M. Sokoloff and J. Yahalom, 'Christian Palimpsests from the Cairo Geniza', *Revue d'Histoire des Textes* 8 [1978] 115–16). Similarly, the Coptic upper script of 086 and the Syriac overwriting of 064/074 have not been dated by the editors. 0168 is apparently lost. 090 (one manuscript with 064 and 074) and 0246 were cleaned but never reused. Sources of information have failed me for 0225.

The tenth-century manuscripts are mostly a group with Georgian upper writing now in St Petersburg.[9] 0133 0269 0271 0272 0273 and 0297 (with the minuscule *l334*) were all used for a manuscript written in 1431 (London, B.L. Add. 31919). 0248 and 0249 were both used in making one new manuscript (Oxford, Bodl. Auct. T 4.21).

Some of these manuscripts were reused for lectionary or minuscule copies: 040 as *l299*, 0132 as 639, 0134 as *l26*, 0209 as *l1611*, 0233 as *l1684*, 0257 as *l2094*. 0208 was used in the first part of the eighth century, probably at Bobbio, in a copying of Prosper's *Chronicon*.[10]

The majuscule lectionary palimpsests were rewritten, for the most part, at a rather later point:[11]

X	*l559a l559b*
X-XI	*l316 l317*
XI	*l2201*
XI/XII	*l1952* (if XI, then 1067)
XII	*l135 l205 l286* (1150) *l293 l486b l586 l1836*
XIII	*l65 l66 l171 l220b l269 l1193a* (1263?) *l1837 l1953 l1954 l2125*
XIII–XIV	*l1854b*
XIV	*l155 l338 l363? l444 l482 l511 l668* (1311) *l703 l907* (1350) *l1214 l1955 l2008* lower script? *l2123 l2124*
XIV–XV	*l481 l2121*
XV	*l368 l370 l1317*
XVI	*l362*

Ten of these were rewritten as New Testament texts: *l135* as *l136*, *l220b* as *l220a*, *l269* as *l1944*, *l586* as 713, *l668* as 982, *l1193a* as *l1193b*, *l1214* as *l1235*, *l1854b* as *l1854a*, *l1954* as *l26*, and *l1955* as *l27*. The eleventh-century manuscript 1904 shared its fate with *l703*. The upper script of *l1317* is by the same scribe as that of British Museum Add. 31919, containing 0133 etc. (as we have seen) *l559a* and *l559b* were used in the same manuscript as 048 (Vat. Gr. 2061).

The scarcity of medieval corrections and marginalia is a further indication that majuscules were little used during this period. Sinaiticus has a couple of medieval corrections.[12] Codex Vaticanus was

---

9   065, 066, 067 and 088 are in the Public Library as Gr. 6; 078 and 079 as Gr. 13; 096 as Gr. 19; 097 as Gr. 18.
10 Lowe, *Codices Latini Antiquiores*, Vol. 9, item 1274.
11 *l1276* (not given as a majuscule in *Liste*[1] or *Liste*) is from the Cairo Geniza and, like 093, its upper script cannot be dated. (This fragment could be from a continuous text manuscript rather than a lectionary, according to C.R. Gregory, *Textkritik des Neuen Testamentes*, 3 vols., Leipzig, 1900–09, 3.1272–3.) For various reasons, I do not provide information for *l1429, l1601, l1637, l1687, l1849, l1885* and *l2158*.
12 Gregory (in his *Prolegomena* to C. Tischendorf's *Novum Testamentum Graece . . . editio octava critica maior*, Leipzig, 1894, 346) notes that there are 'paucissima' twelfth-

restored by someone in the tenth or eleventh centuries.[13] Codex Bezae shows no signs of use between the ninth and sixteenth centuries.[14] The Freer Gospels have no corrector later than the sixth century. Codex Alexandrinus was probably removed from Constantinople to Alexandria in 1308 – an act betokening some kind of interest in it.[15] The Laudian Acts contains eighth- and ninth-century Latin uncial annotations.

The emergence of the pre-minuscule manuscripts into the light of scholarship was late and gradual. Codex Vaticanus is first mentioned in a letter to Erasmus by Bombasius, Prefect of the Vatican Library, in 1521.[16] But it was to be another two and a half centuries before more than a small part of its readings were to become available.[17] Codex Bezae was probably cited at the Council of Trent in 1546.[18] It is certainly one of the first two majuscules to have been cited in an apparatus. The other was the eighth-century Gospel manuscript Codex Regius (L 019). They were among the fifteen witnesses used by Stephanus in his third (1550) edition, the first to contain a critical apparatus. Codex Claromontanus is first mentioned by Beza in the preface to his third edition of 1582. It was subsequently used for Walton's Polyglot. Codex Alexandrinus was an object of some interest from its arrival in London in 1628. It too was collated for Walton's Polyglot. K of the Gospels, Codex Cyprius, was brought to Paris from Cyprus in 1673, and collated by Simon. D^{abs1} was first used by Fell in his edition (1675). It was treated as a separate manuscript until Sabatier showed it to be a copy of D^p. Even as late as the end of the last century, it was given a separate letter (E^p).

In 1707, Mill was able to describe and cite eight majuscule manuscripts: those which we have listed (he only used L as cited by Stephanus), and two more that first appear in his edition: Basiliensis

[26]

---

century corrections, and specifically notes ones to Mt 19.3 and 1Tim 3.16. See also Milne and Skeat, *Scribes and Correctors of the Codex Sinaiticus*, 65.

13 Martini, *Il problema del codice B*, 3–4.
14 Parker, *Codex Bezae*, Chapter 3.
15 T.C. Skeat, 'The Provenance of the Codex Alexandrinus', *JTS* 6 (1955) 233–5.
16 J.J. Wettstein, Prolegomena, *Nouum Testamentum Graecum*, 2 vols., Amsterdam, 1751–2, 1.23–4. Erasmus Ep. 1213 (P.S. and H.M. Allen, eds., *Opus Epistolarum Des. Erasmi Roterodami*, Oxford, 1906–58, Vol. 4, 528–31, ll. 67–81).
17 F.H.A. Scrivener, *A Plain Introduction to the Criticism of the New Testament for the Use of Biblical Students*, 4th ed., revd E. Miller; 2 vols.; London and New York, Cambridge, 1894, 1.109–19.
18 F.H.A. Scrivener, *Bezae Codex Cantabrigiensis, Being an Exact Copy, in Ordinary Type*, Cambridge, 1864 (reprinted Pittsburgh Reprint Series 5, Pittsburgh, 1978), viii.

(E^e 07) and the Laudian Acts (E^a 08). Küster, in his 1710 edition of Mill, added three more: Codex Ephraemi Rescriptus, which had arrived in western Europe in the first part of the sixteenth century, and had recently been drawn to the attention of scholars; the Pauline bilingual Codex Boernerianus (012), which in the sixteenth century had belonged to Paul Junius of Leiden; and the Codex Campianus of the Gospels (M 021).

Wettstein cites twenty-two majuscules in his edition. To describe them he used the system of letters which has been in use ever since: for the Gospels A(02), B (03), C (04), D (05), E (07), F (09), G (011), H (013), I (022, the London leaves), K (017), L (019), M (021), N (022, the Vienna leaves), O (*l*295); for Paul, A (02), B (03), C (04), D (06), E (D^{abs1}), F (010), G (012), H (015); for Acts, A(02), B (03), C (04), D (05), E (08), F (Paris, Bibl. Nat. Coislin. 1), G (020); for Revelation, A (02), B (046), C (04). The witness he called F of the Acts is a Septuagint Octateuch. Wettstein found Acts 9.24–5 in the margin. Tischendorf (who knew it as F^a) found nineteen other such references, from the Gospels, Acts and the Pauline corpus. These readings have dropped out of sight, since the manuscript is no longer officially listed.

During the nineteenth century, a twofold process was carried on. The first was the appearance of collations and transcriptions superior to those that had hitherto been available, advanced still further in later years by the publication of facsimile editions of some manuscripts. The second was the discovery of more manuscripts. The most sensational find was, of course, that of the Sinaitic manuscript in 1844. By the time that Gregory came to write Tischendorf's *Prolegomena*, Wettstein's twenty manuscripts had become eighty-eight. Sixty-five of these are amongst those counted as majuscules today. Two were papyri (P 11 and P 14). Eleven were lectionaries. On the other hand, Tischendorf counted among the minuscules thirteen manuscripts now listed as majuscules.

By 1909, Gregory was able to double that number to 166. The two-hundred mark was passed by von Dobschutz in 1933, and the Münster *Liste* included the round sum of 250 when it appeared in 1963.[19]

Among the most important of those manuscripts to have been discovered since Tischendorf should be noticed the Freer manuscripts, one of the Gospels (W) and one of the Pauline epistles (I), bought in Cairo in 1907 and published in 1912 and 1918 respectively; and the

---

19 For a full account and bibliographical details, see J.K. Elliott, *A Bibliography of Greek New Testament Manuscripts* (SNTSMS 62) 1989, 3–7.

Koridethi Codex of the Gospels (Θ 038), which became known in 1901, and was published in facsimile in 1907.

Today, the list has reached three hundred.[20] The place of a manuscript in the list does not indicate the sequence of discovery or of publication. 0235 was first discussed in 1899,[21] 0234 in 1903, 0237 in 1912. The last two of these manuscripts were cited by von Soden as ε 49 and ε 014, though they did not receive a Gregory-Aland number until 1954.[22]

Although there is a list of three hundred items, there are not three hundred majuscule manuscripts.[23] Some manuscripts are assigned to several different numbers. Graeco-Coptic codices are prone to this, since it has been the practice of dealers to divide them into small portions to be sold separately. 070 has suffered particularly badly – portions of the manuscript are found under eleven other numbers.[24] The numbers 0152 and 0153 were reserved for talismans and ostraka respectively, and are no longer used. 0129 and 0203 are parts of the same manuscript as *l*1575; 0100 and 0195 belong with *l*963; 0192 belongs with *l*1604. These codices should be classified with the lectionaries. 055 is actually a commentary, without the complete text. 0212 is a manuscript of Tatian's Diatessaron, and it is a moot point whether it belongs in the *Liste* at all. Finally, two numbers are doubled – we have 092a and 092b, and 0121a and 0121b. Including 0212, the correct number of extant majuscule manuscripts (in 1992) is therefore 265.

We may note in passing that, with their removal from the list of majuscules, certain kinds of evidence have dropped out of sight. We have referred to the marginalia of the Paris manuscript of the Octateuch, and to the talismans and ostraka. In addition, there are a

---

20 Münster *Bericht*, 1992, 108–9.
21 Elliott, *Bibliography*, 3–7.
22 *Ibid.*, 6.
23 H. Bachmann, 'Nur Noch 241 statt 276 Majuskelhandschriften', Münster *Bericht* 1982, 69–70. Two of the new manuscripts from Mount Sinai have been assigned numbers, but belong to manuscripts already numbered. See Aland and Aland, *Text*², 104–6. There are discrepancies in their figures. According to their information, the figure should be 262, not the 263 they state.
24 F.-J. Schmitz, 'Neue Fragmente zur bilinguen Majuskelhandschrift 070', Münster *Bericht* 1982, 71–92. (The discovery of another fragment, in the British Library, was announced by H.-M. Bethge at the SNTS Textual Criticism Seminar in August, 1994.)

number of inscriptions, epigraphic and painted, that are not part of any list of the evidence available to us.[25]

3. Pre-Constantinian Majuscule Manuscripts

There are five manuscripts which may be plausibly dated to a date before 312, although the case is not proven for all of them.

The oldest is 0212, the Diatessaron fragment from Dura. Discovered in 1933, its text (containing part of a Passion narrative) was first published in 1935.[26] It is dated between 222 and 256;[27] the *terminus ante quem* is established by archaeological data. The manuscript is unique among the majuscules in that it is a roll. The hand is, in Roberts' words, 'rounded and delicate and is written with a fine pen. It stands midway between the earlier rounded hands . . . and the later "Biblical" style'.[28] A recent commentator seems doubtful that the work can be shown to be Tatian's Diatessaron.[29]

0220, containing Rom 4.23–5.3; 8–13, appears to have been found in the neighbourhood of Old Cairo. It is dated by Hatch to 'the latter part of the third century rather than early in the fourth'.[30] The text is identical with that of B, except that at 5.1 it reads ἔχομεν (א¹ B² F G P Ψ 1739 *al*) and not ἔχωμεν (א* A B* C D K L 33 *pler*).

---

25   See most recently, D. Feissel, 'La Bible dans les inscriptions grecques', *La monde grec ancien et la Bible*, ed. C. Mondesert (Bible de tous les Temps 1), Paris, 1984, 223–31, esp. 229–31. The fullest study of the subject (in Greek and Latin inscriptions) dates back to 1914; see L. Jalabert, 'Citations bibliques dans l'épigraphie grecque' and H. Leclercq, 'Citations bibliques dans l'épigraphie latine', in F. Cabrol and H. Leclercq, eds., *Dictionnaire d'archéologie chrétienne et de liturgie*, Vol. 3.2, Paris, 1914, cols. 1731–56, 1756–79.

26   C.H. Kraeling, *A Greek Fragment of Tatian's Diatessaron from Dura* (SD 3), London, 1935; a corrected edition is C.B. Welles, R.O. Fink, and J.F. Gillian, eds., *The Parchments and Papyri: The Excavations at Dura-Europos . . . Final Report*, Vol. 5, Pt 1, New Haven, 1959, 73–4.

27   C.H. Roberts, *Greek Literary Hands 350 B.C.-A.D. 400*, Oxford, 1956, 21. He provides a very clear plate (21b). See also Cavallo, *Ricerche*, 1.47 n. 7.

28   Roberts, *Greek Literary Hands*, 21.

29   William L. Petersen, 'The Diatessaron', in Helmut Koester, *Ancient Christian Gospels. Their History and Development*, London, 1990, 403–30, 412–13.

30   W.H.P. Hatch, 'A Recently Discovered Fragment of the Epistle to the Romans', *HTR* 45 (1952), 81–5. A plate is provided by Aland and Aland, *Text²*, plate 17.

0171 contains verses from Matthew 10 and Luke 22. The Lukan fragment (PSI 2, 124) was the first to be found.[31] The leaf containing Matthew (P. Berol. 11863) was published by Treu in 1966.[32] Placed by the first editor and by Cavallo in the fourth century, it is dated to about 300 by Treu and the Alands.[33] The text was deemed by Lagrange (who of course knew only the Lukan section) to be a witness to the D text.[34] The matter has been thoroughly considered more recently, notably by K. Aland, E.J. Epp, and J.N. Birdsall.[35] While Lagrange, Aland and Epp discuss the Lukan section, the Matthaean portion of the manuscript is examined by Birdsall. He noted eleven disagreements with Codex Bezae and nine agreements, including the addition at Matthew 10.23. He drew attention also to agreements between 0171 and the Old Latin Codex Bobbiensis (k).[36]

[29]

0189 (P. Berol. 11765) is a manuscript of Acts (5.3–21), published just too late to be used by Ropes.[37] The script is a book hand that had been in use since the late third century, here written well and carefully, with even pen strokes. The characters lean a little to the left. Analogies in Cavallo and Maehler are Plates 2a and 2b, the latter the Chester Beatty Ecclesiasticus (Sirach), of the early fourth century. Attempts to

---

31   Published in G. Vitelli, M. Norsa, V. Bartoletti et al., eds., *Papiri greci e latini* (Pubblicazioni della Società Italiana per la ricerca dei Papiri greci e latini in Egitto), 14 vols., Florence, 1912–57, I, 2–4 and II, 22–5.
32   K. Treu, 'Neue neutestamentliche Fragmente der Berliner Papyrussammlung', *APF* 18 (1966), 23–38, 25–8 and Plate 1.
33   Cavallo, *Ricerche*, 1.66; Treu, 'Neue neutestamentliche Fragmente', 25 (without explanation); Aland and Aland, *Text*², 123.
34   M.-J. Lagrange, *Critique Textuelle. II La Critique Rationelle*, Paris, 1935, 71–6.
35   K. Aland, 'Alter und Enstehund des D-Textes im Neuen Testament, Betrachtungen zu P⁶⁹ und 0171', in *Miscellània Papiролògica Ramon Roca-Puig*, ed. S. Janeras, Barcelona, 1987, 37–61; E.J. Epp, 'The Significance of the Papyri for determining the Nature of the New Testament Text in the Second Century: A Dynamic View of Textual Transmission', in *Gospel Traditions in the Second Century. Origins, Recensions, Text, and Transmission*, ed. W.L. Petersen; Christianity and Judaism in Antiquity 3; Notre Dame, 1989, 71–104, 98–100; J.N. Birdsall, 'The Western Text in the Second Century', in *Gospel Traditions in the Second Century*, 3–18, 6–7.
36   The Lukan portion of 0171 has recently been most carefully reconstructed by Birdsall, with a view to determining whether its text ever included 22.61. His conclusion that it did not is well sustained ('A Fresh Examination of the Fragments of the Gospel of St.Luke in ms. 0171 and an Attempted Reconstruction with Special Reference to the Recto', in *Philologia Sacra: Biblische und patristische Studien für Hermann J. Frede und Walter Thiele zu ihrem siebzigsten Geburtstag*, ed. R. Gryson, 2 vols., GLB 24, 1993, 1.212–17, with two plates).
37   A.H. Salonius, 'Die griechischen Handschriftenfragmente des Neuen Testaments in den Staatlichen Museen zu Berlin', *ZNW* 26 (1927) 97–119, 116–19 and plate.

bring the date down to 'third/fourth' seem to the present writer to be over-optimistic. The text is characterized by K. Aland as 'normal'.[38]

0162 (P Oxy 847) contains Jn 2.11–22. It was dated by its editors to the fourth century, and has been brought down to third/fourth century by the Alands.[39] The script is described in the *editio princeps* as follows: 'The rather large calligraphic script is more closely related to the sloping oval type of the third and fourth centuries than to the squarer heavier style which subsequently became common for biblical texts' (i.e. biblical majuscule).[40] There is, however, rather as in P. Oxy. 2699 (Apollonius Rhodius, *Argonautica*),[41] some influence of biblical majuscule – sigma is not markedly narrow, nu is square. Comparison with a hand like P. Herm. Rees 5,[42] dated to about 325, brings out the point. The dating of this type of hand continues to be rather problematical (Turner's dating of P. Oxy. 2699 rejects the first editor's, who considered it to be of the third century).[43] Without more detailed justification, one should be cautious in assigning 0162 to an earlier date. The text is described by Aland as 'normal'.[44] It agrees with P in all but five places, and with B in all but six.

The five manuscripts I have been discussing have one feature in common: they are none of them written in biblical majuscule, the hand which became almost standard for New Testament codices. Nor do they show a common hand. Instead, they present us with a variety of styles, as do the early papyri. One might say that they belong with those papyri in the period before the production of monumental calligraphic codices, an event which had a considerable impact on the development of the copying of New Testament texts.

---

38 K. Aland, 'Der Textcharakter der frühen Papyri und Majuskeln', Münster *Bericht* 1982, 43–58, 54. Note that by some slip, Aland and Aland, *Text*², table 4 and plate 27 assign this manuscript to the 'second/third century'. The description (104) is correct.
39 B.P. Grenfell and A.S. Hunt, eds., *The Oxyrynchus Papyri*, London, Vol. 6, 4–5 and plate VI; Aland and Aland, *Text*², 104.
40 Grenfell and Hunt, *Oxyrynchus Papyri*, Vol. 6, 4.
41 Plate 49 in E.G. Turner, *Greek Manuscripts of the Ancient World*, Oxford, 1971.
42 *Ibid.*, plate 70.
43 *Ibid.*, 88.
44 'Textcharakter der frühen Papyri', 53–4.

3.1 Biblical Majuscule

This name has its origins in Schubart's 'Bibelstil'[45] and Grenfell and Hunt's 'biblical uncial', a recurrent phrase in their Oxyrynchus volumes. We owe the detailed description of the hand to Cavallo.[46] According to his reconstruction, the hand passed through three stages: development, perfection in its 'canonical form', and decline. It is possible, according to his method, to date examples according to their place in this history. The view has been sharply criticised by E.G. Turner as a 'metaphysical concept': 'unless this hand can be proved to have emanated from a single centre, it too is unlikely to have developed and degenerated in linear fashion. If it was written in several centres it is likely that cross-influences will have affected this style, as they did other styles'.[47] If Turner is not altogether fair, it is because Cavallo's account is rather more subtle (he describes various sub-groups within this simple linear theory), and because the biblical texts were increasingly treated in a special way that is likely to have produced a special style, without the influence of a single geographical centre.

Turner describes the hand as one of three types of formal round hands, itself one of the three groups into which he divides literary hands of the first to fourth centuries.[48] In his definition, it is similar to his first type, 'in which each letter (ι only excepted) occupies the space of a square ... and only φ and ψ reach above and below the two lines', with the addition that 'υ regularly and ϱ often reach below the line'.[49] A more recent definition of the hand 'in the phase of its greatest formal perfection' endorsed by Cavallo is 'a preference for geometric forms; letters can be fitted into squares (the only exceptions being Ι Ρ Φ Ψ and Ω); a contrast in thickness between compact vertical strokes, thin horizontal and ascending strokes, descending diagonals of medium thickness (these differences in thickness are due to the angle of writing of about 75 degrees); absence of decorative crowning dashes or ornamental hooks. As for the shapes of the letters, as a general rule they repeat forms and basic structures of the alphabet of classical Greece'.[50]

[31]

---

45 W. Schubart, *Griechische Palaeographie* (Handbuch der Altertumswissenschaft 1.4.1), Munich, 1925, esp. 136–46.
46 G. Cavallo, *Ricerche*.
47 Turner, *Greek Manuscripts*, 26.
48 Ibid., 25–6.
49 Ibid., 25.
50 Cavallo and Maehler, *Greek Bookhands*, 34.

3.2 Other Hands

Cavallo and Maehler divide the book hands of the fourth to the ninth centuries into four types, of which biblical majuscule is the third.[51] The first is sloping pointed majuscule, a group which subdivides into three. The best-known example of the first of these is W, variously known as the Washington Codex and the Freer Gospels. This manuscript is regarded as so early an example of the hand by Cavallo and Maehler that they concluded that a date 'at the end of the iv century cannot be ruled out completely'.[52] For the second group we must point to a papyrus manuscript of Acts, P33. The third group is represented by 0229, a fragment of Revelation.[53] According to the *Liste*, 0229 is destroyed. New Testament majuscule manuscripts in sloping hands are not rare, and specimens may easily be found in the standard collections of plates.[54] Manuscripts in upright pointed majuscule are rarer anyway, and biblical examples scarcely exist. It is used in the captions to miniatures in 042, Codex Rossanensis. The fourth group is Alexandrian majuscule found, for example, in 0232 and P35.

In addition, there are majuscules whose hand has been influenced by local conditions. The Koridethi Codex is strange enough for one to conclude that the scribe's principal avocation was to copy Georgian characters. Codex Bezae was copied by a scribe more at home with Latin than with Greek characters, although it does not forfeit its claim to be good biblical majuscule. Carolingian bilinguals like the codices Augiensis and Sangallensis (F of Paul and Δ of the Gospels) represent an attempt to revive a lost tradition.[55]

4. Scribal Practice and Ancillary Material

In this rather general heading we include a number of topics of importance in studying our manuscripts.

---

51 *Ibid.*, 4–5.
52 *Ibid.*, 38 and plate.
53 Another part of the same codex, written by the same scribe and containing a dialogue between Basil and Gregory, is Cavallo and Maehler's Plate 28b.
54 See, e.g., the invaluable collection of W.H.P. Hatch, *The Principal Uncial Manuscripts of the New Testament*, Chicago, 1939.
55 For the copying of Greek manuscripts in the early medieval period, see G. Cavallo, 'La Produzione di Manoscritti Greci in Occidente tra Età Tardoantica e alto Medioevo. Note ed Ipotesi', *Scrittura e Civiltà* 1 (1977), 111–31.

The first is the *nomina sacra*. These are abbreviations of a number of common words, title and names of the New Testament.[56] The increase in the number of words that came to be included among the *nomina sacra*, and the use of different forms of abbreviations, help to track the development of copying in the early centuries. These matters were studied in detail by Traube; subsequent work has extended his investigation by examining the papyri.[57]

[32]

Secondly, we refer to the collection of material known as the Euthaliana. This is the name given to material provided in some manuscripts of Acts and the epistles, including brief prologues and chapter lists. It was first edited by Zacagni in 1698; it has more recently been usefully studied by L.C. Willard.[58]

A general survey of chapter divisions, canon tables, lectional notes, neumes and miniatures, all of which appear in majuscule manuscripts, is given in Professor Metzger's *Manuscripts of the Greek Bible*.[59]

5. Majuscule Manuscripts and the Papyri

Until the present century; indeed, until the middle of it, classification of texts was made on the basis of a comparison of our major majuscule witnesses – Alexandrian (ℵ and B), Caesarean (W and Θ), 'Western' (several notable bilinguals), Byzantine (A E (07) and the majority). The re-appearance of papyri has led to the beginning of a re-appraisal. In the next few paragraphs, I attempt to give an account of some of the

---

56 The list includes the following: κύριος, υἱός, Ἰησοῦς, χριστός, πατήρ, πνεῦμα, οὐρανός, Ἰσραήλ, ἄνθρωπος and σταυρός.

57 L. Traube, *Nomina Sacra: Versuch einer Geschichte der christlichen Kurzung* (Quellen und Untersuchungen zur lateinischen Philologie des Mittelalters 2), Munich, 1907; A.H.R.E. Paap, *Nomina Sacra in the Greek Papyri of the First Five Centuries A.D. The Sources and Some Deductions* (Papyrologica Lugduno-Batava 8), Leiden, 1959; J. O'Callaghan, *"Nomina Sacra" in Papyris Graecis Saeculi III Neotestamentariis* (AnBib 46), Rome, 1970; *idem.*, '"Nominum sacrorum" Elenchus in graecis Novi Testamenti papyris a saeculo IV usque ad VIII', *Studia Papyrologica* 10 (1971), 99–122. For a general survey, see C.H. Roberts, *Manuscript, Society and Belief in Early Christian Egypt* (The Schweich Lectures of the British Academy, 1977), London, 1979, 26–48. For the *nomina sacra* in Codex Bezae, see Parker, *Codex Bezae*, 97–106.

58 L.C. Willard, 'A Critical Study of the Euthalian Apparatus', unpublished doctoral dissertation, Yale, 1970.

59 Metzger, *Manuscripts of the Greek Bible*, 40–6.

studies which have addressed the relationship between papyrus and majuscule copies.[60]

The Michigan papyrus of Acts (P38) appeared, like 0189, too late for Ropes. [61] Silva New contributed a note on it to the fifth volume of *The Beginnings of Christianity*.[62] It was used, and fully discussed, by Clark.[63] Sanders claimed that 'the papyrus represents an older text, portions of which have survived in later manuscripts'.[64] Clark wrote that this papyrus 'proves beyond doubt that a Z text of Acts similar to that found in D and *c.Th.* [the text used by Thomas of Harkel in his marginalia] existed in Egypt, as well as elsewhere, at a very early date'.[65] New argued that the manuscript showed many Neutral readings, as well as larger Western readings; and therefore that it represents the kind of Western text from which she believed the Neutral text to have been produced. We can see that, in these studies, later recensions are used to classify earlier manuscripts. What was needed was a way of evaluating the older material on its own terms, and then seeing whether the Hortian recensions could have developed out of such beginnings.

The publication of P45 in 1933–4 led at once to a reappraisal of the Caesarean text.[66] Ayuso argued that the Caesarean 'text' divided into two: one, 'pre-Caesarean', contained P45 W fam. 1, 28, fam. 13; the other, Caesarean, comprised P45 Θ 565 700 Origen, Eusebius, Sinaitic Syriac, Old Georgian and Old Armenian.[67] More recently, L.W.

---

60 For a recent and very full survey of the past century of New Testament textual criticism, see J.N. Birdsall, 'The Recent History of New Testament Textual Criticism (from WESTCOTT and HORT, 1881, to the present)' (ANRW Part II: Principate, Vol. 26.1; Berlin and New York, 1992), 99–197, especially 103–9.

61 The editio princeps is by H.A. Sanders, 'A Papyrus Fragment of Acts in the Michigan Collection', *HTR* 20 (1927), 1–19.

62 S. New, 'Note 23. The Michigan Papyrus Fragment 1571' (with plate), in *The Beginnings of Christianity. Part I The Acts of the Apostles*, ed. F.J. Foakes Jackson and K. Lake, Vol. V, *Additional Notes to the Commentary*, ed. K. Lake and H.J. Cadbury, London, 1933.

63 A.C. Clark, *The Acts of the Apostles. A Critical Edition with Introduction and Notes on Selected Passages*, Oxford, 1933, 220–225.

64 Sanders, 'Papyrus Fragment', 13.

65 Clark, *Acts of the Apostles*, 220.

66 The article by C.A. Phillips, 'The Caesarean Text with Special Reference to the new Papyrus and another Ally', *BBC* 10 (1932), 5–19, preceded publication of Kenyon's edition.

67 T. Ayuso, 'El texto cesariense del papiro de Chester Beatty en el Evangelio de San Marcos', *Estudios bíblicos* 6 (1934), 268–82; '¿Texto cesariense o precesariense? su realidad y su trascendencia en la crítica textual del Nuevo Testamento', *Biblica* 16 (1935), 369–415.

Hurtado has re-examined the whole question in the Gospel of Mark.[68] He found that W and P45 form a group with the less closely related f 13. They are not related to 565 and Θ and the designation 'pre-Caesarean' must be abandoned. W and P45 are not connected to the Caesarean group.

One should note here that it is not only new materials that have contributed to a refinement in our understanding. Methods of studying the manuscripts and analysing variant readings have developed dramatically in the second half of the twentieth century. Thus Hurtado may claim greater scientific accuracy than Ayuso in his methods and conclusions.[69]

The contribution of P46 to the majuscule text of the Pauline corpus (already enriched by the discovery in 1879 of minuscule 1739) proved very fruitful. Zuntz's study of 1 Corinthians and Hebrews found a 'proto-Alexandrian' text of the *Corpus Paulinum* comprising P46 1739 B, the Sahidic and Bohairic versions, Clement of Alexandria, and Origen.[70] He used P46 to overturn Lietzmann's theory (shared, as we have seen, by New) that the Alexandrian text was based on the Western text. The oldest manuscript furnished him with evidence that it represents the original text – restored, certainly, by Alexandrian philologists, but purer than the early but corrupt Western text.

The effect of P47 on our appreciation of the text of Revelation was analogous to that of P45 on the Gospels. It enabled Schmid to divide the previously established group ℵ A C into two: the better group consists of A C; the other of P47 ℵ.[71]

[34]

P72, published in 1959, caused a reconsideration of the majuscule witnesses to the Petrine letters and Jude. J.N. Birdsall showed that in Jude it has a number of agreements with Clement of Alexandria, the Liber Commicus, and the Philoxenian Syriac.[72] He drew a parallel between this rather 'wild' text with a wide and early attestation, and the 'Western' text of the Gospels and Acts. The papyrus has more recently been described as 'normal text' in 1 and 2 Peter and 'free text'

---

68 L.W. Hurtado, *Text-critical Methodology and the Pre-Caesarean Text: Codex W in the Gospel of Mark* (SD 43), Grand Rapids, 1981.
69 See the contribution of Thomas Geer, Jr in Chapter 16 of this volume [Ehrman and Holmes, *Contemporary Research*, 253–67].
70 Zuntz, *The Text of the Epistles*.
71 J. Schmid, *Studien zur Geschichte des griechischen Apokalypse-Textes*, 2. *Die alten Stämme*, Munich, 1955.
72 J.N. Birdsall, 'The Text of Jude in P72', *JTS* 14 (1963), 394–9.

in Jude, both 'with certain peculiarities'.⁷³ J. Duplacy and C.-B. Amphoux found P72 to belong in the same group as ℵ A B C etc (agreement with B is the highest of any two manuscripts of 1 Peter in this group).⁷⁴

The publication of P75 led to similar discoveries about the earlier textual history of Luke and John. C.M. Martini, in his study of P75 and B in Luke, concluded that the remarkable relationship between these two manuscripts demonstrates them to be descended from a common archetype that was itself written not later than the end of the second century.⁷⁵

In an article published in 1968, G.D. Fee examined the text of P66 and ℵ in the Gospel of John.⁷⁶ Using the Quantitative Relationship method of analysis, he showed that there was a break in the textual character of ℵ at 8.38 or thereabouts. In John 1–8, the first hand agrees more with D, and thereafter more with P75 and B. Thus, rather than presenting an Alexandrian text with some 'Western' readings, ℵ is a divided text. Fee also concluded that in 1.16–3.16 (for which D is lacking), ℵ is our best witness to the Western text.

In his study of P66, Fee concluded that 'the alleged close relationship between P66 and ℵ exists only in John 6–7, and is the result of agreement in readings within the Western tradition'.

In a study of the text of Jn 6.52–71 published in the same year, Kieffer reached somewhat different conclusions: that there was a second Alexandrian text, 'quelque peu sauvage, fruit de modifications plus ou moins arbitraires (activité «recensionelle») operées en Égypte, probablement à Alexandrie . . . au cours du IIe s.'.⁷⁷ This wild text is partly preserved in P66-ℵ. Another revision was made in Egypt (known to us primarily from and B), which both sought out better witnesses than the P66-ℵ tradition, and corrected the primitive text. The scribe of P66 also knew a manuscript of this recension.

---

73 Aland and Aland, *Text*, 100.
74 J. Duplacy and C.-B. Amphoux, 'À propos de l'histoire du texte de la première Épître de Pierre', C. Perrot, ed., *Études sur la Première Lettre de Pierre* (Lectio divina 102), Paris, 1980, 155–73; reprinted in J. Delobel, ed., *Études de Critique Textuelle du Nouveau Testament* (BETL 78), Leuven, 309–27,
75 Martini, *Il problema del codice B*.
76 G.D. Fee, 'Codex Sinaiticus in the Gospel of John: A Contribution to Methodology in establishing textual relationships', *NTS* 15 (1968–9), 23–44.
77 R. Kieffer, *Au delà des recensions?* (Coniectanea Biblica New Testament Series 3), Lund, 1968, 222.

In a study of John 4, J. Duplacy placed ℵ in Group III, with D and the Old Latin manuscripts e and b; P66 was placed in Group II, with B Origen P75 and C.⁷⁸

In a study to which I have already referred, K. Aland has discussed the relationship of P69 to D. As in his examination of 0171, he is reluctant to find significant agreement with D.⁷⁹ Again, he prefers to consider it to be a periphrastic text, characteristic of the *kind* of text we find in D, rather than the text itself.⁸⁰

Although the preceding paragraphs may appear to have been about the papyri as much as about the majuscules, it is hoped that the shape of the story will be beginning to emerge. There have been two difficulties. The first is that the groupings of manuscripts – Alexandrian, Caesarean, and so forth – have proved problematical. Dissatisfaction with the 'genealogical method' and with the resultant theory of text-types, expressed by E.C. Colwell from 1947 onwards,⁸¹ was not only due to the impact of the papyri. Lake had called Hort's theory 'a failure, though a splendid one' as long ago as 1904. Since then, the growth in the number of witnesses has highlighted the cause of this problem: the fact that allocation to a group does not do justice to the character of individual witnesses. The more manuscripts in a group, the less individuals conform to the details, and the vaguer the criteria for admittance.

To formulate the second problem is really to express the first in a different way. Too much attention has been paid to discovering manuscript groupings, at the expense of the individuality of witnesses. How little work has been done on the majuscules (with one obvious exception) is a wonder of modern scholarship. The story that I have been unfolding is only occasionally that of the examination of witnesses on their own terms. It is nearly all the placing of manuscripts

---

78 J. Duplacy, 'Classification des États d'un texte, mathématiques et informatique: Repères historiques et recherches méthodologiques', *Revue d'histoire des textes* 5 (1975), 249–309; reprinted in J. Delobel, ed., *Études de critique textuelle du Nouveau Testament* (BETL 78), Leuven, 193–257.

79 K. Aland, 'Alter und Enstehung des D-Textes im Neuen Testament. Betrachtungen zu P und 0171', S. Janeras, ed., *Miscellania Papirologica Ramon Roca-Puig*, Barcelona, 1987, 37–61.

80 This conclusion has similarities with my arguments that a free text cannot, by its very nature, share readings with other manuscripts in the way that representatives of fixed texts (e.g. P75 and B) can. See Parker, *Codex Bezae*, 258.

81 E.C. Colwell, 'Genealogical Method: its Achievements and its Limitations', *JBL* 66 (1947), 109–33; reprinted in *Studies in Methodology in Textual Criticism of the New Testament* (NTTS 9), Leiden, 1969, 63–83.

into groups, with the principal members of which they more or less closely conform. We are in danger of losing sight of the significance of particular readings as opposed to the trend of a set of readings.

With these thoughts in mind, we turn in the final section of this study to describe the contribution to our understanding of individual majuscule witnesses in the past half century.

6. Recent Studies of the Major Majuscule Witnesses

With the dramatic exception of Codex Bezae, little enough has been written about our witnesses, except where they relate to the papyri. Since such studies have already been described, we shall not refer to them here.

The major study of Codex Sinaiticus remains that of Milne and Skeat. A series of studies of Codex Alexandrinus and Codex Petropolitanus by J. Geerlings and R. Champlin has extended Silva Lake's earlier study.[82] This has helped to refine our understanding of the place of A in the development of the Byzantine text. The palaeography of the Alexandrinus is examined with particular care by Cavallo.[83]

The standard edition of Codex Ephraemi Rescriptus (C 04), notoriously hard to read as it is, remains that of Tischendorf (1843). The most recent study is that of R.W. Lyon.[84] He produced a list of corrections to Tischendorf's transcription. This has its own problems. The edition of the Catholic Epistles in *Das Neue Testament auf Papyrus* frequently dissents;[85] in particular, Lyon does not seem to distinguish between, or at least does not indicate, readings *prima manu* and corrections. Nor does the edition of Luke made by the International Greek New Testament Project, which like the Münster edition used photographs, always concur with Lyon.[86] The production of a facsimile edition is greatly to be desired.

---

[82] S. Lake, *Family Π and the Codex Alexandrinus. The Text according to Mark* (SD 5), 1937; J. Geerlings, *Family Π in Luke* (SD 22), 1962; *Family Π in John* (SD 23), 1963; R. Champlin, *Family Π in Matthew* (SD 22), 1964. Alexandrinus is deficient down to Mt 25.6.

[83] Cavallo, *Ricerche*, 1.77–80.

[84] R.W. Lyon, 'A Re-examination of Codex Ephraemi Rescriptus', NTS 5 (1958–9), 260–72; cf. esp. 266–72.

[85] W. Grunewald, *Das Neue Testament auf Papyrus*, Vol. 1, *Die Katholischen Briefe* (ANTT 6), Berlin and New York, 1986.

[86] The Münster Institut possesses ultraviolet photographs.

One group of manuscripts to have fared pretty well is the major Graeco-Latin bilinguals.[87] H.J. Frede has dealt thoroughly with the textual tradition of the Pauline bilinguals 06 (Claromontanus), D^{abs1}, D^{abs2}, 010 (Augiensis), and 012 (Boernerianus).[88] He concluded that the first three comprised one branch, and the second two another, both derived from an archetype Z, produced in sense-lines in about 350. The relationship between F and G remains, in the present writer's opinion, rather unsatisfactorily explained.[89] The most recent study of the Claromontane codex is that of R.F. Schlossnikel.[90] By analysing the translation, in particular by isolating a distinctive vocabulary, he is able to substantiate A.C. Clark's claim that Hebrews was added to an earlier manuscript of twelve epistles.

[37]

Another ancient Graeco-Latin bilingual that has attracted some attention is 0230, a fragment of Ephesians. The Latin column is a rarity amongst our Christian manuscripts: it is written in capitalis (rustic capitals). That the Greek shows Coptic mu is no evidence that the manuscript is Egyptian in origin.

One manuscript to have suffered from almost total neglect is the Laudian Acts (08). No publication has been devoted to this manuscript since the 1930s.[91]

We come finally to Codex Bezae. This manuscript is the only majuscule to have received extended and extensive treatment in recent decades. The present writer has expressed his own opinions at length on the subject.[92] This account will attempt to describe the development of contemporary research. By analysing how study of this manuscript has developed, we shall best be able to descry the future for research on the majuscules.

The most significant development in study of the Codex Bezae in the immediate past has been the appearance of a form of *Tendenzkritik*. The earliest exponent of this in its modern form was E.J. Epp, who has

---

87 For further details, see Parker, *Codex Bezae*, 59–69.
88 H.J. Frede, *Altlateinische Paulus-Handschriften* (GLB 4), 1964.
89 See Parker, *Codex Bezae*, 66.
90 R.F. Schlossnikel, *Der Brief an die Hebräer und das Corpus Paulinum. Eine linguistische "Bruchstelle" im Codex Claromontanus (Paris, Bibliothèque Nationale Grec 107 + 107A + 107B) und ihre Bedeutung im Rahmen von Text- und Kanongeschichte* (GLB 20), 1991.
91 O.K. Walther's doctoral dissertation remains unpublished ('Codex Laudianus G35: A Re-Examination of the Manuscript, Including a Reproduction of the Text and an Accompanying Commentary', Ph. D. Dissertation, University of St Andrews, 1979).
92 Parker, *Codex Bezae*.

concentrated on anti-Judaic tendencies in Codex Bezae's text of Acts.[93] A number of smaller studies examined similar questions. It was not universally agreed that such tendencies exist.[94] More recently, methodology has been refined. Rather than isolating certain tendencies from the text, the whole shape of passages or books in the manuscript have been analysed (no doubt under the influence of literary criticism). Exponents of this method include Mees, Rice and M.W. Holmes.[95] The text of Codex Bezae is treated, in this method, not as a collection of individual variants from a standard text, but as a separate and distinctive telling of the story.

7. Conclusions

What wishes may we express for the future? First, that New Testament textual critics will not neglect to study individual codices. And, that such study will be made: best of all, with reference to the original leaves; failing that, by using reproductions. The publication of more facsimile volumes of our witnesses would contribute greatly to improving the methodological basis of our discipline. Without the study of manuscripts as physical entities, textual criticism can become a discipline out of touch with reality, dealing in variants with neither historical context nor manuscript tradition. If the examination of manuscripts were to cease, the *apparatus critici* would no longer possess meaning.

It is here that recent study of the text form of Codex Bezae, and Hurtado's conclusions with regard to the text of W, become significant.[96] Such study represents a move away from treating the manuscript tradition as a corpus containing an authentic text and a bundle of variants, to a view that sees the sum total of each bundle of variants (individual manuscripts) as an autonomous text. Duplacy's phrase 'état d'un texte' (state of text) expresses this solidity very well. When we are dealing with very fragmentary manuscripts such as most

---

93 Eldon J. Epp, *The Theological Tendency of Codex Bezae Cantabrigiensis in Acts* (SNTSMS 3), 1966.
94 For details of the debate, see Parker, *Codex Bezae*, 189–92. That bibliography may be supplemented by further references in C.D. Osburn, 'The Search for the Original Text of Acts – The International Project on the Text of Acts', *JSNT* 44 (1991), 39–55, notes on 43–4.
95 Bibliographical details in Parker, *Codex Bezae*, 189 (Rice, Holmes) and 192 (Mees).
96 Parker, *Codex Bezae*, Chapter 16; Hurtado, *Text-Critical Methodology*, 86–8.

of the papyri and majuscules, it is hard to recover a sense of solidity, to find the state of the text. The extensive majuscules, and the most distinctive minuscule groups, enable us best to do this.

Computer technology may encourage the development of this insight, by enabling us to see the text of manuscripts in two ways: as variants in an apparatus; and, with a touch of a key, as a continuous text. This technology will enable us to map the shape of our witnesses far more effectively and to determine the theological and cultural influences that led to their formation. Once that is done, we may begin to talk about the recovery of older text forms. Meanwhile, the study of the majuscules is certainly not complete. It may prove scarcely to have begun.

Note

This article was written before the second edition of the *Liste* was published. I have updated it as necessary on several occasions.

5 Was Matthew Written before 50 CE?

The Magdalen Papyrus of Matthew

The Times of 24 December, 1994 carried an article headed 'Eyewitness to Christ', followed two days later by 'In Search of Gospel Truth'. This double contribution to the festive season inaugurated a lively correspondence (29 December onwards) about the issues it covered, which spilled over into *The Tablet* and *The Church Times*. The articles were generated by a claim by a German writer C.P. Thiede that a papyrus fragment of Matthew's Gospel now in Magdalen College, Oxford, dates from the middle of the first century and that the Gospel itself was therefore written before that date. Both they and much of the correspondence were rendered inadequate through their confusion of two separate questions. The first and proper issue is a palaeographical one: what is the age of this fragment of Matthew's Gospel? It can only be examined and solved by the proper application of the science of palaeography. The second question is the claim that an early date for the papyrus establishes or enhances the historical value of Matthew's Gospel. The question arises here of the uses of palaeography. Some people who know nothing whatsoever about palaeography, but have very clear ideas about the Gospels and biblical scholarship, have responded rather enthusiastically to Thiede's claims. In this study, I shall offer my comments on the date suggested by Thiede for the papyrus[1] and place them in the context of some reflections on the disciplines of palaeography and papyrology and their role in biblical studies. I shall deal with these wider questions first.

The History

The modern science of palaeography has its origins in Bernard de Montfaucon's *Palaeographia Graeca*, which was published in 1708. Palaeography may be defined as the comparison and analysis of

---

1 Thiede's arguments are set out in the *Zeitschrift für Papyrologie und Epigraphik* 105, (1995), 13–20 and plate 17. The same article, with minor corrections may be found in *Tyndale Bulletin* 46 (1995), 29-42.

ancient hands, leading to their classification and dating. It has often been taken to include other aspects of book production, though today these are often placed under the separate heading of codicology.

There are three principal reasons why palaeography has developed to its present sophistication. The first is the increase in the numbers of manuscripts known to us, both by the systematic exploration of libraries leading to the production of catalogues and by the recovery of materials, especially tens of thousands of papyri, from the sands of Egypt. The second is the development of transport. The train, the steamship, the motor car and the jet aircraft have made it increasingly easy for the scholar to travel from library to library, examining at first hand the raw materials of the trade, and building up a fund of knowledge which would have been the envy of a scholar of an earlier generation. The third reason is the photograph. The camera has made it possible to examine, without even moving from the study, reproductions of thousands of different manuscripts.

The Discipline

Under these favourable conditions, the palaeographer is able to date most manuscripts with a high degree of confidence to a period of half a century. The process of dating may be divided between those manuscripts for which we have some precise piece of information, and those on which we have to depend solely on palaeography. It was common during the Byzantine period to provide the date on which a manuscript was completed. The oldest dated manuscript of the New Testament (indeed, it is the oldest dated minuscule) is dated 7 May 835.

Sometimes there is archaeological or even historical evidence which gives some help. The Herculaneum papyri must have been copied before 79, when the town was engulfed by molten larva; the Qumran texts were hidden in their caves in the late sixties of the first century. Sometimes the character of a manuscript will help. A copy of a chronicle cannot be older than the latest date which it records.

All these are somewhat unusual circumstances, but such fixings will help us to date undated manuscripts by their similarity to ones that are, or may corroborate conclusions already drawn from palaeographical evidence. Most of the time, the only evidence is what may be found on the open page. There are two lines of approach.

The first is codicological. The form (roll or codex), material (papyrus or vellum), size, layout, quality of materials, type of ink, use of coloured inks, running titles, headings and colophons, page numbers, quire signatures, lines of ruling, may all be significant in locating the manuscript in time and place. Scribes worked in scriptoria, where they were trained in the house style and whose traditions they will have preserved. Different fashions were in vogue at different times.

The second line of approach is palaeographical. It proceeds from analysis to comparison. It needs to be emphasised that the analysis of a hand depends primarily not on the *shape* of letters, but on their *formation*: on the sequence of letter strokes and their comparative thicknesses, on the angle of the pen, on the proportions of height and breadth in the characters, on the use of serifs and flourishes at the end of strokes. Having analysed a hand, one then makes and tests a comparison with other similar hands. Here too formation and not shape is the guide. An obvious similarity between two letters in two manuscripts may be misleading. The precise way in which the scribe formed them may have been quite different. An important part of the comparison of two hands is that the comparison of *all* the letters of the alphabet is required. Twelve may be similar, but then as many more will be dissimilar and one would be mistaken in claiming that the hands were similar.

[41]

The consequence of analysis and comparison is the placing of an individual hand within a group. Those that concern us here are book hands. These are, to a greater or lesser extent, high-quality calligraphic achievements, written for ease and pleasure in reading. There are, apart from the variation of individual hands, many types. The most noted for the copying of New Testament manuscripts is the famed 'biblical majuscule' in which such fine manuscripts as the codices Sinaiticus and Vaticanus are copied. It contains various sub-groups, and its development has been carefully charted, so that it is possible to date a hand within it rather precisely.

Apart from the assistance of dated manuscripts, or helpful *termini ante et post quos*, it will have become clear that we date manuscripts by placing them in a sequence. The comparison leads us to conclude that y is younger than x but older than z, so that the chronological sequence must be x–y–z. If we can determine that x is younger than w, which can be dated from the archaeological evidence of its provenance to the year 300, then we know that x, y and z are all fourth century or later. Of course, it is particularly gratifying when some piece of external evidence is found which supports a dating previously reached only on palaeographical grounds.

Within the sequence, there must be some caution in offering an absolute date. One reason is that a scribe may have learned a hand in his youth, and used it for the rest of his professional life. Another is that fashions are unlikely to have changed everywhere at precisely the same time and same rate. An outer limit of half a century is a safe margin.

The comparison of the datings offered by palaeographers leads us to the conclusion that some are bold, and offer dates as early as they dare, while others are excessively cautious and estimate the latest conceivable date. Wisdom suggests that we keep within these extremes. With manuscripts of the New Testament there is an added complication: the pressure felt by some to reject more cautious dates as somehow born of scepticism, and to glory in an early date as proof of the Gospel. Here I turn to the limits of palaeography.

Palaeography and the Gospels

Palaeography is a discipline which at the very best can reach these conclusions: when a manuscript was written and where; where and when it was corrected; how well trained and competent the scribe was; something of the social and cultural context of the manuscript and its copyist; if we are fortunate, there may be evidence in the manuscript which tells us something about earlier manuscripts from which it is descended. All of this is of great significance, for the knowledge of the way in which it was copied and passed down is of great value in our finding out how a text was changed as it was copied, and so recovering its earlier forms. We learn too about the text's reception and use, and so about early Christianity. But palaeography can tell us nothing directly about the origins of the text preserved in a manuscript, nor can it offer any comments on the historical value of that text. The most that it can do is provide a date by which a text must have been produced.

For example, P52 is a fragment of John that was copied in the second quarter of the second century. When it was found, the hypothesis that the Gospel of John had been written as late as the middle of the second century had to be abandoned. But because the Fourth Gospel was composed somewhat earlier than some had supposed, before the year 125 CE, it does not follow that it offers a more accurate verbatim record. Even were a manuscript dating from the year 40 to be discovered, thereby demonstrating that the Gospel was written in the thirties, the question of its value for recovering the genuine deeds and words of Jesus would be a quite separate one.

This is part of a more general point: the dating of a Gospel and the assessment of its historical value are separate. A tradition is not necessarily accurate because it is early, nor false because it is late.

> Here is a tale of things done ages since;
> What truth was ever told the second day?

Palaeography has nothing to contribute to such a debate, and the independence of its methods is jeopardised when it is pressed into such dubious service.

Papyrology

I conclude these general points with a brief description of the science of papyrology. Its origins lie in the late eighteenth century, with the discovery of the Herculaneum papyri. It was with the discovery of the large collections of materials in Egypt that it developed. Such extensive finds as the Oxyrhynchus papyri, with over fifty volumes published and more still to appear,[2] have revolutionised not only the study of ancient manuscripts, but our knowledge of the ancient world. For the study of the New Testament, we now have approximately one hundred papyri registered. A number are extensive, the majority are not. Apart from their textual significance in providing evidence hitherto lacking of the New Testament text of the third and even the second century, they are also of great palaeographical value. The papyri dating from the fourth to the seventh centuries have increased our knowledge of the hands of that period, and those that are older enable us to chart from an early stage the hands used in the copying of the New Testament.

The science of papyrology is divided into the study of documentary papyri and of literary papyri. It is in the decipherment of documentary papyri that it reaches its greatest heights. The ability to transcribe a damaged and badly written text about whose contents there are no prior clues ranks among the greatest achievements of the ancient historian. But the reading of any papyrus (or, indeed, any ancient manuscript) will often call for patience, experience and careful judgement. Sometimes only part of a letter or a sequence of letters will

[42]

---

2   The early volumes were edited by B.P. Grenfell and A.S. Hunt, of whom more below.

be extant, and the decision how the text may be restored should not be made too quickly. Sometimes a ridge or a blemish on the papyrus sheet will show up (especially in a photograph) as uncommonly like a pen stroke. Sometimes letters will be blurred, or a correction will have made the passage hard to read. Sometimes a scribe may have been careless, or even have written so poorly that each letter is not clearly distinguishable.

The papyri have brought palaeography down to the second century of the Christian era. But there is still a gap between the earliest literary stages of the New Testament and the oldest extant manuscripts. It is to an attempt to deny that gap that we now turn.

The Magdalen Papyrus

This papyrus fragment contains parts of Matthew 26. It is numbered P64 in the list of New Testament Greek manuscripts, and is listed as Gr. 18 in the Magdalen College Catalogue. Another fragment of the same codex, containing fragments of Matthew chapters 3 and 5 and numbered P67 is in Barcelona. Yet a third probable part of this book is in Paris, numbered P4 and containing parts of Luke chapters 1, 2, 3 and 5.[3] The date generally given to P64 and P67 is about the year 200 (remembering that we take this as the median point of half a century).

Thiede suggests that the Magdalen papyrus of Matthew dates from between 70 and 100. To carry his argument, he has to achieve three objectives. The first is the satisfactory analysis of the hand under discussion with which one should begin. This stage is simply lacking. The other two are both based on the process of comparison which we have seen to belong with the first to the essence of palaeographical study. He needs to demonstrate that the parallels used by others to support a date of around 200 are false, and to establish that there are convincing parallels between the papyrus and first-century hands.

---

3 Thiede initially dismisses the connection between P4 and the other leaves as though it had been abandoned. The matter is taken up by P.W. Comfort in the same issue of *Tyndale Bulletin* as Thiede's article: 'Exploring the Common Identification of Three New Testament Manuscripts: P[4], P[64] and P[67]', *Tyndale Bulletin* 46 (1995), 43–54. Although his article contains some useful information, it lacks a scientific comparison of the hands. Thiede makes a contribution to the subject in the same issue, 55–7 ('Notes on P[4] = Bibliothèque Nationale Paris, Supplementum Graece 1120/5'). They both seem to believe that P4 is by the same scribe, but is from a different book written at a different time.

C.H. Roberts, the first editor of the Magdalen fragments, argued for a date in the late second century from comparison with four papyri.[4] Thiede does not challenge the comparisons. He does not even comment on them. He introduces the claim that some papyri have been dated too late because Hunt and Grenfell believed no codex to be older than the third century. This is not pertinent, since all of Roberts' examples are rolls and not codices, and since Roberts had already dealt with this matter. Thiede does not assay the necessary task of tackling more recent studies of Greek palaeography, such as Cavallo's *Biblica maiuscola*, in which there are many examples of hands similar to the Magdalen papyrus, whose dating supports Roberts' conclusions.[5]

Thus Thiede does not even attempt the first objective. What about his claim that there are similar first-century hands? He suggests five parallels. One is from Herculaneum. He does not offer any direct comparison, merely observing that this manuscript is 'another first century analogy'.[6] There is no evidence offered here, so we have to set it aside. The other four are Greek manuscripts found at Qumran. Thiede's method of comparison is to list letters which he considers to be the same shape, and to claim this as evidence that the manuscripts are contemporaries. It will be clear from my description of palaeographical method that there are two basic errors of methodology here. The first is that the analysis of a hand depends primarily not on the shape of letters, but on their formation. The second error is that the comparison of two hands requires the comparison of *all* the letters of the alphabet. Thiede does not even discuss the dissimilar letters. Granting all this, is there any parallel between the Magdalen papyrus and these Qumran manuscripts? His first item for comparison is a papyrus fragment known as $7Q6_1$. He claims similarity solely on the grounds that in both eta (H) has 'the horizontal stroke above the median'. This is worthless. The feature is found in all but the squarest book hands, in all periods. Two other examples containing Leviticus (4QLXXLev[a] and [b]) are simply not used with enough precision for one to make a reasoned response. The former has eight letters 'etc' which are 'identical or near-identical';[7] the other 'shows several letters resembling [the Magdalen papyrus], such as the Alpha, the Beta, etc'. Unless we know the scope of 'etc', and the criteria according to which

[43]

---

4   C.H. Roberts, 'An Early Papyrus of the First Gospel', HTR 46 (1953), 233–7 and plate, 235f.
5   Cavallo, *Ricerche*.
6   Thiede, *art. cit.*, 17.
7   *Ibid.*

such words as 'resembling', 'identical' and 'near-identical' are used, we cannot comment.

Turning to his main example, a fairly extensive Minor Prophets Scroll, there is another fault in Thiede's study. This scroll is the work of two scribes, and Thiede does not tell us which of them he is offering for comparison. But whichever we take, his argument cannot be substantiated. He claims that alpha is one of six letters which are particularly alike in the two manuscripts. But even a brief glance shows that he is mistaken. The Qumran alphas are generally (not invariably) written like our upper-case A, the Magdalen letter is written with the equivalent of our two left hand strokes as a curved bow, with the third stroke at a more acute angle to the line of writing. Iota, rather than 'particularly close',[8] is almost as different as so simple a letter could be (though less markedly so in Scribe B of the Qumran manuscript). Taking the questions of formation ignored by Thiede, the Qumran hands have narrower letters, while those in the Matthew papyrus could each be placed within a square. The pen strokes at Qumran are thinner in proportion to the size of the letters, giving a more spindly appearance to the script. The Qumran hands (especially Scribe A) have pronounced horizontal serifs to many of the verticals, while the Matthew hand has only the slightest of stops of the pen. So different are these two manuscripts, that I had to check more than once to ensure that I had in my hand the right volume of *Discoveries in the Judaean Desert*.[9]

This is not an exhaustive description of the shortcomings in Thiede's paper. It is a list of the chief of them. They are so basic as to render his paper worthless. I find it extraordinary that any one could even have thought of comparing the Magdalen papyrus with these hands from Qumran or, having done so, find it closer to them than to the early stages of biblical majuscule. Thiede has failed to achieve his necessary objectives. It is a matter for sorrow that such a claim should have been made in so public a manner.

This debate at least serves to illustrate the value, scope and methods of palaeography. This piece is written in the hope that it will encourage general appreciation of both palaeography and papyrology, and discourage those who are inclined to give credence to the incredible.

---

8 Thiede, *art. cit.*, 16.
9 E. Tov, *The Greek Minor Prophets Scroll from Nahal Hever (8HevXIIgr) (The Seiyâl Collection 1)* (Discoveries in the Judaean Desert 8), Oxford, 1990.

Addendum

The original cause of this contribution is fast becoming forgotten, and I reprint it not on account of the criticisms of a particular claim, but for its general comments on the history and methodology of palaeography.

6 Codex Bezae and other Greek New Testament Manuscripts in Cambridge University Library

Some manuscripts are famed for the beauty of the hand in which they are written; others because they reproduce an outstandingly pure text; others because they are the oldest or the only copy of that text; others even by association with the author. For none of these reasons could the Codex Bezae Cantabrigiensis commend itself to us. Its copyist, while writing in a regular and professional hand, cannot have been famed for his calligraphy. And while much can be said about the text of the Gospels and Acts which it contains, even most of those who consider it to be valuable confess that it is by no means pure. Nor could Codex Bezae, today at least, be regarded as of remarkable antiquity. Certainly, a century ago it would have been among the dozen or so oldest known copies of the Greek New Testament. But today it is a full two and a half centuries younger than our oldest manuscript. As to uniqueness, it is one among thousands of witnesses to the text of those books it contains. And yet, even though it has no claim to eminence on any of these scores, there can be few other manuscripts in existence about which more has been written. No other New Testament witness could even begin to rival its bibliography of monographs, articles and editions. In what lies its fascination?

Before attempting to answer that question by calling for the two dark green boxes in which the manuscript is kept, let us order to our desk in the Manuscripts Reading Room a few of the other New Testament manuscripts kept in the University Library, and see whether a comparison will help us to understand. There are 46 Greek New Testament witnesses (if we include ones that belong to other institutions but are held in the Library). Just over half of them were, as one might expect, copied in the period 1000–1300. Although a small collection by some standards (there are about 370 each in Paris and Rome, and the world's largest concentration, on Mount Athos, contains 900) it is still the fourteenth largest collection of Greek New Testament manuscripts, and more than makes up in variety and interest for what it lacks in bulk. Time restricts us, so we must sample carefully.

We begin with the oldest, the fragmentary remains of a papyrus codex of Romans (Add. 7211, numbered P27 in the listing of Greek New Testament manuscripts). Containing verses from chapters 8 and 9, it was copied in the course of the third century, and thus pre-dates Codex Bezae by over a century. There is one other papyrus witness in the library (Add. 5893, P17), a fourth-century witness containing parts of eight verses of Hebrews 9. Compared to these tiny papyrus remains, Codex Bezae is extensive, containing as it does, on the 406 out of its original 534 parchment leaves, most of the four Gospels and Acts. Its only extensive gaps are 67 folios between the Gospels and Acts (which perhaps contained Revelation and the Johannine Epistles), and the last six chapters of Acts. P17 and P27 are the only two University Library manuscripts older than Codex Bezae. Four more approach it in age. The first is a palimpsest manuscript, containing fragments of the first eleven chapters of Luke's Gospel (BFBS MSS 213, 040 in the listing of New Testament Greek manuscripts). Called Codex Zacynthius, because it was found on the Ionian isle of Zante, it is given a letter as well as a number: Ξ, 040. The use of letters for majuscule manuscripts of the New Testament pre-dates the use of numeral indicators. Codex Bezae is known as D (a demonstration that it was one of the first majuscules known). Although generally dated to the sixth century, it is in this writer's judgement, of the seventh. This manuscript is of great interest, because it contains an excellent text, because it has the same division into chapters as the famous Codex Vaticanus (along with at the most two other witnesses), and because it is the oldest witness to contain a commentary (in the form of a catena of patristic comments) as well as the text. It is a matter of great regret to modern scholarship that it was re-used in the thirteenth century to make a lectionary text of the Gospels (*l*299). The other three manuscripts are of the sixth century. The first of them (Ms/Add. 1875, *l*1354) is a lectionary. More notably, it is bilingual: it contains the readings in Greek and Coptic. In this respect it is like Codex Bezae, which is a Greek–Latin bilingual, one of only four surviving from the early church. Bilingual manuscripts are not uncommon. There are two others in the Library, also lectionaries; one (Add. 1879.13; *l*311) is four pages of a Graeco-Arabic witness, of the twelfth century, the other (Or. 1699; *l*1575) consists of two leaves of a ninth-century Graeco-Coptic witness. Other leaves of the same manuscript survive in Vienna, Paris and London. The other two sixth-century witnesses belong with Codex Bezae as codices written on parchment in majuscule (also known as uncial) letters, containing the continuous text. They are a Cairo Genizah manuscript, Taylor-Schechter 12, 189.208 (093), a palimpsest of two leaves of Acts and 1 Peter, which were re-used to copy a Hebrew text; and 0246. The latter, the property of Westminster College, Cambridge, is a fragment of the Epistle of James. The page was later scraped for re-writing, but never used.

We have now looked at eight manuscripts; three of them palimpsests, all extremely fragmentary. This indicates how fortunate we are that any manuscripts so extensive as Codex Bezae should have survived from antiquity.

And now the time has come to return this large pile of manuscripts to the long-suffering counter, and beg for a sight of one of the most intriguing manuscripts of Antiquity. We will not be allowed to see it unless we have good reason. And rightly so, for the metallic-based ink which the scribes used has released an acid which has slowly eaten through the fine parchment, weakening it. Animal skin is a strong and durable substance, but it cannot be expected to survive for 1600 years unscathed. The very fine thicknesses achieved here lead to the pages curling very sharply as soon as the pressure that keeps the volumes closed in their boxes is released. The codex was rebound thirty years ago by Douglas Cockerill of Grantchester, in a vellum binding similar to that which he employed for the Codex Sinaiticus. It has been bound into two volumes, matching the two of the facsimile edition.

I have anticipated much of what is before us when we open a volume at random: written in majuscule letters in about the year 400, we see a page of the four Gospels and Acts. The parchment is fine and pale in colour, the ink an attractive olive-brown. Each page is 26 cm high and 21.5 cm across. On the left page (verso) is the Greek text, and on the right (recto) a Latin version of it. The lines are uneven in length, written in units of sense (or at least meant to be). There is quite a generous margin, and a running title at the top of each page. What is the history of this 1600-year-old bundle of skins?

We begin in uncertainty. Debate about the area in which it was produced continues. I have argued that it was made in Berytus (modern Beirut) by a Latin copyist who spent most of his time turning out legal texts and documents. There are two lines of argument, the one palaeographical, the other based on the early history of the manuscript.

Other suggestions recently canvassed include Jerusalem, Egypt and the Rhône valley.[1]

The manuscript was frequently corrected and annotated. There is a sequence of about eighteen hands, of whom the most important worked in the first hundred years or so. Nearly half of all corrections are to the text of Acts, and every corrector but the earliest worked principally on the Greek text. Some of the most unexpected secondary material is the addition in the margin (sometime between 550 and 650) of sentences for use in fortune telling. An example is 'If you lie, they will condemn you'. The manuscript is not unique in containing them. There is a similar set in a later manuscript from St. Gall, and there is a whole group of papyrus manuscripts of John in which each page shows a short passage from the Gospel followed by such a sentence. By my reconstruction of events, all this happened in Berytus, or at least in Syria. We now move on to surer ground, for without doubt we find the manuscript in Lyons in the middle of the ninth century. Some pages were replaced at that time, and the proof is found in the replacement pages. They contain blue ink and a particular form of interrogation mark. Both features are *lyonnaise*. Further evidence is that some of the New Testament citations of a writer of Lyons called Ado show close similarities to the text of Codex Bezae. In addition, I have recently proposed that the restored leaves were copied from a surviving *lyonnaise* manuscript (Lyons, Bibliothèque Municipale 431). The thesis has been advanced that the leaves were penned by the famous Florus of Lyons. This is, however, hard to sustain; but that his was the inspiration behind the manuscript's restoration, only one of many marks of respect to antiquity with which early medieval Lyons is associated, can hardly be doubted.

For the next 600 years there is – silence. Then, in the sixteenth century, renewed interest. The manuscript is cited in 1546 at the Council of Trent as witness to a reading at the end of John's Gospel. It is collated for Cardinal Sirleto (1514–1585). In 1550 it features as one of the fifteen witnesses cited in the first Greek New Testament to contain variant readings. In 1562 Lyons was sacked during a religious war, and the manuscript was removed from the Monastery of St Irenaeus to Geneva, where it passed into the possession of the Reformer Théodore

---

1 Parker, *Codex Bezae*; J.N. Birdsall, 'The Geographical and Cultural Origin of the Codex Bezae Cantabrigiensis: a Survey of the *Status Quaestionis*, mainly from the Palaeographical Standpoint', in W. Schrage (ed.), *Studien zum Text und zur Ethik des Neuen Testaments (Festschrift H. Greeven)* (BZNW 47), Berlin and New York, 1986, 102–14.

de Bèze (latinised as Beza). Although Beza produced a number of editions of the Greek New Testament, only in the first did he make any use of his venerable possession. Indeed, thereafter he rated it very low, so low that when he gave it to the University of Cambridge in 1581, he took some of the generosity out of the deed in his accompanying letter, saying that it was 'better hidden than published', and that he suspected that its corruption was the work of ancient heretics. The University's gracious acceptance of the gift avoided any comment on the gift itself.

But if Bezae thought that this dubious manuscript would be safely lost to view in its new home, he was mistaken. From within fifty years of its removal to Cambridge it was the frequent object of study. Such famous scholars as Mill, Wettstein and Tischendorf collated it. In 1793 Thomas Kipling published a transcript of the manuscript, and in 1864 F.H.A. Scrivener produced another and extremely accurate one, which contained lists of the corrections. A facsimile was printed in 1899.

Such is the history of the manuscript. A Greek–Latin bilingual, with its numerous early correctors and annotators, its flourishing in the ninth-century renaissance of Lyons, and its re-appearance in the Renaissance of the sixteenth century, it almost provides a history in miniature of the dealings between Greek-speaking and Latin-speaking Christendom.[2] But even the interest of the history of the manuscript pales before the fascination of its text, and it is an attempt to illuminate its unique significance in early Christianity that will occupy our remaining space. The best approach is to take a passage as illustration. The text of the Revised Standard Version (RSV) (with a few changes to bring out the underlying Greek text more clearly) and the Greek text of Codex Bezae (I have made my own translation for the occasion) are set in parallel columns. Where the latter contains additions, they are given in bold type; where one word is substituted for another, it is in italics. Changes in word order in the Greek are indicated by underlining (with double underlining where there are minor changes in order within a larger re-ordering of material). Words found in the RSV and omitted in Codex Bezae have a line through them in the former. The passage is the beginning of Luke 6.

[40]

[41]

---

2 Parker and Amphoux, *Codex Bezae*.

RSV	Codex Bezae
¹ And it came to pass on a sabbath, that he was going through the grainfields, and his disciples plucked and ate some heads of grain, rubbing them in their hands.	¹ *And* it came to pass on a **second-first** sabbath that he was going through the grainfields, *and* his disciples **began to** pluck the heads of grain and rubbing them in their hands ate.
² But some of the Pharisees said, 'Why are you doing what is not lawful to do on the sabbath?'	² But some of the Pharisees *said* **to him** '**See** *what your disciples* do on the sabbath which is not lawful.'
³ And Jesus answering them said	³ *But* Jesus answering them *said*
... (⁴) and also gave it to those with him?	... (⁴) and also gave it to those with him?'
⁵ And he said to them, 'The Son of man is lord of the sabbath.'	
	The same day, seeing someone working on the sabbath, he said to him, 'Man, if indeed you know what you are doing then you are blessed. But if you do not know, then you are accursed and a transgressor of the law.'
⁶ On another sabbath, when he entered the synagogue and taught, a man was there whose right hand was withered.	⁶ *And when he entered again* into the synagogue on a sabbath, *in which there was* a man *who had a withered hand*,
⁷ And the scribes and the Pharisees watched him ... (¹⁰) and his hand was restored.	⁷ the scribes and the Pharisees watched him ... (¹⁰) and his hand was restored **so as to be like the other one.**

	⁵ And he said to them **that** The son of man is lord **even** of the sabbath.
¹¹ But they were filled with fury ...	¹¹ But they were filled with fury ...

... There are three ways in which the text of Codex Bezae is distinctive. Generally, it may be seen that there are numerous small changes which, tiny in themselves, together constitute a writing of the text. Of the 172 words of Codex Bezae that we have printed, only 53 are in ordinary Roman type. Secondly and most evidently, there is the length. The RSV passage contains 108 words against Codex Bezae's 172. Besides minor additions, a whole passage has been added, the story of the man working on the sabbath, dubbed by Dr Ernst Bammel the *pericope cantabrigiensis*.[3] Found in no other source, it is an event in the life of Jesus which some scholars (mostly notably Joachim Jeremias) have claimed to be authentic.[4] Thirdly, the simple act of placing verse five after verse ten makes a triplet of stories on the theme 'The son of man is lord of the sabbath', and thus radically revises Luke's structure.

I have chosen the passage, of course, because its divergences are so marked. It is universally agreed, however, that Codex Bezae offers a separate edition of the Gospels, even though its 'text of Matthew and John is less evidently distinctive than that of Luke and Mark. As for Acts, its text is even more markedly different. Considerably longer than that of the other early majuscule manuscripts such as the codices Sinaiticus and Vaticanus, it has long been recognized that it constitutes a separate edition of Luke's second book. Recent study has demonstrated that although Codex Bezae is a principal witness to the longer text, it contains a form of it that has undergone further development. Some scholars have suggested that both texts come from Luke's pen. A few have argued in favour of the authenticity of the longer text. The majority have favoured the shorter version.[5]

In writing of addition and revision in the passage from Luke 6, I am, of course, assuming that Codex Bezae does not present the original text. But the question must be raised whether it in fact *is* authentic, and that it is most other manuscripts that are wrong. There are, and long

---

3 E. Bammel, 'The Cambridge Pericope. The Addition to Luke 6.4 in Codex Bezae', *NTS* 32 (1986), 404–26.
4 J. Jeremias, *Unknown Sayings of Jesus*, London, 1957, 49–54.
5 W. Strange, *The Problem of the Text of Acts* (SNTSMS 71), Cambridge, 1992.

have been, scholars who maintain that Codex Bezae provides the authentic text. They have always been in a minority. There are a number of possible positions:

1. Codex Bezae presents us with a hopelessly corrupt text of the Gospels and Acts.
2. Although Codex Bezae is largely corrupt, it does on occasion preserve the original text. This is the majority position.
3. Codex Bezae is a corrupt representative of one of the earliest types of text. This is not incompatible with (2).
4. Codex Bezae preserves the original text.
5. The original text cannot be recovered, but Codex Bezae is the oldest and best text available to us, dating from the second century.
6. Codex Bezae is a late example of a way of copying the text that felt quite free as regards the precise wording.

[43]   It is the last alternative that the present writer favours. I have argued that the manuscript is a late survivor of the period when the precise letter was of less value to Christians than the spirit of the tradition. Thus, stories could be added from oral tradition before they were lost, and a Gospel could be subtly revised to bring out the evident meaning, the moral pointed and the tale adorned. Such revision is similar to the ways in which the earliest Gospel (Mark) was altered by its successors, Matthew and Luke. This is not to say that the manuscript's text is altogether a late creation. In the Gospels, Codex Bezae's Greek text is close to the earliest (late second- or third-century) translations of the Gospels into Syriac and Latin. Its Latin text shows signs of being influenced by two third- and fourth-century traditions of Latin translation, the African and the European. The Greek text has, moreover, close affinities to the texts of second-century writers (where we can recover them).

While the majority of its readings are not original, and although its text continued to be freely altered, Codex Bezae is a key witness to the most widely used text of the second century. And, apart from the age of the text, the manuscript's value rests in its character. For it manifests that freedom in copying which typified the early Christian attempt to honour not the wording of the tradition but its spirit.

7 A New Oxyrhynchus Papyrus of Revelation: P115 (P. Oxy. 4499)

The publication of this papyrus in the latest (66th) volume of the Oxyrhynchus series is a significant contribution to our understanding of the text of the book of Revelation.[1] Since the exhaustive studies of Josef Schmid have succeeded in providing a definitive reconstruction of the text's history, we are able to build on a sure foundation.[2] Before looking at the text of the papyrus, I shall describe its contents and offer some very brief palaeographical comments.

1. Description

The extant portions consist of nine different leaves, containing Rev 2.1–3, 13–15, 27–9; 3.10–12; 5.8–9; 6.4–6, and (with gaps) 8.3–15.7. The editors suggest original dimensions of at least 14.5 x 22 cm, with a written area of 12.5 x 18.5. It may well have been copied into a codex that had already been bound, since the left-hand pages tend to have a narrower written area than the right-hand ones. It is not possible to know whether the codex contained other texts.

Palaeography offers the date of late third or early fourth century, largely on the grounds of some older elements, such as rounded alpha and beta, and the forms of delta, kappa and nu. We therefore have a manuscript probably somewhat older than Codex Sinaiticus (ℵ), but not as old as P47.[3] Textually, it may shed light on a crucial period in the development of the text of Revelation.

[160]

---

1   N. Gonis, J. Chapa, etc., *The Oxyrhynchus Papyri*, London, 1999, 10–37. The papyrus' editor, J. Chapa, deserves our congratulations.
2   J. Schmid, *Studien zur geschichte des Griechischen Apokalypse-Textes* (Münchener Theologische Studien), 1. Teil, *Der Apokalypse-Kommentar des Andreas von Kaisareia*, 2 vols., Munich, 1956; 2. Teil, *Die Alten Stämme*, Munich, 1955.
3   I favour dating ℵ at or slightly after the middle of the fourth century, and P47 at the end of the third.

2. Orthography and Punctuation

This is pretty good, with care in the use of diaeresis over initial iota and upsilon, and diastolle. Itacisms include[4]

    6.5 ϊδ[ον] for ειδον (and in more than a dozen other manuscripts)
    9.2 κ[α]μεινου for καμινου
    9.19 αιχου[cαι] for εχουcαι
    10.3 μοι[καται] for μυκαται (and also in C)
    14.6 ϊδον for ειδον (and in more than a dozen other manuscripts).

3. Corrections

There are twelve corrections. Some appear to be by the first hand, others by a corrector. They are as follows:

Page/Line	Ref.	Originally written	Correction	How written	Hand
5/3	2.27	αυτου[c]	OM	line written over word	?
6/1	3.10	[τ]ους τ[ους]	τ[ους]	line written over 1st word	?
6/4	3.12	] γαου [		ω written above ου	scribe
13/13	8.7	γ″	τρι[τ]ο[ν]	γ″ changed to τρι, τον added above	corrector
15/97	9.20	[προcκυνη]coυcι[ν]	[προcκυνη]cωcι[ν]	ω written above ου	scribe
16/113	10.4	φωνην .. [ ]	φωνην [ ]	line written over letters[5]	?
17/163	11.9	τα [πτωματα]	κα[ ]	κα written above	corrector
17/175	11.12	.	OM	line written over letter?[6]	?
18/199	11.18	διαφθειρ]ονας	διαφθειρ]οντας	τ written above	scribe

---

4   I do not include ϊc[τηκει] at 12.4 here, but as a variant at 4.4.5. below.
5   There is too much space in the papyrus for what one would expect from other witnesses, suggesting that something extra has been written by mistake.
6   All that is visible is a trace of ink with a line over it. Since the text of other witnesses does not provide either a *nomen sacrum* or any other abbreviation such as a numeral sign, a mark of deletion as at 2.27 seems the best explanation.

20/273	13.3	OM	εκ	added above the line	scribe
21/323	13.18	[ ]η	OM	line written over letter[7]	?
23/380	14.15	ωρ[α]	η ωρ[α]	η written above line	corrector

[161]

At present it is not clear to me whether the corrections with a superline are by the first hand or the corrector. This is awkward, because the first of them presents a variant reading. Three of the corrections (2.27; 9.20; 13.3) are textual changes known from other witnesses. They are discussed at 4.2 below. Three more correct evident errors: 3.10, 12; 11.18. At three more it is no longer possible to know what was corrected: 10.4; 11.12; 13.18. The change at 8.7 is an expression of scribal preference. For the correction at 11.9, see 4.4.4 below. That leaves 14.15. The omission of the article by the scribe is likely to be his error.

4. Examination of the Text

4.1 Introduction

It will be recalled that Schmid found four main text-types, of which the best is that represented by the majuscule codices Alexandrinus (A) and Ephraemi Rescriptus (C) and some minuscules containing ancient readings, in particular 1611 1854 2329. In looking over the drafts, I was very quickly struck by the number and character of the agreements between P115 and Codex Ephraemi Rescriptus. I therefore made a complete comparison of the two texts, using Tischendorf's transcription of the palimpsest.[8] In order to test out my findings, I also made a full collation of P115 and the facsimile editions of P47, Sinaiticus and Alexandrinus.[9]

---

[7] There is too much space in the papyrus for what one would expect from other witnesses, suggesting that something extra has been written by mistake.

[8] C. Tischendorf, *Codex Ephraemi Syri rescriptus sive Fragmenta Novi Testamenti*, Leipzig, 1843.

[9] F.G. Kenyon, *The Chester Beatty Biblical Papyri*, Fasciculus III, *Revelation, Plates*, London, 1936; H. and K. Lake, *Codex Sinaiticus Petropolitanus. The New Testament*, Oxford, 1911; *Codex Alexandrinus in reduced facsimile*, London, 1909. It should be noted that Codex Vaticanus (B) is not extant in Revelation. The fifteenth-century minuscule supplement 1957 is a representative of the Byzantine text.

I set aside those places where there is either too little or too much space in P115 for any known reading, and where one has not been able to make anything grammatically possible to fit. That is, the probability is that there is a nonsense reading, probably a repetition or omission, in the manuscript. These passages are at[10]

3.12	[cτε]φανον [ ] γαου τ[ ]υ [ ] και [
6.5	ηνο[ιξεν λεγον]τ[ο]ς
11.2	κ[αι] αυτην [ ] εθνεcιν
11.13	[εδωκαν].[.]..τω
12.10	και η [εξουcια] αυ[του
12.15	[ποταμον ινα αυτην ποτα]μοφορ[ητον]
14.10	[κα]ι ενω[πιον βαcανιc]μου

To these one could add the places in the list of corrections at 10.4, 11.12 and 13.18 where the remains of a deletion sign are visible. In several places where a space seemed initially the only solution to the problem of restoring the text, further reflection suggested that we can fill the space after all. At 9.11 the reading seems to have been [δ]ε. This was conjectured as the restoration before the minuscule attestation for it was noted by looking in Hoskier's apparatus.[11] There seems to be the right amount of space to read [εχουcιν] before it, if one accepts the shortenings [ανουc] and [ε′].

At 11.19, the inclusion of [και αcτραπαι] after φ[ωναι] fills the gap perfectly.

At 14.15 (line 377) I would prefer to restore [αυτου] after [ναου], the reading of Sinaiticus.

At line 342 (14.5), the problem of space in the lacuna is solved by positing the reading [γαρ].

There are of course many places where one cannot be certain what the papyrus read. For example, at 10.9 it could be reconstructed either as [κοιλ]ιαν or as [καρδ]ιαν, at 11.2 either as [πατηcουcιν] or as [μετρηcουcιν], at 11.19 either as [αυτου] or as [του κυ], at 12.10 either as η [εξουcια] or as η [cωτηρια], at 13.10 either as [αποκτανθηναι] or as [αποκτενει δει], the reading of C. There are many places where the difference between an omission or an inclusion requires little difference of space. At 9.13 the papyrus cannot have read τεccαρων, but might just have had δ′ (though I think it unlikely), so here I have not recorded

---

10 I follow the normal conventions of transcription, as they are found in the edition: a dot under uncertain letters (that is, those which are not beyond doubt the one preferred, not letters that are damaged), a dot on its own to indicate illegible traces of ink, and square brackets around restorations of lacunae.

11 See 4.4.3 below.

a variant. I have also of course excluded places where one of the other manuscripts has an error where P115 has a lacuna.

I have not included the itacisms listed in Section 2, in any of the following lists.

Even with all these exceptions, it is surprising how often one feels justified in finding variation between the papyrus and other witnesses. My full list contains 165 readings. This includes all the variations, including evident scribal errors in one of them, between the papyrus and one or more of the other four witnesses.

4.2 The Corrections

Three of the corrections exhibit textual variation known from other witnesses. Particularly noteworthy are those where it seems that it is the first hand that has made a change between the readings of text-types. In what follows, the reading of the papyrus always precedes the colon, those of other manuscripts come after it.[12]

2.27   αυτου[c] at end *; OM * or *c: OM cet
9.20   [προcκυνη]coυcι[v] *; -cωcι[v] *c: προcκυνηcουcιν P47 ℵ A C pc; προcκυνηcωcι(v) **M**
13.3   OM *; εκ c: OM 046* 1854 2053 2329 **M**A; εκ P47 ℵ A C

There are two possible explanations for these readings. The first is that the exemplar contained notes or corrections towards another text. The second is that the scribe either had knowledge of or consulted another copy or copies. Two of the three variants bring the text into agreement with C. The deletion at 2.27 corrects a reading that agrees with the LXX (Ps 2.9).[13] The support of three important minuscule witnesses to the 'A C text' at 13.3 is the first of a number of such instances. Their agreement with P115 is particularly interesting, since it demonstrates that their reading, which previously one might have supposed to have originated with the Andreas text, is in fact a variation within the A C text group. It is the poorer reading, a stylistic improvement which is regularly to be found in some manuscripts where this usage occurs (5.5

---

12   From here on, I have tried to provide a controlled apparatus. The minuscules 1611, 1854 and 2329, the principal ones with A C readings, are always cited, in addition to P47 ℵ A C and the **M** text. The bold **M** represents the black letter M, for the majority text. **M** sometimes divides into two strands, **M**A (the text descended from that found in the Andreas commentary, and **M**K, the Byzantine text).

13   There is no variant recorded in the Göttingen edition.

etc.). The agreement of A C with P47 ℵ suggests that theirs is the true group reading.

4.3 Singular readings

I exclude both the places described in 4.1 where the text of the papyrus cannot be reconstructed and the corrected errors noted in Section 3 (3.10, 12; 11.18; 14.15).

2.27   αυτου[c] after [cυντριβε]ται *: OM *c cet
8.12   OM: και το τριτον της cεληνης ℵ A cet (def. P47 C)[14]
9.19   [εκ του cτο]ματος: εν τω cτοματι P47 ℵ A C cet
       ουραι: ουραι αυτων P47 ℵ A C cet
11.19 φ[ωναι και αcτραπαι]: αcτραπαι και φωναι ℵ A C cet (def P47)[15]
12.4   OM οταν τεκη P47 ℵ A C cet
13.13 OM: εκ του ουρανου P47 ℵ A C cet[16]
14.6   [αλ]λον ιδον αγ'γ[ελον]: ειδον αγγελον P47 ℵ*; ειδον (ιδον A) αλλον αγγελον A C
14.20 $\overline{βχ}$: χειλιων εξακοcιων P47 ℵ^a A C 1611 1854 2329 cet; χιλιων διακοcιων ℵ*; χειλιων εξακοcιων εξ 2036; *mille quingentis* gig

That there are only nine readings is a testimony to the quality of the manuscript. That it is outweighed by the number of corrections is a testimony to the care taken in correcting. This becomes clear when we see how many, or rather how few, of these readings are obviously false: the reading at 8.12 (hom.); the first reading at 9.19 (followed by the normal dative εν ταις [ουραις]; the error was suggested by 9.17–18, with εκ repeatedly and εκ των cτοματων twice); 12.4; 13.13 (OM) are clearly errors. The same is probably true of the second reading at 9.19, since it is normal for the seer to include his third person pronouns.[17]

---

14   The editors leave a gap, but the omission seems to me to be the best explanation of the available space. The fifth-century Old Latin manuscript h also omits the equivalent of these words. I consider this to be accidental agreement in error.
15   The editors leave a gap here. Von Soden cites his I^{b2 400} (= Gregory-Aland 628) for this reading, but Hoskier (69 in his system of sigla) records it as reading φωναι αcτραπαι. H.C. Hoskier, *Concerning the Text of the Apocalypse. Collations of all Existing Available Greek Documents with the Standard Text of Stephen's Third Edition, together with the Testimony of Versions, Commentaries and Fathers*, 2 vols., London, 1929. Volume 2 contains the collations.
16   Hoskier cites *boh pl.* for the omission.
17   The editors leave a gap, though they suggest that the letter given only as . could be omicron.

This leaves four new readings. Do any of them have a claim to originality? We may quickly discount 14.6, since the author's unvarying formula is Καὶ εἶδον or Καὶ εἶδον ἄλλον. The situation at 11.19 is more complicated, since the words come in both orders: αστραπαι comes first at 4.5, though here 385 (Hoskier's 29) reads φωναι και αστραπαι και βρονται. At 8.5 and 16.18 there is variation. Probably we should accept the reading here as a scribal alteration (perhaps under the influence of 8.5). The reading at 2.23 is best understood as a harmonisation (maybe an unconscious one) to the LXX.

The remaining reading is at 14.20, where we are fortunate that the numeral comes in an extant piece of papyrus. What is the number? It is probably 2,600. But it is just worth noting that χ is used in inscriptions to represent χιλιοι. This would give the number 2,000. However, this does seem rather unlikely, and since I do not know of any instances of the inscriptional usage occurring in manuscripts, I assume that the number is 2,600.[18] Other possibilities in the manuscripts are 1,606, 1,600, 1,500 and 1,200. 2,600 is no more easy to explain than any other of the numbers. 1,600 must remain the most likely reading.

The conclusion therefore is that none of these readings is original.

4.4 Comparison with A C

4.4.1 General comments

A general sense of the relationship between the papyrus and P47, ℵ*, A and C may be gained from the figures, containing all the differences, from my original list of 165 readings.

> P47 differs from P115 in 79 readings out of 131 (it is lacunose in 34 of the 165 places)
> ℵ* differs from P115 in 84 readings out of 165
> A differs from P115 in 58 readings out of 165
> C differs from P115 in 43 readings out of 137 (it is lacunose in 28 of the 165)

These figures are simply intended to show that the papyrus has far fewer disagreements with A C than with P47 ℵ*, and that within its

[165]

---

18 Since the fragment is broken immediately after χ, it is possible that there could have been one or even two numerals which have been lost.

group it is closer to C than to A, while outside it differs more from P47 than from ℵ*.[19]

The places where the papyrus agrees with A C against P47 ℵ* are important in that may provide much older testimony to the reading of the group. They also provide the opportunity to test its quality, by seeing whether they are places where the A C text is superior. P47 is extant in readings that concern us from 9.11, with some lacunae (one reading in 10.8, one in 11.4, one in 11.19, and one in 13.16). Readings where P115 agrees with A C against P47 ℵ* are as follows (the brackets and dots show restorations in P47 and P115):

Ref	P115 A C	P47 ℵ*
9.11	[ονομα] εχει (def. C)	εχει (εχι ℵ*) ονομα
9.20	π[ληγαις ταυταις]	π[ληγαις αυτων ταυταις]
10.9	και κ[αταφαγε αυτο]	αυτο και καταφαγε
11.14	[η ουαι η τριτη ερχ]ετ[αι]	ερχεται [η] ουαι η τριτη
11.19	ο ε[ν]	εν
12.14	[α]ι	OM
13.8	[το] ον[ο]μα	τα ο[νοματ]α[20]
14.7	[θαλασσαν]	την θαλασσαν
14.19	εις	επι
15.7	εν	OM

In these ten readings, P115 A C are almost invariably superior. Only at 14.7 are P47 ℵ* likely to be correct.

Agreements of P115 A C against P47 but not ℵ* are also usually in the favour of the former. There are 43 of these readings. A good number of them, of course, are errors in P47.[21]

---

19 Unfortunately, it is not possible to compare the papyrus with some other interesting witnesses, simply because it and they are too scrappy. For example, if we take P85 (fourth/fifth century), the results are (P115 before the colon, P85 after it): 9.20 [τα ξυλινα]: ξ[υλινα]; 9.21 [ουτε]: a large omission by hom; 10.9 [πικρανει . . . εν]: a large omission by hom. But they both appear to have read βιβλαριδιον at 10.8. This reading is discussed at 4.4.4 below. I also compared the papyrus with the other new Oxyrhynchus fragment, 0308 (fourth century): they overlap in 11.15 and 18, and there is one variation, in v. 18: P115 [τοις δουλοις σου τοις π]ροφητα[ις]: P116 [τοις δουλοις σο]υ και [τοις προφηταις].

20 See below for variants surrounding the pronoun.

21 The 43 readings are: where C is extant: 9.20 [και τα] ειδω[λα]: OM; [και] τα λιθινα [και τα ξυλινα]: και τα λιθινα και ξυλινα; [δυ]νανται: δυναται; 21 ου[τε εκ των κλεμματων αυτων]: OM; 10.4 ζ̄: OM; 8 ηνεωγμε[νον]: ανεω[γμ]ενον; 9 [μοι]: [OM]; 10 [βιβλαρ]ιδιον: βιβλιδιον; 11.8 [και ο κ̄c̄ αυτων]: ο κ̄c̄; 10 [ουτοι οι β̄]

With regard to the readings of P115 A C together against ℵ*, I do not think that any of the ℵ readings has a claim to be correct, even when the many scribal errors have been discounted. There are 47 of these readings.[22]

But these readings remain less important than those places where the papyrus differs from A C. For where they differ it may have the better reading, or may provide the reading of the archetype, or may at least cast light on the way in which the tradition has developed. We divide this part of the enquiry into three sections: those readings where it differs from C and not A, those where it differs from A and not C, and those where it differs from both of them.

προφηται: οι προφηται οι β̄; 11 [και το ημισυ]: ημισυ; 12.1 [η σελ]ηνη: την σεληνην; 3 [αυτου]: OM; 9 [και ο σ]ατανας: και σατανας; [αυτου μ]ετ αυτου: μετ αυτου; 13 [εδιωξεν]: απηλθεν εκδιωξαι; 14 [εδοθησαν]: εδοθη; 15 εκ: απο; 16 η γη²: OM; [αυτης]: της; 13.2 [ην]: OM; 6 τους εν τω ο̄ῡν̄ω̄ σκηνουντας: εν τω ουρανω; 7 και λαον: OM; 11 [ε]λ[α]λει: λαλει; 13 καταβα[ινειν]: καταβηναι; 15 [του θηριου]... [οσοι εαν]: του πο[ι]η[ε]αν; 14.7 [λεγων]: λεγοντα; [δ]οτε αυτ[ω]: δοξασατε αυτον; 14 [δρ]επανον: δραπαν; [εν]: OM; [δρεπανον]: δραπαν; [θερισον οτι ηλθε]ν... [εξηρανθη]: θερισμ[ον ε]ξηλθεν ο θερισμος οτι [   ]; 18 [δρεπανον]: δραπαν; 19 τον με[γ]ᾱ: του μεγαλου; 20 αχ[ρι]: μεχρι; 15.4 [εφαν]ερωθη[σαν]: εφανερωθη; 6 οι: OM; ζωων: OM. Where C is deficient: 9.11 [ονο]μα αυτω: ω ονομα; 14 [ευ]φρατη: ευφρατου; 18 [αυ]των: OM; 19 [η γαρ]: ην γαρ η; 11.1 [καλαμ]ος ομοιος: [κ]αλαμον ος.

22 Where P47 C are extant: 9.20 [και] τα λιθινα [και τα ξυλινα]: και τα ξυλινα και τα λιθινα; 10.3 [OM]: ως; 4 βροντα[ι]: φωναι; 8 θαλασσης και επι της γης: της; 10 [βιβλαρ]ιδιον: βιβλιον; 11.5 [αυτ]ους θελ[ει: θελει αυτους; 8 [και ο κ̄ς̄ αυτων]: και ο κ̄ς̄; 10 [ουτοι οι β̄] προφηται: ουτοι οι προφηται οι β̄; 14 απηλ'[θεν]: παρηλθεν; 15 [ε]γεν[ο]ν[το: εγενετο; 19 OM: ανω; 12.9 [και ο σ]ατανας: ο σατανας; 14 του αετου του μεγαλου: αετου μεγαλου; 13.2 λεοντο[ς]: λεοντων; 6 [το ονομα αυτου]: αυτον; 7 [ε]ξουσια: εξουσιαν; 14 γης π[οιησαι]: γης και ποιησαι; 18 [vo]υν: νους; 14.1 αυτων: αυτω; 2 [μεγαλης]: OM; 7 [λεγων]: OM; 19 τον με[γ]ᾱ: την μεγαλην; 20 [εξωθε]ν: εξω; 15.6 [λινον] καθαρο[ν λαμπρον]: καθαρους λινους λαμπρους. Where P47 C are both deficient: 8.8 [αγγελος]: OM; 13 [ενος]?: OM; [εν]: OM; 9.2 η[νοιξεν... αβυσσου]: OM; [εκ]: επι; 2–3 του φρεατος και εκ του καπνου: OM; 4 χλωρον ουδε παν: OM. Where P47 is deficient: 2.2 [κοπον]: κοπον σου; 14 [κατα σου]: OM; τω [βαλακ]: OM; 27 αυτου[ς * (OM *c): OM; 3.12 ποιησω αυτον: ποιησω αυτω; 8.3 το ενωπιον: ενωπιον; 4 ο καπνος: καπνος; 11.4 [αι]: OM; 19 εγενοντο: εγενετο; 13.16 [τους] μεγ[αλους]: μεγαλους. Where C is deficient: 9.11 επ αυτῳ̄: εαυτων; [βασιλεα]: τον βασιλεα; [ονο]μα αυτω: ω ονομα αυτω; 15 οι [ητοιμας]μ[ε]νοι: ητοιμασμενοι; [και ημεραν]: OM; 11.1 [λεγων]: λεγει.

4.4.2 Agreements between P115 and A against C

The number of places where P115 and C differ is very small. In all there are only twenty-one,[23] once we have excerpted the scribal errors of the papyrus and C.[24] In seven of them P115 and A agree.

Ref	P115 and A (02)	Support for them	C (03)	Support for C
2.14	[οτι]	ℵ (def. P47) Oec[25]	OM	1611 1854 min pc
9.20	[ουτε]	1611 (ουδε P47 ℵ)	ου	1854 K[26]
11.11	του[c θεωρουντας]	P47 ℵ 1854 1611 2329 cet	των θεωρουντων	P min pc
11.12	[φω]νην μεγα[λην ... λεγουcαν	1611 2329 cet	φωνηc μεγαληc ... λεγουcηc	P47 ℵ P 1854
11.18	[διαφθειρ]οντας	P47 ℵ cet	διαφθειραντας	051 1611 1854 2329 pc
13.8	τ[ω]	ℵc 051 2329 M	OM	ℵ*
14.6	κατοι[κουντας]	051 pc	καθημενους	P47 ℵ 1611 1854 2329 pler

In some of these places, the added agreement of one or more of the minuscules containing readings of this text-type (1611 1854 2329) encourages us to believe that P115 provides added evidence that this is the reading of the text-type, and indeed the superior reading.

It is rather striking that at 2.14; 9.20; 11.11, 18 the other ancient group (P47 ℵ) should support P115 A. In all four of them the external and internal evidence already seemed in favour of the reading of A. The support of the papyrus strengthens the case.

The variant at 11.12 is not easy to resolve.[27] There are places where the author prefers the accusative when φωνη follows ακουω, and

---

[23] 10.2 has a particular problem, since the reading of C is apparently uncertain. According to *Nestle-Aland*[27], the first hand reads βιβλιδαριον. Tischendorf prints it as βιβλαριδιον, with a note on p. 358: 'BΛAPIΔI rescripsit B. Pro eo prima manus habuisse videtur BΛIΔAPI. Unde efficitur, BIBΛIΔAPION primae manus esse. Quod etiam Wetstenius notavit legi in codice nostro.' In view of the apparent uncertainty, I set this reading aside.

[24] The discounted readings of C are 10.2 τον δεξιον, 8 OM εν τη χειρι; 12.14 OM και ημιcυ καιρου; 13.6 OM και την cκηνην αυτου, 15 OM δουναι, 15 OM ινα ... του θηριου; 14.1 οροc, 1 OM cιων, 2 OM αυτων, 3 OM και των πρεcβυτερων. It will be noted that C is rather prone to omission.

[25] 2329 reads ει.

[26] 2329 reads και ου.

[27] See Schmid, *Die Alten Stämme*, 102, who one still assumes expresses a preference for the accusative by placing it first.

places where he favours the genitive.[28] This is the only place where the major witnesses disagree. The external evidence suggests that the genitive may be the more ancient reading, for here the support of P47 ℵ goes with C.

The same is true of καθημενουc at 14.6.

At 9.20, Schmid concludes that ουδε is 'wahrscheinlich die ursprüngliche Lesart'.[29] The support, admittedly by no means certain, of the papyrus adds weight to this.[30]

The text at 13.8 contains more variations than I have detailed, with the forms βιβλω and βιβλιω:

βιβλω *ℵ 1611 1854 pc
βιβλιω C
τη βιβλω P47 2344 al
τω βιβλω ℵc
τω βιβλιω A 051 2329 M
τ[ω βιβλιω] P115

This is another place where the author's usage (he has both η βιβλοc and το βιβλιον indiscriminately) is of little help where the tradition divides. Schmid prefers τω βιβλιω on the external evidence. The most that our papyrus can be said to do is to strengthen the case for an article.

[168]

On the whole, A is superior in quality to C. In these readings, the new papyrus shows similar quality, for in nearly all of these readings it and A are right. Only at 14.6, where κατοικουντας looks like an attempt to get rid of καθημενους, and probably at 11.12, is C superior. A harsher test comes with the next group.

4.4.3. Agreements between P115 and C against A

There are 25 variants between P115 and A.[31] Eleven of them are places where the papyrus differs from A and agrees with C.

---

28 Ibid., 200.
29 Ibid., 225.
30 The line would be a little shorter than one might expect if one read ου, but not impossibly so. Of course, the papyrus cannot help to resolve the choice between ουδε and ουτε.
31 Again, excluding errors from A (even if it is sometimes supported – one would expect a degree of agreement in error): 6.6 του δηναριου; 9.2 OM ως, 11 τον αρχοντα της αβυccου τον αγγελον, 14 OM εκτω; 10.2 OM ηνεωγμενους, 9 γλυκυ ως μελι; 11.4 κυ, 5 OM ουτως, 12 OM αυτοις, 18 τους αγιους και τους φοβουμενους; 12.10 εξουςια; 14.7 φωνη, 10 βαcανιcθηcονται, 10 των αγγελων, 15 κραζων εκ του ναου. At 14.15 the papyrus is in error with ωρ[α] * (see Section 3 above). At 10.8 the editor of P115 restores απηλθα, but the C reading απηλθον is at least equally likely.

C is deficient between 8.4 and 9.17, so the following variants between the papyrus and A cannot be compared with it.

Ref	P115	Support for P115	A (02)	Support for A
8.5	κα[ι] φωναι κα[ι α]ϲ[τραπαι]	ℵ 1611 M[K]	αϲτραπαι και φωναι	2329 pc[32]
8.6	εα̣[υτουϲ]	ℵ[c] 1611 1854 2329 M	αυτουϲ	ℵ* pc
9.3	[α]υτοιϲ	ℵ 046 2329	αυταιϲ	0207 1611 1854 M
9.5	[βαϲανιϲ]θω[ϲιν]	1611 2329 M[K]	βαϲανιϲθηϲονται	ℵ P 1854 pc
9.11	[δ]ε	1611 2329	OM	cet
	ο α̣[πολλυων]	pc	απολλυων	cet

C then resumes:

Ref	P115 and C (04)	Support for them	A (02)	Support for A
10.9	[βιβλαρ]ιδιον	1 pc	βιβλαριον *; βιβλιαριδιον corr	βιβλαριον 2329

C is again deficient at

Ref	P115	Support for P115	A (02)	Support for A
10.10	[εγε]μ̣[ι]ϲθη	ℵ* 2329 [33]	επικρανθη	P47 1611 M

and then resumes:

Ref	P115 and C (04)	Support for them	A (02)	Support for A
11.3	[περιβεβλημ]ενοι	1611 1854 M	περιβεβλημενουϲ	ℵ* P 046 2329
11.15	[λ]εγουϲαι	P47 ℵ 051 1611 1854 2329 M[A]	λεγοντεϲ	046 pc
13.18	χιϲ̄	mss teste Irenaeus	εξακοϲιοι εξηκοντα εξ	P47 ℵ (-ϲιαι) 051 1611 1854 2329 M P (-ϲια)

These eleven readings are particularly illuminating. Everybody's attention will no doubt turn to 13.18. Certainly the new support for C suggests that this was the original reading of the A C text-type. Unfortunately, there is no room here for an adequate discussion of the variant, beyond expressing a preference for the authenticity of the A reading. In any case, more may be learned from some of the other readings. One is especially struck by places where agreement with P47 ℵ provides strong external evidence in favour of the reading of P115

---

32 There is also a v.l. with φωναι first: φωναι και βρονται και αϲτραπαι 1854 M[A].
33 ℵ[c] 1854 2329 read εγεμιϲθη, adding πικριαϲ after μου.

and C. I single out 9.3 [α]υτοιc; 10.10 [εγε]μ[ι]cθη; 11.15 [λ]εγουcαι. There is a *prima facie* case for reading αυτοιc at 9.3, 4, 5, as *constructiones ad sensum*. However, Schmid rejected the reading, describing the support of ℵ as 'durchaus ungenügend und darum zu verwerfen'.[34] But the added weight of our papyrus at the first occasion (sadly we cannot know what it read at verses 4 and 5) removes the objection.

Schmid considered the reading περιβεβλημενουc at 11.3 to be a mechanical error caused by the following word, cακκουc.[35] The support of P115 increases the external evidence in favour of his conclusion.

The situation at 11.15 is quite different, and here it is A which preserves the author's usage.[36]

What about the reading at 10.10? I would like to propose that (1) it is the harder reading, (2) the A reading is harmonisation to verse 9, (3) the external evidence is at least tilted more in its favour by the witness of the papyrus.

At 10.9, the whole picture is:

βιβλαριδιον P115 A^c C pc
βιβλαριον A* 2329
βιβλιδαριον 1611 M
βιβλιον P47 ℵ 1854

The author's usage is not very helpful here. But I suspect that the reading of our papyrus is right, and that some of the variants are due to different forms of the word at v. 8. If the reconstruction at 10.8 (see below) is correct, then P115 is consistent in the whole passage, and may well be correct in this variant.

That leaves the insertion of δε at 9.11. Although the restoration has to be regarded as tentative, it is possible.[37] There seems to have been some uncertainty over the asyndeton here, since P 1854 2351 al supply καὶ before ἔχουcιν, while the Koine text replaces the finite verb with a participle. Our δε, if that is indeed what we have, should probably be regarded as a similar attempt. In any case, δέ is rare enough in Revelation, and none of its seven occurrences in the Nestle-Aland/UBS text is quite like the usage here.[38] But the agreement with 1611 and 2329 is very important, showing that this reading is 600 years older than the previous extant evidence.

[170]

---

34 *Die Alten Stämme*, 237.
35 *Ibid.*, 101.
36 Evidence in *ibid.*, 236, 240.
37 The editors leave a blank (see 4.1 above).
38 They are 1.14; 2.5, 16, 24; 10.2; 19.12; 21.8.

The reading at 8.5 is not dissimilar in support for the papyrus. It is preferred by Nestle-Aland, presumably on the grounds of the range of attestation. If so, the papyrus adds weight to the case.

The remaining readings are less impressive. The reflexive at 8.6 looks like a correction.[39] So do the subjunctive at 9.5 and the insertion of the article at 9.11.[40]

I conclude that the papyrus is right at 8.5; 9.3; 10.9, 10; 11.3, and wrong at 8.6; 9.5, 11 (*bis*); 11.15; 13.18. That gives five good and six poor readings where it differs from A. The five readings are especially important, for they are places where the superiority of the best manuscript is questioned. It is worth noting that in three of them (8.5; 10.9; 11.3) the Nestle-Aland/UBS text has already adopted the reading now given added support by P115. There is now a case for changing it in the other two. Unfortunately, C is also extant in only two of these five readings, neither of them one of the two where the Nestle-Aland/UBS text needs revising.

4.4.4. The Readings where the Papyrus Differs from both A and C

There are not many of these either. In fact, there are only fourteen, of which three (10.8; 12.10; 14.5) have to be regarded as very uncertain restorations.

Ref.	P115	Support for P115	A C	Support for A C
2.27	αυτου[c] at end *	none	OM	P115ᶜ cet
10.8	Βιβλαριδιον	P85ᵛⁱᵈ ℵ P pc	βιβλιον	1611 1854 pc[41]
11.9	τα [πτωματα] *	2329 Mᴬ	το πτωμα (πτω[μα] A)	P47 ℵ 1611 1854 cet
11.19	φ[ωναι και αcτραπαι]	none	αcτραπαι και φωναι	cet (def P47)
12.9	[ο οφιc ο μ]εγαc	P47 pc	ο μεγαc ο οφιc	1611 1854 2329 cet
12.10	[του θ̄ῡ]	1 al	του θεου ημων	1611 1854 2329 cet
13.3	OM *	046* 1854 2053 2329 Mᴬ	εκ	P115ᶜ cet
13.7	και εδοθ[η] … νικηcαι αυτουc	ℵ 051 1611 1854 2329 al Mᴷ	OM	P47 Mᴬ
13.8	OM	ℵ² P 051 al M	αυτου	1854 2053 pc

---

39 So also Schmid, *Die Alten Stämme*, 75.
40 For the latter, see *ibid.*, 199.
41 Other readings here include βιβλιον 2329.

14.2	ω[ϲ] φωνην κιθαρωδων	P47 2053	ωϲ κιθαρωδων	cet
14.5	? [γαρ]	P47 1 (051) ℵ 2329 M^K	OM	P 1854 2053 al
14.6	[αλ]λον ιδον αγ′γ[ελον]	none	ειδον (ιδον A) αλλον αγγελον	ℵ^c P 051 1611 2329 cet
	ευαγγελιϲαι	051 M	ευαγγελιϲαι επι	P47 ℵ P 1611 1854 2053 2329
14.20	β̄χ̄	none	χειλιων εξακοϲιων	P47 ℵ^a 1611 1854 2329 cet

First, we must clear away the singular readings which were discussed in Section 4.3 (11.19; 14.6; 14.20) and the two corrections discussed in Section 4.2 (2.27; 13.3). All these were shown to be of poor quality. Once that is done, and one has stripped away scribal errors from the text, it begins to become clear that the significance of this papyrus is considerable, for it gives us a much better chance of recovering the family reading where A and C differ from it. And where it agrees with a member of the P47 ℵ group against them, we have a very good chance of a superior reading. Perhaps the best example is at 13.7. On internal grounds, the omission of the first part of the verse looks suspiciously like homoeoarcton, and editors have generally taken this view. The main ancient support is Sinaiticus. Given this manuscript's tendency to omit, its weight in the opposite situation is all the greater. Now the new witness adds a good deal more external weight. One does not even need to suppose there to be a genealogical connection between the omission by P47 and by A C: it would be an easy enough mistake for them to make independently.

[171]

At 14.2, the new witness agrees with P47 in repeating φωνην. This would be in keeping with the style of the author. The agreement of the two oldest witnesses, from the two more ancient texts, encourages us to read it. The removal of the word is an understandable amelioration of the style.

At 11.9, the odd correction suggests that there is something awry in our papyrus, and it is likely that the plural is caused by its appearance later in the verse; there is also variation at the beginning of the verse.[42] In any case, the plural looks like a stylistic improvement.

---

42 I wonder whether the corrector became confused with the occurrence of το πτωμα/τα πτωματα earlier in the verse, and wrongly inserted the initial και. If so, then it is likely that the papyrus read the plural there also.

The reading shared with P47 and a few minuscules at 12.9 is interesting. (Note that there is a third reading in ℵ: ο μεγας οφις.) The AC reading provides two balanced phrases, each consisting of article–noun–article–adjective. Does this neatness suggest a little editorial tampering? But we are encouraged by 12.3 to place 'great' with 'the dragon', and so what we have in our papyrus is probably a confusion.

[172] The slightly doubtful restored reading at 12.10 in the new papyrus is a poor one.

At 13.8 there is some uncertainty as to the number of the pronoun, amongst other variations:

το ονομα P115 **M**
το ονομα αυτων 1611 pc
το ονομα αυτου A C 1854 pc
τα ονοματα ℵc P 051
τα ονοματα αυτων P47 ℵ* 2329 al

Does the omission in the new papyrus, which anticipates the **M** text, reflect this uncertainty? At any rate, the pronoun either singular or plural is likely to be original.

Coming to 14.5 and the insertion of γαρ – but we should note that the reading cannot be regarded as certain – we find that the agreement of our papyrus with P47 ℵ raises the possibility that this is a very ancient, pre-recensional reading. Yet there are good reasons against its being original, since it could be harmonised to verse 4 παρθενοι γαρ εισιν, and is perhaps an improvement.

The omission of επι at 14.6 is more certain in the papyrus. It is also quite possibly original, since we can see from 10.7 (where there is no variation) that the transitive use of the verb is the author's preference. Even so, Schmid and Nestle-Aland both prefer to insert επι.[43]

We therefore find several variants where the new witness seems to have the original text: 13.7; 14.2, and 14.6. It is noteworthy that in two of these, it is the only member of the text-type to have this reading. In the other five places it is either a poor text, or the restoration is too uncertain for us to reach safe conclusions.

What is rather striking is that it is not certainly superior at 14.5, the only reading (if reading it is) where it agrees with both P47 and ℵ against A C.

---

43 Schmid, *Die Alten Stämme*, 78.

4.4.5 Two other readings

Two other readings need to be discussed separately, because of the particular problems of reconstructing the text of the papyrus. The first is at 12.3:

[πυρ]ροc μεγ[αc] P115 P47: πυροc μεγαc ℵ 2053 al
μεγαc πυρροc A P 051 pm
πυροc μεγαc C 046 1611 1854 2329 pler

Although the editor fills the lacuna with [πυρ], it could equally read [πυ], and the text of A C 1611 1854 2329 makes that more likely. The history of this reading is rather interesting. Δρακων πυροc μεγαc is a very strange phrase. One could conceive that πυρροc μεγαc was an amelioration of it, followed by a transposition in A P. The variant πυρροc for πυροc is also found at 8.5 in 757; 14.18 in 2067. There is no v.l. recorded by Hoskier where πυροc comes elsewhere (1.14; 2.18; 3.18; 4.5; 8.8; 9.18; 10.1; 19.12, 20; 20.14, 15.) At 6.4 πυροc is read by A P 1854 2329 **M**; πυρροc by ℵ C 1611 1841 2053 al. Is it significant that two later witnesses to the A C text (1854 2329) agree in πυροc in each place? Unfortunately, it is also possible that they both follow the Byzantine text here.

The second reading is at 12.4. The papyrus reads ïc[τηκει].[44] A has εcτηκεν, C εcτηκει, and 2053 (a minuscule that has many of its reading) has ειcτηκει.[45] Westcott and Hort everywhere prefer the form of the pluperfect without the epsilon, and it seems that behind the orthographical variation we have some valuable support for a rather interesting reading. It is one which should be included in the apparatus, and deserves serious consideration. The pluperfect of ἵcτημι is also found at 7.11. There it is spelt as ιcτηκειcαν by A and εcτηκιcαν by C. Its use there is as an imperfect.[46] Similar usage in 12.4 makes excellent sense.

---

44 The pluperfect of ιcτημι without epsilon is everywhere the preferred form of Westcott and Hort. For their rationale, see Vol. 2, 169.
45 This reading is found in the commentary, but not in the lemma (according to Hoskier).
46 See G. Mussies, *The Morphology of Koine Greek as used in the Apocalypse of St. John. A Study in Bilingualism* (NovT Suppl 27), Leiden, 1971, 347.

4.4.6 P115 and 2329

At one point it seemed worth testing the relationship between the papyrus and 2329. This tenth-century commentary manuscript (Meteora 573, foll. 210–45) was highly praised by Hoskier.[47] He writes that 'we can say confidently that a document directly underlies Apoc. 200 coeval with our oldest uncial witnesses'.[48] Schmid, although he regularly cites the manuscript, does not have any comment to offer on its value beyond a brief statement.[49] Certainly, P115 agrees with 2329 in most of the significant readings which Hoskier singles out as representing what he calls 'our "uncial" transmission'.[50] The manuscript contains other interesting materials: Hippolytus' *On the Blessings of Jacob*,[51] and Origenian scholia edited by Diobouniotis and Harnack.[52]

A complete comparison of the two witnesses would be unlikely to be profitable. It is those places where they agree against A C that are most valuable, for here we must ask whether it could be that the new support for the reading of 2329 changes our view of the textual history. Only at 13.7 is the answer that there are indeed grounds for preferring a reading that they share against A C.

---

47 H.C. Hoskier, 'Manuscripts of the Apocalypse – Recent Investigations. I', *BJRL* 7 (1922–23), 118–37, 120–37 and 2 plates; revised in *Concerning the Text of the Apocalypse*, Vol. 1, 637–52. It was cited by him as 200. See also N. Beis, 'Die Kollation der Apokalypse Johannis mit dem Kodex 573 des Meteoronklosters', *ZNW* 13 (1912), 260–65. Since Beis' collation is against Mai's 1859 edition of minuscule 1957 (i.e. the supplement to Vaticanus), it is not of much practical use.

48 Hoskier, *Apocalypse*, 641.

49 'Die Minuskeln 2329, 1854 und 1611, die er als Zeugen eines alten, neben oder vielmehr vor dem "kirklichen Standardtext" stehenden Textes nennt, sind gerade dort, wo sie von K abweichen, mit P47 S und AC verwandt', Schmid, 1.2, 9f.

50 Hoskier, *Apocalypse*, 640.

51 K. Diobouniotis and N. Weis, *Hippolyts Schrift über die Segnungen Jakobs...* (TU 38, 1), Leipzig, 1911.

52 K. Diobouniotis and A. Harnack, *Der Scholienkommentar des Origenes zur Apokalypse Johannis nebst einem Stück aus Irenaeus, Lib V, Graece* (TU 38, 3), Leipzig, 1911. R.H. Charles, *A Critical and Exegetical Commentary on the Revelation of St. John*, 2 vols., Edinburgh, 1920, Vol. 1, clxxvif rejects Harnack's view of the materials.

5. Conclusions

1. This manuscript is the oldest member by over a century of the A C text-type. It sometimes agrees with minuscule members of the group against A C.
2. Agreement between P115 A C against P47 and/or ℵ confirms the high quality of P115.
3. The conclusions to be drawn from comparing the papyrus with A and C are that it is usually right where it follows A against C, and usually wrong when it disagrees with both of them. It is right less than half the time when it disagrees with A.
4. The evidence from Conclusion 3 confirms yet again the superior quality of A to C.
5. Quite a number of the poorer readings of P115 are due to attempts to improve the style – this may be regarded as a feature of the papyrus.[53] It may be taken all the more seriously where it seems to retain a harder reading, as at 10.10.
6. P115 is more often right with Sinaiticus than with P47.
7. None of P115's singular readings has a claim to be correct.
8. Agreement with later minuscules reminds us yet again that new discoveries sometimes show late witnesses to contain variants that are far older than we could have known.
9. There are a number of readings where the papyrus' evidence makes a case for a change to the text of Nestle-Aland/UBS. Perhaps most noteworthy are 9.3 [α]υτοιc and 10.10 [εγε]μ[ι]cθη. Also to be considered are 10.8 [βιβλαριδιον], 14.2 add φωνην after ωc, 14.6 omit επι. One may add the pluperfect (ε)ιcτηκει at 12.4.

The process of examining a new witness is a slow one, and it is generally years before the necessary reappraisal of the known tradition in the light of an important new discovery can be achieved. The present paper is offered in that knowledge,[54] but in the hope that it may contribute towards the evaluation of this important new witness.

It is sometimes suggested that the papyri have not had any genuine effect on the printed text of the New Testament. The example of this witness alone is sufficient to disprove the claim.

---

53 Indeed, it is a feature – hardly surprising, given the nature of the Greek – of many manuscripts of Revelation, certainly of P47 and ℵ, and occasionally of A and C as well.
54 Reading the proofs, I already wonder whether I should have considered more seriously the reading $\overline{\chi\iota c}$ (13.18).

Note

This papter was first read to the Textual Criticism Seminar of the 1999 SNTS meeting in Pretoria.

I am grateful to members of the seminar for their comments and suggestions, which influenced the printed version. Inevitably, there has been much interest in the reading σισ of 13.18, which I am now firmly convinced is the older reading (see note 54). For further evidence, see Gryson's edition of the Apocalypse for the Vetus Latina.

8 Some New Manuscripts of the Greek New Testament in Boston and Cambridge
(with M.B. Morill)

A visit in November 1999 to libraries in Boston and Harvard in order to view the Greek manuscripts of the New Testament yielded two groups comprising six manuscripts not – so far as we are aware – widely known. The purpose of this article is to offer a description of the manuscripts, with an account of what we have been able to discover about them.

I. Manuscripts belonging to the Endowment for Biblical Research

The first group of manuscripts was brought to our attention while we were examining Gregory-Aland 2811, a Gospels manuscript in Boston University's School of Theology Library. The librarian kindly showed us an exhibition catalogue of 1985.[1] The following accounts pertain to entries which either do not seem to match any manuscripts known from the *Liste*,[2] or add to what is known about a witness. The new manuscripts have now been assigned Gregory-Aland numbers by the Institut für Neutestamentliche Textforschung, Münster.[3]

1. Entry 4 (page 3) is headed 'leaves from a Greek Gospel Lectionary'. A twelfth-century date is offered. It consists of two leaves, measuring 399 x 236 mm, of two columns and twenty-five lines; the first leaf contains readings from Mark (with the pencilled foliation 84), the second readings from Luke (pencilled foliation 105). The leaves contain forged miniatures of Mark and Luke, probably the work of Demetrios Pelekasis, who was active in the 1920s and 1930s.[4] The

---

1 J. Oliver (ed.), *Manuscripts, Sacred and Secular: From the Collections of the Endowment for Biblical Research and Boston University*, Boston, 1985.
2 *Liste*.
3 We are grateful to Dr Michael Welte for supplying the numbers, and providing some additional information about *l*1840.
4 See G. Vikan, 'A Group of Forged Byzantine Miniatures', in *Aachener Kunstblätter*, 1973.

manuscript was purchased from A. Marguerite Smith in 1954. It is also noted that two other leaves of the same manuscript are housed in the Houghton Library at Harvard University. These leaves are described below. The manuscript has been given the Gregory-Aland number *l*2415.

2. Entry 5 is a Greek Gospel lectionary, dated to the second half of the fifteenth century. This is *l*1840 in the *Liste*. Written on paper, it consists of 219 folios, 200 x 140 mm, with one column of 22 lines. The watermarks of scales in circles and crossed arrows are typical of Italy in the second half of the fifteenth century. The provenance is a sales catalogue (London, Maggs 1945, no. 597) and A. Marguerite Smith in 1954. An undated manuscript note by Harry Buck gives the number L–1840 and promises a report in *ZNW*.[5] The manuscript was subsequently (and is so recorded in the *Liste*) in the Zion Research Library Brookline, Mass., s.n. Further enquiry in the University Library revealed that these manuscripts have recently been sold. We have not yet been able to establish their present whereabouts.

2. Manuscripts in the Houghton Library at Harvard University

The Houghton Library is the rare-book and manuscript library at Harvard University. We are particularly grateful to the library staff for their kind help, and for drawing to our attention the possibility that there might be manuscripts of whose existence we were unaware.[6]

These manuscripts are all from the bequest of Philip Hofer, made in 1984, and our initial information was taken from the typed checklist of manuscripts in this category.[7] Philip Hofer (1898–1984) was founder and first curator of the Department of Printing and Graphic Arts in the Houghton Library, and secretary of the Fogg Art Museum, and a distinguished collector in his own right.

---

5   All information taken from Oliver, *op. cit.*, 4.
6   We are grateful to Dr James F. Coakley, who answered several questions which arose subsequent to our visit, and suggested several improvements to the paper.
7   Manuscript Typ 243, a Synaxarion, does not contain biblical text. For some reason the title inside the front board describes it as Gregory Nazianzen.

3. MS Typ 267 (now Gregory-Aland *l*2415)

This is the other part of the manuscript already described (1 above). We are able to confirm the date offered by Oliver.[8] This part also consists of two folios, containing two portaits of evangelists in the same style as those in the Boston leaves. The number of lines varies between 24 and 25. The first leaf contains the pencilled foliation 50, and contains:

Mt 10.14 ἐξερχομένοι – 15
Mt 10.23–30 τρίχες

The second leaf (foliated 176) contains the lections

ending ρως αὐτὸν παραδῷ (Mk 14.11)
Lk 22.1
Jn 13.3–11
Jn 13.12–17
Mt 26.2–8 (breaking off at οἱ μαθηταὶ αὐτοῦ)

A collation of the two Johannine readings against the Oxford 1873 Textus Receptus yielded one variant (TR reading before the bracket):

verse 8 ὁ] OM

4. MS Typ. 294

This manuscript contains the four Gospels and, in a second hand, Revelation. There is an *ex libris* label for Frances Hofer on the reverse of the flyleaf, and a manuscript note 'Bought of [?] B. Zoumboulakis Athens. 12/60 pr CUED. Anatolia? 13th C? HS. Ask Kurt Weitzmann'. Byron T. Zoumboulakis was a dealer. The size of the manuscript is 14.6 × 19.1 cm. It has been paginated in a modern hand, perhaps of the seventeenth or eighteenth century. There are no quire signatures in either part of the manuscript.

The contents are as follows:

[240]

Page	1	Hypothesis (Εὐσέβιος Καρπιανῷ)
	3	Canon tables (Canon X is present only as far as 81 in the Matthew column, and equivalents – the rest is missing)
	9	a note in a later hand
	10	portrait of Matthew
	11	inc. Matthew
	80	expl. Matthew
	81	blank
	82	portrait of Mark

---

8 Oliver, *op. cit.*, 4.

83	inc. Mark	
130	last extant leaf of Mark, ending at 16.19 μετά τὸ λαλῆ[. Presumably the following folio contained the end of Mark on the recto and on the verso a portrait of Luke	
131	inc. Luke	
205	expl. Luke	
206	portrait of John	
207	inc. John	
262	expl. John	
263	inc. Revelation	
297	expl. Revelation	

Manuscripts consisting of the Gospels and Revelation are quite scarce. There are only ten in the *Liste*:

792	saec. XIII	Athens, Nat. Bibl. 107
1006	XI	Athos, Iviron 728
1064	XVIII	Athos, Kuttumasiu 286
1328	XIV	Jerusalem, Orthodox Patriarchate, Saba 101
1551	XIII	Athos, Vatopedi 913
1685	1292	Athens, Byz. Mus. 155
2323	XIII	Athens, Mus. Benaki 46
2643	1289	Riverside/California s.n.
2656	1650	Athens, Nat. Bibl. 3110
2794	XII	Vienna, Mechitaristenkolleg

The fact that Typ. 294 is in two hands (as are some other manuscripts containing Revelation and one or more other parts of the New Testament)[9] prompts one to suppose that they are two separate manuscripts that have been bound together for convenience, and to protect the smaller section. This is borne out by the dates of the two parts. An analysis of the binding might cast further light on the manuscript's history. Given these separate origins, our remaining comments will treat the two parts as separate manuscripts.

4a. MS Typ. 294 (F1–262)

The manuscript has been given the Gregory-Aland number 2863.

The Gospels are written in a twelfth-century upright minuscule, with some of the exaggerated strokes which were becoming increasingly common. A rather inadequate initial comparison was Vat.

---

9 See J.K. Elliott, 'The Distinctiveness of the Greek Manuscripts of the Book of Revelation', *JTS* 48 (1997), 116–24, 118. On the analogy of 60, previously classified as containing the Gospels and Revelation, but now divided into two manuscripts (60 e and 2821 r), the present manuscript should receive two numbers in the Münster listing.

Pal. Gr. 13, dated 1167.[10] But the Karahissar style is a better analogy.[11] The manuscripts most closely associated with the Karahissar tetraevangelion (St Petersburg, Russian National Library 105, Gregory-Aland 574) are:[12]

> the Rockefeller McCormick New Testament (Chicago, University Library MS 965, Gregory-Aland 2400)
> Palermo, Biblioteca Centrale, Dep. Mus. 4, Fol. 1–229 (Gregory-Aland formerly 1815, now 2127
> Athos, Lavra B 26 (Gregory-Aland 1505)
> Paris, Bibliothèque Nationale Suppl. Gr. 1335 (Gregory-Aland 2327)
> Paris, Bibliothèque Nationale Coislin 200 (Gregory-Aland 38)

These manuscripts were all dated by Colwell to the second half of the thirteenth century, on the grounds not only of palaeography (which would admit also an earlier date) but also of internal evidence. His evidence with regard to the palaeography deals largely with the question of the presence of majuscule forms of certain letters.[13] The preponderance of majuscule over minuscule forms of eta and lambda is, in Colwell's method, evidence for a date later than 1150 plus or minus, while the preponderance of majuscule epsilon requires a date after 1166 plus or minus. The analogy of Paris, Coislin. 200 (given a twelfth-century date by some authorities) encourages us to believe that a date in the second half of that century remains the best date for MS Typ. 294 (F1–262).

[242]

The Gospels contain Ammonian sections, but no Eusebian canon numbers.[14] There are very few other helps for the reader. Sometimes there is περὶ τοῦ etc at the head of the page, but that is all. In these features too it is very similar to the Karahissar group. There is one

---

10 Plates in P.F. de Cavalieri and H. Lietzmann, *Specimina Codicum Graecorum Vaticanorum* (Tabulae in Usum Scholarum 1), Berlin and Leipzig, 1929, pl. 30; K. and S. Lake, *Dated Greek Minuscule Manuscripts to the year 1200*, 11 vols., Boston, 1934–45, Vol. 8, MS. 319, Pl. 585–6; E. Follieri, *Codices graeci bibliothecae Vaticanae selecti* (Exempla scripturarum edita ..., IV), Vatican, 1969, pl. 28; R. Barbour, *Greek Literary Hands A.D. 400–1600*, Oxford, 1981, Pl. 47; H. Hunger, *Handschriften aus Bibliotheken Roms mit dem Vatikan*, Repertorium der griechischen Kopisten 800–1600 3, Vienna, 1997, entry 105 (pl. 57).
11 We are indebted to Mr Nigel Wilson for this observation, and for several other helpful comments which he made on a draft of this paper.
12 E.C. Colwell, *The Four Gospels of Karahissar*, Vol. 1, *History and Text*, Chicago, 1936, especially 104–18.
13 The evidence and argument are fully set out in the appendix (225–41), and reprinted as 'A Chronology for the Letters E, H, Λ, Π, in the Byzantine Minuscule Book Hand', in *Studies in Methodology in Textual Criticism of the New Testament*' (NTTS 9), Leiden, 1969, 125–41.
14 C.R. Gregory, *Textkritik des Neuen Testamentes*, Leipzig, 1900–09, Vol. 2, 862, for a list of other manuscripts with this feature.

column to the page, and there are usually 37 lines, with a range of 35–38. There are illuminated initials, and a design at the head of each Gospel. There are a few corrections, including the insertion of some lines omitted in John 10, but several absurdities and homoioteleuta are uncorrected. Red dots above letters are used to indicate deletion.

Page 234 originally ended with Jn 9.41 ἡ οὖν ἁμαρ [. . .], and page 235 originally started with approximately seven letters, now obscured, then continued with 10.6] ἃ ἐλάλει αὐτοῖς. A later hand, in a brown ink, has added the end of 9.41 and 10.1–6 in the bottom margin of page 234 and top margin of page 235.

Text

A collation with the Oxford 1873 Textus Receptus in John Chapter 18 yielded the following evidence (TR text before the square bracket):

2. συνήχθη] + καὶ
8. ὁ] OM
11. σου] OM
20. πάντοτε] πάντες
25. ἠρνήσατο] + οὖν
    οὐκ εἰμί] οὐ
28. πρωΐα] πρωΐ
32. ἤμελλεν] ἔμελλεν
36. ὁ Ἰησοῦς] ἰ(ησοῦ)ς
    ἔστιν²] OM *; txt corr.
37. ὁ Ἰησοῦς] ἰ(ησοῦ)ς

An initial survey in Münster bears out the conclusion that the manuscript is a witness to the Byzantine text.

4b. MS Typ. 294 (F263–297)

The manuscript has been given the Gregory-Aland number 2864. Revelation is written in a hand of a similar date to the Gospels part of the manuscript (although our first impression was that it might be of the second half of the eleventh century). There is one column to the page, each of 29 lines. There are rubricated initials. We have not examined the text. First studies in Münster indicate that it is Byzantine in character.

5. MS Typ. 491

MS Typ. 491 is a manuscript containing Acts, the Catholic and Pauline Epistles and patristic extracts. The verso of the flyleaf states that it was given by 'Philip Hofer, Class of 21'. There are some scribblings in Greek below. The manuscript has had folio numbers stamped on the top right-hand corner of each recto.

The volume is composed of two manuscripts. The first, extending so far as F219b, contains Acts and the New Testament epistles. The second, beginning at F220, consists of the patristic texts. Again, the binding may be able to cast light on the history of the constituent parts. The two will be discussed separately.

5a. MS Typ. 491 (F1–219)

The manuscript has been given the Gregory-Aland number 2865. It contains one column, and 26 lines to the page. Its size is 18 x 26 cm. The quire signatures are found at the inside bottom corner of both the first and the final page of each quaternion.[15] The manuscript contains ἀρχή and τέλος indications in the text. There are decorated illuminated bands at the beginning of each book, and rubricated initials. There are a considerable number of corrections in the text and margins, some comparable in date to the first hand.

	Contents
1	inc. Ac
56ᵛ	expl. Ac
57	inc. Catholic epistles, each with ὑπόθεσις and κεφάλαια
88ᵛ	expl. Jude
	inc. Pauline epistles, each with ὑπόθεσις and κεφάλαια
157	Hand Three, on paper (Eph 1.1–16 προευχῶν)
162	Hand Three, on paper (Eph 5.3 δὲ ὀνομαζέσθω – 28 ὁ ἀγαπῶν τὴν)
190	Hand Three, on paper (1 Tim 5.9]νυῖα ἑνὸς – 6.4 λογομαχίας)
217	(Heb 11.38 ταῖς ὀπαῖς) Hand Two takes over to the end of the manuscript. 23 lines to the page. Paper.
219	expl. Hebrews, followed by a note containing the date 1583 (see below).

---

15 For this position, see B. Mondrain, 'Les signatures des cahiers dans les manuscrits grecs', in P. Hoffmann, ed., *Recherches de codicologie comparée. La composition du codex au Moyen Âge, en Orient et en Occident*, Paris, 1998, 21–48.

Folio 99, lines 9-end (Rom 6.19–7.2) has been rewritten. In addition, corrections have been made throughout in at least four hands. There are vellum repairs to damaged leaves, some made with pieces from a minuscule manuscript. Altogether, this manuscript shows signs of having been extensively and respectfully used.

The main hand of the manuscript may be dated to the twelfth, or even to the end of the eleventh century. That it was written before the middle of the twelfth may be established on the basis of the earliest marginal corrections, which contain square breathing marks.

Hand Two, who wrote Folios 217–9, is fifteenth, or may be even sixteenth century.

Hand Three, responsible for three paper leaves, worked in the fifteenth century.

There is extensive evidence of sixteenth-century use. This may be very precisely dated, by means of two notes. The first, in the bottom margin of F 17, reads:

μακάριος ἀνήρ ως οὐκ επορευθ᾽ εν βουλ(η) ἀσεβῶν / 1583 χῦ

A second note on F219 also contains the date 1583. Chapter numbers for Acts have been added in a sixteenth-century hand. In addition, there are textual notes in Acts, including most noticeably the addition of Acts 8.37 (from a printed copy?) in the margin at the appropriate place.

A collation of the manuscript with the Oxford, 1873 *Textus Receptus* in Acts 8.30–40 yields the following variants:

32 ἣν ἀνεγίνωσκεν] OM; supplied by a twelfth-century corrector
κείροντος] κείραντος
αὐτοῦ] OM; supplied by the sixteenth-century corrector
33 ἐν τῇ ταπεινώσει] OM; supplied by the sixteenth-century corrector
34 τοῦτο] OM

The reading κείραντος is not particularly common, according to the Nestle-Aland[27] apparatus. The extent of correction by subsequent readers is, at least on this page, as remarkable as the number of omissions.

The small amount of textual evidence that has been gathered here, and the fact that this manuscript seems to have been used extensively over a long period of time, encourage one to believe that a detailed study of it would prove valuable (although initial surveys in Münster suggest that the manuscript is a witness to the Byzantine text).

5b. MS Typ. 491 (F220-)

The hand appears perhaps older than that of Ff1–219b. A date in the late tenth or first part of the eleventh century seems reasonable. The breathings are fairly square. The letter forms suggest that date. These leaves contain majuscule marginalia. F 220 has been rewritten. The text consists of a sequence of patristic extracts.

9 Codex Bezae: The Manuscript as Past, Present and Future

The open page of a manuscript appears essentially two-dimensional. In fact, it contains a third dimension, a perspective through time. The more interesting and complicated a textual history it represents, the more evident this third dimension will be. As Umberto Eco wrote, in a phrase which I have quoted elsewhere, 'It is impossible to write except by making a palimpsest of a rediscovered manuscript'.[1] In our own field, this re-use of the labours of a predecessor is most productively found not in the dramatic palimpsesting of a codex, but in that process of improving and annotating which is so significant a feature of certain manuscripts. By observing the annotations in the manuscript we can see its use and development, and sometimes even its influence, and by reconstructing the alterations that must have been made in earlier copies for the scribe to have written what he did, we can discern the ghostly palimpsests of lost texts. Codex Bezae is not the least suitable manuscript for such treatment, since it had a sequence of correctors, and a complicated earlier history which, thanks to the stereophony of its twin Greek and Latin columns, we can recover with remarkable frequency. To attempt this journey through time, we will take a fairly full double page of the manuscript, although we may need to turn to others to produce a complete picture. The opening selected is F423b/424, containing Acts 2.42–3.4. This passage is easily legible and contains some interesting annotations.

We start in the middle of time, as it were with the manuscript's present rather than its past or future, that is with the scribe.[2] He wrote

---

1   *The Island of the Day before*, quoted by me in *The Living Text of the Gospels*, 148.
2   I am rather well aware that all the matters with which I deal briefly here are handled, often at considerable length, in my study *Codex Bezae*. I do not reproduce here the evidence for my statements, though I provide a reference where it draws the reader's attention to a case which I have made. Altogether, in my relationship with Codex Bezae I am beginning to feel too like David Copperfield's friend Mr Dick, who was unable to keep King Charles' head out of any conversation. So I have used this paper as the opportunity to imitate the amiable Mr Dick in another of his habits, that of flying kites. This paper is an attempt to present some of the main

in Greek and Latin, a scribe trained in copying Latin, perhaps legal texts. Berytus has been suggested as a likely place in which he worked.[3] The style of writing used is known as b-d uncial for the Latin and biblical majuscule for the Greek.[4] He used the same letter forms for Greek and Latin characters of similar appearance. Thus, the Greek upsilon is written as Latin Y; a genuine Greek upsilon would be different. As for the text which he used, I will come to that later.

The manuscript contains the four Gospels, Acts and the end of 3 John.[5] The Greek is written on the left page, the Latin on the right. The layout is significant, for the following reasons. First, it allows us to locate the manuscript in a tradition of Graeco-Latin manuscripts.[6] Second, each column had an influence on the other, at least on the visual level and sometimes as the scribe tried to keep the two texts in tandem. This is not to adopt the outmoded view that the distinctive character of the Greek text is due to extensive 'Latinization'.[7] But it would be surprising in such a manuscript if there was *no* reciprocal influence at work.

[44] After that briefest of glances at the scribe, we need to step into the future, first by noting the numbers 338 and 424 in the top right-hand corner of the right-hand page. This is nineteenth-century foliation inserted in Cambridge University Library. The lower figure numbers the extant pages, the higher one takes account of missing leaves. In the bottom right-hand corner of the right-hand page is Hh2, another nineteenth-century addition in pencil, this time of quire numeration.

---

findings of my study of Codex Bezae from a particular perspective and according to a particular idea. For full bibliographies, the reader is referred to my book and to the Lunel conference papers.

3   *Codex Bezae*, Chapter 15. For a full survey of various theories that itself advocates Jerusalem, see J.N. Birdsall, 'The Geographical and Cultural origin of the Codex Bezae Cantabrigiensis: a Survey of the *Status Quaestionis*, mainly from the Palaeographical Standpoint', *Studien zum Text und zur Ethik des Neuen Testaments* (Festschrift H. Greeven), ed. W. Schrage, Berlin, 1986, 102–14. More recently, see J.N. Birdsall, 'After Three Centuries of the Study of Codex Bezae: the *Status Quaestionis*', Parker and Amphoux, *Codex Bezae*, xix-xxx; A.D. Callahan, 'Again: the Origin of the Codex Bezae', Parker and Amphoux, *Codex Bezae*, 56–64.

4   *Codex Bezae*, 27–30.

5   In my opinion it originally contained Revelation and the Johannine epistles between Mark and Acts: *Codex Bezae*, 8–9. A different view has been advanced by C.-B. Amphoux: 'Schéma d'Histoire du Texte grec du Nouveau Testament', *New Testament Textual Research Update* 3/3 (1995), 41–6. See my reply, 'Professor Amphoux's History of the New Testament Text: A Response', *New Testament Textual Research Update* 4/3 (1996), 41–5.

6   *Codex Bezae*, Chapter 4.

7   *Codex Bezae*, Chapter 12.

These numberings are evidence of the recent conservation of the manuscript. The pale oblong of parchment in the bottom right corner of the left page in the facsimile is probably a nineteenth-century repair. The leaves at that time were disjoint and the manuscript disbound. But in 1965 the pairs of leaves were re-joined, and the manuscript bound. The paler parchment visible between the leaves in modern photographs is what joins the leaves together.

Elsewhere (there is no example on this page) one finds an occasional mark or phrase of eighteenth-century date. These are likely to be from the pen of Richard Bentley, who had the manuscript on loan from Cambridge University Library for a number of years. The manuscript had by then already been in Cambridge for 150 years, in fact since 1581. It was a gift from the Genevan Reformer Theodore Beza, who had himself acquired it from a monastery in Lyons, after the town's sacking in 1562.

Moving back another 200 years, we find evidence of sixteenth-century use: on line 19, there is a half bracket in the left margin and *IV Cap⁻* in the right margin of the right-hand page; there is also *II.III* in the top left corner of the left page and bottom right corner of the right page. This is evidence of reading and consulting the manuscript in the Renaissance and Reformation. We know that the manuscript was owned by Bezae between 1562 and 1581, and that he used it as an authority in his first edition of the Greek New Testament, and that in 1550 it was one of the witnesses cited in the first ever *apparatus criticus*, that of Robertus Stephanus. Perhaps the chapter numbers were inserted by one of these two scholars.

Stepping up through the centuries even more briskly, we find ourselves in ninth-century Lyons. The manuscript was probably there throughout the Middle Ages. In the ninth century, supplementary leaves (abbreviated as d^{suppl})were added in order to replace several lacunae, consisting of Mt 3.7–16 (Greek), 2.21–3.7 (Latin); Jn 18.14–20.13 (Greek), 18.2–20.1 (Latin); Mk 16.15–20 (Greek), 16.6–20 (Latin). Why do we know that Lyons was the place where this was done? Because of the form of the question mark, and because of the use of blue ink in the replacement colophon to Mark.[8] It has for some time now been possible

---

8   *Codex Bezae*, 45–8, building on the work of others, including especially E.A. Lowe ('The Codex Bezae and Lyons', *JTS* 25 (1924), 270–4, reprinted in *Palaeographical Papers 1907–1966*, ed. L. Bieler, Oxford, 1972, Vol. 1, 182–6), and C. Charlier ('Les Manuscrits personnels de Florus de Lyon et son activité littéraire', *Mélanges E. Podechard*, Lyons, 1948, 71–84). There is now scientific evidence to substantiate the blue ink theory: B. Guineau, L. Holtz, J. Vezin, 'Étude comparée des tracés à l'encre

to associate this work with Florus, a Lyonnaise scholar of great distinction. Florus died in 860, and so this restoration may be dated rather precisely to the middle of the ninth century. Amongst other things, he was responsible for the preservation of a number of ancient texts and manuscripts, including without a doubt Codex Bezae. Another point of connection with Lyons is that it is possible that the Latin column of these replacement leaves was copied from a manuscript of a similar date also produced in Lyons. This one, unlike Codex Bezae, has remained in Lyons to the present day.[9] The texts are close, there are corrections in Lyons 431 which are followed in d^{suppl}, and one whole line of Lyons 431 is missing in d^{suppl}. The Greek text which was copied was of good quality.

The manuscript's future from this point lay in western and northern Europe. But provenance is no indication of origin, and there is no reason to suppose that because the manuscript was found in Lyons it must have been written there. Rather, there are a number of good palaeographical reasons against this.[10] The preceding centuries are at first glance somewhat less certain. However, a study of the successive hands reveals useful information about the kind of contexts in which the manuscript was used, although to associate these contexts with particular places must contain an element of speculation. What we do not know is the stage at which the manuscript came to Lyons. A date in the seventh century, as a result of the Arab conquests in the eastern Mediterranean, seems possible. Certainly, one may say that it was between approximately 650 and around 800. Before that, the evidence of the correctors and my theory of Berytus as its place of origin suggest that the manuscript had been moved in the middle of the sixth century. While I had suggested a local move at that time, perhaps to Sidon,[11] Birdsall has advanced the theory that the manuscript was removed from Berytus to Sicily or southern Italy in the sixth century, and from there to Lyons as a safe place in the eighth.[12] It is to the period just before 650 that we now move. A symbol indicating a beginning of a lection may be observed to the left of line 19 of the Greek page,

---

bleue du ms. Lyon, B.M. 484 et du fol. 384v du Codex de Bèze', Parker and Amphoux, *Codex Bezae*, 79–94.

9   Lyons, Bibl. Mun. 431. *Codex Bezae*, 172–3.

10 E.A. Lowe, 'A Note on the Codex Bezae', *BBC* 4 (1927), 9–14, reprinted in *Palaeographical Papers 1907–1966*, ed. L. Bieler, Oxford, 1972, Vol. 1, 224–8. Yet see recently L. Holtz, 'L'écriture latine du Codex de Bèze', in Parker and Amphoux, *Codex Bezae*, 14–55. See further J.N. Birdsall, 'The Geographical and Cultural Origin'.

11 *Codex Bezae*, 282.

12 'After Three Centuries', Parker and Amphoux, *Codex Bezae*, xxii-xxiii.

opposite 3.1. This is written by a hand known as M⁴, which added indications of the beginnings and ends of lections in Mark and Acts.[13] It may be dated to the period 550–600. Evidently, the manuscript was at that time being used for the public reading of the Scriptures. The markings are slightly later than the other lectionary annotations on the page, just above, opposite line 12 (2.46, but referring to 3.1). Later cropping of the margin has reduced what was originally

Αννα]γνοσμα [his usual spelling] [περ]ι του σα[ββατου τ]ω της [δια]κονι[σι]μου (scil. διακινησιμου) ('Reading for the sabbath on the making to walk').

This hand, datable to the second half of the sixth century, provided the Ammonian Sections in the Gospels, and lectionary annotations throughout the codex. Palaeographically, it is perhaps closest to a group of manuscripts of Syrian and possibly Antiochene origin.[14] There was thus a fairly lengthy period of lectionary use of the manuscript.

From the same period come the *sortes* in Mark's Gospel, a sequence of sentences at the foot of the page, used for telling fortunes or determining one's future.[15]

The remaining annotations are all to the text.[16] There are just over 800 to Acts all told. That is a dozen to a page, a rather large number. The most recent is in lines 10–11. It is by Corrector F. Before this correction can be understood, it is necessary to explain one of the most significant things about Codex Bezae: its text of Acts. It is far longer than that found in other witnesses, and in addition contains many re-writings. Here, it reads (2.45–6)

---

13 The original listing of correctors, each with a letter of the alphabet, was made by F.H. Scrivener in his transcription of the manuscript. It was subsequently emended by J.R. Harris, in *The Annotators of the Codex Bezae (with Some Notes on Sortes Sanctorum)*, London, 1901. I have further revised their findings.
14 *Codex Bezae*, 42–4, citing Cavallo, *Ricerche*.
15 There are other manuscripts with these, including a number of papyri and parchment manuscripts of John's Gospel. See especially B.M. Metzger, 'Greek manuscripts of John's Gospel with "Hermeneiai"', *Text and Testimony. Essays on New Testament and Apocryphal Literature in Honour of A.F.J. Klijn*, ed. T. Baarda, A. Hilhorst, G.P. Luttikhuizen and A.S. van der Woude, Kampen, 1988, 162–9; B. Outtier, 'Les *Prosermeneiai du Codex Bezae*', Parker and Amphoux, *Codex Bezae*, 74–8.
16 The full sequence of correctors who supplied lectionary notes of various kinds are
550–600   J, M¹/M² (probably only one hand), L
600–650   I, M, M⁴, N, O, O²

ΚΑΙ ΔΙΕΜΕΡΙΖΟΝ ΑΥΤΑ ΚΑΘ ΗΜΕΡΑΝ ΠΑΣΙ ΤΟΙΣ ΑΝ ΤΙ ΧΡΕΙΑΝ ΕΙΧΕΝ ('And parted them day by day to all those who had need')[17]

Most other manuscripts read

Καὶ διεμέριζον αὐτὰ πᾶσιν καθότι ἄν τις χρείαν εἶχεν καθ' ἡμέραν . . . ('and distributed them to all, as any had need. And day by day . . .')

Corrector F changes the text of D to read

Και διεμεριζον αυτα καθ ημεραν πασι καθ τοις αν τι χρειαν ειχεν καθ ημεραν ('And distributed them day by day to all those who had need. And day by day . . .')

[46] In fact it makes a fudge, a compromise between the two readings. This line thus shows a new form of the text in process of coming into being. A copy taken from this emended text would be distinctive in this error. As it happens, no manuscript is known to have this correction, either because Codex Bezae was never copied in Acts, or because no descendant of such a copy has survived, or because a copyist rejected Corrector F's version.

In line 1 there is a quite small correction, the addition of καί ('and'). This is made by the corrector who is probably the most interesting hand to have revised the Greek text, Corrector B. This work may be dated to before the middle of the fifth century. What is particularly interesting is that the reading which the corrector introduces is often that introduced into Codex Sinaiticus by the so-called C group of correctors (abbreviated as ℵc).[18] So it is here. In this instance we have a grammatical point – is Luke giving a sequence of four items or two pairs of items? B was the most active corrector, making over 300 changes, half of them to the text of Acts. This is an average of two a page. I have suggested that the relationship between D^B and ℵc may be a sign of contact between Codex Bezae and the scholarly traditions of Caesarea.

The next corrector, still working backwards in time, is found three times on the left-hand page, in lines 4, 21 and 30. This is C, to be dated shortly before B. The addition of τε follows most manuscripts. The reading of D* may simply be an error. In line 24 D^C changes ενατη τη προσευχης to της προσευχης την ενατην, that is to the text of other manuscripts. Finally, in line 30 it alters ειναι to εισειεναι (sic). These corrections show a careful reader who is tidying up the text.

---

17 The translations of D are taken from J.M. Wilson, *The Acts of the Apostles TRANSLATED from the CODEX BEZAE with an INTRODUCTION on its LUCAN ORIGIN and importance*, London, New York and Toronto, 1923. Translations of the text of most manuscripts is from the RSV.

18 *Codex Bezae*, 139–49.

We move back now to A, the oldest corrector to concentrate on the Greek column. In line 29, ιδων is changed to ειδων. Again, this was a corrector who was keen on tidying up the text here and there.

There are also correctors who are hard to identify. In line 13, αν is erased (unless there is a substitution, an erasure is anonymous, though if there is a washing out of letters, this must have been done by the scribe before the ink had dried). In lines 22 and 27 there is the deletion of ιδου and αυτων. Certain habits in this can sometimes be discerned, but if two or more correctors use the same method of indicating a deletion (for example with a point or a cancelling line), it may be impossible to distinguish between them. In line 26, παρ αυτων is changed to παρα των. Finally, in line 33 ν και has been erased.

All these correctors were concerned almost exclusively with the Greek column. They show that the text of D fascinated as much in the fifth and sixth centuries as it does today. A number do not feature on this page. They are D, who appears to have been a scholar, and who went to some pains to change the text to agree with that of good manuscripts; E, who made about forty-five changes to Acts; H, the majority of whose fifty-two changes to Acts are orthographic, but some others of which show a somewhat distinctive text; and J[1], who added some missing text on one double opening of John.

We turn now to a quite different hand, the oldest. This corrector works almost exclusively with the Latin column, and almost wholly in Matthew and the early part of Acts. Known as G, it is contemporaneous with the scribe. There are several corrections on this page: line 13, the addition of *in*; line 18, the correction of *cottie* to *cottidie*; line 23, the substitution of *u* for *o* in *baiolabatur*. G may also have been responsible for the deletions in lines 17 and 29: the way that it is done is consistent with his methods elsewhere.

These corrections are rather dull compared to G's activities elsewhere. In Matthew he was active, not just in correcting the Latin but in improving it. 17.25 is a good example, where he wrote *facit aut prae*[*stat*] in the margin against *ETIAM*. The fact that this corrector felt so confident led F.C. Burkitt to conclude that he was the bishop of the church for which the codex was produced.[19] He makes a good case, though it cannot be proven.

We come at last to the scribe. He makes one of his own corrections at line 18: αυ is washed out under εν.

[47]

---

19 F.C. Burkitt, 'The Date of Codex Bezae', *JTS* 3 (1902), 501–13.

So far, this survey has dealt with the easy part, the physically visible levels of the text. A copy made from Codex Bezae would have been different between each stage of correction. These processes of correction led to endless complications and confusions in the text of the New Testament, and we may see the process in action on these open pages. However, the text as the scribe produced it was already the product of over three centuries of such processes. How do we move back to discern older levels of the text beneath what is before us? First, by examining the scribe's habits, practices and typical errors. These can be used to eliminate distinctive aspects of the manuscript, including singular or unusual readings, from further investigation. Second, with D, there are in fact *two* texts, the Greek and the Latin, and the opportunities to compare them furnish unique opportunities for recovering and examining the earlier strata of the tradition.

Various theories have been put forward to explain the relationship between the two columns. Eberhard Nestle, for example, believed that the 'Latin text d is not translated directly from its own Greek but from the Greek of the parent manuscript'.[20] He was right in recognising that the texts represent different generations. My own method has been to look for differences between the two columns, and to find a theory that accounts for them. There are two of them on these two pages. In lines 8–9 (2.45), there are the following readings: in the Greek:

ΚΑΙ ΟϹΟΙ ΚΤΗΜΑΤΑ ΕΙΧΟΝ Η ΥΠΑΡΞΕΙϹ ΕΠΙΠΡΑϹΚΟΝ

In the Latin:

ET QUI POSSESSIONES HABEBANT ET FACULTATES DISTRAHEBANT

The reading of most other Greek manuscripts is

καὶ τὰ κτήματα καὶ τὰς ὑπάρξεις ἐπίπρασκον

The reading of the Latin column of Codex Bezae seems to show a compromise between the two.

In lines 13–14 (2.46), we find in D

ΚΑΙ ΚΑΤΟΙΚΟΥϹΑΝ ΕΠΙ ΤΟ ΑΥΤΟ ΚΛΩΝΤΕϹ ΤΕ ΑΡΤΟΝ ΜΕΤΕΛΑΜΒΑΝΟΝ ΤΡΟΦΗϹ

The Latin has

ET PER DOMOS (+ IN D^G) IDIPSUM CAPIEBANT PANES ACCIPIENTES CIBUM

[48] The reading of other Greek manuscripts is

κλῶντές τε κατ' οἶκον ἄρτον, μετελάμβανον τροφῆς

---

20 *Introduction to the Textual Criticism of the Greek New Testament*, London, Edinburgh, Oxford and New York, 1901, 65.

Again, D seems to present a halfway house between the Greek texts. One is reminded of the correction by F in the previous verse, and sees that the attempt to improve the text to another standard often led to fresh corruptions and to conflations of different forms. This pattern is common in the D text of Acts. It provides strong evidence that the D text of Acts is evolving rather than the product of a single individual and occasion. The Latin column is derived from a Greek text which contains some of the distinctive features of the Greek column in particular points of variation, but not all of them – that is, it is in some ways older, lacking many of the characteristic additions and paraphrases of D. There is similar evidence elsewhere in the manuscript, particularly in Luke and Mark. I consider this finding to be an important conclusion of my study of the manuscript.

There are a number of other features which enable one to trace the earlier history of the text that are not particularly evident on this page. These include the *nomina sacra*. The examples on this page are not significant, but others make it possible to discern the hands of several scribes in the antegraphs of Codex Bezae.[21] Secondly, there is the orthography.[22] One interesting example on this page is the spelling ΪΩΑΝΗΝ in lines 29 and 33. This form with a single nu is found in Luke and Acts, while the double-nu form (ϊωαννης) is found in Matthew and Mark; the use changes from double- to single-nu in John in the course of Chapter 5. In the Latin, we find *Iohannes* in Matthew, Mark and Acts, *Iohanes* in Luke, and a slightly less clear situation in John. Thirdly, there is the evidence of the sense-lines, the division of the text into lines irregular in length containing units of sense.[23] In fact, on this page they accord between the two columns, but elsewhere there are many differences in line-breaks between the two columns. This evidence has led me to the conclusion that the scribe of the manuscript ran together shorter lines from his exemplar of the Gospels, but preserved those of its text of Acts, which was probably a separate manuscript.[24] From the first two classes of evidence, I concluded that the Gospels part of the manuscript was copied from one that contained the Gospels in Greek and Latin in the order Matthew–Mark–John–Luke, and that it was the work of two scribes, who divided their work somewhere around the end of the first third of John.[25] This in turn was

---

21 *Codex Bezae*, Chapter 6.
22 Ibid., Chapter 7.
23 Ibid., Chapter 5.
24 Ibid., 95–96.
25 Ibid., Chapter 8.

derived from another bilingual copy, also with the Gospels in the order Matthew–Mark–Luke–John.[26] Behind this may lie monolingual copies, but I could not discover any evidence for earlier copyings.

Again, this evidence points to a text that evolved. This is not to deny that through this evolution there emerged a distinctive text, nor that there may have been points in this evolution that were particularly important in the attainment of this distinctive character. Holmes has shown that Codex Bezae in Matthew is definitely a recension,[27] but it is not a recension that was reached in a single stage. Moreover, behind the development may be discerned a yet older textual layer. It has long been agreed that where D agrees with the earliest Old Latin witnesses and with the Old Syriac, we have evidence of a second-century text. This is a matter which deserves continuing examination. The importance of the Latin column in understanding the development of the Old Latin versions cannot hardly be overstated.[28]

Starting with the composition of Codex Bezae, we have looked from that point both forwards at the manuscript's use, and backwards through the earlier strata which may be recovered. The findings should encourage us to look forwards to new developments in our discipline, and backwards to the exploration of the most interesting of all the challenges of our discipline, the text of the early second century and before.

---

26 The diagram on page 119 of *Codex Bezae* has the blatant error of 'Mt-Mk-Jn-Lk' for this manuscript. It should of course read 'Mt-Mk-Lk-Jn'.

27 M.W. Holmes, 'Codex Bezae as a Recension of the Gospels', in Parker and Amphoux, *Codex Bezae*, 123–60.

28 See J.-M. Auwers, 'Le texte latin des Évangiles dans le Codex de Bèze', in Parker and Amphoux, *Codex Bezae*, 183–216.

10 The Date of Codex Zacynthius (Ξ): A New Proposal

In the Festschrift presented to Kirsopp Lake in 1937,[1] W.H.P. Hatch wrote an article in which he suggested new dates for two uncial manuscripts of the New Testament, namely the Codex Zacynthius (Gregory-Aland Ξ: or 040: Cambridge University Library, British and Foreign Bible Society MS, 213) and the Codex Cyprius (Gregory-Aland K or 017: Paris B.N. Graec. 63). It is with the former of these (with which Hatch dealt first) that this article is concerned.

The manuscript designated Ξ is the palimpsested underwriting of the first 89 leaves of a thirteenth-century lectionary (Gregory-Aland *l*299). It was presented to the British and Foreign Bible Society in 1821 by General Colin Macaulay, who had received it as a gift in the previous year from Prince Comuto in Zante (whence its Latin name). It was numbered in their library as No. 24 until, fairly recently, it was moved to Cambridge University Library, where it holds the number British and Foreign Bible Society MS 213.

Samuel Prideaux Tregelles edited it in full in 1861.[2] Scrivener and Gregory dated its hand to the eighth century.[3] Until recently, the date of seventh or eighth century was accepted by all editors.[4] In the article

[118]

---

1   W.H.P. Hatch 'A Redating of Two Important Uncial Manuscripts of the Gospels – Codex Zacynthius and Codex Cyprius', *Quantulacumque. Studies Presented to Kirsopp Lake*, ed. R.P. Casey, S. Lake and A.K. Lake, London, 1937, 333–8.

2   S.P. Tregelles, *Codex Zacynthius... deciphered, transcribed, and edited*, London, 1861. This remains the only edition. For corrections to the transcription, see J.H. Greenlee, 'A Corrected Collation of Codex Zacynthius (Cod. Ξ)', *JBL* 76 (1957), 237–41. See further his 'Some Examples of Scholarly "Agreement in Error"', *JBL* 77 (1958), 363–4, in which various errors in citation are tracked through the critical editions.

3   C. Tischendorf, *Novum Testamentum Graece*, ed. octava critica maior, Vol. 3, *Prolegomena*, scripsit C.R. Gregory, Leipzig, 1884, 407f; C.R. Gregory, *Textkritik des Neuen Testamentes*, Vol. 1, Leipzig, 1900, 90–1. See also F.H.A. Scrivener, *A Plain Introduction to the Criticism of the New Testament*, 4th edn, London, New York, and Cambridge 1894, Vol. 1, 161.

4   Including Tregelles (*op. cit.*). Nicholas Pocock, 'The Codex Zacynthius', *The Academy* 19 (Feb. 19, 1881), 136–7, anticipates Hatch in favouring (though hesitantly) a sixth-century date: 'it is noticeable that the character of the writing is very like that of the recently discovered Codex Rossanensis' (137). His grounds are that the *nomina sacra*

of 1937, Hatch proposed that this be emended to the earlier date of the sixth century. That date now appears to have been tacitly taken as correct by recent editors of the Greek New Testament, being given, for example, in the publications of the Münster Institut für Neutestamentliche Textforschung and the United Bible Societies. We propose to reconsider Hatch's judgement, Professor Parker discussing the strictly palaeographical arguments, and Professor Birdsall the other component in Hatch's reasoning. His argument was based upon the structure of the text which the palimpsest hides from us, namely the text of Luke, chapters 1–11, with a marginal catena. It is unique amongst catenae to the New Testament in the respect that both text and marginal commentary are written in majuscule, a rare feature in any case of a manuscript with marginal apparatus. The catena is in fact the earliest to be preserved in manuscript.

1. The Palaeography

The study of the development of Greek hands was far more advanced in 1937 than it had been in 1821. But it has been refined a great deal since 1937. The period between the sixth and ninth centuries has proved especially troublesome to scholars, especially biblical scholars, since there happens to be a shortage of comparative material from these years. It will become apparent that this remains a problem.

Codex Zacynthius is written in two hands (a point on which Hatch does not comment).[5] Biblical majuscule is used for the text and headings, and upright pointed majuscule for the catena. While materials illustrating the development of the former are plentiful, examples of the latter are rarer, and its history is less certain. There is

---

used in the manuscript provide evidence for date (although he does not advance beyond listing the forms). But there is no sufficiently specific evidence.

5 He was aware of the custom of using two different hands (either one majuscule and one minuscule, or two forms of minuscule), but writes 'Unfortunately, with the exception of Codex Zacynthius, there is no New Testament manuscript extant which has both the biblical text and the commentary in uncial script' (335). The essential difference between the two hands was already noted by Tregelles: 'The *Text* is in round full well-formed Uncial letters, such as I should have had no difficulty in ascribing to the *sixth* century, were it not that the Catena of the same age has the round letters (EΘOS) so *cramped* as to appear to belong to the *eighth* century' (Tregelles, *Codex Zacynthius*, ii).

concomitantly less secondary material.[6] These two hands will be studied separately.

a. The Biblical Majuscule

One of the characteristics of this hand is that *epsilon* sometimes jumps slightly above the line. This habit may be observed in other manuscripts, including the Codex Rossanensis (042).[7] And, indeed, one may understand why Hatch found our manuscript to be so similar to sixth-century hands. There is the same fastidious contrast in thickness between horizontal and vertical strokes, the same attention to uniformity. However, the fact is that in two respects the hand is different. Principally, it lacks the regularity of square shapes which is in some ways even more marked in the sixth century than previously. This squareness, so magnificently attained in the Vienna Dioscorides (Nationalbibliothek MS Med. gr. 1), datable to 513, is still the goal of the scribe of the Rossanensis. By contrast, a number of letters in Codex Zacynthius are compressed: *mu, epsilon, delta*; the crossbar of *tau* is shorter. Secondly, one or two letters depart markedly from the classical shapes of biblical majuscule. *Upsilon* in particular has lost its symmetry, and its descender has become very fine; the junction of the upper strokes can even be below the line. The two strokes of *lambda* sometimes meet at the very apex of the letter.

Certainly, this hand shows none of the excessive elaboration and confusion of forms that characterise attempts at biblical majuscule from the eighth century onwards. But it lacks the features that would place it in the sixth century. A date in the seventh places it best. It may help to set the hand in relation to the specimens in Cavallo's *Ricerche*.[8] He dates 026 (Plate 92) to 'intorno alla metà del [VI] secolo o anche un po' più tardi'. Another example is placed at the end of the sixth century (P. Vindob. G. 1384, Plate 91b). 0107 'probably' belongs to the beginning of

---

6 For the history of biblical majuscule, we rely above all on Cavallo, *Ricerche*, and on Cavallo and Maehler, *Greek Bookhands*. For upright pointed majuscule, see E. Crisci, 'La maiuscola ogivale diritta. Origini, tipologie, dislocazioni', *Scrittura e civiltà* 9 (1985), 103–45.

7 For this manuscript, see A. Muñoz, *Il codice purpureo di Rossano e il frammento sinopense*, Rome, 1907, and works cited there. See also Cavallo's illustrated guide *Codex Purpureus Rossanensis*, Rome, n.d. (Italian, French and English texts).

8 Cavallo, *Ricerche*, 105–7, 121–3, plates 91–7.

the seventh.[9] Wolfenbüttel, 75a Helmst. (Homilies of John Chrysostom, Plate 95) is later.[10] Our hand is definitely older than the last of these. It is younger than the Vienna papyrus. The closest analogy is 0107, but there is no strong similarity between the two. Zacynthius retains a lightness lacking in the other manuscript, while 0107 better preserves the forms of biblical majuscule. It is thus very hard to fit our manuscript into the sequence proposed by Cavallo. But a date earlier rather than later in the century seems appropriate.

b. The Upright pointed Majuscule

This script is described by Cavallo and Maehler as 'fairly well-attested in its initial phase, in the second and third centuries, but it very rarely appears in the fourth to eighth centuries (there are hardly more examples than those illustrated in plates 12, 40, 48a). But it seems likely that this form continued in use during the later centuries in parts of the Greek East outside Egypt'.[11] The hand is most fully described by E. Crisci, who also finds little material prior to the ninth century. The script had three main features at its purest: a contrast between narrow and broad letters; uniformity in thickness of stroke; and absence of decoration, and even of thickening, at the end of strokes. The hand in Codex Zacynthius preserves only the first of these characteristics. Otherwise here, both the degree of contrast between thick and thin strokes and the amount of ornamentation with serifs is as great as that in the biblical majuscule hand. It is thus principally the difference in proportion that distinguishes the two hands on the page.

Turning to individual letters, *rho* is noteworthy for its long and elegant descender (more reminiscent perhaps of sloping than of upright pointed majuscule); *alpha*, though not pointed, is in three strokes; the first stroke of *kappa* is clearly separated from the rest of the letter; the crossbar of *theta* extends beyond the width of the letter, with a bar at each end of it. *Upsilon* is developed well beyond the simple and symmetrical form found in earlier versions of the hand. Its left stroke is thicker than the right, and the descender is a very fine stroke. It is extremely similar to that in the biblical majuscule hand. The body of *phi* is rounded.

---

9   Illustrated in W.H.P. Hatch, *The Principal Uncial Manuscripts of the New Testament*, Chicago, 1939, pl. XXXV.
10 This manuscript also contains upright pointed majuscule; see Crisci, 116, n. 39.
11 Cavallo and Maehler, *Greek Bookhands*, 4.

If we compare the hand with other examples, then some broad indications at once appear. It is far more mannered than that found in the *Auszeichnungschrift* of the Rossano Gospels, which in the sixth century preserves the simplicity of fourth- and fifth-century representatives of the script. But it is distant also from the artificiality of eighth-century examples, such as Patmos Cod. 171, a manuscript containing LXX Job with a catena.[12] The Zürich Psalter (Cod. RP 1), dated to the seventh century, affords points both of similarity and of difference.[13] The degree of ornamentation is not dissimilar, though it is somewhat more advanced in Ξ (somewhat stronger serifs, somewhat more elaborate superlines). Some letters are very alike, especially *omega*, *mu*, and *nu*, all in the traditional form for the script (but note that in Zürich Psalter the forms of *mu* and *nu* are simpler on some occasions than on others). The traditional form of *epsilon* is better preserved in Zacynthius – in the Zürich manuscript it tends to be more closed. The base of *delta*, which in the Zürich manuscript extends to the left, as in earlier forms of the hand, stops at the corner in Zacynthius.

The relationship between these two manuscripts in the development of the hand is not easy to establish. But it is safe to say that that they are approximately contemporary. A date in the seventh century is the best conclusion.

This view is substantiated by the analysis of Crisci, who suggests that the Rossano and Zürich codices 'provengano dal medesimo ambito grafico. La datazione più probabile resta la prima metà del secolo VII'.[14] By offering this assessment, he rules out a sixth-century date for Codex Zacynthius, even though he does not discuss it beyond accepting the date claimed by Hatch.[15]

We thus find that both hands of the manuscript appear to be of the seventh century. The general appearance of the biblical majuscule is somewhat older than that of the upright pointed majuscule. A tendency to archaise in biblical majuscule is the best explanation of this. So, although we have hardly provided any evidence to rule out a later sixth-century date for the biblical majuscule, the appearance of the two hands together is more certainly of the seventh.

The difficulty of placing the hands is not only to be ascribed to the paucity of comparative materials. It is also due to the way in which, in this particular manuscript, the two forms have influenced each other.

---

12 Cavallo and Maehler, *Greek Bookhands*, plate 48b.
13 *Ibid.*, plate 48a.
14 Crisci, *art. cit.*, 115.
15 *Ibid.*, 116 n. 39.

[122]

As we have seen, neither retains the classical appearance of the script, and neither has advanced into the later heavily ornamented and artificial forms which each came to assume. We have here a manuscript which, both in the combination of hands and in the form of each, is unique.

Can any conclusions about origin be reached from this investigation? The most fruitful line of investigation is the combination of these two hands for main text and *Auszeichnungschrift*. An earlier example is – again – the Rossano Gospels. According to Cavallo and Maehler, the 'probable origin of this manuscript appears to be Syria or Palestine'.[16] At a later date, according to the same writers, 'very many manuscripts of the ix and particularly the x century, written entirely or partly in "upright pointed majuscule", come either from regions in the Greek East other than Egypt, or from Byzantine southern Italy'.[17] Thus, Egypt seems to be improbable, but almost anywhere else a possibility. There are one or two possible links with southern Italy: one *might* be the much later evidence of southern Italian manuscripts in upright pointed majuscule; and given that, another *might* be the location of Zante (granting all the difficulties of provenance as evidence for origin). But we are without the materials to trace this phenomenon back into the period which saw the production of our manuscript. It is better to admit ignorance than to offer speculations. To have established a better date must be the extent of our study.

In conclusion, the presence of two hands to some extent compensates for the lack of comparative material for each hand individually, both by providing two chronologies and by making it possible to compare the manuscript with others containing two hands. Palaeographically, a seventh-century date appears to be the most secure. However, the evidence of the catena must also be considered.

2. The Catena

[130]

...

---

16 Cavallo and Maehler, *Greek Bookhands*, plate 40. This hypothesis had already been advanced by Cavallo, *Ricerche*, 98–105, where he placed N (022), Sinopensis (023), Rossanensis and Beratinus (Q, 043) in an 'Ambiente siriaco-antiocheno'. He is following older authorities in this: see A. Muñoz, *Il codice purpureo di Rossano e il frammento sinopense*, and works cited there, and Cavallo, *Codex Purpureus Rossanensis*.

17 Ibid., 106.

Conclusions

The palaeographical evidence points to a date in the seventh century. This corrects the too-late date of Tregelles and his successors, as well as the too-early one suggested by Hatch. The evidence of the catena even more clearly rules out the sixth-century dating. A date of the seventh century is more probable on palaeographical grounds, and one of the eighth from the nature of the catena. The combination of the palaeographical and catena evidence leads to the conclusion that Codex Zacynthius must have been produced at a date which accommodates the two, that is, around the year 700.

[131]

11 Manuscripts of John's Gospel with *Hermeneiai*

The phenomenon of *sortes sanctorum*, ἑρμηνεῖαι or προσερμηνεῖαι, as they have variously been called, a system of divination consisting of prophetic sentences written in full or partial copies of biblical texts, was first studied by James Rendel Harris, initially in his monograph on the Codex Bezae, and subsequently at greater depth in *The Annotators of the Codex Bezae*.[1] Harris concentrated his attention on a comparison between the system in Codex Bezae which, uniquely, is found in the margins of Mark's Gospel, and that of the Latin Codex Sangermanensis, the most complete available system. Since 1901, a considerable body of analogous material has come to light. The origin and development of the use of sacred texts in sortilege (including sets of *sortes* found in the margins of the Psalter) has been explored by van der Horst.[2] Those texts to which most attention has been paid include a number of papyri, generally Graeco-Coptic, and manuscripts in Armenian and Georgian.[3] Most of the papyri were separately described by B.M. Metzger.[4] They have subsequently been edited with the other Johannine papyri for the International Greek New Testament Project.[5] In our subsequent work on the parchment manuscripts of the Fourth Gospel, we have examined several more fragments with *hermeneiai* (one – Gregory-Aland 0210 – is also described by Metzger). This paper is not

---

1   London, 1901.
2   P.W. van der Horst, 'Sortes: Sacred Books as Instant Oracles in Late Antiquity', L.V. Rutgers *et al.*, (eds.), *The Use of Sacred Books in the Ancient World* (Contributions to Biblical Exegesis and Theology 22) Leuven, 1998, 143–73.
3   For a valuable survey, see B. Outtier, 'Les *Prosermeneiai* du Codex Bezae', Parker and Amphoux, *Codex Bezae*, 74–8, and the same author's 'Réponses oraculaires dans des manuscrits bibliques caucasiens', in C. Burchard (ed.), *Armenia and the Bible* (University of Pennsylvania Armenian Texts and Studies 12), Atlanta, 1993, 181–4.
4   B.M. Metzger, 'Greek Manuscripts of John's Gospel with "Hermeneiai"', T. Baarda *et al.* (eds.), *Text and Testimony. Essays on New Testament and Apocryphal Literature in Honour of A.F.J. Klijn*, Kampen, 1988, 162–9.
5   W.J. Elliott and D.C. Parker (eds.), *The New Testament in Greek IV. The Gospel According to St. John*, Edited by the American and British Committees of the International Greek New Testament Project, Volume One *The Papyri*, NTTS 20, Leiden, 1995.

concerned with the *hermeneiai*, but with the character of the documents as witnesses to the text of the Gospel, and their consequent value for the editor. It is sensible to ask whether, if someone scribbles down a sentence from John, and under it a brief sentence of the kind found in the astrological section of a popular newspaper, we are entitled to find the result of much use for textual criticism, however valuable it may be for other lines of research. Of course, we need also to ask whether 'scribbles down a sentence' is a fair description of the process by which these documents were produced. The question promoting this survey is this: Can we treat the copies as serious and reliable witnesses to the text of the Gospel of John? To that end, a description of the parchment codices will be offered, followed by an evaluation of all the documents. They are:

    P55 Vienna, Österriechische Nationalbibliothek, Pap. G. 26214
    P59 New York, Pierpont Morgan Library, P. Colt 3
    P60 New York, Pierpont Morgan Library, P. Colt 4[6]
    P63 Berlin, Staatliche Museen, Ägyptische Abteilung, P. 11914
    P76 Vienna, Österriechische Nationalbibliothek, Pap. G. 36102[7]
    P80 Barcelona, Fundació Sant Lluc Evangelista, P. Barc. 83
    0210 Berlin, Staatliche Museen, Pap. 3607 and 3623
    0302 Berlin, Staatliche Museen Pap. 21315

A justification must be added for the inclusion of P60. Unfortunately no evidence of any *hermeneiai* survives. However, apart from its very close similarity to P59, with which it was found, two pieces of evidence support the conclusion that it originally did contain them. One is the fact that almost every page begins with a new sentence or idea, sometimes quite a brief one so that there is a blank space below it (such as Fragment X verso).[8] The second is that the apparent layout as it may be reconstructed contained enough space for a heading and a *hermeneia*.[9] I have therefore included this document in my survey.

---

6   Not described by Metzger.
7   Not described by Metzger.
8   Elliott and Parker, plate 35 (d).
9   See L. Casson and E.L. Hettich, *Excavations at Nessana*, Vol. 2, *Literary Papyri*, Princeton, 1950, 94f: 'It seems almost certain that the layout of the page in the two documents [sc. P59 and P60] was similar, i.e. that [P60] bore at the bottom of each page a ἑρμηνεία consisting of a center-head and a line or line and a half of descriptive or interpretive text'.

1. Descriptions of the Parchment Codices

0210
Pap. 3607 contains Jn 5.44 on the recto and 6.1–2 on the verso, while Pap. 3623 has 6.41–2 on its recto and nothing on the verso. The fragments were first edited by Otto Stegmüller in his article on the *hermeneiai* in Codex Bezae.[10] They are to be dated to the seventh century. Beneath the text of each biblical passage is the heading *hermeneia* and a phrase.

0302
The manuscript contains Jn 10.29–30 on the recto, followed by the heading ἑρμενεία followed by empty parchment (probably the *hermeneia* itself was on the missing left side of the page). The verso contains illegible traces of text followed by a *hermeneia*, in Greek and in Coptic. The first editor, Kurt Treu,[11] read fragments of a first line on the recto which, even after using a microscope, Dr Elliott and I were unable to confirm when we studied the manuscript in June 1999. The manuscript is dated to the sixth century. The mixture of Greek and Coptic in a *hermeneia* manuscript is not unique. Treu points to P63, to Paris, Bib. Nat. Copt. 156 (not a New Testament witness) and to a fragment in the Louvre, which he describes as having *hermeneiai* to John, but with no extant biblical text (van Haelst 1124).

[51]

2. An Analysis of the documents

Since the goal of this enquiry is the value of this group of witnesses for the editor of John, it is worth considering the ways in which they might be compared with each other and contrasted with other witnesses. I suggest that there are four ways in which we may test this. The first is to look at their script, to attempt an opinion on the place they come as written documents. The second is to look at their presentation. The third is to assess the standard of their orthography. The fourth is to compare their text with that of other witnesses, to see what variants they contain, and how seriously they should be taken.

---

10 'Zu den Bibelorakeln im Codex Bezae', *Biblica* 34 (1953), 13–22, 18–19. Transcriptions of 0210 and 0302 based on fresh examinations of the manuscript have been made for the IGNTP edition of the majuscule manuscripts.

11 K. Treu, 'P. Berol. 21315: Bibelorakeln mit griechischer und koptischer Hermeneiai', *APF* 37 (1991), 55–60.

2.1. Date

The comparative list of dates in the IGNTP papyrus volume leads to the following summary of the wider period in which they have been dated:

P55	VI-VII
P59	VII-VIII
P60	VII-VIII
P63	V-VI
P76	VI
P80	V-VI[12]
0210	VII
0302	VI

It is certainly noteworthy that they all fall into the same broad period. It is the same period as the addition of the *sortes* to Codex Bezae.[13] The fact is striking, and even with so small a sample it seems to be a reasonable conclusion that the practice of making such books began in the fifth century.[14]

2.2. Script

Treu describes 0302 as well-written, and I agree. It is a competent square hand. The same cannot be said for 0210, written somewhat sprawlingly with an inconsistent slope to the right. P55 is evenly written in a rather compressed hand. P59 is in a similar style, while P60 is sufficiently similar to P59 for the first editors to have taken a while to realise that they were dealing with two manuscripts rather than one. P63 is no better, even rather worse, than 0210. P76 is a good piece of writing, very much the product of a Coptic scribe. P80 is very similar in appearance to 0210.

---

12 The original editor dated this manuscript to the second half of the fourth century (R. Roca-Puig, 'Papiro del Evangelio de San Juan con «Hermeneia»', *Atti dell'XI Congresso Internazionale di Papirologia*, Milan, 1996, 225–36). Turner, however, dated it to V-VI (*The Typology of the Early Codex*, Pennsylvania, 1977, 150), and there is no doubt in my mind that he is right with regard to this sloping majuscule hand.

13 Parker, *Codex Bezae*, 43, 49, where they are dated to the period 550–600.

14 We need to annotate van der Horst in two respects therefore. So far as the *sortes* in Codex Bezae are concerned, he follows the broad dating of former scholarship, describing them as 'between the seventh and ninth century' ('Sortes', 166). And he follows Metzger's acceptance of Roca-Puig's dating of P80 when writing that 'one already finds this kind of oracular *hermêneiai* in eight early papyri of the Gospel of John dating from circa 300 to 600 CE' (167, n. 101).

We thus have one well written manuscript (0302), four good but not quite as good (P55 P59 P60 P76) and three poor ones (P63 P80 0210). The three poor ones have hands of a similar type, and so do three of the middle group. They are none of them either among the worst or best productions among the manuscripts of John, and it should be observed that it would not be hard to find similar examples among manuscripts containing other texts. P28 must rank at the bottom, and witnesses at the top must include P45, P75 and P95.

2.3 Presentation

It would be tempting to suspect that the less well-written manuscripts also let themselves down orthographically, so let us start with them. P63 immediately disproves the hypothesis. The scribe is careful with diaeresis and apostrophe, and corrects himself once (in 4.9). On the other hand, there is a complete absence of punctuation. An interesting feature of this copy is that *nomina sacra* are scarcely found. All such words are written in full, with the exception of $\overline{θυ}$ at 3.18 and 4.10. The layout is generous, with a clear delineation between biblical text and *hermeneia*. P80 is very brief, containing only six words wholly or partially surviving. Here πνευμα, the only word which is a *nomen sacrum*, is written in full. There is no space between the text and the *hermeneia*. 0210 has page numbers, but is otherwise rather featureless, with no punctuation or diacriticals. There is no consistent attempt to separate the Gospel text from the *hermeneia*. It has *nomina sacra*.

[53]

In the next group, P55, while lacking punctuation, has diaeresis sometimes but not always, and a rather careful layout, with a lot of space around the *hermeneia* heading. P59 also has a generous layout, as may be seen from the largest surviving part, Fragment IV (a) and (b), and the smaller fragment IX (papyrological) verso. We find fairly consistent use of diaeresis (in the form like a circumflex accent). The first letter of the page (which begins with a new section) is enlarged, usually with paragraphus supplied. *Nomina sacra* are used. The original layout of P60 is not so clear, but like P59 it may have been quite generous. Certainly what may be seen of the upper margin gives this impression. It has the same form of diaeresis as P59, and occasionally the first letter of the page is enlarged or ekthetic. It uses *nomina sacra*. The layout of P76 is very similar to the other three, with the addition of some ornamentation around the *hermeneiai*. There is nowhere in this small fragment a place where a diaeresis or *nomen sacrum* could be written. We do have one punctuation mark.

Finally, 0302 is again frustratingly small (only seven words of John). It clearly distinguishes the two categories of Gospel text and *hermeneia*, and our picture clearly shows the degree of decoration. There is a punctuation mark.

Apart from P63, is it wishful thinking to find any distinguishing marks for the groups? It seems to me that, with the exception of P63, there is – hardly surprisingly – a correlation between quality of script and clarity of layout. The absence of *nomina sacra* may be associated with the poorer hands.

2.4 Orthography

Again, one approaches this aspect of production with the question of correlation of quality with hand and layout.

As for P63, there is one possible peculiarity, at 3.18, where it reads καικρ[ι]νεται. But it might deserve the benefit of the doubt here – the first editor preferred to read this as two words. P80, as I say, is so short that the fact that its six words contain no oddities tells us nothing. Finally, 0210 reads ουκ instead of ουχ at 6.42.

Coming to the next tentative group, P55 shows no peculiarities, since ειδε for ιδε at 1.36 is by no means a rare spelling. Since it contains approximately three dozen complete or nearly complete words, this seems fairly accurate, although most of the complete words are ones with little room for variation, such as articles or *nomina sacra*.

P59 shows fairly consistent orthography, especially in writing iota for epsilon-iota:

11.42	ηδι[ν]
11.44	[υπ]αγιν
11.47	[αρχιε]ρις
11.48	[ελευσον]τε
11.51	εκινου
18.2	εκι
18.22	[υ]περαι[των]
	ραπει[cμα]
21.15	πλι[ον]
21.20	[βλε]πι

P60 has very similar habits:

16.33	[εχε]ται
17.8	ρειματ[α]

	απεϲτιλα[ϲ]
17.11	ερχομε
17.21	[απεϲ]τιλαϲ
17.22	ημιϲ
17.23	[τε]τελιωμενοι
	απ[εϲ]τιλα[ϲ]
18.1	[ϲυν τοιϲ μαθ]ητεϲ
18.4	ζητιτε
18.7	[ζ]ητιτε
	ναζωρεον
18.10	ηλκυ[ϲεν]
	επεϲεν
18.12	[οι υπηρε]τε
18.15	ηκολουθι
	ϲυνιϲηλθεν
18.24	απεϲτιλεν
18.25	[θε]εμενομ[ενοϲ]
18.32	ϲημενων
18.36	υπηρετε[15]
18.39	[ϲυ]νηθια
	[βουλεϲ]θαι
19.6	[υπηρε]τε
19.7	ημιϲ
	[ο]φιλι
19.10	[απ]ολυϲε
	ϲαι
	ϲταυρωϲε
19.12	ι (for ει)
19.25	[ει]ϲτηκιϲαν

[55]

The consistency in writing iota for *epsilon-iota* is even found in a preference for πιλατος over πειλατος. It and P59 present a fairly consistent picture, although it has to be said that P60 exchanges *epsilon* for *alpha-iota* more than P59 does.

P76 also replaces *epsilon-iota* with *iota*, reading μιζω[ν] at 4.12. This brief fragment (17 words preserved, only four of them in full) has no idiosyncrasies.

0302 has none either, but there is little enough evidence, as we have seen.

Given the difficulty of adjudging such very fragmentary texts, none of these shows any consistent habits which cannot be paralleled from

---

15 The reading follows the first editors (Casson and Hettich, cited above). The piece of parchment containing the *pi* is missing.

other papyri and majuscules, as the IGNTP editions of these texts makes clear.

2.5. Text forms

I turn finally to the question which for many editors is likely to come first. In the first place, one notes that the documents were all produced in the fifth to eighth centuries. There are no third to fourth–century witnesses, and none from a period when the Byzantine Text had become fully developed.

Secondly, it must be pointed out that these documents are not like Codex Bezae, to which the *hermeneiai* were added a long time after it had been produced. These are purpose-written, and most notably did not necessarily contain the continuous text of John. A *hermeneia* manuscript can be non-continuous in two possible ways. First, it may contain a selection of pieces of text. Second, it may contain continuous text, each page beginning with a new division of the text, with the *hermeneia* beneath. The surviving material of each witness needs careful scrutiny before one can decide to which type it belongs.

We cannot reach a conclusion with regard to the single leaf comprising P55, of which the upper and lower margins are both missing. The first side contains most of 1.31–3, and the second 35–8. Although there are no codicological difficulties with the possibility that the second side contained the missing text, it is worth noting that the first letter of verse 35 seems to be preceded by a paragraphus. On the analogy of P59, this suggests that the page began here. But given the fragmentary nature of the evidence, certainty cannot be attained.

P59 has clear evidence of belonging to the second type. Fragment IV (easily the largest) consists of two conjoint leaves, the central sheet of a gathering. The sequence of material on these pages is Jn 11.40–43 + *hermeneia* – 11.44–6 + *hermeneia* – 11.47–8 (no *hermeneia* on surviving material) – 11.49–52 + *hermeneia*. As has been noted, each page usually begins with an enlarged letter and paragraphus. Fragments VII (17.24–6 and 18.1–2) and XII (21.17 and 21.18) also support the view that the entire Gospel text was contained.[16]

---

16 Note also the possibility that the beginning of 11:47, found on Fragment IV(c) recto had been begun on the bottom of the previous page. See Elliott and Parker, 79.

Turning to P60, the evidence is sufficiently conclusive that it contained the continuous text. Fragments XII (18.26–7 on one side and 18.28–9 on the other) and XIV (18.34–5 and 18.36) are good examples.

P63 consists of two conjoint leaves, with Jn 3.14–15 and 16–18 on the first recto and verso, and 4.9 and 4.10 on the second pair. It is not very easy to work out very much about further textual divisions in the manuscript. If we assume that the manuscript contained all the text between 3.17 and 4.8, then a division into an even number of sections of a similar size could suggest eight blocks (3.19–21, 22–4, 25–6, 27–8, 29–31, 32–6, 4.1–4, 5–8), in which case the surviving sheet would have been the second of a quaternion. With twelve slightly shorter blocks, it would have been the outermost sheet. It therefore appears to be of the second type.[17]

P76 is part of a single leaf, containing 4.9 on the papyrological verso and 4.12 on the recto (we do not have the beginning of either). It could have contained the verses in between if it had been approximately 34 cm in height, which is perfectly possible.[18]

Since our fragment of P80 only preserves writing on one side, nothing can be said.

The first leaf of 0210 clearly did not contain 5.45–7 (at any rate, not in sequence between 5.44 and 6.1). It is the only certain example of the first type of non-continuous text witness.

As with P80, we cannot say anything about 0302.

The conclusions to be drawn then with regard to the text contained by these witnesses is:

Selection of passages   0210
Possibly selection of passages P76
Most likely continuous sequence of text divided into blocks P59 P60
Possibly continuous sequence of text divided into blocks P63
No evidence P55 P80 0302

It is at least likely that the preference was for reproducing all the biblical text.

---

17   At such a rate, a book containing the entire Gospel would have been very large.
18   The existing material, containing 77 letters in the IGNTP reconstruction (which lacks a probable 4 letters at the beginning and 5 at the end), is in six lines, with a total vertical measurement of 7 cm. The number of letters in the *Nestle-Aland*[27] text for 4:10–11 is 193. Calculating 15 letters to the lines (86 divided by 6), verses 10 and 11 would have taken up 13 lines. Allowing 1 cm between the top of one line and the top of the one below, this would require 13 cm. When one adds 11 cm for the material below the last line of biblical text (containing *hermeneia* and bottom margin) and calculates a similar 3 cm for the top margin, one reaches a total of 3 + 13 +7 + 11.

[58] With regard to the text, the first question that occurs is whether the way in which the text is presented – as discrete blocks – affected the wording. There is a possible analogy with the lectionaries, in which standard opening phrases, incipits, are used, with appropriate changes to the biblical text. For example, P63 immediately shows signs of not being a continuous-text manuscript by omitting και in 3.14, against all other papyrus and majuscule witnesses.

We have the following places where the beginning of a passage is extant in one of the eight witnesses. The variants are provided which are found in the IGNTP's editions of the papyri and the majuscule manuscripts.[19]

P55	1.35	τ[η επαυριον παλιν]	παλιν is omitted by P75 036 044
P59	11.40	Λεγει αυ[τη ο ιc]	P66 02 omit ο
	11.44	Εξ[ηλθεν ο τεθνη]κωc	Omission of και with P45 P66 P75 03 04* 019 044
	11.47	Cυν[ηγαγον ουν οι]	No variation
	11.49	[Εις δε τις εξ αυτων]	P66 omits τις
	12.35	Ειπεν ουν	No variation
	21.17	Λεγει αυτ[ω το τριτον]	No variation
	21.19	Και το[υ]τ[ο ειπων]	No variation
P60	17.1	[ταυτα ελαληcεν] ο ιc	ο is omitted by 01 03 038 0109
	18.15	ηκολουθι δε [τω ιυ]	No variation
	18.26	λεγει εις εκ τω[ν]	No variation
	18.28	[αγουcιν ου]ν τον	ουν is omitted by 019 021 030 0211
	18.31	Ειπεν ουν αυ[τοις]	No variation
[59] | | 18.32 | [ ] του ιυ | There is too little room for ινα ο λογος, but the fact that what lies above looks to be the top margin leaves one wondering whether this page ran |

---

19 U.B. Schmid, with W.J. Elliott and D.C. Parker, *The New Testament in Greek IV. The Gospel According To St. John Edited by The American And British Committees Of The International Greek New Testament Project*, Volume Two, *The Majuscules* (New Testament Tools, Studies and Documents 37), Leiden, 2007. Of course there could be relevant information in other witnesses, but this restriction has the virtue of providing a complete record for the two oldest classes of manuscript.

			continuously from the other side
	18.34	[απ]εκριθη ο̣	o is omitted by P66 03 019 033 0109; αυτω o is read by 01 04^C2 07 011 013 017 028 034 036 037 039 045 047; P60 is in agreement with 02 04* 05 etc
	18.36	[απεκριθη ι̅ς̅] η	o ι̅ς̅ is read by 022 037; P66 and the rest omit o
	19.7	[απε]κριθη̣ς̣α[ν αυτω]	αυτω is omitted by P60 P90^vid 01 032
	19.10	[λεγει τοις αυτω ο] πιλατος	Omission of ουν with 01* 02 against P66 and the rest
	19.12	Ο̣[ι] δ[ε ε]κραυγ[αζον]	All other witnesses read δε ιουδαιοι εκραζ.
	19.14	[λεγει τοις ι]ουδα[ιοις]	Probably no room for και against all other papyrus and majuscule witnesses
	19.23	Ο̣[ι ο]υ̣ν	No variation
P63	3.14	καθως μωϋσης	Omission of και against all other papyrus and majuscule witnesses
	3.16	ουτως γαρ ηγα[πη]σεν	063 omits γαρ
	4.9	λεγει ουν αυτω	ουν read with P66 P75 and most majuscules; 01* 028* 031* 047 omit it
	4.10	απεκριθη ο ι̅ς̅ και ειπ[ε]ν̣	o read with 05 022 038; P66 P75 and all other majuscules omit it
0210	5.44	[π]ω̣ς δυνασθε πισ[τευσαι]	No variation
	6.1	[μ]ε̣τ̣α̣ ταυτα απηλθε̣ν̣	No variation
	6.41	[ε]γογγυζον ουν οι ϊουδ[αιοι]	05 reads δε for ουν

The witnesses come out of this examination very well. If one were to take the analogy of lectionary manuscripts, a non-continuous witness would be quite likely to remove conjunctions. Only three times does a manuscript omit against all other witnesses cited (P60 at 19.12, 14 and P63 at 3.14). But both manuscripts retain a conjunction elsewhere (P60

[60]

at 18.15, 28, 31; 19.12, 23 and P63 at 3.16 and 4.9. The other manuscripts with an opening phrase all contain a conjunction at least once. Moreover, there are a number of places where a word found in one of these manuscripts is omitted elsewhere in the tradition.

It may therefore be concluded that this class of manuscripts retains significance in these opening phrases. An example of the significance of this is at 19.10. If P60 regularly omitted conjunctions, then the likelihood of its omission of ουν along with 01* and 02 being genealogically significant would be reduced. As it is, the reading may be regarded as possibly significant genealogically. There is no difference observable in this tiny sample between witnesses likely to contain selections and those with the continuous text.

Turning to the rest of the text, how much do these witnesses show readings which we know from the other papyri and majuscules? P55 has these noteworthy readings:

1.31 υδατι with P66 P75 03 04 011 019 024 029 032 038 039 044 083 0233 0260
τω υδατι 01 cet

1.32 ως with P75 01 03 cet
ωσει P66 017 021 024 030 033 034 037 039 041 063 0101 0211 0233
εμεινεν with P66 P75 02 03 cet
μενον 01 032

1.35 παλιν is omitted by 036 044 (see above)
ο is omitted by 03 019

1.36 P66* 04 032ˢ add ο αιρων την αμαρτιαν του κοσμου

1.37 probably reads και with P5 P66 P75 cet; omitted by 01* 044
οι δυο μαθηται αυτου (what survives is ο[ ]του) with 01 03
οι δυο αυτου μαθηται P66 P75 04* 019 032 033 044 083
οι δυο μαθηται P5 04ᶜ²
αυτου οι δυο μαθηται cet

1.38 probably read δε with P5 P66 P75 cet; omitted by 01* 07 09 013 021 031 036 039 045 063 083 0233
αυτοις is omitted by 01*

With no errors, no singular readings, and agreement always with either P75 or 03 (in fact a direct comparison with 03 shows that the two differ only in orthography), the text is of excellent quality.

The following readings in P59 are worth singling out;

1.26 omits δε after μεσος with P66 P75 01 03 04* 019 083

2.15 probably added αυτων after τραπεζας (reads [ ]ων against all other witnesses)

11.40 probably read ο before ι̅ς̅ with P75 01 03 cet, against P66 02, which omit it (see above)

11.41 omits ου ην ο τεθνηκως κειμενος with P66 P75 01 03 04* 05 019 032 033 038 044 0233; 02 017 041 omit ο τεθνηκως κειμενος probably omitted δε before ι̅c̅ with 0233 (και ο 05; ο ουν 038), but is alone in the word order [ηρεν] ο ι[c̅]

11.43 omitted φωνη μεγαλη against all other witnesses

11.44 omission of και with P45 P66 P75 03 04* 019 044 (see above) possible insertion of και before λεγει against all other witnesses probable insertion of αυτον before υπαγειν with 03 04* 019 038

11.46 reads ο against 03 04 05 019, which omit it

11.51 reads με[λλει] against all other witnesses omitted ο with P45 P66 and all majuscules except 038 041^C 070 0211

11.52 reads δ[ιες]κορπισμενα with P75 and nearly all other witnesses (εσκορπισμενα P45 P66 05)

17.25 omits και ουτοι εγνωσαν against all other witnesses

18.17 τω πετρω η παιδισκη η θυρωρος with 04* 019 033; 03 omits τω πετρω; the rest have η παιδισκη η θυρωρος τω πετρω

18.22 in word order των παρεστηκως υπηρετων (but not necessarily the precise form) agrees with 01^Cca 04* 019 032 033 044 054

21.18 reads αλλοι (and presumably plural verb forms) with 01 05 032 (041 also has plural verb forms) reads [α]ποισου[σιν] with 01^Cca 032 041

21.20 reads δε with most witnesses (02 03 04 032 041* omit)

21.23 supports ουκ ειπεν δε with 01 03 04 032 against και ουκ ειπεν cet [62]

This papyrus has five readings not attested in any other extant papyrus or majuscule. In two it omits (11.43; 17.25), in two it adds (2.15; 11.44) and in one (11.51) it changes a form. There is no direction of change different from that usually found in manuscripts – that is to say, individual manuscripts tend to lose words, even though the text as a whole expanded in the course of transmission. There are no grounds for doubting that, whatever the purpose of the book in which it was written, this document was written to a good standard of attention.

Turning to P60, the following readings are worth noting:

16.29 the reconstruction suggests that the manuscript may have read εν before παρρησια, with 01* 03 04 05 032

16.33 the reconstruction suggests that the manuscript omitted εγω, against all other witnesses

17.1 seems to have omitted both και and σου, either side of ο υιος, with 01 03 032 0109* 0301 and against P66 and the rest (02 05 033 038 omit only και)

17.9 seems to have omitted περι αυτων ερωτω ου; this slip was not made in any other of the manuscripts under review

	17.12	omitted εν τω κοσμω with P66 01 03 04* 05* 019 032 η before γραφη is omitted, without other support
	17.22	omits εcμεν at the end of the verse with P66 03 04* 05 019 032
	17.24	reads ο for ουc with 01 03 05 032
	18.4	[εξηλ]θεν εξω κ[αι]; εξηλθε(ν) και is read by 03 04* 05; but εξω is not read by any other witness[20]
	18.5	omits ο ῑc̄ with 03 05 0211 (and probably P66)
	18.10	reads ωταριον against ωτιον with 01 03 04* 019 032 033
	18.13	reads απηγαγον against P66 01* 03 05 032; omits αυτον with P 66 01 03 04* 05 022 032 033 037
	18.14	is alone in omitting ο before cυμβουλευcαc [21]
[63]	18.18	reads και ο πετροc μετ αυτων with P66vid 01 03 04 019 033
	18.24	has ουν with 03 04* 019 022 032 033 037 038 041ᶜ 044 according to the IGNTP reconstruction, read ῑν̄ for αυτον, an otherwise unattested reading
	18.25	adds μετ αυτ[ου] after πετροc, not otherwise attested[22]
	18.33	reads εξηλθεν instead of ειcηλθεν, with no support omits και εφωνηcεν τον ιηcουν, again with no support[23]
	18.34	omits αυτω with P66 02 03 04* and others reads ο against P66 03 019 033 0109 omits cυ, with 01*
	18.36	reads οι εμοι ηγο(ω)νιζοντο αν with P90 019 032 033 044 0109
	18.37	omits ο before ιηcουc with 019 032 033 036 037 044 omits εγω with P90 01 03 019 032 044 054 0290
	18.39	reconstructed as reading [cυ]νηθια υμ[ιν απολε]cθαι το π[αcχα]; the closest reading is that of 0211, cυνιθεια υμιν απολυcω εν το παcχα
	18.40	omits παντεc with 01 03 019 032 033 045* 0109
	19.2	reads [πορφυ]ρουν ιμ[ατιον], with no support
	19.5	reads ιδου against ιδε with P90 01 019 032 033 044 054
	19.10	supports απολυcαι . . . cταυcωραι with 01 02 03 022
	19.11	reads αυτω with 01 03 019 032 044 0211 reads κατ εμου ουδεμιαν with P66 01 03 017 019 032 033 044
	19.12	omits ιουδαιοι against all other witnesses (and see above)

---

[20] This includes the minuscules according to the complete collation of John 18 made by the IGNTP.

[21] The reading is supported by two minuscules, 2291 and 2656*.

[22] Minuscule 895 reads μετ αυτου cιμων πετροc. Without this evidence, one would be tempted to reconstruct P60 as μετ αυτ[ων].

[23] Minuscule 1555 also omits the words, though it then reads λεγει not ειπεν.

19.13	reads τουτων των λογων with 07 013 028 034 ᶜ* 037 038ᶜ* 054	
19.15	adds λεγοντες with 022 030	[64]
19.16	supports the phrasing παραλαβοντες... απηγαγον, with 021 (reads παρελαβοντες) 022 032 (λαβοντες... απηγαγον 01*; παραλαβοντες... ηγαγον 01ᶜᵉᵃ)	
19.17	supports εαυτω τον σταυρον with P66 01 019 032 041 044 0290 (αυτω 03 033)	
19.20	according to the reconstruction supports the order εβραιστι ρωμαιστι ελληνιστι with 01ˢ¹ 03 019 022 033 044; only the second ιστ is visible, but the space requires that it be from ρωμαιστι, and there is scarcely room for ελληνιστι before it and in any case neither P66 (the only other papyrus for this passage, itself partly lacunose) nor any majuscule places ελληνιστι first	
19.25	according to the reconstruction omitted μαρια η του κλωπα και, with no support	

There are twelve readings here supported by no other papyrus and by no majuscule.

16.33	omits εγω
17.9	omits περι αυτων ερωτω ου
	omits η before γραφη
18.4	adds εξω after [εξηλ]θεν
18.14	omits ο before συμβουλευσας
	reads ιν̄ for αυτον
18.25	adds μετ αυτ[ου] after πετρος
18.33	reads εξηλθεν instead of εισηλθεν
	omits και εφωνησεν τον ιησουν
19.2	reads [πορφυ]ρουν ιμ[ατιον]
19.12	omits ιουδαιοι
19.25	omits μαρια η του κλωπα και

Seven are omissions. Although this is the kind of tendency one expects from most scribes, it might be arguable that this copyist shows it somewhat strongly. On the other hand, we also have two places where wording is expanded. There are two substitutions and one change of order. The three longer omissions are all understandable as the omission of a clause leaving some kind of sense (at 17.9 and 19.25 *saut du même au même* is a likely explanation). We have a couple of articles omitted, evident confusion once (εξηλθεν at 18.33), and a few minor alterations which do not affect the sense of the text. The omission of ιουδαιοι at 19.12 may or may not be associated with a new section. With regard to the quality of text, it has to be said that this manuscript

[65]

often agrees with manuscripts showing a form of text which may well be the source of the other variants.

Compared to P59 and P60, the remaining witnesses are too slight to provide much evidence. Nevertheless, P63 has some interesting readings

3.14	omits και with no support (see above)
3.15	includes μη απολαηται αλλ against P36 P66 P75 01 03 019 029 032 083 086
3.16	includes αυτου after υιου against P66 P75 01* 03 032 adds εις το[ν κοσμ]ον after εδωκεν, with 022
3.17	omits ινα κρινη τον κοσμον, with P66*
4.9	reads γυναικος σαμαριτιδος ουσης with P66 P16vid 01 019 022 032 02 03 04* 019 022 032 044 083 086
4.10	adds ο before ιησους, with 05 022 038 the scribe first wrote ζω υδωρ, and corrected it to υδωρ ζων (the reading of all other witnesses)

There are several longer readings here, as well as several omissions. The parablepsis at 3.17 is an error apparently also committed (and corrected) by the scribe of P66. It is difficult to decide on so small a sample whether its agreements with 022 indicate a noteworthy similarity or not.[24]

P76 probably shares the P63 reading γυναικος σαμαριτιδος ουσης at 4.9. At 4.12 it reads οστις instead of ος with 01 and 038, and in the same verse omitted και οι υιοι αυτου (with 0211 – probably a coincidence in parablepsis). This manuscript is too lacunose to draw any conclusions from that.

P80, although so brief, has a noteworthy reading at 3.34, where it has μερου[ς] with 030 (μερου P66*), against μετρου.

Reading from 0210 are as follows:

5.44 omits υμεις with 019
includes θεου against P66 P75 03 032

6.1 omits the article before ιησους, with no support
omits της γαλιλαιας with 022 047

6.2 probably asyndetic, with no support
reads εθεωρουν, with p66*c 03 05 019 022 044
omits επι των ασθενουντων, with no support

6.41 has the word order εκ του ουρανου καταβας, with 021 036 044 047

---

24 The only differences between them are (022 first): 3:14 και] OM; 3:17 ινα κρινη τον κοσμον] OM; 3:18 κεκριται] καικρ[ι]νεται; 4:9 πιειν] πειν; 4:10 πιειν] πειν; εδωκεν] εδωκεν αν.

Three readings with no support in this fragment, all of omission, does seem quite high.

Finally, what about 0302?

10.29   includes μου after πατρος, against P66 P75 01 03 019

If one starts with the hypothesis to be tested, that these manuscripts by their nature are unlikely to be very useful in textual study and comparison, then they come out of the test very well. They regularly show good readings and cannot often be condemned for lack of care in the reproduction of the text. Certainly they do not fare worse than continuous text manuscripts.

3. The Use of Manuscripts Containing *Hermeneiai* in Editing John

In order to keep track of the large number of witnesses to the text of the New Testament, we need to categorise, list and number them. A result of this is that we can very easily fall into the trap of treating all witnesses which we have then captured as though they were of a single kind, while totally ignoring those which fall outside our parameters. The witnesses with fortune-telling sentences demand that we think differently. In their nature and in how they have been used, they link two areas of research.

[67]

What we have concluded with regard to their textual character suggests that, with caution in certain respects, they deserve to be used alongside continuous-text manuscripts as useful, albeit fragmentary, weapons in the study of the development of the Johannine text.

At the same time, in appearance and purpose they have less in common with the continuous-text manuscripts than they do with various texts which have long been excluded from the reckoning of witnesses to the New Testament text. These texts include amulets and other kinds of documents as they have been described by Stuart Pickering.[25] It is arguable that such materials *should* be taken into account by students of the Johannine text. Pickering argues that the likely extent of scribal interference in producing these non-continuous-text manuscripts is precisely what makes them so interesting. It is also worth wondering whether care in the wording may have been viewed

---

25   S.R. Pickering, 'The Significance of Non-Continuous New Testament Textual Materials in Papyri', *Studies in the Early Text of the Gospels and Acts*, ed. D.G.K. Taylor (Texts and Studies Third Series 1), Birmingham, 1999, 121–41.

as necessary for the magic to take effect. Certainly, if we are interested in every question we can think of regarding the use that early Christianity and its scribes made of its texts, then these scraps, catching copyists and users *not* on their best textual behaviour, are as important as any other. Here I set aside questions of category and inclusion – if we exclude 0212 because it is a harmony fragment, and P. Vindob. G 2312 because it contains excerpts (from Psalm 90, Romans 2 and John 2), then why should we include excerpts with *hermeneiai* in an edition? Should we distinguish between the ones which seem to have contained a continuous text and those consisting of excerpts?

We return to the question behind this study: Can we treat these copies as serious and reliable witnesses to the text of the Gospel of John? The answer lies in the fact that with regard to book production – script, presentation and orthography – we find the group not distinguishable from other copies of John, showing a similar range of abilities. With regard to the text, we find evidence that the wording of the text was relevant to the scribe, who produced a good copy. Comparison with other papyrus and majuscule witnesses shows a high degree of agreement and an unremarkable number of singular readings. It must therefore be concluded that these are documents which are of use to the editor of John.

12 Greek Gospel Manuscripts in Bucharest and Sofia

I had the opportunity to visit both Bucharest and Sofia in September 2001, and examined many of the New Testament Greek manuscripts in the two cities.[1] My researches were directed specifically towards the study of continuous-text manuscripts of the Gospel of John, as part of the Principio Project. The character of this report will be more understandable if a brief explanation of this project is provided.

The International Greek New Testament Project (IGNTP), having published an *apparatus criticus* of the Gospel of Luke, decided to break the formidable task of producing a critical edition of the Gospel of John into smaller stages of production. The first stage was the publication of transcriptions, an *apparatus criticus* and plates of the papyri in 1995.[2] The second stage, given the title of the Principio Project, was funded by the Arts and Humanities Research Board, the UK Higher Education Funding Council for research in the humanities. With funding for the years 2000–03, it had as its remit the completion of two further tasks facing IGNTP. The first is an edition of the majuscule manuscripts, of which there are approximately forty-one fragmentary and twenty-nine more or less complete. This edition, to appear in 2007, will be comparable to that of the papyri, but with the major difference that it is being published both on a website and in book form.[3] The second is an

---

1 I am greatly indebted to the many people who made my work possible: Dr Simon Crisp and Mrs Clare O'Driscoll of the United Bible Society for setting up contacts in Romania and arranging the travel; Caroline Blaj of the Romanian Bible Society for making arrangements with the libraries there and for guiding me around Bucharest; Dr Gabriela Dumitrescu, Librarian of the Romanian Academy and her staff; Carmen Tănăsoiu of the National Art Museum; Professor Ivan Dmitri for the initial arrangements in Bulgaria; Desislava and Michael Pulieva for looking after me; and to the library staff of the various institutions I visited, in particular Professor Axinia Džurova of the Ivan Dujček Centre for Slavo-Byzantine Studies.
2 W.J. Elliott and D.C. Parker (eds.), *The New Testament in Greek IV. The Gospel According to St. John Edited by the American and British Committees of the International Greek New Testament Project. Volume One The Papyri* (NTTS 20), Leiden 1995.
3 U.B. Schmid, with W.J. Elliott and D.C. Parker, *The New Testament in Greek IV. The Gospel According To St. John Edited by The American And British Committees Of The International Greek New Testament Project*, Volume Two, *The Majuscules* (New

analysis and grouping of all Greek manuscripts, in order to select those which will appear in the final apparatus. According to our database, there are 1,934 Greek manuscripts which contain the Gospel of John, in whole or in part. Apart from the formidable logistics of accessing and recording the data which will form the basis of the analysis, there are significant decisions to be made with regard to the method of grouping to be used. There are a number of methods currently in use. The IGNTP developed and continues to use the Claremont Profile Method.[4] This in its conception consisted of taking three sample chapters, collating a sample of manuscripts in order to determine the significant group readings, drawing up a profile of readings for each group, and then noting the readings of each manuscript in the selected readings. Although individual manuscripts of course have more or less distinctive texts, it is possible to observe the distinctive set of readings of particular groups. Even if an individual witness does not contain all the group readings, it may be shown to match the profile of a particular group more closely than that of any other. The Principio Project used this method, with two modifications. The first is that, instead of profiling three chapters, it took only one, Chapter 18. We profile the earlier part of the Gospel by using the database of variants in 152 Teststellen in John 1–10 created by researchers of the Institut für Neutestamentliche Textforschung (INTF) in Münster.[5] Besides providing sufficient material for the job without duplicating each other's work, we are able to compare the results of the two methods. In a recent study, I have demonstrated that the IGNTP and INTF methods are closer than has sometimes been assumed, and may complement each other very satisfactorily.[6] The second is that we are able to make a complete transcription of all witnesses in the test passages, and to determine the group readings from all the witnesses rather than from a sample.[7]

Testament Tools, Studies and Documents 37), Leiden, 2007, and published also in an electronic edition (see www.iohannes.com).

4 F. Wisse, *The Profile Method for Classifying and Evaluating Manuscript Evidence*, SD 44, Grand Rapids, 1982.

5 K. Aland, B. Aland, K. Wachtel, K. Witte, *Text und Textwert der griechischen Handschriften des Neuen Testaments*, V. *Das Johannesevangelium, I. Teststellenkollation der Kapitel 1-10*. (ANTT 35-36), Berlin and New York, 2005.

6 'A Comparison Between the *Text und Textwert* and the Claremont Profile Method Analyses of Manuscripts in the Gospel of Luke', *NTS* 49 (2003), 108–38.

7 M.B. Morrill and D.C. Parker, *Text und Textwert der griechischen Handschriften des Neuen Testaments*, V. *Das Johannesevangelium, 2. The Full Collation of Chapter 18* (ANTT 37-38), Berlin and New York, forthcoming.

The reason for this second modification is that instead of using the traditional method of making paper and pencil collations, the project has used the Collate program, developed by Dr Peter Robinson of the Centre for Technology and the Arts, De Montfort University, for the Canterbury Tales Project. Collate will automatically compare transcriptions and produce a list of differences, which can then be manipulated in various ways to achieve the editors' aims. I should here describe the level of detail in our transcriptions. Those of the majuscule manuscripts are more detailed, even though it is not our goal to add all possible information in our transcriptions at this stage. Our current standard is that each will include page, column and line breaks, punctuation (including initial letters, hanging lines and spaces in some transcriptions), of course all corrections, all words spelled as in the manuscript, and reconstructed text tagged so that it can be marked separately and if required excluded from collation. Anybody who wants to can later add Eusebian Canon numbers, lectionary equipment, marginalia, and provide more tagging. In the John 18 transcriptions of minuscules we do not record page or column or line breaks. We do record all variations, corrections, *nomina sacra* and spelling variations, including movable-nu but excluding iota adscript. Not all of this will be of value in grouping manuscripts, but the data will be of interest to other groups. A collection of such variants in a thousand manuscripts, with every orthographical aberration and every error that a scribe managed to make will be a resource which – we hope – will be put to uses that have not yet been devised.

[5]

Out of these transcriptions will come a merged database of variant readings in John 18. The passage contains 800 words of the 16,000 of the Fourth Gospel, and thus represents 5 per cent of the total text. As well as profiling according to the Claremont Method, we should be able to perform other tests such as, for example, finding manuscripts with identical texts and the manuscript closest to each witness. The database will also be made available to the Stemma Project, a group which is applying mathematical models developed in the study of genetics to the analysis of manuscript textual traditions, for whom such a large population of manuscripts will be a valuable specimen.[8]

If a manuscript was not available in the IGNTP or the INTF microfilm holdings, we have tried to examine the original. However, the restraints of time and money have not always permitted this. Even

---

8 See e.g. Christopher Howe, Adrian C. Barbrook, Matthew Spencer, Peter Robinson, Barbara Bordalejo and Linne R. Mooney, 'Manuscript Evolution', *Trends in Genetics* 17 (2001), 147–52.

so, in pursuit of either difficult majuscule or unfilmed minuscules members of the team have paid visits to libraries in Wolfenbüttel, St Petersburg, Thessaloniki, Tirana, Durham (N.C.), Paris, Moscow, Dublin, all libraries in the UK holding relevant material, Rome and the Vatican, and Chicago. So it was that, having occasion to visit Bucharest in September 2001, I decided to add a visit to Sofia into my journey, and to examine the Greek New Testament manuscripts in both places. In time, with the publication of the results of the project, it will be possible to augment the rather bald statements offered below with regard to the textual character of manuscripts.[9]

The manuscripts are to be found in five libraries, two in Bucharest and three in Sofia. As well as finding one or two manuscripts not previously known, I was able to gather additional information on others. All the manuscripts are either continuous-text minuscules or lectionaries. The full textual data will become available at a later date. While some of the information below reflects my purpose and what I was able to do in the time available, I hope that even the most desultory of these annotations may prove of use to someone.

Bucharest, National Art Museum

The national art collection, housed in the former royal palace, contains five manuscripts:[10]

1	(Gregory-Aland 2472)
3	(Gregory-Aland 2554)
14	(Gregory-Aland 2555)
25	(Gregory-Aland *l*2146)
32	(Gregory-Aland 2767)

I examined the four continuous-text manuscripts, and am able to add some additional information about them. They spent a part of the twentieth century in Russia (1916–56).[11] For a thorough analysis of the

---

9   For a more detailed version of what is outlined here, see D.C. Parker, 'The Principio Project: a Reconstruction of the Johannine Tradition', *Filología Neotestamentaria* 13 (2000), 111-18, also published in C.-B. Amphoux and J.K. Elliott (eds.), *The New Testament in Early Christianity* (Histoire du Texte Biblique 6), Lausanne, 2003, 21-29.

10 Two (3 and 14) are placed in the Romanian Academy in the *Liste*. It is with deep gratitude to those responsible for the *Liste*'s creation and revision, which makes the planning of such trips as mine a much simpler activity, that I offer corrections in the notes below. In each case, I place the *Liste* entry in brackets.

11 As a consequence, MS 14 has acquired the confusing additional class mark 3 in the front, which is to be ignored.

illuminated manuscripts (1, 3, 14, 32) we are deeply indebted to the excellent recent study by a team of Romanian scholars.[12] They help us to refine the dating and extend considerably our knowledge of the history of these witnesses.

MS 1 is a twelfth-century copy of the Gospels.[13] It was produced in a Byzantine scriptorium. The miniatures and canon tables are fourteenth-century. The text is Byzantine.

MS 3 is of particular interest as one of a very small number of manuscripts to contain all of the New Testament.[14] It has 382 folios.[15] The numeration is by stamped page numbers, in which numbers are sometimes missed out. The date has a *terminus ante quem*, a note written in 1434. The script supports the early fourteenth-century date to which the decoration points. Unlike some other 'complete' manuscripts, which appear to be composites made from several originally independent manuscripts, this one is the work of a single scribe. The order of books is Gospels – Acts – Catholic Epistles – Pauline Epistles – Revelation.[16] There is no further material. The presentation of Revelation is somewhat different from that of the rest of the books in that there is a series of brief marginal notes. Some of the illumination was added in the sixteenth century.

MS 14 is a tetraevangelion of the thirteenth to fourteenth centuries,[17] produced in a Byzantine scriptorium. Portraits of the evangelists were added in the sixteenth century.

MS 32, another manuscript of the Gospels, was produced between the end of the thirteenth century and the first decade of the fourteenth.[18]

Bucharest, Romanian Academy

There are twelve manuscripts here:
    94   (Gregory-Aland 2314)
    234   (Gregory-Aland 2318)

---

12 Liana Tugearu with Mihail Carataşu, Pavel Mircea Florea and Carmen Tănăsoiu, *Miniatura şi Ornamentul Manuscriselor din Colecţia de Artă Medievală Românească. Vol. 1 Manuscrise bizantine şi greceşti medievale tîrzii*, Bucharest, 1996. The foreword by Virgil Cândea is also given in English, as is the general introduction.
13 Correction to the *Liste* (XIV). Tugearu, 45–64 and colour plates I-V.
14 Tugearu, 95–113 and colour plates XIII-XV.
15 Correction to the *Liste* (397).
16 It does have 2 Cor, *contra* the list of contents in Tugearu, 96.
17 Correction to the *Liste* (XVI). Tugearu, 79–94 and colour plates XI-XII.
18 Correction to the *Liste* (XIV). Tugearu, 65–78 and colour plates VI-X.

360	(Gregory-Aland 2316)
665	(Gregory-Aland 2315)
695	(Gregory-Aland 2317)
932	(Gregory-Aland 2476)
933	(Gregory-Aland 2477)
934	(Gregory-Aland 2761)
935	(Gregory-Aland *l*1737)
936	(Gregory-Aland *l*1738)
1175	(Gregory-Aland 2760)
1543	(Gregory-Aland 2868)

[8] Of these I did not look at 234, 935 or 936, the former because it does not contain the Gospels, the latter two because they are lectionaries. There are also a few manuscripts of the eighteenth and nineteenth centuries containing New Testament abstracts. These are written in modern Greek.[19] For example, MS 353, a paper manuscript of the eighteenth century with 81 leaves, contains excerpts from the four Gospels. A typical example is:

1,46 Εκ Ναζαρεθ δυναται τι αγαθον ειναι;
Ερχου και ιδε
47 Ιδε αληθωσ ισραηλιτησ εν ω δολοσ ουκ εστι
48 Ποθεν με γινωσκεισ;

MS 1543 is worth a fuller description, since it is not known to New Testament scholars. I was kindly given access to the unpublished part of the catalogue of Greek manuscripts, and found the entry for this further addition to the *Liste*.[20] It contains the four Gospels, written on 276 parchment folios. The dimensions are 16.5 x 11 cm after trimming. I suggest a thirteenth-century date. It contains no canon tables, but does contain chapter lists. There are illuminated headbands to the Gospels. The binding is incorrect: for example, F226 (which is within the text of John) contains Mk 11.2 – γετε – 17 γέγραπται, while the leaf that contains Jn 4.53–5.7 was not in or near the right place. Unfortunately, I did not have time to undertake a full collation of the leaves. There are two colophons, on folios 220v and 273v, both naming the scribe as one Mark. The text of John represents that of one of the Byzantine sub-group (it is not yet possible to be more precise). It contains Jn 7.53–8.11 without comment.

MS 94 is well written, a twelfth-century manuscript, and not late.

MS 933 breaks off at Jn 11.33 και εταρα.

---

19 See also the *Liste*, 195, n. 6.
20 The published catalogue volumes extend as far as cod. Gr. 1066.

Sofia, National Library Cyril and Methodius

There are twelve manuscripts given under this location in the *Liste*, consisting of the two continuous-text Gospel manuscripts Gr. 7 and Gr. 14, and ten lectionaries. But the full number is 13, since there is an additional lectionary to be listed.

I was shown two new lectionary fragments. The first comprises another two leaves of MS Gr. 6 (Gregory-Aland *l*1883). The number of leaves under its entry should therefore be increased from two to four. The second is most of one parchment leaf that had been used in binding. It may be thirteenth century, and contains two columns of 26 lines (23 survive). The original size cannot be reconstructed. The recto contains Jn 19.38–42, followed by the reading IB, Mt 28.62ff, continued on the verso. The verso is difficult to read, having been darkened by exposure and used as a writing surface for one or two scribbles and comments, and time was too limited to recognise any further passages. So far as I am aware, no catalogue number has yet been assigned to this item.

Gr. 15 is a lectionary with the Gregory-Aland number *l*2403. It has 296 folios (the printed catalogue of Stojanov is wrong in this respect).[21] It is datable to the sixteenth century. I did not undertake any textual analysis.

More extended comment on MS Gr. 7 (Gregory-Aland 2748) is necessary, since this should probably be treated as two manuscripts rather than one. The *termini inter quos* of the book are Mt 12.44 λεγει επιστρεψω and Lk 7.32 λεγουσιν ηυλησα, but what comes between contains several hiatuses.

The first manuscript consists of Ff 1–91, and contains Mt 12.44 to the end (which is on F67v) and Mk 1.1–8.10 ηλθε. Leaves 49–52 – Gathering 7 (a later hand has numbered the gatherings in arabic numerals) – are replacement leaves, and I suggest were copied in the sixteenth century. They contain Mt 24.50 η ου προσδοκα – 26.38 μεινατε ωδε και γρε.

The second manuscript consists of F92 (beginning at Mk 8.24 βλεπω τους) to the end of the manuscript (Lk 7.32, F127). The first manuscript could be older. I suggest a twelfth-century date for it, and one of the twelfth/thirteenth century for the second. While I suppose that it is conceivable that we have here one manuscript and two hands, the gap between the two blocks (Mk 8.10–24) makes my suggestion more likely. Nor do we have marked similarity in layout between the

---

21 (Latin title) *Codices Graeci Manuscripti Bibliothecae 'Cyrilli et Methodii'*, Sofia, 1973.

two parts. Admittedly, there is some inconsistency in the first manuscript, which initially writes the Eusebian numbers in black, then changes to red.

The whole ensemble has evidently had a chequered and interesting history. There is a sequence of folio numbers and chapter indications written in a western style of hand in the later sixteenth or seventeenth century which runs down to around F100 (subsequent cropping of the leaves makes certainty rather difficult). What is essential is that analysis of the text of the constituent parts of this manuscript must not treat it as a single entity.

MS Gr. 14 requires no addition to what is already known, except to point out that it contains 238 folios.[22]

Institute for Church History and Archive of the Bulgarian Patriarchate

The Institute is in the same building as the University's Theology Faculty, on Sofia's main square, the Ploshtad Sveta Nedelya. Of the twenty-two manuscripts of the New Testament, six contain the Gospel of John. The manuscripts all have two numbers: one (the first given in the *Liste*) contains the Greek manuscripts; the second (the one in brackets in the *Liste*), which will be used here, is of all manuscripts in the collection.[23]

MS 475 (Gregory-Aland 2462) is lost after Jn 21.23 εξηλθεν ουν.

MS 342 (Gregory-Aland 2773) is a fifteenth-century paper copy with some lacunae.

MS 421 (Gregory-Aland 2463) is dated 1354/55.

MS 852 (Gregory-Aland 2774) is of the fourteenth century (I follow Getov, against the *Liste*, which has XIII/XIV).

MS 905 (Gregory-Aland 2775) is a fourteenth-century parchment manuscript, with some fifteenth-century replacement leaves. These are:

      Ff 1–9   Preliminary material for Matthew and Mt 1.1–4.23 νοσον και πασαν

      F 122   Mk 15.17 τιθεασιν αυτω – 32 οι συνεσταυ

      F 129   Lk 1.17 ετοιμασαι – 30 ο αγγε

      F 138ff   Lk 3.17 καυσει πυρι – Jn 21.25

---

22 Correction to the *Liste* and the catalogue (233). A revised catalogue is planned.

23 There is a valuable checklist: Dorotei Getov, *A Checklist of the Greek Manuscript Collection at the Ecclesistical Historical and Patriarchal Institute of the Patriarchate of Bulgaria*, Sofia, 1997.

MS 949 (Gregory-Aland 2856), of the twelfth century, has one replacement gathering on paper, I suggest of the fourteenth century, containing Jn 11.54 διεριβεν to 15.18 μισει γινωσ.

Of these manuscripts, the more interesting textually are 421 (Gregory-Aland 2463) and 905 (Gregory-Aland 2775). Both may turn out to be members of a smaller and more distinctive Byzantine sub-group.

Ivan Dujčev Research Centre

These holdings comprise the largest collection of Greek New Testament manuscripts in Bulgaria. Of the twenty-eight lectionaries and twenty-five continuous-text manuscripts, there are twenty-one containing the Gospels. I was able to examine all, with the exception of MS 351 (Gregory-Aland 1794), which was undergoing conservation. Many of these manuscripts came from Kosinitza during the First World War, and their whereabouts were a mystery until recently (they are reported as of unknown location in the first edition of the *Liste* (1963).[24]

MS 328 (Gregory-Aland 1784) is particularly intriguing. The first hand is lost from F211v, Jn 11.20 υπηντησαν. This hand, of the thirteenth/fourteenth century on parchment, is of a southern Italian type. The lacuna is replaced by paper leaves. Ff234–5 also belong with the supplementary leaves. Containing Jn 8.26 καγω – 44 εκεινοσ αν, and filling only three and a half pages (the rest of F235v is blank), they properly belong between Ff211 and 212. But they only partially fill the lacuna – F211 breaks off at 8.26 αληθησ εστιν. The watermark is a scissors device. This symbol, unique to Italian manufacture, dates the paper to the last third of the fourteenth century.[25] The similarity of origin of the two hands is all the more significant when an initial textual analysis suggests that *both* parts of the manuscript may belong to Family 13. This seemed fairly likely from transcribing John 18. It also emerged from an examination of the Teststellen in Chapters 1–10. Looking briefly at a few well-known family readings, the manuscript lacks the insertion of Jn 19.24 at Mt 27.35. Unfortunately, I did not check the position in the manuscript of Jn 7.53–8.11. An initial

---

24 See also M. Richard, 'La recherche des textes hier et demain', D. Harlfinger (ed.), *Griechischer Kodikologie und Textüberlieferung*, Darmstadt, 1980, 3–13, 4.
25 V.A. Mosin and S.M. Traljic, *Filigranes des XIIIe et XIVe siècles*, Zagreb, 1957, e.g. samples 2620, 2626.

impression is that the supplement may be a stronger family member than the older leaves.[26]

MS 177 (Gregory-Aland 1684), formerly in Serres, is a large commentary manuscript, measuring 32 x 24 cm.[27] It has fourteen different hands. This variety seems to be the result of slow growth and not of repeated damage. The oldest is early eleventh century, though my first thought was that it might be late tenth century. The last hand is of the thirteenth century.[28] Ch. 18 is by two hands, both of the thirteenth century.

MS 274 (Gregory-Aland 1783) is copied by two hands. The change seems to be at about F100 (out of 227), in Matthew 27.

MS 233 (Gregory-Aland 2214), dated 1371, is another commentary manuscript (the commentator is Theophylact of Achrida). The colophon is on Fol 410v. The biblical text is in blocks within the main text – i.e. the *mise en page* consists of one block of text and commentary.

MS 193 (Gregory-Aland 2249) is dated 1330 in the colophon (fol. 334v). Folios 1–39 are of the sixteenth century. The final folios, 335–72, are a lectionary (Gregory-Aland *l*2418).

MS 56 (Gregory-Aland 2250) is one of those manuscripts that has the outer sheet of each gathering parchment, the inner ones paper. It contains portions of Matthew, Mark and Luke. The final gathering in the present folio numeration (95–102) is in fact the second extant gathering, containing part of Matthew.

---

26 The evidence from *Text und Textwert* V.1-2 does not seem to support this conclusion.
27 For information on all these manuscripts see A. Dzurova *et al.*, 'Checklist' de la Collection de manuscrits grecs conservés au Centre de recherches slavo-byzantines «Ivan Dujčev» auprès de l'Université «Clément d'Ohrid», Thessaloniki, 1994.
28 Correction to the *Liste* (X-XIII).

II. TEXTUAL CRITICISM

13 The Development of Textual Criticism Since B.H. Streeter[1]

When in *The Expository Times* for November 1938 Sir Frederick Kenyon reviewed the fifty years since Westcott and Hort's edition of 1881, his main point was that there had been an amazing increase of material – papyri, Bell and Skeat's *Fragments of an Unknown Gospel*,[2] the Washington Codex, the Sinaitic palimpsest, and the unearthing of Family Θ and the Caesarean group. In the thirty-six years that have elapsed since then, this increase has continued, with the discovery of 1,020 manuscripts between 1933 and 1969.[3] Apart from the many new variant readings that have been recorded, this growth of the material has led to much discussion of methodology. Reaction to the old criticism represented by Westcott and Hort has been concentrated on two aspects: first, on the genealogical method, the basis of their theories; and second, on the collation of the texts and the practical problems of preparing a critical edition and an *apparatus criticus*.

The genealogical relation of manuscripts was developed as the basis of preparing a text in the editing of classical works, mainly by the three German scholars Wolf, Bekker and – especially – Lachmann. By the genealogical method it should be possible to determine the history of the text, and the claims of every manuscript to authenticity in its variant readings. An example of a stemma incorporating all the extant manuscripts of a document is provided in the preface to A. E. Housman's *editio minor* of Manilius.[4] The critic is not always, however,

---

1 This article is an abridgement of an essay that was awarded the St Andrews University Gray Essay Prize in 1974.
2 H.I. Bell and T.C. Skeat (ed.), *Fragments of an Unknown Gospel and other Early Christian Papyri*, London, 1935.
3

	v. Dobschütz IV (1933)	Aland VII (1969)	
pap.	48	81	+33
majusc.	208	267	+59
minusc.	2370	2764	+394
lect.	1609	2143	+534
Total	4235	5255	+1020

4 M. Manilii *Astronomica*, recensuit A.E. Housman. Editio minor, Cambridge, 1932, ix.

[150] so fortunate as to be able to draw up an exact plan of the manuscripts at his disposal. So it is, for example, with Lucan: 'The five manuscripts on which we chiefly depend ... cannot be divided and united into families or even classes ... The true line of division is between the variants themselves, not between the manuscripts which offer them. The manuscripts group themselves not in families but in factions.'[5] Such is to some extent the case with the New Testament, where a stemma can be composed only in the most general way. This is evident from a glance at the diagram of Westcott and Hort's textual theory in Streeter's *The Four Gospels* (26). The problem really arises when there is a mixture of texts in a given manuscript. But if sufficient manuscripts exist for the whole history of the text to be recovered, even this ceases to be a source of confusion. It is easily forgotten that Hort was himself aware of the limitations inherent in the genealogical method when he first applied it to the New Testament.[6] Too often criticisms are confined to the section where he deals with the theory of the method; more may be learnt from his application of it to several selected passages.[7] Two illustrations are noteworthy – Acts 6.8 and Mark 6.33. The history of the readings in the passage from Acts is clear;[8] from the second example the conclusion is drawn that 'the common original of the documents attesting β must have been older than the common original of the documents attesting δ'.[9] By analysing a further group of readings (Mark 8.26, 9.38, 49; Luke 9.10, 11.54, 12.18, 24.53) Hort is able to come to more detailed conclusions with regard to the grouping of manuscripts; the picture thus sketched is filled in by a discussion of the patristic and versional evidence.

The interpretation of the evidence arrived at by Westcott and Hort continues to be widely accepted. Thus a study with its subject the development of criticism since Streeter can only interpret and explain that subject if its chief inspiration is understood.

The ink of *The New Testament in the Original Greek* was scarcely dry before the work was under attack. The first criticisms in our period are those of Joseph Bédier, whose objections to the genealogical method were the result of his editing several medieval French documents. In an

---

5   M. Annaei Lucani *Belli Civilis*, Libri Decem, ed. A.E. Housman, Oxford, 1926, vif.
6   Westcott and Hort, Vol. 2, 39–59, especially 53–7.
7   *Ibid.*, 90–107.
8   Cf. also Metzger, *Text of the New Testament*[2], 221–3.
9   Westcott and Hort, Vol. 2, 99.

article published in 1928[10] he discussed the application of the developing methods of textual criticism to *Le Lai de l'ombre*. He is able to produce a number of possible relationships, and so concludes that 'le schéma reste malléable comme le plomb'.[11] 'La base de la construction, le rez-de-chaussée, est solide. Mais il en va autrement des parties hautes ... on peut, presque toujours, en modifier la disposition'.[12] Bédier's method was to choose, purely on internal grounds, the manuscript to be regarded as preserving the best text, and to make it the basis of his edition, using the other manuscripts to correct it. The method of Westcott and Hort themselves might be parodied as being just this, since they followed the Vatican Codex as much as they could, turning elsewhere when that failed them. And the choice of the best manuscript on internal grounds is as much a part of the genealogical as it is of Bédier's method.

[151]

His views were largely followed by Léon Vaganay: 'De surcroît elle [cette methode] est incomplète: elle peut établir la parenté, mais non l'absence de parenté. Enfin, et surtout, son application devient impossible dans le cas fréquent des textes contaminés ... En somme, poussé à fond, le systeme de Lachmann aboutit trop souvent à des constructions de fantaisie, hypothèses plausibles sans doute, mais pas plus que d'autres...'[13] These are the arguments also of E.C. Colwell,[14] whose chief complaint appears to be that the genealogical method is not a panacea for every ill. Because it will not solve every problem for him, he will not admit it to be able to solve any. 'Genealogical method can trace the tree down to the last two branches, but it can never unite these last two in the main trunk – it can never take the last step'.[15] 'If genealogical method takes the investigator only as far as the penultimate station, his reconstruction cannot justifiably be described as achieved by the genealogical method'.[16] Our attention might well be drawn at this stage to Lachmann, who in his edition of Lucretius was able not only to reconstruct the archetype of all the existing manuscripts, even though the two oldest manuscripts were probably not copied directly from it, but to advance beyond that archetype to the

---

10   'La tradition manuscrite du Lai de l'ombre, réflexions sur l'art d'éditer les anciens textes', *Romania* 54 (1928), 161–96, 321–56. Separately published under the same title, Paris 1970.
11   *Ibid.*, 338.
12   *Ibid.*, 356.
13   *Initiation à la critique textuelle néotestamentaire*, Paris, 1934, 60.
14   'Genealogical Method: its Achievements and Limitations', *JBL* 66 (1947), 109–33.
15   *Ibid.*, 113.
16   *Ibid.*, 114.

very times of the poet, demonstrating some passages to be interpolations by Lucretius himself – an example of what Colwell deems impossible. But he has another line of attack – the claim that Westcott and Hort did not, after all, use the genealogical method. There are two branches to the method – 'genealogical study of manuscripts and genealogical study of groups of manuscripts'.[17] It is plainly the latter with which Westcott and Hort approached the New Testament, and with this weapon that they demolished arguments in support of the Textus Receptus. Having gone thus far, Westcott and Hort were forced, in the face of the problem of mixture of manuscripts, to that counsel of desperation, the conflate reading. This Colwell regards as an illogical bulwark of an indefensible position. The rejection of the theory of conflate readings leads, of course, to the rejection of the whole genealogical method. Like Vaganay, Colwell finds the consequences of the mixing of manuscripts to be the chief problem. Thus he rejects the reading χάριτος at Acts 6.8. Logically, the critic finds no guide to the correct reading in the history of the text. But Colwell does not want to say this. In this article, written in 1947, he had no alternative to offer, and thus could provide no firm conclusion.

Later, in partnership with M.M. Parvis, while working on the International Greek New Testament Project, Colwell produced an alternative method, that of 'Multiple Readings'.[18] They define a Multiple Reading as 'one in which the minimum support for each of at least three variant forms of the text is either one of the major strands of the tradition, or the support of a previously established group (such as Family I, Family Π, the Ferrar Group, K¹, Kⁱ, Kʳ), or the support of some one of the ancient versions (such as af, it, sy^s, sy^c, bo or sa), or the support of some single manuscript of an admittedly distinctive character (such as D)'.[19] Since only Jn. 1.1-4.40 is used as the test passage to show this method at work, it is possible that the true nature of a manuscript could be quite different. This is clearly a serious problem. In a later article[20] Colwell and Parvis developed the Multiple Readings further as the 'Claremont Profile Method', to deal with the greater number of medieval minuscules. A manuscript is checked against the Textus Receptus at chapters 1, 10 and 20 of Luke, and

---

17 Ibid., 109.
18 E.C. Colwell, 'Method in Locating a Newly-discovered Manuscript within the Manuscript Tradition of the Greek New Testament', TU 73 (1959), 757–77.
19 Ibid., 759.
20 E.C. Colwell with I.A. Sparks, F. Wisse, P.R. McReynolds, 'The International Greek New Testament Project: a Status Report', JBL 87 (1968), 187–97.

compared in its results with known groups and families. Out of this emerges the 'profile' of the manuscript.

It may appear from this that Colwell's dislike of the genealogical method of Westcott and Hort is paralleled by his use of Multiple Readings. A method has to be used indifferently, whatever the circumstances. If it fails under these conditions, it must be rejected. We are undoubtedly reminded of the work of Dom Henri Quentin. In editing the Vulgate Old Testament, he worked out his *règle de fer*, a method in which the relation of the manuscripts is determined by examining them in groups of three. He reduced the main manuscripts of the Vulgate, those nearest the archetype, to three. Although E.K. Rand, in reviewing Quentin's work,[21] criticised, he also praised it, concluding that the results are to be admired, but the method by which they were reached is to be rejected.[22]

With the illumination of Quentin's example, the fault in Colwell's own method, and in his rejection of Westcott and Hort's procedure, is more easily discernible. The errors of scribes and characteristics of manuscripts obey no laws; they only contain phenomena which may be observed. But their vagaries cannot be reduced to a mathematical formula whereby every reading can be categorised. The methods of both Colwell and Dom Quentin fail to recognise a factor of variation in the texts with which they are intended to deal. No method is to be followed blindly through thick and through thin, the genealogical no more than any other. Textual criticism becomes an art at the stage at which the rules become flexible. The critics of the genealogical method have sought to judge it by an inapplicable standard, and to replace it by a rule of thumb which will save them from thinking. It must be seen whether those who have followed in the line of Westcott and Hort have committed this error, or whether they have criticised and developed their method.

Development of the genealogical method was distinctive of Streeter's generation, in the isolation of smaller groups of manuscripts, and in Streeter's theory of local texts. In the former task Kirsopp Lake was a leading figure. In 1902 he had published *Codex 1 of the Gospels and its Allies*.[23] He later wrote, with Dr R.P. Blake, 'The Text of the Gospels and the Koridethi Codex',[24] in which the relation was established between Θ, Family 1, Family 13, 28, 565 and 700. The conclusion was

---

21 E.K. Rand, 'Text of the Vulgate', *HTR* 17 (1924), 197–264.
22 *Ibid.*, 262f.
23 *Texts and Studies* 7, 3, Cambridge, 1902.
24 *HTR* 16 (1923), 267–86.

reached that all these manuscripts represent mixtures of the 'family-text', a combination of Western and Neutral readings with the Antiochian text.[25] Streeter then named the whole group 'Family Θ', and argued that it represents the old text of Caesarea, identifying it as that used by Origen after his arrival there.[26] Lake and Blake, assisted by S. New, amplified this suggestion,[27] but it did not go uncriticised. F.C. Burkitt, reviewing The *Four Gospels* in the *Journal of Theological Studies*, considered the unity of Family Θ to be 'the unity of Undenominationalism, the unity of Baptists, Congregationalists, &c, united in opposition to Catholicism'.[28] In a later number of the same periodical Streeter defended his views, and in an appended note to this, Burkitt modified his criticisms so far as to write that he considered Fam. Θ to be in fact 'only one group with syr. S'.[29]

The Lakes carried on the task with studies of Family Π,[30] and the Ferrar group.[31] Apart from its useful elimination of material, the use of the genealogical method on these families has plainly assisted in the development of methods for grouping manuscripts, even if the Lakes were some times over fussy in their treatment, following too slavishly the methods they had developed.

Turning from the genealogical method of Westcott and Hort, we must now look at the chief problem in their legacy. If the nineteenth century saw the triumph of the great uncials over the ecclesiastical text, the twentieth has seen a certain amount of warring on Olympus between the uncials themselves. The problem of the 'Western' text must here be raised. The problem is that, particularly in Acts, but also to some extent in the Gospels, the Codex Bezae (D) contains additions not found elsewhere or, alternatively, that the codices ℵ, B, etc., lack portions of the original text retained by D. According to Griesbach the canon is *brevior lectio potior:* but this maxim was criticized by Professor A.C. Clark, in his book *The Primitive Text of the Gospels and Acts.*[32] He showed, conclusively for classical authors, that 'a text is like a traveller who loses a piece of luggage every time he changes trains'. There are

---

25 Ibid., 285f.
26 B.H. Streeter, *The Four Gospels, a Study of Origins*, fourth impression, revised, London, 1930, 91–100.
27 'The Caesarean Text of the Gospel of Mark', *HTR* 21 (1928), 207–404.
28 *JTS* 26 (1925), 278–94; 285.
29 Ibid., 378–80.
30 S. Lake, *Family Π and the Codex Alexandrinus*, SD 5 (1937).
31 K. and S. Lake, *Family 13 (the Ferrar Group)*, SD 11 (1941).
32 Oxford, 1914.

many omissions in the text of Cicero, and also of the New Testament, which Clark considered to be due to homoioteleuton. This theory of wholesale accidental omission was taken up by Streeter with some enthusiasm,[33] but Kenyon in reviewing Clark's work had no praise for it.[34] Kenyon's criticisms, however, do not come to grips with the salient points of Clark's argument, and his paper is finally a prejudged reaffirmation of the priority of the Neutral text, phrased as if nothing had happened since 1881. In his later book *The Acts of the Apostles*[35] Clark placed much less weight on this theory, and argued instead for an intentional alteration of the original form of the text – that of D. This was carried out by an abbreviator who 'having before him a manuscript written in στίχοι similar to those found in D, frequently (not, of course, always) adopted the rough and ready method of striking out lines in his model, botching from time to time to produce a construction'.[36]

If the abbreviator intentionally excised passages, then he must have had good reason to do so. It is by the actual variants that Clark's theory stands or falls. He finds six kinds of excision.[37] 'The first thing which an abbreviator would do would be to excise passages which he considered otiose'. Such are the readings of Z (Clark's Western text) at Acts 6.8, 9.17, 40; 14.10; 16.4; 18.4, 8. But such phrases tend elsewhere in the tradition to be additions rather than to have any great claim to originality (6.8 has been referred to already as an example of a growing text). There is a comparable example at 4.33, where the reading of P8 etc. accounts for the others; B is a variation of the same one, 808 etc. alter κυρίου to χριστοῦ, D E and ℵ B both conflate the two, and 629 etc. and it^ph etc. add ἡμῶν. There is a similar example at Rom. 3.26.

The problem of the passages in D showing close local knowledge not to be found in the B ℵ text is a harder one. Are they the observations of an eye witness, later omitted through lack of interest in all areas except where the events occurred, or the additions of those possessing local knowledge who wished to preserve local traditions and to make the story more precise? Clark's suggestion that they are original is simpler, and more probable. The additions have every claim to originality (cf. Acts 12.10; 19.9; 20.15; 21.16; 28.16).

[155]

---

33 Streeter, *op. cit.*, 129–48.
34 'The Western Text in the Gospels and Acts', *PBA* 24 (1938), 287–315.
35 Oxford, 1933, reprinted 1970.
36 *Ibid.*, viii.
37 *Ibid.*, xlv-lii.

The third class of excisions Clark lists is of those 'botched texts' already mentioned. The reading which Clark considers the best champion of his cause is at 24.7. Here the longer text is surely to be preferred. The B ℵ text should not be allowed to get away with such readings.

Of further geographical variants discussed by Clark, one, at 20.4, has a very strong claim to originality. At 12.25 too the reading of D seems to be the only sensible one – ἀπὸ Ἱερουσαλήμ for εἰς Ἱερουσαλήμ. 13.1–3 requires that Saul and Barnabas be in Antioch. It is consistent that they should leave Jerusalem (12.25), where they had been according to 11.30; this finishes the section neatly, begins the story of Paul's missionary journeys, and puts them in the right place for 13.1. The number of variants testifies to an early confusion in the text. It only needed the words Ἀντιοχείαν ἀπό to drop out for such an error as that of ℵ B etc. to arise. At these passages then – 12.10, 25; 19.9; 20.4, 15, 21.16; 28.16 – we agree with Clark that the longer reading is to be preferred.

With regard to the Gospels the situation is different. Even Westcott and Hort were willing to admit the inferiority of their favoured text in respect of the so-called 'Western non-interpolations'. Klyne Snodgrass, in a recent article,[38] considers that the term should be relegated to history, and most of the passages be given free access into the text. D, he writes, does not carry enough weight to convict the heavenly twins ℵ and B of corruption. A similar attitude, possibly wrongly, has been held concerning the *Pericope Adulterae.*

No sure conclusion is yet attainable over the relation of the two text-types. But in Acts at least the tendency of partisans of both B and D to cry 'My codex right or wrong' is to be deplored, It would be strange if D were not sometimes right against B. Both texts have their merits and their defects. It is by the critical use of both that the older text will be uncovered.

Such is the state of affairs in which the debate over the text of Acts, and partly also of the Gospels, is placed. The critic who approaches the *Corpus Paulinum* is in a happier position. There is no great diversity of text-types; he is left free to push back into the textual history of the second century. This is what Günther Zuntz sets out to do in *The Text of the Epistles.*[39] It was the great achievement of the early pioneers that they established the fourth-century text; it is the task of their successors

---

38 'Western non-interpolations', *JBL* 91 (1972), 369–79.
39 Zuntz, *The Text of the Epistles.*

to improve on this: 'modern criticism stops short before the barrier of the second century ... The ... "recensions" which were its lodestars vanish in primeval darkness. The ensuing task has been formulated by Sir Frederick Kenyon; it is "to express the later recensions in terms of this primitive stage"'.[40] Zuntz's target is the recovery of the primitive *Corpus Paulinum,* to be dated at AD ± 100. The manuscript which is the foundation stone of his structure is P46. Although it provides only an imperfect example of the second-century text, it is still a valuable criterion for assessing the quality of other manuscripts. Zuntz therefore discusses 'the main groups of the evidence in their relation to P46'.[41]

[156]

To outline his conclusions: Western readings in non-Western witnesses are, generally, ancient survivals;[42] Byzantine readings which occur in Western witnesses reach deep back into the second century; the Alexandrian group of manuscripts is better defined if P46 B 1739 sah boh Clem Orig are described as 'proto-Alexandrian'.[43] This group provides attestation for more than seventy Western readings, of which the vast majority are correct. Other variant readings in the second-century basis which reappear later in Western and late Eastern witnesses are almost all of them wrong. This allows Zuntz to make six statements.[44] First, that the evidence of late witnesses becomes important whenever they are anticipated by P46, B or some Western witness. Second, that the 'Alexandrian' family as a whole, from P46 onwards, stands a good chance of being right against all other witnesses. Third, that the Western witnesses alone sometimes, but very rarely, preserve the original wording. Fourth, that the Western witnesses joined by P46 or B or 1739 are more often right than wrong; they are hardly ever wrong when joined by the whole 'proto-Alexandrian' group. Fifth, that the (rare) combination of other 'Alexandrians' (against P46 etc) with the Western witnesses is right only at 1 Cor. 8.8. Sixth, that P46 alone with one Western witness can be right against the rest of the tradition. Thus,

> the farther you work back on the 'Alexandrian' line, the more you meet with 'Western' elements; and the greater the Byzantine support for Western readings, the more often they are shared by one or other of the oldest 'Alexandrian' witnesses. And the vast majority of such readings are genuine. We thus begin to discern, beyond the later 'families', the second-

---

40   *Ibid.,* 11.
41   *Ibid.,* 58–159.
42   *Ibid.,* 142ff.
43   *Ibid.,* 156.
44   *Ibid.,* 158f.

century reservoir from which derive all those readings, whether right or wrong, which are found in more than one of them ... From this 'reservoir' – it is not a 'text' – issued both the remarkably pure 'Alexandrian' stream and the muddy Western tradition.[45]

The Western evolved in no very clear or ordered fashion. But for the 'Alexandrian' so haphazard a process is inadmissible. The Alexandrian codices – in inverted commas no longer – derive their attitude and technique from 'that Greek philology of which Alexandria was the centre'.[46] Zuntz's hypothesis is that the archetypal *Corpus Paulinum* was produced in about AD 100, from manuscripts of varying quality, in an edition which noted variant readings; possibly its place of origin was Alexandria. In spite of general corruption, the text-type was preserved with relative purity in the 'proto-Alexandrian' tradition.

One may see Zuntz's method as the latest refinement of the classical genealogical principle, in using which he sees himself as the heir of Bentley and Tregelles, Lachmann and Griesbach, rather than of Westcott and Hort. He realises what, we may now say, Westcott and Hort did not – that even their form of the genealogical method is inapplicable to the mass of New Testament manuscripts. The evidence divides into streams, not into stemmata. Nevertheless, the genealogical method it still is. If, then, the modern period of New Testament textual criticism began with Westcott and Hort, we may say that so far its culmination has been in the work of Zuntz, who has used their achievement in a more far-seeing way than the generation of which we may take Streeter to be representative. If Zuntz's conclusions go beyond the work of his predecessors, his method has much to teach those following the present trends in textual criticism. For, as he says, the critic still needs the same abilities and the same attitude to his problem. Although there exists an 'unimaginable and unmanageable mass of "variants"', the vast majority are irrelevant, and only a fraction recorded.

> Supposing that some day, such a collection of all the variants should be made available, the first step in using it would still have to be in discarding the overwhelming proportion of chaff which it must unavoidably contain. Criticism begins with selection. Therewith it is implied that the textual criticism of the New Testament cannot be carried out by statistical methods ... None but commensurable entities can be reduced to figures, and no two variants are strictly commensurable.[47]

---

45   Ibid., 214.
46   Ibid., 271.
47   Ibid., 58.

To discover whether a reading is right or wrong 'we have got to use our critical faculties and methods'.[48] In this there are no mechanical short cuts; as Zuntz concludes, criticism 'is not a matter of clever tricks or of dry schematism: it is a matter of experience and labour, of patience and knowledge'.[49]

The critic of today, then, is in essentially the same position as the critic of two or of eighteen centuries ago. Our conclusion therefore to this discussion is that the genealogical method has been vindicated by events, and that attacks on it rest on a basic misunderstanding.

It will be remembered that the other matter with which we wish to deal is the critic's task of bringing his labours to fruition in the editing of the Greek New Testament and the preparation of an *apparatus criticus*. It is to this that we now turn.

E. Reuss listed, in all, 745 editions of the New Testament in Greek printed between 1514 and 1870.[50] The thousand mark has long since been passed,[51] nor have the presses been idle in the past half-century. The greatest piece of labour in this field to have been published must undoubtedly be said to be that of S.C.E. Legg.

[158]

Legg published two volumes of his projected edition, which was to reproduce Westcott and Hort's text with a new and enlarged apparatus.[52] When T.W. Manson reviewed the volume containing Matthew,[53] he argued that the editor was going about his task in completely the wrong way. He saw the labour of mastering the vast amount of material as being beyond one man's ability, and the publishing of Westcott and Hort's text as unnecessary. Instead, he advocated the preparation of an edition of the Textus Receptus, to be followed by the 'accurate collation and scientific grouping of the pre-Byzantine materials'.[54] This suggestion had already been made by Streeter,[55] Zuntz[56] and Kilpatrick.[57] Manson further advocated the editing of the text by a committee rather than by a single man. If all the

---

48 Ibid., 59.
49 Ibid., 283.
50 Eduard Reuss, *Bibliotheca Novi Testamenti graeci cuius editiones ab initio typographiae ad nostram aetatem impressas quotquot reperiri potuerunt*, Brunswick, 1872.
51 Cf. Metzger, *op. cit.*, 146.
52 Legg, *Mark* and *Matthew*.
53 *JTS* 42 (1942), 83–92. Cf. also the criticisms of G.D. Kilpatrick, 'The Oxford Greek New Testament', in the same volume, 30–4.
54 Manson, *op. cit.*, 89.
55 *The Four Gospels*, 147f.
56 'The Byzantine text in New Testament criticism', *JTS* 42 (1942), 25–30.
57 Kilpatrick, *op. cit.*

material is to be uncovered in one edition, this seems to be necessary. A radically different attitude to the editor's task emerges with this suggestion. Perhaps the most valuable of Manson's proposals, if such huge operations are under discussion, is that the two tasks of editing the text and of collecting the material should be tackled separately.

Legg had completed but not published the Lukan volume when he died, and therefore the question arose concerning the completion of the undertaking. A group in America was interested, Manson's review had a certain effect, and in 1948 the International Greek New Testament Project was founded. Legg's Matthew and Mark were to stand unaltered. Luke was to be published in 1954, the project to be completed in 1965. In a discussion of the project written in the supposed year of its completion, Jean Duplacy had much to say of the speed at which the work was getting done.[58] 'Malheureusement il ne s'agira que de *Luc,* c'est-à-dire d'un seul des huit volumes ... il y a une vingtaine d'années ... si le rhythme du travail s'accélérait quelque peu, quand verrons-nous l'achèvement de l'oeuvre? ... on ne peut répondre que: dans très, très longtemps'.[59] More seriously, he questions whether there do not exist unused forces which could assist in the great task. In his eyes it would be more satisfactory for the different groups at work each to do their own section. Where collations exist, such as that of the *itala* at Beuron, they should be made available for use by the others. The groups not assisting with the IGNT should start elsewhere, with the Catholic Epistles or the Pauline *corpus.* Although this system would pose great problems of coordination, 'un chien vivant vaut mieux qu'un lion mort'.

Parallel to the Anglo-American project a similar German venture has been afoot – that of the Münster Institute. While the original Legg was to be the 'new Westcott and Hort', this is to be the 'new Tischendorf'. Rather than being a separate concern, it is the undertaking of a number of bodies – the Institut für neutestamentliche Textforschung, the Beuron Institute, the Strasbourg Centre d'Analyse et de Documentation Patristique, the Louvain Institute Orientaliste, the Pontifical Biblical Institute, the École Biblique and the Rechenzentrum der Universität Tübingen. Duplacy's recommendations have been followed in as much as the edition is starting with the Catholic Epistles, leaving the Gospels to the IGNT. So far has textual criticism advanced that it is now to the original text that Kurt Aland, Director of the

---

58 Jean Duplacy, 'Une Tâche Importante en Difficulté: l'édition du Nouveau Testament Grec', NTS 14 (1967–8), 457–68.
59 *Ibid.,* 461.

Munster Institute and editor of this edition, seeks to return, leaving the aims of Bentley and Lachmann far behind. Westcott and Hort's 'original' text was that of the fourth-century Alexandrian uncials. Will Aland's be that of the papyri?

With respect to the apparatus, the problem in the undertakings is the same – that of collating the mass of Byzantine minuscules and lectionaries and placing them in the tradition. Instead of seeking a quick way round the labour, such as the' Multiple Readings' method is intended to be for the IGNT, a thousand test passages have been used for each manuscript. The use of computers has saved labour and, we are told, assisted in improving methods. The scope and depth of the German project seems to be greater than that of the IGNT. The co-operation of the different institutes has already proved practical. But perhaps most important is the ultimate responsibility of one man – K. Aland – over both text and apparatus. It is due to the peculiar nature of textual criticism that the committee encounters problems. As a science, it is easily undertaken by a group – as regards the collation of manuscripts and the preparation of an apparatus. But in as much as it is an art – in the evaluation of manuscripts and choice of readings one man will usually be better off on his own. This seems an excellent reason for the IGNT to concentrate on the production of a really reliable thesaurus of readings. The preparation of a text based on it could then be undertaken by either one man or a very small committee.

The influence of these two great editions is in the future. With the exception of Legg's volumes the student and scholar have been indebted to a number of smaller editions. The second edition of the British and Foreign Bible Society text, prepared by G.D. Kilpatrick with the assistance of Erwin Nestle and others, was based on the first edition of 1904 itself following Eberhard Nestle's 1903 edition.[60] A very similar Greek Testament is the Nestle-Aland, now in its twenty-fifth edition. The readings in this are selected on a mechanical principle, following the majority reading of the three editions of Tischendorf, Westcott and Hort, and Bernhard Weiss.[61] Reference must also be made to two editions which are the fruit of Roman Catholic scholarship over the past fifty years. Merk's bilingual edition,[62] like the Nestle-Aland, is intended to show the family readings; unfortunately his citation of manuscripts is often inaccurate. J.M. Bover's edition,[63] also a bilingual

---

60 London, 1958.
61 3 vols., Leipzig, 1894–1900.
62 Rome, 1933; 9th edition, 1964.
63 Madrid, 1943; 4th edition, 1959.

one, is unusual, since his text is more Western or Caesarean than it is Alexandrian.

Most recent of modern editions is that prepared for the United Bible Societies by a committee of – originally – four scholars, and intended for the use of translators.[64] The presence in the apparatus of only significant variants is a handicap for none but the textual critic, and leaves room for fuller citation of manuscripts for those that are recorded. Moreover, it cannot be denied that very few people are really equipped to deal with *textgeschichtliche* minutiae; so far as that goes, this edition may prove of more use than the IGNT. It will be noted that this edition too is the production of a committee. Although this committee is small, divergence of opinion is occasionally recorded in B. M. Metzger's companion *Textual Commentary*.[65] For the collation of evidence, the advantages of a committee may be clearly seen.

In reviewing the past fifty years of criticism, it is apparent that the developments are remarkable. The objectives of a contemporary writer are considerably further removed from those of Streeter than his are from Westcott and Hort. In 1924 the critic was concerned with the text of the fourth century. Now, due both to a clear understanding of this and to the evidence of the papyri, he has moved his frontiers back by the best part of two hundred centuries.

[161]
> The author believes that he has retrieved (except in very few places) the true exemplar of Origen, which was the standard to the most learned of the *Fathers* at the time of the Council of Nice and two centuries after. And he is sure that the Greek and Latin manuscripts, by their mutual assistance, do so settle the original text to the smallest nicety, as cannot be performed now in any *classic* author whatever: and that out of a labyrinth of thirty thousand variant readings, that crowd the pages of our present best editions, all put upon equal credit, to the offence of many good persons, this clue so leads and extricates us, that there will scarce be two hundred out of so many thousands that can deserve the least consideration.[66]

Thus Bentley, who showed an optimism which we can but envy. He reveals an attitude to the *apparatus criticus* which is worth remembering – that the Textus Receptus is to be blamed for the unnecessary presence of Byzantine readings.

---

64 UBS[1] and [2].
65 Metzger, *Textual Commentary*[2].
66 Richard Bentley, *Proposals for Printing a New Edition of the Greek Testament and St. Hierom's Latin Version, with a Full Answer to all the Remarks of a Late Pamphleteer, By a Member of Trinity College in Cambridge* (1721). A. Dyce (ed.) *Bentley's Works*, London, 1838, III, 475–538.

No heathen author has had such ill fortune. Terence, Ovid, &c. for the first century after printing, went about with 20,000 errors in them. But when learned men undertook them, and from the oldest MSS. set out correct editions, those errors fell and vanished. But if they had kept to the first published text, and set the var. lections in the margin, those classic authors would be as clogged with variations as Dr. Mill's Testament is.[67]

Before we condemn Bentley's assurance as arrogance, and his opinion as erroneous, it would be as well to remember that his text of the New Testament can rival any, and that it is as impressive as any of his editions of the classics. Of his thirty-seven departures from the Byzantine text in the specimen printing of Revelation 22, thirty-one are supported by the most recent edition, the United Bible Societies' second edition. When we recollect that Bentley's earliest manuscripts were later than ours are, and that his chief witness was the Alexandrian, his achievement is recognised as clearly remarkable.

Were Bentley alive today, he would doubtless have sorted out the papyri by now. Work on the earliest evidence must take priority, for only when that has been done can the later be properly understood. That is not to deny the value of sifting late material – otherwise we would be unaware of the value of 1739. But the precise value of that manuscript is that, though late in date, its text-type is a much earlier one. Perhaps there is a mental confusion in the quest for yet more and more complete apparatuses not dissimilar to the old system of counting manuscripts for and against a reading. However complete the apparatus, the editor is not a whit nearer the goal of his task. Bentley with his few manuscripts could produce a text very little inferior to one edited today from several thousand manuscripts and with all the tools of modern scholarship. The main danger in the textual criticism of the fifty years we have been discussing lies in the too great reliance on labour-saving automatic methods. 'Scientific' methods are not possible. As A.E. Housman wrote, it would be equally sensible for a dog to hunt for fleas on statistics of area and population as for a critic to use any rule-of-thumb method.[68] Zuntz's *The Text of the Epistles* is the finest example of methodology that we have discussed. And it is certainly no coincidence that he is well aware of his debt to Richard Bentley. 'Textual criticism does not provide the student with a magic wand. We are granted the means for a worthwhile achievement – if only we trouble to use them. Fifty years of laborious, methodical work can bring us as much nearer to the original text as is the distance which separates

[162]

---

67 Bentley's *Letter to Archbishop Wake*, Dyce, *op. cit.* III, 478.
68 A.E. Housman, *Selected Prose*, Cambridge, 1961, 132.

Stephen from Westcott and Hort'.[69] Zunt opens up the way into the second-century text of the Pauline *corpus*. The next step is the application of the knowledge gained by this to the harder problem of the Gospels and Acts, particularly of the Western text. With the ever-present hope of yet older papyri being discovered, exciting prospects lie ahead. Let us look forward, at however close or distant a date, to the situation at which Bentley hoped to have arrived, 'so that that book, which, by the present management, is thought the most uncertain, shall have a testimony of certainty above all other books whatever; and an end be put at once to all var. lectt. now or hereafter'.

Afterword

This essay was my first piece of extended research. Written in the old Durham University Library on Palace Green in June and July 1975, it is associated for me with midsummer days and a bell chiming for Evensong in the Cathedral. I was fortunate in the topic, because it required me to read everything I could find over half a century of research. As it was submitted for the prize it was twice as long. I cannot say that it lost much by being pared down, and it taught me how to be concise.

As my first publication, it is also reasonable to expect it to need the largest number of retractations. The ending I certainly disagree with, and there are plenty of things which are inadequately understood. Whether my account of Colwell is fair I am far from sure, but I think that I spotted a weakness, even if I could not explain it. I gave undue space to Bédier and Vaganay, although that is more obvious now than it was thirty years ago. But one of the duties of a profesor is to be understanding towards those who are starting out, and so I cannot judge this youthful enterprise too harshly. There are plenty of things which I would express differently today, even that I find embarrassing. What are they? Reader, do you expect me to tell you that?

---

69 Zuntz, *The Text of The Epistles*, 13.

14 The Translation of ΟΥΝ in the Old Latin Gospels

This study became necessary in the course of my work on Codex Bezae. I wished to ascertain the degree of consistency with which the version used one Latin word to translate one Greek one, in order to find differences between the manuscripts, to assess their usefulness in supporting Greek readings, and to place the relation between the two columns of Codex Bezae in a new light. The advantages in choosing οὖν were, first its frequency, second its insignificance, with the implication that a reviser would pay little or no attention to it. The disadvantage is that it is not used uniformly, being shunned by Mark but embraced by John. My method was first, by reference to Moulton-Geden,[1] Yoder[2] and Bachmann-Slaby,[3] to compile a list of occurrences (μὲν οὖν was not included). I then collected all the variants in these places, that I could discover, chiefly from Tischendorf,[4] but also from Legg[5] and from Aland's *Synopsis*[6] as well as from various editions of manuscripts. I then ascertained from Jülicher's *Itala*[7] the Old Latin readings (checking Codex Bezae from the facsimile), and finally added the readings of the Vulgate from Wordsworth and White.[8] I set out all this information in columns on the back of computer paper. By this means I collected 64 occurrences of οὖν in Matthew, 16 in Mark, 46 in Luke, and 238 in John – a total of 364. I added to this list, by reference to the concordances of Stone[9] and Fischer,[10] eighteen places where *ergo* is read in some part of the Latin text, but where οὖν is not attested in any Greek manuscript.

---

1 W.F. Moulton and A.S. Geden, *A Concordance to the Greek Testament* etc., 2nd ed, Edinburgh, 1899.
2 J.D. Yoder, *Concordance to the Distinctive Greek text of Codex Bezae* (NTTS 2), 1961.
3 H. Bachmann and W.A. Slaby, *Computer-Konkordanz zum N. T. Gr. von Nestle-Aland 26 Auflage und zum Greek New Testament 3rd edition*, Berlin, 1977.
4 *N.T. Graece, editia octavo critica maior*, Leipzig, 1869–72.
5 Legg, *Mark* and *Matthew*.
6 *Synopsis Quattuor Evangeliorum*, Editio octava, Stuttgart, 1973.
7 Jülicher. I have used the system of brackets found therein.
8 *Novum Testamentum* etc; *Quattuor Euangelia*, Oxford, 1889–98.
9 R.C. Stone, *The Language of the Latin Text of Codex Bezae, Index Verborum*, Illinois, 1946.
10 *Novae Concordantiae Bibliorum Sacrum iuxta Vulgatam Versionem critice editam quas digessit Bonifatius Fischer OSB*, Stuttgart, 1977.

The statistics which I have collected will be misleading without the knowledge of the extent of the manuscripts. I therefore begin with a list of the number of references out of the 364 for which each is defective.

	Mt	Mk	Lk	Jn
a	3	-	2	1
aur	-	-	2	-
b	1	5	10	3
c	-	-	-	-
d	8	1	-	53
f	-	11	-	-
ff²	21	-	1	12
j	all	all	all	135
l	1	-	-	87
q	4	1	-	44
r¹	36	2	2	20
e	35	14	1	5
k	34	1	all	all

It will be observed that, with the exceptions of j and k, I have only taken into account those codices that are extant in all four Gospels.

I have also tried to indicate the presence of Greek variants which may have an effect on the figures I have tabulated. The reader should also realise that there are quite certainly other variants that I have not included, and that statistical analysis is not much more than the joining together of dry bones that need clothing in flesh and imbuing with life.

I divide the results of this study into three parts – the translation of the Gospels into Latin, the Greek texts represented in the Latin witnesses, and the light thrown upon the two texts of Codex Bezae.

1. The Translation of the Gospels into Latin

Overwhelmingly, the word chosen proved to be *ergo*. Other common words are *autem*, *igitur* and *itaque*. *Enim*, *et* and *vero* also occur.[11] Their position in the sentence does not vary from normality in any of the witnesses.

---

11 Cp. W. Thiele, *Die lateinischen Texte des 1. Petrusbriefes* (GLB 5), 1965. He draws attention to the variation of usages between the several text-types of the epistle.

Autem

The first number indicates the total in each Gospel, the second the number of occasions when there is a variant δέ in the Greek.

	Mt	Mk	Lk	Jn
a	5 (3)	2 (1)	3 (3)	17 (7)
aur	3 (2)	1	1 (1)	13 (8)
b	5 (3)	-	1 (1)	32 (9)
c	5 (3)	2	3 (1)	17 (8)
d	2 (2)	-	4 (4)	13 (5)
f	5 (3)	-	2 (2)	28 (10)
ff²	4 (3)	1	2 (1)	22 (7)
j	x	x	x	16 (1)
l	4 (3)	-	-	9 (4)
q	4 (3)	-	3 (2)	16 (9)
r¹	2 (2)	-	3 (3)	63 (15)
e	4 (1)	-	6 (5)	21 (8)
k	1	-	x	x

Enim

The bracketed numbers indicate a variant reading γάρ.

	Mt	Mk	Lk	Jn
a	1	-	-	-
aur	-	-	-	1 (1)
b	2	-	-	-
c	1	-	-	-
d	1	-	-	-
f	1	-	-	2 (1)
ff²	-	-	-	1
j	x	x	x	1
l	2	-	1	-
q	1	-	-	-
r¹	-	-	1	-
e	-	-	-	1
k	-	-	x	x

Ergo

The number in brackets indicates the number of these readings where οὖν is not in any Greek manuscript.

	Mt	Mk	Lk	Jn
a	37 (2)	7	23	114 (1)
aur	47 (1)	11(1)	33 (1)	180(2)
b	41 (2)	7(1)	19	129(4)
c	46(2)	6 (2)	24	164 (2)
d	45	9	29 (2)	137 (1)
f	48 (1)	4	34(1)	157 (1)
ff²	28	8 (1)	21	151 (2)
j	x	x	x	56 (1)
l	45	10(1)	24	95 (2)
q	43 (1)	8 (1)	28	129 (1)
r¹	18	9 (1)	27 (1)	58 (1)
e	16	-	19	102*(2)
k	15	3 (1)	x	X

* Jn 11.47 corr. (om. p.m.) is included.

Et

The number in brackets refers to those places where there is a variant καί in the Greek text.

	Mt	Mk	Lk	Jn
a	2 (1)	1 (1)	2 (2)	15 (3)
aur	2 (1)	-	3 (2)	11 (3)
b	2 (1)	-	2 (1)	14 (1)
c	3 (2)	-	3 (2)	13 (3)
d	-	1 (1)	-	8 (8)*
f	1 (1)	-	3 (2)	8 (3)
ff²	2 (1)	-	3 (2)	11 (2)
j	x	x	x	8 (1)
l	2 (1)	-	2 (1)	12 (4)**
q	2 (2)	1 (1)	3 (2)	8 (1)
r¹	1 (1)	-	2 (1)	12 (5)
e	-	-	-	21 (5)
k	-	-	x	x

* This includes *ergo et* at Jn 11.56.
** This includes *et ... ergo* (11.36) and *et ergo* (*et eras.*, 13.24).

Igitur

	Mt	Mk	Lk	Jn
a	-	1	-	9
aur	1	-	-	3
b	-	1	-	16
c	-	1	1	3
d	-	-	-	4

	Mt	Mk	Lk	Jn
f	1	-	-	3
ff²	-	-	-	4
j	x	x	x	4
l	1	1	1	-
q	-	-	-	-
r¹	-	-	1	41
e	-	-	1	2
k	3	-	x	x

Itaque

	Mt	Mk	Lk	Jn
a	3	-	2	9
aur	2	1	1	5
b	2	-	1	7
c	2	1	3	6
d	-	-	-	1
f	1	-	1	6
ff²	2	1	1	3
j	x	x	x	3
l	2	-	1	2
q	2	-	1	8
r¹	1	-	1	3
e	2	-	3	18
k	7	-	x	x

Other Words

[256]

The details will be given later.

	Mt	Mk	Lk	Jn
a	1	-	-	3
aur	2	-	-	1
b	2	-	1	-
c	1	1	2	1
d	2	1	1	4
f	1	-	1	6
ff²	-	1	2	1
j	x	x	x	1
l	1	-	1	-
q	-	-	1	1
r¹	1	-	1	1
e	-	-	-	1
k	-	-	x	x

Omission

The number in brackets shows how frequently the whole verse or phrase containing οὖν has been omitted.

	Mt	Mk	Lk	Jn
a	12 (2)	5	14 (2)	70 (1)
aur	7 (1)	3	6	24 (1)
b	9 (1)	3	12 (2)	37 (1)
c	6	5	10 (1)	34
d	6 (1)	4	12 (2)	18 (2)
f	6	1	5	28 (3)
ff²	7 (1)	5	16 (2)	33
j	x	x	x	14
1	6	5 (2)	16 (2)	33 (2)
q	8	7	10 (1)	32 (2)
r¹	5 (1)	5	8 (2)	40
e	7 (1)	2	16 (2)	67 (1)
k	4	12 (1)	x	x

With figures of such general uniformity, our attention is drawn at once to some significant divergencies.

Autem and Igitur

The first of these is the use of *autem* in John, by the manuscripts b f j r¹. In the case of f, this may be partly explained by the number of variant readings δέ in the Greek text. But b r¹ also make more use of *igitur* than do the other manuscripts – this is a habit particularly of the Dublin manuscript. They therefore represent a tradition made on freer principles than those used by the other traditions. It should be noted also that in b, *autem* only occurs twice after 9.16, where the Greek is certainly οὖν (11.31, 32), and *igitur* is not used after 9.15. This is indication, either of an imperfect revision, or of an interruption to the transmission of the text. it may be that the Vercellensis has also been slightly affected by this version.

Itaque

Another independent system of translation may be observed in the use of *itaque* in the African manuscripts. In Mt 1.17–19.38, it appears in k at 7 out of 17 places (and in two of these it omits with ℵ). The use by e in the Fourth Gospel, though by no means so high proportionately, is still twice as much as that of any other manuscript. Here the word's use is spread throughout the Gospel. This fragment of information from k (for it may almost be counted out of this study from Mt 15.33 onwards) is hard to assess. But the greater frequency of *itaque* in it than in the less purely African Codex Palatinus, suggests that the word may originally have been very common in this version, and was replaced at successive revisions.

Enim

The use of *enim* (which regularly represents γάρ) is very rare.[12] Twice it translates a variant γάρ.

Mt 18.4 γάρ W: *enim* g¹
Jn 9.30 οὖν D; γάρ cet: *enim* aur f Vg^{exc E}

At most of the other places there is early evidence for omission in the Greek text. *Enim* may be an attempt to supply a particle felt to be necessary.

Mt 5.19 om. L al *l*184: *enim* a b c d f g¹ l q
6.22 om. ℵ pc sy^c: *enim* b; om. a aur c ff¹ l q
Lk 20.44 om. D Mcion Cyr: *enim* l: om. a c d e ff² i q
Jn 6.30² om. ℵ L 33 al: *enim* j: om. l
8.24 om. P66 ℵ 240 244 sy^{s.p}: *enim* ff²; om. a e

On two further occasions there is evidence for omission by some Latin witnesses.

Lk 19.12 δέ D L 247: *autem* d; *enim* r¹; om. e; *ergo* cet
Jn 12.50 *enim* f; om. b r¹

The two other occurrences in this study of the word are:

Mt 23.3 *enim* l; *itaque* e; *ergo* cet
Lk 11.36. The word comes in the addition to the verse that is to be found in f q. The former manuscript reads *enim*, the latter *ergo*.

---

12 Cf. Thiele, *op. cit.*, 54, Augustine on 1 Pt 4.1 for οὖν; 171, use by **V** in Rom, 1 and 2 Cor for γάρ. See also the same scholar's *Wortschatzuntersuchungen zu den lateinischen Texten der Johannesbriefe* (GLB 2), 1958. He says *enim* is used for δέ in free citations (15).

Et

The tendency of *et* to appear is, with the exceptions of d and e, balanced among the manuscripts. Some readings follow a variant καί in the Greek text.

Mt 26.24 καί 118 209 al: *et* c q
  63 οὖν D; δέ U; καί cet: *ergo* d; *et* cet (deest Afra).
Mk 14.61 καί D W f¹·¹³ 565: *et* a d q
Lk 19.23 οὖν D; καί cet: *ergo* d e r¹; om. l; *et* cet
Jn 6.3 καί ℵ*: *et* j
  7.15 καί Γ Δ Λ Π al: *et* aur f
  9.11 καί pc: *ergo* d; *et* cet
    12 καί P75 ℵ B L W 1 33 al: *et* l
    41 καί Δ 69 124 al: *et* l
  10.39 καί D: *et* d
  11.55 οὖν D; καί cet: *et* a e f r¹
  12.2 καί D: *et* aur c d e [r¹]
  13.26 καί P66 A D W Θ f¹: *ergo* a r¹; *et* cet. (deest j)
    27 καί D: *et* d e

It is possible that some of these readings may have arisen independently in the Latin, but it is more likely on each occasion that a Greek variant is represented.

At other places, as with *enim,* an attempt may have been made to supply a word. Besides some of the readings just given, omission occurs at:

Jn 6.10 om. E F al: *et* e j q
  7.47 om ℵ D f¹ 33 al: *et* e; om. a aur c d ff² r¹
  9.20 om. D Θ al f¹ 33 565: *autem* f; *ergo* q; *et* j; om. cet
    25 om. K S 1 33 al: om. a; *et* e
    26 om. ℵ*: om. a e [r¹]; *et* l
  12.4 om. L 33 249 pc: *et* b c ff²; om [a] e r¹
  18.40 om. S al: *et* r¹; om. e

Use of *et* where there is no Greek variant may be due to the varying purposes for which the evangelists employ it, and to the inevitable intrusion of the most common conjunction, The latter tendency may be seen at work in the manuscripts. At Jn 13.24 Codex Rehdigeranus rendered νεύει οὖν by *et innuit ergo* before the *et* was erased; and at 11.36 it has *et dixerunt ergo* for ἔλεγον οὖν. At 21.23 aur reads *Et exiit ergo* for ἐξῆλθεν οὖν (*et* a f; *itaque* e; *ergo* cet.). At 6.24 Vg^R has *ergo et*. At 11.56 the two columns of Codex Bezae have οὖν καί and *ergo et* respectively.

Of the manuscripts, it will have been seen that e is the most prone to adopt *et,* revealing in this respect a certain freedom. At the other extreme, d uses it least. *Et* is never used in it where there is no v.l. καί.

The problem of assimilation of the Greek to the Latin will be examined later.

Other Words

The rest are words that, with the exception of *vero, at* and *sed*, appear only once where οὖν occurs in the Greek.

Mt 21.36 οὖν D: *vero* d
25.3 οὖν D; δέ Z 157; γάρ ℵ B C L 33; om. W Δ al: *sed* aur b c f g¹ l
28.19 νῦν D; οὖν B f¹ 33 al; om. cet: *nunc* a aur b d h n
Mk 12.6 οὖν A C D N etc; δέ W Θ 565; om. cet: *etiam* d
27 οὖν A D Θ f¹³ 33 al; δέ G f¹ 565 700; om. cet: *vero* c ff²
Lk 4.7 *vero* c ff²
Jn 6.14 *vero* f q
19 *sed* d
8.59 τότε D; οὖν cet: *tunc* d
12.50 *quia* e
19.16² *vero* f
38 *ad* f
20.19 *set* [a]
21.6 δέ ℵª D W al: *ad* d
7² *vero* f.

[259]

Only *vero* can be regarded as a *bona fide* rendering of οὖν. I have included the rest only in order to avoid confusion by remaining silent about any readings. *Sed* at Mt 25.3 is likely to follow δέ (on 157 and the Latin text, see n. 28 below). Jn 12.50 *quia* in e (omitting *ego loquor*) may be either a corruption of *quae*, or perseveration of *quia* earlier in the verse. *Set* at Jn 20.19 in a could have been occasioned by a misreading of *sero*. At 19.38 f has a totally independent version of the phrase. *Vero* in d at Mt 21.36 is probably because the word comes in the preceding sense-line.

For the rest, we see that *vero* was used only spasmodically:

c 2
d 1
f 3
ff² 2
q 1

These findings are in agreement with what B. Fischer had to say about freedom of translation. His further observation, that the development was from 'a freer translation to an ever closer correspondence to the Greek',[13] would also seem to be supported here. But the complex

---

13 'Limitations of Latin in representing Greek', in Metzger, *Early Versions*, 362–74 (quotation from 369). This is a translation of his contribution to ANTT 5.

relation between Greek and Latin variants, to be explored shortly, is such that one might be safer in adding to his statement, that the development was also of increasing correspondence to one Greek text instead of to another. It is also clear that it was not a uniform development, since some translations were freer than others in the first place, and because revision was frequently casual or incomplete, as the manuscripts show.

This brings us to another question. Is one justified in finding, from the evidence here set out, a number of separate translations into Latin? The answer to this need not necessarily be the same for all four Gospels, or even for the whole of each. The objection to this possibility might at once be made, that the predominance of *ergo* in all manuscripts is proof that the manuscripts represent a single translation. However, two or more translators might independently have selected the same word to render οὖν; indeed, it is most probable that *ergo* would be chosen by any number of translators. When this is accepted, then we are free to focus our attention on the evidence of the other words. It must also be observed that in the process of development described by Fischer, and observed here, the more common word *ergo* would have tended to be used more and more, at the expense of other and rarer ones.

That this is what happened may be demonstrated by comparison of the Old Latin texts with the Vulgate. The complaints of Jerome and Augustine (to the effect of *quot homines, tot interpretationes*) indicate that piecemeal revision of separate versions did not resolve confusion; the Vulgate did achieve this, by its consistency as well as by its general acceptance in the church. In the figures given below, I have always taken the majority reading, which is invariably that printed by Wordsworth and White. The bracketed numbers have the same significance as in the earlier lists.

	Mt	Mk	Lk	Jn
autem	2 (2)	-	-	11 (6)
enim	-	-	-	1 (1)
ergo	50 (1)	9 (1)	38	179 (2)
et	2 (1)	-	3 (2)	5 (3)
igitur	1	1	-	3
itaque	1	-	1	8
other	2	-	-	-
omit	6	6	4	31

Individual codices do not always maintain this consistency, The Egerton manuscript lettered E shows a tendency to introduce *autem* – three times in Matthew, once in Luke, and five times in John; D (the

Book of Armagh) does the same thing once in Matthew and four times in John. But only at Jn 5.10, where the choice is between *ergo* and omission, and at 9.12 (*et* or omission) is there any doubt as to the true Vulgate reading, and on both these occasions Wordsworth and White seem to have adopted the right one.

When genuine textual variants have been taken into account, the Vulgate shows a smaller number of synonyms than any Old Latin manuscript. Only in failing to replace all the occurrences of *autem* and of *itaque* does the text reveal its reliance on earlier versions.

Having seen the way in which the Old Latin Gospel texts developed, we may now conclude this section by determining what traces of separate translations do remain in our manuscripts. I use three criteria for determining them,
1. The consistent and singular use of one word rather than another. The best example of what I mean is the way in which Cyprian has *felices* instead of *beati* at Mt 5.4–10.
2. A free method, in which a number of words are all used regularly. This was the preference, if the analogy is useful, of William Tyndale.
3. The achievement of a high degree of consistency in a text unlikely to have been standardised or thoroughly revised (e.g. d rather than aur b). In such a text revision might have caused inconsistency, rather than have eliminated it.

[261]

On these grounds, I conclude that there is evidence for the following separate translations:
1. Matthew: (e) k – use of *itaque*.
   d – most consistent.
2. John: b f j r¹ – regular use of *autem* and *igitur*.
   a e – some use of *itaque*, and *et*, and frequent omission.
   l is the most consistent, but it leads by too short a head for the information to be of much value.

It is harder to speak of the other two Gospels, where the total number of references is smaller. But the following points should be noted.
3. Luke: aur f omit least.
4. Mark: k omits twelve times out of sixteen. This concerns the Greek textual basis, not the technique of the translator. We therefore turn our attention to this aspect of the problem.

2. The Greek Texts Represented in the Latin Witnesses

Such is the contamination of the Old Latin witnesses to the text of the New Testament, that study of the various translation techniques is a safer way of distinguishing its different parts, than the more obvious method of looking for the separate Greek *Vorlagen*. I do not intend to try to follow that method here. Instead, I shall look at those places where *ergo* stands in the Latin, or in some part of it, with no corroborative οὖν, to determine whether such a variant ever existed in a Greek manuscript.[14]

As a preliminary, the further use of the words that render οὖν must be recorded.

Enim, ergo, et and *igitur* can on occasion translate ἄρα.
Enim: Lk   12.42 f
Ergo: Mt   12.28 d
                  19.25 a aur b c f l q r¹
                  27 a aur b c f ff² l q r¹
                  24.45 e
            Lk   11.48 a b d f q r¹
Et: Mt   19.25 ff²
Igitur: Mt   12.28 aur l
                  19.25, 27 d
            Lk   1.66 β

When ἄραγε is translated we have:
Mt 7.20 *ergo* k; *itaque* b g¹ h; om. ff¹; *igitur* cet
17.26 *ergo tamen* e; *ergo* cet

Some of the words can also be used for ὥστε:
Ergo: Mt 19.6; 23.31 e
Igitur: Mt 12.12 k
Itaque: Mt 12.12 cet. (desunt e ff² r¹)
          19.6 all except d e; 23.31 all except e
    Mk 2.28 aur f l q
       10.8 all (deest e)

Vero, which we have seen used for οὖν, more frequently renders δέ; this is so at nine of its ten appearances in d. (*Vero* is, as far as I can discover, never a popular word, and always seems to be in contention with *autem*.)

---

14   The question is raised by e.g. G.D. Kilpatrick, 'The Text of the Epistles: the Contribution of Western Witnesses' in the Festschrift for Professor Aland, *Text, Wort, Glaube* (Arbeiten zur Kirchengeschichte 50) Berlin, 1980, and by W. Thiele, 'Probleme der Versio Latina in den Katholischen Briefen', in ANTT 5, 93–119, 102–13.

In the Gospels, d uses *ergo, igitur* and *itaque* in no other connection. Now that the range of *ergo* has been established, we can turn to the places where there is no οὖν as an equivalent to *ergo* in the Greek.

Mt 2.1 om. M* al; δέ cet: *autem* d; *et* k Cypr;[15] *ergo* a aur b c f ff¹ g¹ q Vg.

Use of οὖν in Matthew is restricted to teaching and to conversation. It occurs in narrative (apart from parables) only at 26.63 in D, which is certainly wrong, and at 27.17 in most manuscripts, where the δέ of D Θ f¹³ al is preferable. Οὖν would be so unsuitable here, that the introduction of *ergo* by a translator is more likely.

6.33 δέ: *autem* aur ff¹ l Vg; *ergo* a b c f g¹ h; om. k. Cypr. (deest Codex Bezae).

The preceding commands in the chapter, each concluding a saying, mostly include *ergo*. A scribe once included it here by perseveration.

Mk 13.23 δέ: *autem* k q Cypr; om. [a] c ff² i; *ergo* cet. (desunt e f).

This is the first of a number of readings, where *ergo* has been employed to translate δέ, because it was felt to be the most satisfactory word.[16]

15.14 δέ: *ergo* ff²; *autem* [a] aur c k; *vero* d l r¹.

The reading may have been influenced by v. 12; or it may seek to define the connection between the crowd's demand and Pilate's question.

15.16 δέ: *ergo* c; *autem* aur d ff² k l.

The reading of the Colbertinus is due to Jn 19.1, where a reads *Tunc ergo Pilatus acceptum Iesum . . .*, which affords a very close parallel to it.

Lk 7.31 εἶπεν (δέ) ὁ κύριος τίνι (οὖν) 71ᶜ 372 1200ᶜ; τίνι δέ ℵ; τίνι pc; τίνι οὖν cet: *Tunc [ergo Iesus] dixit Cui ergo* f; *Cui ergo* cet. (b post *similes*).

Ait autem dominus in Vg^cl, and the remarkable *Dixit praeterea Dominus* of Beza's translation are both plainly straight from the printed Textus Receptus. *Ergo* in f (from later in the verse) has no stronger a claim to represent a Greek reading than Beza's *praeterea*.

10.4 om.: *ergo* aur Vg^mss; om. cet. (lac. ff²).

The word was introduced in imitation of the command at v. 2b. Although Greek evidence is not impossible, given the witnesses for the reading, there is no necessity for assuming it.

18.26 δέ: *autem* a e q r¹; *ergo* d; *et* cet: *et* sy^cs.[17]

Here again *ergo* may have seemed suitable to a translator.

---

15 Citations of Cyprian are taken from the edition in *Corpus Christianorum*, Vols. III–IIIA.
16 Cf. Fischer, *op. cit.*, 369.
17 See 181 and n. 19, below.

19.13 καί Δ Λ 124; om. L 69 pc; δέ cet: *ergo* r¹; *et* b c ff² i l q; *autem* cet.

The appearance of *ergo* in r¹ may be due to its use in v. 12.

19.16 δέ: *ergo* d s; *et e*; *autem* cet. (deest r¹).

The *et* of the Palatine manuscript is an assimilation to Mt 25.20, or to vv. 18, 20 here. *Ergo* may have been used because it was better here than *autem*.

Jn 4.25 om. Gr: om. [a] d q [r¹]; *ergo* cet.

This interesting reading should be compared with other occurrences of the phrase ὅταν (δέ) ἔλθῃ, notably 7.27; 16.13; and above all 15.26, which should be studied in conjunction with this passage; b c ff² read *ergo* in both places, and its greater popularity in the first of them suggests that it influenced 15.26 rather than the other way round. If that is so, then *ergo* is more likely to be a translation of οὖν. The introduction of οὖν into the Greek text is explicable as a misreading of ὅταν.

6.59 om. Gr: *ergo* b; om. cet. (deest l).

Ergo has been introduced from the beginning of v. 60.

8.6 δέ: *autem* aur r¹ Vg; *enim* e; *ergo* Vg^R; *ideo* c; om. cet. (deest j).

As at 6.59, we see how a popular conjunction could easily be introduced (here from the last clause of v. 5).

8.7 δέ: *ergo* e; *autem* cet.

e follows aur c [r¹] Vg exactly, apart from *ergo*; the word may be a relic of an earlier rendering and not an accident, but there is no reason why it should have Greek antecedents.

9.30 ἀπεκρίθη δ' ὁ ἄνθρωπος P75*; ἀπεκρίθη ὁ ἄνθρωπος cet: *respondit ergo homo* d; *respondit homo* a q r¹; *respondit ille homo* cet. (responde\<ns\> j).

Two of the three Old Latin readings have their origin in the opening of v. 25, ἀπεκρίθη οὖν ἐκεῖνος: d picks up part of its own *respondit ergo ille*; the *ille homo* of most manuscripts is a conflation of the two phrases; only a q r¹ have preserved the correct text. The appearance in the very next line of ἐν τούτῳ οὖν in D and *in hoc ergo* in d, supported only by e r¹ is further evidence of the ease with which an author's favourite words slip in and out of manuscripts.

13.23 om. B C* L; δέ cet: *enim* Vg^D; *et* e; *igitur* Vg^Z*; *ergo* aur b l Vg^cet; *autem* cet. (deest j).

What is most striking here is the *igitur* of the Harlean codex. *Ergo* could have intruded from v. 22, but the other synonyms could not. Behind some of the variety of Latin readings must lie a variant οὖν. Such a variant may have arisen as a result of the error in B – it is significant that no Latin manuscripts omit.

15.26 δέ A D L Θ Π f¹·¹³ al; om. cet: om. e l; *autem* aur d f q Vg; *ergo* cet (deest j).

See above, on 4.25.

In two of these eighteen readings, the best explanation is that they represent a variant reading οὖν. In eight of them, the reading is due to the influence of another passage, or of the immediate context, an influence which, in the absence of any other evidence, must be set within the Latin tradition. In five of the readings, *ergo* probably translates δέ. It is significant that on none of the occasions does *ergo* command the support of all manuscripts; there are always two readings, and generally three. In the case of Greek variants, and of casual errors, the reason is obvious. Where *ergo* translates δέ, the sense of the passage may have been hard to reproduce; or some translators may have preferred to keep *ergo* for a single use. (ff² is the only manuscript extant in all five of these readings that reads *ergo* in none of them.)

Comparison with two other versions illuminates the conclusions we have reached. A number of synonyms were used for οὖν in the Old Syriac Gospels, roughly corresponding to those in Latin – w- (= *et*), den (= *autem*) and hakil (= *ergo*).[18] The Peshitta regularly corrected the first two in favour of the third. But the presence of *hakil* is not certain proof that οὖν stood in the Greek texts behind the several versions.[19]

Reference to Young's *Analytical Concordance*[20] reveals the many uses to which the word *therefore* is put, in a version whose textual basis is known to us. Besides οὖν, sixteen Greek words are given, including ἀλλά, γάρ, δέ (1 Cor 7.8) and καί (2 Cor 8.11). And a look at the Index-Lexicon to the New Testament at the end of the volume shows that οὖν was translated by eight different English words.

---

18 F.C. Burkitt, *Evangelion da-Mepharreshe*, Cambridge, 1904, Vol. 2, 89.
19 That οὖν lies behind *hakil* is described as a 'general criterion' by S.P. Brock, 'Limitations of Syriac in representing Greek', in Metzger, *Early Versions*, 94. The same writer says elsewhere that 'the appearance of a formal equivalent between the Greek and Syriac can be very misleading, and ... considerable care needs to be exercised in quoting the evidence of the Old Syriac where these particles are concerned'. 'The Treatment of Greek Particles in the Old Syriac Gospels, with Special Reference to Luke', *Studies in New Testament Language and Text*, ed. J. K. Elliott Leiden, 1976, 80–6. Quotation from 85.
20 Eighth ed., Lutterworth, 1939.

Practical observation endorses the view that one would be certain to reach theoretically: that the use of a particle in Latin texts is unlikely to be sufficiently consistent to furnish reliable evidence of the Greek text behind it. But we have achieved one thing at least. The use of *ergo* is so nearly limited to the translation of οὖν, that in those places where the Greek evidence is divided, we can be confident that *ergo* is support for οὖν.

It is not so certain that *autem* is likely to translate δέ, and not οὖν, in such passages. A list of the passages where there is a Greek variant δέ, and *autem* stands in some or all Latin manuscripts, illustrates the uncertainty. I have marked with an asterisk those readings where I consider *autem* to be a translation of δέ.

*Mt 18.26 δέ D *l*184: *ergo* q r²; *autem* cet.
*   31 δέ ℵ^ca C L W pler: *ergo* d e; *autem* cet.
*   24.15 δέ ℵ^c L 157 al: *autem* l
*   25.3 δέ Z 157: *autem* ff¹ q r²
*   27.17 δέ D Θ f¹³: *ergo* aur ff¹ l Vg; *autem* cet.
Mk 12.20 δέ 106 892 *l*14: *autem* a
*Lk 3.7 δέ D 1 13 al: *autem* d e f r¹
*   12.20 οὖν D; δέ cet: *autem* aur b f ff² q r¹ Cypr^ter
*   13.18 δέ A D Π al: *autem* c q
*   15.28 οὖν Γ Δ Λ Π al; δέ cet: *autem* a d e
*   17.22 οὖν D 157; δέ cet: *autem* a e λ r¹ s
*   19.12 δέ D L 247: *autem* d
*   21.36 δέ ℵ B D: *autem* [a] d e
Jn 2.18 δέ Or^bis 239: *autem* r¹
    3.25 δέ ℵ* 47: *autem* b j
    4.6 δέ V al: *autem* d ff²
       33 δέ D: *autem* [a] b q <r¹>
       52¹ δέ 13 69: *autem* e l
    6.3 οὖν D W f¹ 13 69; δέ cet: *autem* q
       10 δέ A W Θ Ψ f¹·¹³: *autem* b q
*   35 δέ A f¹ al pler: *autem* aur c Vg
       61 οὖν ℵ* D 13 61^mg 69; δέ cet: *autem* aur c f ff² q
*   67 δέ D: *autem* b d
*   68 δέ D: *autem* b d
    8.5 δέ D: *autem* c d ff² r¹
    9.25 δέ 13 *l*60: *autem* f r¹
    12.9 δέ D: *autem* [a] e
       19 δέ K al: *autem* c f ff² l r¹
       29 δέ W: *autem* r¹

*   44 οὖν D 240 244; δέ cet: *autem* it exc. d j
        13.30 δέ 80 249: *autem* e r¹
*   18.4 δέ ℵ D L W f¹ 33 565: *autem* it exc. aur^{s.m.} d e
        24 δέ ℵ f¹³: *autem* r¹
        19.15 δέ P60 ℵ* A W Θ pler: *autem* aur f q Vg
        26 δέ ℵª: *autem* it exc. q
*   29 δέ ℵ: *autem* aur f Vg
*   20.17 οὖν ℵª D L 050 pc; om. A; δέ cet: *autem* exc. c d q
        19 δέ 239: *autem* e q
        20 δέ 1: *autem* d q r¹

The probability of *autem* representing οὖν is greatest in the group b d f r¹. Where the Bezan Greek has δέ it is more likely that *autem* translates δέ. When these two principles come into conflict, at Jn 4.33, I concluded that D's reading was repetition from v. 32, and unlikely to have had any influence if d read *ergo*. I have included some of the Greek evidence, indeed some of the variants, for the sake of completeness rather than out of a conviction of its relevance. Some variants are greater in extent than I have indicated.

It is clear that the evidence of *autem* in the fourth Gospel must be treated with caution, and that one might easily be misled by an editor. I therefore examined a number of editions to see how they did treat it. Tischendorf is the only one I opened who refers to all the variants that have just been listed. He generally just cites the manuscripts reading *autem* along with those that have δέ, without telling one what the Latin word is. On seven occasions he states that they do have *autem* (Mk 12.20; Jn 6.61, 68; 9.25; 12.9; 19.15), and so leaves the reader with the choice of agreeing with him or not.

Legg cites the Latin manuscripts that have *autem*, in support of δέ at Mt 18.26, 31; 25.3. On no occasion does he tell us what the wording of them is.

We find a more judicious approach in Aland's *Synopsis Quattuor Evangeliorum*, where the Old Latin support for οὖν or for δέ is rarely given. But I have noticed three places where he does give it: Jn 3.25; 6.10, 35. Only on the third occasion is the testimony valid.

As one would expect, the smaller editions do not include such variants in their apparatus. The third edition of the United Bible Societies' *The Greek New Testament* refers to none of the variants concerned except Jn 12.9, where the editors' concern is with the inclusion or rejection of ὁ.[21] Although it has been said that variants of

---

21   See Metzger, *Textual Commentary*², 237.

particles are not normally included in the latest edition of Nestle-Aland,[22] it still manages to include fourteen of those we have listed, and to include the Old Latin evidence for all but two of these. The ingenious system of symbols designed to indicate disagreement among Old Latin manuscripts allows both editor and reader to suspend judgement on a number of occasions. If (it) at Jn 12.9 is the same as lat(t), then the citation is correct. But lat(t), indicating that 'a part of the tradition apparently presupposes the same Greek translation base, but a certain freedom of translation base makes absolute certainty impossible',[23] should also have been used at Jn 12.29; 18.24 (where in any case the Vulgate has *Et*): or rather, the Latin reading should have been placed with the other variant.

I conclude this section by suggesting three canons to be employed when we assess the relevance of Latin evidence, and attempt to place it in its proper place in the apparatus of a Greek Testament.

1. There must be grounds for believing that a var. lect. was known either to the author or to the reviser of the Latin text in question, from the Greek copy before him or in some other way.
2. There must be grounds for the belief that the Latin word translates the one for which we are seeking support. Such grounds will be harder to find if the word is *autem* in r¹, or *et* in e, when we want corroboration for a reading δέ or καί in John.
3. Citation without certainty is worse than silence. And where there are many Greek variants, and the Old Latin manuscripts translate in a number of ways, leave them out.

3. Codex Bezae

The study has shewn Codex Bezae to be, at least in some particulars, the most consistent of the thirteen principal manuscripts of the Old Latin Gospels. An abstraction of the figures that were given at the beginning indicates this.

	Mt	Mk	Lk	Jn
Autem	2 (2)	-	4 (4)	13 (5)
Enim	1	-	-	-
Ergo	45	9	29 (2)	137 (1)
Et	-	1 (1)	-	8 (8)

---

22 J.K. Elliott, 'An Examination of Nestle-Aland²⁶ and The Greek New Testament³', *JTS* 32 (1981), 19–49.
23 *Nestle-Aland²⁶*, Stuttgart, 1979, Introduction, 55*.

Igitur	-	-	-	4
Itaque	-	-	-	1
Others	2	1	1	4
Omission	6 (1)	4	12 (2)	18 (2)

A translator chose *ergo* to translate οὖν, and then stuck to it with remarkable fidelity. This method was preserved in the subsequent transmission of the version. It is especially significant that this is so in all four Gospels. Only l, and q to a lesser extent, come near to this consistency. Comparison with the Acts of the Apostles shows how greatly the Gospels are in agreement with each other.

autem	4
enim	1
ergo	34
itaque	2
-que	1
quidem	4
vero	6
quidem ergo	1
tunc ergo	1
Total	54

Halfway between Matthew and Luke in the number of times οὖν is translated, it uses twice as many synonyms as Matthew, three times as many as Luke. Particularly striking is the frequency with which *vero* occurs, and the use of *quidem* (used in the Gospels by all manuscripts for μὲν οὖν).

To return to the Gospels. Attention has been drawn more than once to indications that Codex Bezae is descended from a composite text. Blass showed how the spellings Ἰωάνης and Ἰωάννης alternated in blocks,[24] and a study of the *nomina sacra* reveals that the forms used change from one book to another, and once in the middle of one.[25] We are now in a position to affirm the homogeneity of the Latin text, and even to conclude that all four Gospels were translated by one man, or by the same group of men. In many ways, the Acts of the Apostles in d is different from the Gospels, and these differences accentuate the uniformity of the Gospels. While the evidence of spellings and of the *nomina sacra* may testify to a stage at which several scribes were employed, or to the use of more than one exemplar at an earlier copying, the consistency of translation technique in this respect is proof of the unity of origin of the Bezan Latin Gospels.

---

24 *Philology of the Gospels*, London, 1898, 75f.
25 Ludwig Traube, *Nomina Sacra*, Munich, 1906, contains the relevant material. I hope to set out my own conclusions elsewhere.

The possibility that such consistency has been achieved by a process of revision is ruled out by two facts. The first is that the age of the text is well attested by many other features of it. The second, that other revised texts, including the Vulgate, seem to retain some evidence of their earlier nature.

We now turn to what has for long been the main subject of debate in the study of Codex Bezae, the matter of whether the Greek text has been assimilated to the Latin. At this point it becomes necessary to abandon the statistical method, and to examine the singular, or nearly singular readings of D, in order to determine whether they are assimilations to d. I consider singularity to be no more, except in casual errors, than one of the accidental truths of history. Moreover, on some occasions they may only appear to be singular as a result of an accidental lapse by the authorities usually consulted. Some well-attested readings may also be really dependent on an originally singular reading of Codex Bezae. This remains, however, the convenient way in which to proceed. I shall deal first with the singular readings that are in agreement with d, and then turn to those that are not.

Mt 13.28: om. οὖν D 252*: *ergo* f q; om. cet. (deest r^1).

Legg also cites all the versions except one Sahidic manuscript in favour of omission.[26] This error is sufficiently widespread for one to believe that it is Greek in origin. Being accidental, it may have arisen separately in D and 252*. If D were dependent on d, one would be left with the task of accounting for the reading of the versions.

18.26 δέ D 2145 *l*184 sy^{hl} cop^{sa}; καί 299 sy^{cp}; om. sy^s; οὖν cet: *ergo* q; *autem* cet.

Again, apart from some support for D that has the appearance of having been haphazardly gathered by Legg,[27] the consensus of most of the Old Latin suggests that it followed the text read by D (see above, p. 182).

25.3 οὖν D; δέ Z (Θ 1) 157; γάρ ℵ B C L 33 al; om. cet: *autem* ff^1 q r^2; *ergo* d ff^2; *sed* cet. (desunt a e k).

---

26 There is a brief reference to the relation of Coptic conjunctions with their Greek equivalents in J.M. Plumley, 'Limitations of Coptic (Sahidic) in representing Greek', Metzger, *Early Versions,* 149. A great deal can also be gathered from W.E. Crum, *A Coptic Dictionary,* Oxford, 1939.

27 Scrivener mentions D in connection with *l*184, *A Full and Exact Collation of about Twenty Greek Manuscripts of the Holy Gospels,* Cambridge, 1853, lxii.

Sed indicated that a reading δέ was known.[28] *Autem* is more likely to be another translation of it than an alternative for οὖν. *Ergo* might be one also, but of the five readings on p. 179-80 above where *ergo* seemed to render δέ, ff² was a party to none of them. Against this probability must be balanced the absence of any reason why D should have introduced οὖν. Those who like the theory of assimilation, will find assimilation here.

    26.63 οὖν D; δέ U; καί cet: *ergo* d; om. aur ff¹ g¹ l; *et* cet. (desunt e k)

οὖν/*ergo* is assimilation either to Mk 14.61 067 pc k, or (more probably) to Jn 18.19 Gr. omn. aur b c ff² q. At the former place D is καὶ λέγει αὐτῷ, d *et ait illi*; at the latter the codex is deficient. Although certainty is impossible, it may be more likely that the Latin text follows the Greek, since the existing Greek witnesses are agreed at Jn 18.19, while the Latin are not.

    28.19 νῦν D; οὖν B Δ Π 1 33 al; om. cet: *nunc* a aur b d h n; *ergo* cet. Cypr (desunt k r¹)

νῦν is a corruption of οὖν. The further change of πορευθέντες to πορεύεσθαι (= -θε) is also an easier one in Greek than the *ite* of d e from *euntes* (cet.).

    Mk 13.33 οὖν D; δέ W Θ Σ f¹³ al; om. cet: *ergo* d f i q; *itaque* aur c ff²; om. cet. (desunt b e)

The reading οὖν lies behind both *ergo* and *itaque*. It must therefore be a genuine Greek variant.

    Lk 3.10 om. D al Or; οὖν cet: *ergo* a aur f [r¹] Vg; om. cet.

The reading is in imitation of Acts 16.30. The difference between the Latin in these two places (here *simus*, in Acts, *fiam*) shows that the change was first made to the Greek text of the Gospel, which the Latin then followed (note that at Acts 16.30 *sim* is read by gig Lucif) .

    5.7 οὖν D; καί cet: *ergo* d; *itaque* e; om. b; *et* cet.

Itaque in e is proof that οὖν is independent of the reading in d. Moreover, the fact that D has βοηθεῖν for συλλαβέσθαι, while all Latin manuscripts have *adiuvarent*, indicates the autonomy of the Greek text.

    12.20 οὖν D; δέ cet: *ergo* [a] c d e i l Cypr^ter; *autem* cet.

Introduction of the stronger particle may be intended to make this verse, rather than 21, the purpose of the story. Such a change, though

---

28 For the relation of 157 to the bilingual tradition of D, see H.C. Hoskier, 'Evan. 157 (Rome Vat. Urb, 2)', II, *JTS* 14 (1913), 243–5.

not impossible in the Greek text, may have been more likely to occur in the Latin. The reading *autem* is to be taken as a translation of δέ.

17.22 οὖν D 157; δέ cet: *ergo* d; *autem* a e λ r¹ s; *et* cet.

All three Latin readings may be traced to οὖν (compare Mt 18.29, *autem* e f; *ergo* d q; *et* cet., where all Latin manuscripts have οὖν). But the nature of the variant is very similar to that at 12.20, and should therefore be ascribed to the same cause.

19.12 δέ D L 247 pc; om. 252*; οὖν cet: *autem* d; *enim* r¹; om. e Vg^Q; *ergo* cet.

This is the only place in our survey where r¹ has *enim*; it may be another witness to the reading of D. The Greek tradition will have found it very easy to introduce the common phrase εἶπεν δέ.

19.23 οὖν D; καί cet: *ergo* d e r¹; om. l; *et* cet.

[270]   The reading of D is assimilation to Mt 25.27; the order of μου τὸ ἀργύριον has been altered for the same reason (and in Matthew τὰ ἀργύρια has been put into the singular).

20.25 οὖν Γ al; om. D; τοίνυν cet: *ergo* aur c f r¹ Vg; om. cet (deest b).

οὖν is from Mt 22.21. Omission is due to Mk 12.17, with which both columns of Codex Bezae are identical; assimilation is again reciprocal.

20.29 om. D; οὖν cet: *autem* e ff²; *enim* Vg^B; om. a d i q; *ergo* cet. (deest b)

The text has been assimilated to Mt 22.25 (where D alone omits δέ) in the whole phrase. The Greek of the third parallel, Mk 12.20, has been similarly altered, with the addition of οὖν. But d at Mk 12.20 has *fuerunt*, not the *erant* that is read here. It therefore appears that the alteration in these texts must have been made in the Greek first.

20.44 om. D Mcion Cyr; οὖν cet: *enim* l; *ergo* aur f q r¹ Vg; om. cet. (deest b)

Omission seems to be under the influence of Mk 12.37.

21.7 om. D f¹ 13 al; οὖν cet: *ergo* s δ; om. cet. (deest b)

The omission is by assimilation to either Mt 24.3 or Mk 13.4. Both its popularity in the Latin tradition, and its support among Greek manuscripts show this to be an old variant in the original language.

Jn 6.67 δέ D; om. G; οὖν cet: *autem* b d; om. a; *ergo* cet. (deest r¹)

The immediate explanation, that *autem* in d for οὖν has occasioned the reading in D, is less likely than that the passage has been harmonised to Lk 9.20 rather than Mk 8.29. The fact that, at Mt 16.15, Codex Ephraemi and some minuscules have been affected by the Johannine version, shows that these texts did influence each other.

6.68 εἶπεν δὲ αὐτῷ D; ἀπεκρίθη οὖν αὐτῷ Γ Δ 0250 pler; ἀπεκρίθη αὐτῷ P66 P75 ℵ B C L Λ Π al: *autem* b d; *ergo* aur l q Vg^{exc. D Δ}; om. cet.

Here D has adopted the reading that it has at Mt 16.16 but d has *illi*, not *ei*. The δέ is not, therefore, a translation of *autem*, but the Latin is from the Greek.

7.23 οὖν D; om. cet: *autem* <j> Vg^Q; *ergo* a d f; om. cet.

The reading *autem* is additional support for D, showing that it represents the text influential in the formative period of the Old Latin texts.

8.5 δὲ νῦν D; οὖν cet: *ergo* aur e Vg; *autem nunc* d; *autem* e ff^2 r^1

νῦν is, as at Mt 28.19, οὖν corrupted. Δέ may well have been added after comparison with the Latin column, by someone who was aware that the text was faulty. *Autem* here may certainly be taken to represent οὖν. It is much less likely that δέ has been written because it occurs twice in the immediate context.

8.59 τότε D; οὖν cet: *igitur* r^1; *itaque* [a]; *tunc* d; *ergo* cet. (deest j)

If *Tunc* arose by some confusion over *tulerunt*, then the Greek has been assimilated to the Latin.[29]

9.18 om. D 69 72; οὖν cet: *ergo* aur c q Vg$^{exc\ T^*}$; om. cet. (deest j)

The agreement of the Leicester Codex is important. Along with the general support of the Latin tradition, it may be taken that this slip was Greek in origin.

9.30^2 οὖν D; γάρ cet: *enim* aur f Vg$^{exc\ E}$; *ergo* d e r^1; om. cet.

d (alone) has *ergo* at the beginning of the verse also, and was presumably once in some confusion. Its reading with e r^1 may be a conjectural restoration, in a text that omitted, to which D has been assimilated. Alternatively, the evidence for omission in the Latin may indicate the reading of a Greek *Vorlage* (or *Vorlagen*), in which case D could represent the conjecture, followed by d e r^1.

9.41^1 οὖν D *l*184 al; δέ S Γ 1241 al; καί Δ 69 124 543; om. cet: *ergo* d; *et* l δ Vg$^{K\ V\ W\ Z}$; om. cet. (deest j)

οὖν may have found its way here from its place later in the verse, where it is read by A pler, and [a] <j> l r^1. There is no reason to doubt that the Latin follows the Greek.

10.39 καί D; δέ P45; οὖν P66 ℵ A K L al; om P75 B Γ Θ Λ al: *autem* f; om. Vg^E; *et* d; *igitur* r^1; *ergo* cet. (desunt j q)

---

29 The shape of letters in the context can be shown to be a major cause of casual error in the codex.

Omission is due to the preceding word ἐζήτουν; the readings καί and δέ are attempts to restore the text (compare 7.30 οἱ δὲ ἐζήτουν ℵ; 11.56 below).

11.41² καί D; οὖν 1; om. P59^vid 69; δέ cet: *et* d; *ergo* Vg^T; *autem* cet. (desunt j q).

D is also alone in prefixing ὅτε to the verse. This is an alteration which demands the omission of the particle here altogether. The Latin is equally strange. If ὅτε is due to *cum*, then it seems improbable that καί can be due to *et*.

11.55 οὖν D; καί cet: *autem* l; *ergo* aur b c d ff²; *et* a e f r¹ Vg.

The reading of l inclines me to the belief that the reading of D is not in imitation of the Latin.

11.56 οὖν καί D; οὖν cet: om. Vg^Δ; *ergo et* d; *ergo* cet. (desunt j lq r¹).

Omission in Codex Dunelmensis may reflect a Greek error similar to that at 10.39. In that case, the reading of D will be a conflation of the true reading and a conjectural one, aided by the presence of καί on the other side of τον ιην. It is necessary to assume, as at 10.39, that the Latin follows the Greek.

12.2 καί D; om. P66* 122; οὖν P66^c cet: *autem* Vg; *ergo* b f ff²; om. ⟦a⟧; *et* aur c d e [r¹].

This is a most likely case of the Greek being assimilated to the Latin, since *et* may well be an alternative translation of οὖν.

12.34b οὖν D; om. cet: *ergo* d; om. cet. (desunt j q).

The appearance of οὖν here is the result of its omission earlier in the verse, and subsequent restoration to the wrong place in the text. This probably occurred in the Greek text, where its omission is widespread.

12.35b οὖν D; om. cet: *ergo* d; *itaque* e m; om. cet. (desunt j q).

Again, the support of e frees D from the suspicion that it has followed the Latin.

12.44 οὖν D 240 244; δέ cet: *ergo* d; *autem* cet. (deest j).

There is dislocation in W and recasting in Θ 69. The reading of D may be the result of one of these, or of a similar error.

13.27 καί D; om. 59 86 249 254; οὖν cet: *et* d e Cypr; om. a f l Vg^{exc. D}; *ergo* cet. (deest j).

καί had occurred three times in the preceding lines. The error may have been made in the copying of either text.

20.26 οὖν D f¹ pc; om. cet: *ergo* d; *itaque* f; om. cet. (desunt j ff² l).

The reading of f justifies the belief that d follows the Greek text.

In many of these readings it has been shown that the error may have arisen in either text. In others it may more easily be discovered in the Greek tradition; in yet others it is likely that the Greek has been assimilated to the Latin. In other words, we find what on reflection one would expect in a bilingual tradition – a reciprocal influence. When a scribe or corrector thought that the text was at fault, he tried to restore it by comparing the columns; subconsciously also, he will have been influenced by both.

On the whole, the preceding examination has shown that assimilation to the Latin was not the most important factor in the history of the Greek column. The force of other circumstances becomes clear in the study of those passages where the two columns disagree.[30]

Mt 21.36 οὖν D; δέ 487; καί ℵ*; om. cet: *autem* Vg^E; *et* Vg^R; *vero* d; om. cet. (deest k).

καί is from Mk 12.4; δέ is from v. 37. The word *vero* comes in d immediately before, in v. 35. The reading of D remains inexplicable, unless it is derived from v. 40, or Mk 12.61//Lk 20.15.

26.24 οὖν D Z al Chr; καί min pc; om. cet: *et* c q Vg$^{D\,E\,Q}$; om. cet (desunt e k).

This is most likely a palaeographical error in D, a misreading of ὁ μέν.

Mk 3.11 οὖν D; om. cet: om. lat (desunt k r^1).

This too is a palaeographical error, caused this time by the preceding ὅταν.

10.9 om. A D Cl Or; οὖν cet: om. k*; *ergo* cet (deest e).

It may be suspected that this reading has the same cause as the last two. Here the abbreviation ὁ for οὖν could have been mistaken as a reduplication of the definite article.[31]

12.6 ἔτι οὖν A C D N etc.; ὕστερον δέ W Θ 565; ἔτι cet: *autem* a aur c ff^2; *ergo* l q Vg; *etiam* d; om. b i k r^1 (all translate ἔτι).

I have already suggested that *etiam* represents a recollection of ἔτι οὖν.

13.23: See above, p. 179.

---

30 J.A. Findlay, 'On Variations in the Text of d and D', *BBC* 9 (Feb., 1931) 10–11, gives as the total number of discrepancies, 107 in Matthew, 106 in John, 176 in Luke, 469 in Mark, and 607 in Acts. His theory is that someone assimilated the Greek text to the Latin, but had had enough by the end of Luke. Scrivener, *Bezae Codex Cantabrigiensis*, xxxix, claimed to have found a total of 1919 differences – 251 in Matthew, 229 in John, 428 in Luke, 380 in Mark, and 631 in Acts. My provisional figures are: 103 in Matthew, 122 in John, 229 in Luke, 343 in Mark, 600 in Acts.

31 P. Glaue, 'Der älteste Text der geschichtlichen Bücher des NT', *ZNW* 65 (1954), 90–108, puts forward evidence that Codex Bezae had an ancestor in cursive.

Lk 10.2 om. D; οὖν cet: om. e; *ergo* cet. (deest ff²).

The support of sy^s for D, as well as of e, shows the age of this omission. Unless d has been revised, it testifies to a difference between its Greek base and the text of D. The opinion of Blass, who considered οὖν to be an assimilation to Mt 9.38, is worthy of consideration.[32]

12.40 δέ D; οὖν A Δ al; om. P75 ℵ B L Θ al: *ergo* d δ; om. cet. (deest a).

Omission is very probably in imitation of Mt 24.44. For καὶ ... δέ, see Blass-Debrunner §447(9).[33] Here the reading οὖν, represented in d, is more evidently spurious, following καί.

13.18 δέ A D Γ Δ Λ Π al; οὖν P75 ℵ B al: *autem* c q; *ergo* cet. (deest r¹).

δέ is used by consuetude, and – more immediately – because of its use in v. 6. Whether it is supported by *autem* must be uncertain, but with c and q, it is likely that it is.

18.26 See p. 179 above.

19.16 See p. 180 above.

Jn 4.33 δέ D; om. ℵ* sy^c s p; οὖν cet: *autem* [a] b q <r¹>; om. d e; *ergo* cet. (deest j).

It is preferable to regard *autem* as an alternative translation of οὖν rather than as support for D (see p. 182 above). The following words are replaced in D with ἐν ἑαυτοῖς οἱ μαθηταί, which is modelled on v. 32. The version in the Latin is dependent on the Greek, not on v. 32; the change in its word order will have occurred later – transposition in this way is common in d.

6.19 οὖν: *autem* ff²; *et* b j r¹; *itaque* e; *sed* d; *ergo* cet. (deest a).

This inexplicable reading in d may indicate just that a copyist was thinking of the end of the story and of the significance of Jesus' arrival.

6.41 δέ D; οὖν cet: *igitur* b r¹; *itaque* e; *autem* m; *ergo* cet. (deest l).

Den in sy^c s p may support D. Aland (*Synopsis Quattuor Evangeliorum, ad loc.*) also cites sah. The error certainly arose in the Greek (οὖν is at its most popular in John 6).

6.62 om. ℵ*; οὖν cet: *autem* f; *ergo* aur c ff² Vg; om. cet. (desunt j r¹).

The Latin reading may have its origin in the same error as that of ℵ – the superficial similarity of EAN and OYN.

7.6 om. ℵ* D W 106 pc sy; οὖν cet: *autem* j q r¹; om. e; *ergo* cet.

---

[32] F. Blass, *Euangelium secundum Lucam ... secundum formam quae videtur Romanam*, Leipzig, 1897, ad loc.

[33] *A Greek Grammar of the New Testament*, trans. by R.W. Funk, Chicago, 1961.

Tischendorf is incorrect in placing an asterisk against D^Gr to indicate that it has been corrected. There is no obvious or particular cause for this error of omission.

9.30[1]

This verse has already been discussed above. Although I argued (p. 180) that the reading in d comes from v. 25, there may still be a connection with the second *ergo* (p. 189).

12.9 δέ D; οὖν cet: *autem* 〚a〛 e Vg^G; *ergo* aur d f Vg^cet; *et* b c ff^2; *igitur* r^1; om. Vg^F.

D also adds ἤκουσαν after Ἰουδαίων, in imitation of the Johannine phrase (v. 29 etc.), with all the Old Latin except aur f r^1. We see again how it has influenced part of the Latin tradition.

12.28 καί D; om. X*; οὖν cet: *autem* a r^1; om. d; *ergo* cet. (desunt j q). [274]

The reading in D is due to the addition of the previous phrase, which comes from 17.5. Omission in d is the result of the word before – *fieret*.

Some of the differences between the two columns are the result of error in the copying of one or the other. In others, it may be seen that the Greek text lying behind d is by no means identical to that of D. In most of these places, there seems to be other Old Latin support for the Greek of Codex Bezae, showing it to be closely related to the text on which d is based. Thus, much of the singularity of D is Greek in origin. When this fact is taken with what we saw of those singular readings in which it concurs with the Latin column, it must be concluded that the theory of assimilation does not account for the differences between Codex Bezae and most other Greek manuscripts. Some of them may be explained in this way, but many more cannot.

Of particular interest are those passages where D is alone, or nearly so, in reading δέ against the Latin *autem* (Mt 18.26; Lk 19.12; Jn 6.67). For each of these I have suggested alternative explanations to that of assimilation. There are, in fact, a greater number of places where D alone has δέ, against *ergo* in d (Lk 12.40; 13.18; 18.26; 19.16; Jn 6.41; 12.9).

There is a further point to be made concerning the readings where D is more or less on its own with οὖν, when d has *ergo*. Since the consistency of the translation is clearly established by the figures with which we began, it is impossible that *ergo* should have been used in the wild way that would be necessary at these singular readings of D. Nor can it be suggested that alterations to the Greek text hide such a wildness. For the Latin is most consistent in Luke, where Findlay recorded a higher number of discrepancies than in Matthew or in John. The consistency of d throughout prohibits the view that it can represent the δέ, καί or γάρ found in the manuscripts which disagree with D.

Comparison with d reveals that D agrees with it more than disagrees, when its Greek reading is singular. This partly reflects the measure of assimilation – of both sides – that has occurred. It also indicates how closely allied D is to the text on which its Latin column is based.

When the theory of assimilation to the Latin has failed, one has to account for the unique nature of the Greek column in other ways. Again and again we have seen how readings are due to the influence of parallel passages in other Gospels. H.J. Vogels collected about 1500 harmonisations in D.[34] His conclusion that the Diatessaron was responsible for this had better not be resurrected. But, however it is explained, the role of Synoptic assimilation plays a large part in the composition of the text of Codex Bezae (a glance at the Lord's Prayer in Luke will convince anyone of that).

The material we have studied provides evidence for three main factors in the development of the text of Codex Bezae: Synoptic harmonisation; the influence upon each other of the two columns; and a stage of indifferent copying in the transmission of the text, that resulted in corruptions and false emendations.

Final Summary

1. οὖν is translated by *autem, enim, ergo, et, igitur, itaque* and *vero*. None of these words are limited to this use, and in fact *autem, enim, et* and *vero* are predominantly used in other ways.
2. A bewildering double process may be observed in the translations of οὖν. The main one was of increasing standardisation, culminating in Jerome's Vulgate. But the comparing of one manuscript with another led to greater confusion, in the mixing up of separate methods of translation. This confusion was compounded by the inconsistency which marked some parts of the tradition from the first.
3. The result of this is that considerable care must be exercised when Old Latin readings are being incorporated into the *apparatus criticus* of a Greek Testament.

---

34 *Die Harmonistik im Evangelientext des Codex Cantabrigiensis* (TU 36), Leipzig, 1913.

4. The Latin of Codex Bezae is very consistent in all four Gospels, which are therefore closely related in their origins. Acts was translated separately, according to a less rigorous system.
5. The main influence on the Greek text is that of harmonisation to Gospel parallels. Assimilation to the Latin has a subordinate role, as does the corruption of poor copying.

Afterword

In one respect the approach taken in this study needs serious modification. It assumes that the Latin tradition is split between a fluid Old Latin text and a fixed Vulgate. I was naive in presupposing a fixed Vulgate text, even in the Gospels. To be sure, Jerome made a revision, and that revision influenced the subsequent history of the Latin Gospels. But the Vulgate also is a broad stream, containing not only mixed texts with a blend of Old Latin readings and Vulgate readings, but also a variety of readings which grew up within the Vulgate tradition. If this article is read with this different understanding of the whole tradition in mind, then the findings make more sense.

I find myself also commenting on the limitations of statistical data, a view which I had expressed even more firmly in 1976. It has to be said that for such a sceptic, I have used this kind of material a great deal. The truth is that for too long I was convinced by Housman's comments about the dangers of statistical analysis, confusing wit with substance. Of course figures have to be interpreted on the basis of historical knowledge and practical experience, but (especially where they are based upon complete sets of available data) they provide the basic material for useful research. No more apologies for statistics.

15 "The Principles and Practice of New Testament Textual Criticism"

Collected Essays of G.D. Kilpatrick. A Review

The authoritative and detailed contributions of G.D. Kilpatrick form one of the most important and distinctive contributions to textual criticism in the period since Westcott and Hort. Since they were wholly in the form of articles, the collection of these pieces into a single volume is a significant event. Moreover, the tragic abandonment of his revision of the Bible Society's *Greek New Testament* (the 1958 edition, though produced by him, only partially represents his preferred text) means that we are often dependent on these essays for our knowledge of the Kilpatrick text. The editor's announcement in the Introduction that he hopes that 'Kilpatrick's labours can be brought to completion and published' (xix) signals an event eagerly to be anticipated. Meanwhile, the present volume is an opportunity to offer some reflections on the character and significance of Kilpatrick's work.

The volume is divided into two parts. In the first ('The Principles') are eight papers, written between 1957 and 1981. They include the seminal 'Atticism and the Text of the Greek New Testament' (1963), and 'The Greek New Testament of Today and the Textus Receptus' (1965). The second part ('Practice') is subdivided into three: 'General' (the three papers on the significance of the Western text in the Gospels, Acts and Epistles); 'Vocabulary and Grammar' – another eighteen pieces on various questions of style and usage; and finally forty articles on the text of specific passages. In addition, we are given a short biography with a *mise en scène* of the subject's text – critical principles, and a full bibliography of Kilpatrick's publications. The editor, Kilpatrick's most distinguished pupil and now the leading proponent of his theories, is to be congratulated on setting this feast before us.

It is well known that Kilpatrick is the propounder of what has come to be known as 'thoroughgoing eclecticism'. This method is partly founded on the eclecticism applied so elegantly to classical texts by A.E. Housman, and in describing his own views, Kilpatrick draws our attention to this (63, 115). In addition, we may note the influence of

C.H. Turner's 'reasoned eclecticism' (123; see also, 63, 113). To state it at its baldest, Westcott and Hort advocated the 'cult of the best manuscript'. Kilpatrick insists against this that, in determining in any one instance the correct reading, we must accord precedent to the criteria by which we first decided which manuscript was best. 'The important thing to remember is that the decision rests ultimately with the criteria as distinct from the manuscripts, and that our evaluation of the manuscripts must be determined by the criteria' (115). In practice, Kilpatrick concerned himself mainly with establishing the criteria significant in questions of style and wording. His thesis is that the New Testament texts were fairly extensively atticized from an early point in their transmission. It should be noted that he means precisely this – atticized, not classicized in a broader sense. The Attic authors are 'Thucydides, Plato, the Ten Orators and for the most part Aristophanes. To this we may add more recent discoveries like *Hellenica Oxyrynchia*, Menander, and Epicurus and the fragments of Attic Comedy and Oratory' (77).

Let us pause and consider the virtues of this kind of textual criticism. In the first place, it maintains the place of the New Testament texts and their transmission within the longer history of Greek literature. He is able to show, by his own extensive knowledge of the language, how words and forms disappeared and reappeared. And his evidence is that of contemporary writers rather than modern scholars. For example, on the question of whether ζήσω or ζήσομαι is correct, we are referred immediately to the *Antiatticista*: ζήσει: Πλάτων Πολιτείας ἕκτω, οὐ ζησεται (25, 75–8).

We can also see that Kilpatrick does not study readings in isolation from other readings. Variants are set, not only in the context of the history of the Greek language, but also of the style of the individual writer, and therefore indeed of the development of early Christianity (see, for example, 'Scribes, Lawyers, and Lucan Origins', 245–9).

Next, we can see that the Kilpatrick method does not permit the unthinking short cut which notes a concurrence of two significant manuscripts (perhaps P75 and B), and with no further consideration decides that this must be the correct reading. Whether or not you choose to dub this 'thororoughgoing eclecticism', the fact is that it is genuine textual criticism. It positively insists that we use our critical faculties in determining the original reading.

There is a question to be raised about this method, and it concerns the place of the history of the text. Housman, after all, drew up stemmata of his codices, and he was happy to talk about 'good' and 'bad' manuscripts. Kilpatrick has no comment to make on the character of manuscripts. And we discover that he delights in finding good readings in rejected texts: we find these ideas fully expressed in 'The Greek New Testament of Today and the *Textus Receptus*' (1965) and the papers on the western witnesses. But it would be wrong to say, as it is sometimes claimed, that he had no theory of textual history, or that he considered the question to be of no importance. Here it is necessary to discuss one aspect of his rejection of 'best manuscripts' theory that is not properly understood.

This is his endorsement of Vogels' theory that virtually all variant readings had been created by the year 200. He comes back to it regularly, and used the evidence of the papyri to support the claim (19). Later, the agreement of Aland is keenly noted (81). As soon as we have accepted Vogels' theory, then we can see that the date of our source for a given reading, be it fourth-, seventh-, or eleventh-century manuscripts, does not matter. We can be sure that the reading itself dates back to the period before 200. The importance of this aspect of Kilpatrick's theory is considerable. For he has set all the variants in a period from which virtually no manuscripts survive. It can therefore be said that there is no external evidence to be considered. We may note that he ably uses the evidence of P66 in support of his views. This manuscript has about seventy places where the scribe substituted one reading for another. This indicates that 'many of the differences between what our scribe first wrote and his subsequent corrections go back well into the second century' (5).

It should also be noted that Kilpatrick accepted the Westcott-Hort division of the materials into three major recensions, besides accepting the existence of the Caesarean text. Given his theory and his style of working with individual variants, he had no particular reason to try to replace these broader opinions with anything different. Rather, his intention is to challenge in detail the too easily made assumption that the 'Neutral' text is superior.

[213]

Thus we can see that Kilpatrick has a reconstruction of the history of the text. We could be forgiven for believing that he had not, for it is one in which individual manuscripts have no role. Where it is, I think, weak, is that it does not raise the question about how readings can in fact be typical of a given tradition. Kilpatrick seems to have been aware of this, and on the penultimate page of 'Western text in Gospels and Acts' he addresses the matter. Here he describes his view of the history of the text-types, going on to insist that he has 'no desire to make light of the importance of knowledge of the manuscripts and the principles of palaeography ... The problem of the original text and that of the various textual types are interdependent ... We may then conclude our inquiry by suggesting that ... although the Alexandrian text and especially B are our best authorities, yet all the early types and witnesses contribute something of value, and none can be rejected' (126f). How far this goes to meet the criticism may remain a question. I would suggest also that, even if most variants date from before 200, some information can be gathered from a study of the kinds of readings preferred by different traditions. For example, it may be true that some conflations in the Byzantine text are second century, but I find it hard to believe that the Syrian text's preference for such conflations tells me nothing about the place of such readings in the development of a standard ecclesiastical text; or that the characteristics of B anticipated in P75 do not provide evidence about the vital transition between the fluid period of the second century and the establishment of fixed types from the time of P75 onwards. The question of the credentials of this latter text is one of some importance. This is recognised in the closing paragraphs of 'Eclecticism and Atticism', a response to an article by C.M. Martini about Kilpatrick's methodology.

If we attempt to place his work within the history of textual criticism, we can see that the early modern critical period (Griesbach to Lachmann) attempted to find criteria for selecting readings, and sought out the oldest materials as the most worthy to which to apply these criteria. Westcott and Hort as it were brought these two strands together, arguing that certain manuscripts were generally to be followed on both counts. The period after them has often forgotten about the criteria, and followed manuscripts regarded as somehow more likely than not to be right. Kilpatrick sets his face against such mechanical and unthinking procedures by insisting on the criteria.

Let us return to the criteria. We find that they operate for certain kinds of variant, but not so frequently for ones of a more purely theological kind. (It must of course be said that to draw such a distinction between kinds of variants is not always wise.) There are of course exceptions. One is the argument that the original reading at Acts 7.56 was θεοῦ not ἀνθρώπου. I am not suggesting that the criteria of eclecticism cannot be applied to theologically motivated readings. Nor am I in any sense implying that the variants which he discusses, to some of which he returns several times, are not of significance and interest. But it suggests that Kilpatrick's use of his own principles was in practice often limited to variants in style and wording (does this reflect a limitation in the help that the textual criticism of classical literary texts practised by Housman can afford the theological New Testament?). The need for a copy of his preferred text, from which his views on other readings may be discovered, is all the more urgent. Already, a comparison of his text with Nestle-Aland[26] shows a marked divergence. To see how he handles certain important readings would help to redress the imbalance in the way that the currently available texts do not reflect the range of opinions in the text-critical debate.

Textual criticism advances, on the whole, by slow and patient reflection on detail. In an era during which many people have been blinded by the wonders of new discoveries, George Kilpatrick has continued the scholarly tradition of painstakingly applying internal criteria to the evidence. It is a strange irony that his method has been sometimes regarded as innovative or aberrant. We will understand his work better when we appreciate the influence of traditional British criticism upon his development.

Note

This is the only review in the book, and I included it because it is an assessment of an approach of some significance in English-speaking scholarship, namely thoroughgoing eclecticism. The later essay on the text of James (Chapter 16) shows that as a result of that study I became less confident that an 'anti-Atticising' approach improves the quality of our text.

16 The Development of the Critical Text of the Epistle of James

From Lachmann to the *Editio Critica Maior*

The appearance of the first fascicle of the *Editio Critica Maior* of the Institut für Neutestamentliche Textforschung, Münster, has already made a great impact on our perception of what a critical edition should achieve.[1] Its presentation is novel, and in its thoroughness and scope it amply deserves the sobriquet 'the new Tischendorf'. So what of the text? What does it contribute to the security of our knowledge of the text? When the exegete comments on the Epistle of James, what exactly will the words that comprise his study be? It is this question which will occupy us here.

The most noted point hitherto is probably the similarity to the text of Nestle-Aland[27]. In only two places has the wording of the text been changed: at 1.22 from μόνον ἀκροαταί to ἀκροαταὶ μόνον, and at 2.3 from ἐκεῖ ἢ κάθου to ἢ κάθου ἐκεῖ. In addition, the editors have jettisoned the brackets found in the Nestle text (for example at 4.12). Instead, they place • against variant readings which they consider as likely to be original as the text selected. This is in fact done in the second place where the new text differs from Nestle-Aland[27]. It is thus arguable that there is only one difference between the two editions.

In all there are eleven • readings. In all of them, there are two equal variants (never three or more):

Ref.	Text	• reading
1.20	οὐκ ἐργάζεται	οὐ κατεργάζεται
2.3	ἢ κάθου ἐκεῖ	ἐκεῖ ἢ κάθου
19	εἷς ἐστιν ὁ θεός	εἷς θεὸς ἐστιν
3.4	ἀνέμων σκληρῶν	σκληρῶν ἀνέμων
8	οὐδεὶς δαμάσαι δύναται ἀνθρώπων	οὐδεὶς δύναται δαμάσαι ἀνθρώπων
15	αὕτη ἡ σοφιά ἄνωθεν κατερχομένη	ἡ σοφιά αὕτη ἄνωθεν κατερχομένη

---

1   *Editio Critica Maior* 1. Lieferung *Der Jakobusbrief*. Teil 1 *Text*. Teil 2 *Begleitende Materialen*, Stuttgart, 1997.

4.12	ὁ	omit
14	τὸ	τὰ
	ποία	ποία γὰρ
5.10	ἐν τῷ ὀνόματι κυρίου	τῷ ὀνόματι κυρίου
18	ὑετὸν ἔδωκεν	ἔδωκεν ὑετὸν

While the editors have been criticised for changing the text so little, two things should be offered in their defence. The first is that the same materials on which they based their edition were available to the editors of Nestle-Aland[27]. The relevant volume of *Text und Textwert* was in preparation a long time ago.[2] The second is that, if a textual tradition has been studied afresh, and the text constituted agrees with what had already been considered good, then what can one do but be pleased to find that the critical decisions had been along the right lines all along?

One further question remains here: if the readings are of equal value, why is the one printed rather than the other? The answer, so far as may be ascertained by observation, is that the reading printed in the text is generally that read by 03 (Codex Vaticanus). There are three exceptions: the readings at 2.19, where the principal witnesses which the text follows are P74 01 02; 4.12, where they are 01 02; and 4.14, where the only major support is 01 (03 omits and does not support the other • reading, which is found in 02). One would expect the 03 text also at 2.19 and 4.12, where it is supported by P74 P100. But there may be some rationale which has escaped me. Every editor has to take a manuscript as the base text, and so one would not be surprised to find an individual witness such as B at all • readings. It may in fact be that the editors have operated in the same way as Westcott and Hort (see below), and to have felt a slight, even a very slight preference for the text reading over the alternative.

It was the study of these features, that is the similarity to the text of Nestle-Aland[27] and the use of •, which prompted me to compare the new text with that of some distinguished editors of the past, and to enquire how the manuscript evidence had influenced their decisions.

A measure of the distance that we have come is found when we note that a collation of the *Editio Critica Maior* against the Stephanus text of 1550[3] yields 67 variants, excluding movable nu and sigma, the variation -ημψ-/-ηψ-, and counting multiple mood differences in a

---

2   K. Aland (ed.), in Verb. m. A. Benduhn-Mertz, K. Witte u. G. Mink, *Text und Textwert der griechischen Handschriften des Neuen Testaments*, Bd. I, *Die Katholischen Briefe*, 3 vols. (ANTT 9–11), Berlin and New York, 1987. Of course, P100 was made available just in time for inclusion in the apparatus, but not for revision of the text.

3   Η Καινη Διαθηκη. *Novum Testamentum Textûs Stephanici A.D. 1550*..., ed. F.H.A. Scrivener, Cambridge and London, 1877.

sentence as one variant. This tally also excludes those places where the Textus Receptus has the alternative reading not in the text of *Editio Critica Maior* (1.20; 3.4; 4.14 OM/γάρ; 5.10).

Against this background, a good place to begin seems to be with the new edition's illustrious predecessor, Tischendorf's *Editio octava critica maior*. The results are somewhat predictable. It is sufficient to give the main witnesses supporting Tischendorf's choice of text.

Ref.	ECM	Tischendorf	Support
1.22	ἀκροαταὶ μόνον	μόνον ἀκροαταὶ	P74 01 02(*f) 04
27	τῷ θεῷ	θεῷ	01T 04C2
2.3	ἐπιβλέψητε δὲ	καὶ ἐπιβλέψητε	P74V 01 02
	• ἢ κάθου ἐκεῖ •	ἐκεῖ ἢ κάθου	02
6	ὑμῶν	ὑμᾶς	P74 01* 02
22	συνήργει	συνέργει	01* 02
3.6	καὶ ἡ γλῶσσα	ἡ γλῶσσα	01*
	ἡ σπιλοῦσα	καὶ σπιλοῦσα	01*
8	• δαμάσαι δύναται ἀνθρώπων •	δύν. ἀνθ. δαμ	**Byz**
14	καὶ ψεύδεσθε κατὰ τῆς ἀληθείας	τῆς ἀλ. καὶ ψεύδ.	01T 398
4.2	πολεμεῖτε οὐκ ἔχετε	πολεμ. καὶ οὐκ ἔχετε	01 025 044
4	τοῦ θεοῦ ἐστιν	ἐστιν τῷ θεῷ	01
9	καὶ κλαύσατε	κλαύσατε	01 02
	μετατραπήτω	μεταστραφήτω	01 02 044
14	• ποία •	ποία γὰρ	P74 P100 01Z 02 025 044
5.4	ἀπεστερημένος	ἀφυστερημένος	01 03*
	εἰσεληλύθασιν	εἰσεληλύθαν	03 025
9	ἀδελφοὶ κατ' ἀλλήλων	κατ' ἀλλ. ἀδελφ.	**Byz**
14	ἀλείψαντες αὐτὸν	ἀλείψαντες	03 025
18	• ὑετὸν ἔδωκεν •	ἔδωκεν ὑετὸν	02 044

There is a marked preference for Codex Sinaiticus in these twenty readings. But there is also a willingness to adopt late readings if they seem good enough, notably at 3.8 and 5.9. In fact, neither of these readings commends itself,[4] but we learn a little about Tischendorf's methods.

Textually, there seems to be no great affinity between these two editions. Since the edition of Westcott and Hort is often hailed as that which set the seal on the critical text of the New Testament, it is likely that the comparison between it and the *Editio Critica Maior* will be

---

4 The position of the vocative in 5.9 in the Münster text is consistent with that found elsewhere in the letter.

closer. It is also perhaps the one in which the reader will be most interested.[5] Since Westcott and Hort also operated a system of alternative readings, there are quite a few readings within this category, and it is worth providing them for both editions. I do not include various matters of punctuation for which Westcott and Hort provided alternatives:

Ref.	ECM text	alternative	WH text	margin
1.18	αὐτοῦ	-	αὐτοῦ	ἑαυτοῦ
20	οὐκ ἐργάζεται	οὐ κατεργάζεται	οὐκ ἐργάζεται	-
26	αὐτοῦ[1]	-	ἑαυτοῦ	αὐτοῦ
	αὐτοῦ[2]	-	ἑαυτοῦ	αὐτοῦ
2.3	ἢ κάθου ἐκεῖ	ἐκεῖ ἢ κάθου	ἢ κάθου ἐκεῖ	ἐκεῖ ἢ κάθου
4	οὐ	-	οὐ	OM
19	εἷς ἐστιν ὁ θεός	εἷς θεός ἐστιν	εἷς θεός ἐστιν	εἷς ὁ θεός ἐστιν
26	γὰρ	-	OM	γὰρ
3.4	ἀνέμων σκληρῶν	σκληρῶν ἀνέμων	ἀνέμων σκληρῶν	-
8	δαμάσαι δύναται	δύναται δαμάσαι	δαμάσαι δύναται	-
15	αὕτη ἡ σοφιά	ἡ σοφιά αὕτη	αὕτη ἡ σοφιά	-
4.9	μετατραπήτω	-	μετατραπήτω	μεταστραφήτω
12	ὁ νομοθέτης	νομοθέτης	νομοθέτης	ὁ νομοθέτης
14	τὸ	τὰ	OM[6]	τὰ
	OM	γὰρ	OM	γὰρ
	ἡ[2]	-	OM	ἡ
15	θελήσῃ	-	θέλῃ	θελήσῃ
5. 10	ἐν τῷ ὀνόματι	τῷ ὀνόματι	ἐν τῷ ὀνόματι	-
11	ὁ κύριος	-	ὁ κύριος	κύριος
16	εὔχεσθε	-	προσεύχεσθε	εὔχεσθε
18	ὑετὸν ἔδωκεν	ἔδωκεν ὑετὸν	ὑετὸν ἔδωκεν	-
20	αὐτοῦ ἐκ θανάτου	-	αὐτοῦ ἐκ θανάτου	ἐκ θανάτου αὐτοῦ

Several of these readings appear below, when the two possibilities in the one edition are not the same pair as those in the other. It should be noted that Westcott and Hort do not state that their two readings are absolutely on a par: 'Wherever it has been found impossible to decide that one of two or more variant readings is certainly right, alternative readings are given; and no alternative reading is given which does not appear to have a reasonable probability of being the true reading. The primary place in the text itself is assigned to those readings which on the whole are the more probable, or in cases of equal probability the better attested'. It could thus be argued that the text reading of the Cambridge editors should be included in the list of genuine differences,

---

5 Westcott and Hort.

6 Westcott and Hort themselves place this and the next variant together in the alternative text: τὰ τῆς αὔριον· ποία γὰρ ἡ ζωὴ ὑμῶν; ἀτμίς ἐστε ἡ.

but that the wording of the *Editio Critica Maior* description of alternatives does not allow one to include their text reading. However, I take only those readings where the actual texts differ.

There are nine readings where the two differ.[7] Since Westcott and Hort has no *apparatus criticus*, I have supplied the deficiency from the *Editio Critica Maior*, concentrating on those witnesses which I think could have been known to the editors.

Ref.	ECM		MS Support
2.14	ECM	τὸ	02. 03. 04C2. 044. 63 minuscules. **Byz**. Cyr. PsOec
	WH	OM	B C*
16	ECM	τὸ	all witnesses except 03. 04* and those which are deficient or ambiguous
	WH	OM	B C*
19	ECM	εἷς ἐστιν ὁ θεός	P74. 01. 02. 442. 621. 1735. 1842. 2464. L596. AnastS. Cyr
		εἷς θεὸς ἐστιν	see next line
	WH	εἷς θεὸς ἐστιν	B. 19 minuscules. L1440
		εἷς ὁ θεὸς ἐστιν	C 33 81 five other minuscules
4.8	ECM	ἐγγιεῖ	all witnesses except 03 and those which are deficient or ambiguous
	WH	ἐγγισεῖ	B
14	ECM	τὸ /	01. 044. 35 minuscules. **Byz**. GregAgr. PsOec
		OM	see next line
	WH	OM /	B
		τὰ	A P 33 81 36 other minuscules, one lectionary, and Syr^h
5.4	ECM	ἀπεστερημένος	all witnesses except 01 03* and those which are deficient or ambiguous
	WH	ἀφυστερημένος	ℵ B*
	ECM	εἰσεληλύθασιν	all witnesses except those cited below, those which are deficient or ambiguous, and those few supporting two other variants
	WH	εἰσεληλύθαν	B P 81 four other minuscules
20	ECM	γινωσκέτω	all witnesses except those cited below, those which are deficient or ambiguous, and those few supporting other variants
	WH	γινώσκετε	B 69 88 (a few other minuscules with sub-variants)

What is the explanation of the differences? It is really very simple. Every single time, Westcott and Hort follow Codex Vaticanus. Other editors have rejected the reading of B at these places. Yet again, we find an instance of a particular editor showing partiality towards a particular manuscript.

---

7 Excepting a few matters of orthography, such as 3.14 ἐριθείαν ECM] ἐριθίαν WH; 16 ἐριθεία] ἐριθεία; 5.10 κακοπαθείας] κακοπαθίας.

The two are quite close. But the degree must be tested by further comparisons. The first is with the edition prepared by G.D. Kilpatrick.[8] There are a total of thirty-six differences, of which only two are orthographic, and not including places where Kilpatrick has the apparatus • reading.[9]

Ref.	ECM	Kilpatrick
1.25	OM	οὗτος
26	OM	ἐν ὑμῖν
2.3	ἐπιβλέψητε δὲ	καὶ ἐπιβλέψητε
	OM	αὐτῷ
6	ὑμῶν	ὑμᾶς
10	τηρήσῃ, πταίσῃ	τηρήσει, πταίσει
13	OM	καὶ
18	τῶν ἔργων	τῶν ἔργων σου
	σοι δείξω	δείξω σοι
	μου τὴν πίστιν	τὴν πίστιν μου
26	γὰρ	OM
3.8	δαμάσαι δύναται	δύναται δαμάσαι
12	οὔτε	οὔτως οὐδὲ
17	OM	καὶ
4.2	οὐκ ἔχετε	καὶ οὐκ ἔχετε
4	OM	μοιχοὶ καὶ
7	ἀντίστητε δὲ	ἀντίστητε
8	ἐγγιεῖ	ἐγγισεῖ
12	σὺ δὲ	σὺ
	ὁ κρίνων	ὅς κρίνεις
13	ἢ	καὶ
	OM	ἕνα
15	θελήσῃ	θέλῃ
	ζήσομεν καὶ ποιήσομεν	ζήσωμεν καὶ ποιήσωμεμν
5.4	ἀπεστερημένος	ἀφυστερημένος
	εἰσεληλύθασιν	εἰσεληλύθαν
5	OM	ὡς
9	κριθῆτε	κατακριθῆτε
11	ὑπομείναντας	ὑπομένοντας
13	statements	questions
16	οὖν	OM
	εὔχεσθε	προσεύχεσθε
20	γινωσκέτω	γινώσκετε

Probably the most obvious difference may be expressed as the observation that James' Greek is better in the *Editio Critica Maior* than in

---

8   *A Greek-English Diglot for the use of Translators. The General Letters*, London, 1961.
9   1.20 οὐκ ἐργάζεται: οὐ κατεργάζεται; 2.3 ἢ κάθου ἐκεῖ: ἐκεῖ ἢ κάθου; 4.14 τὸ: τὰ; 5. 18 ὑετὸν ἔδωκεν: ἔδωκεν ὑετὸν.

the Kilpatrick text. That is to say, that Kilpatrick's version, by consistently refusing the better writing, presumably on the grounds that it is an Atticism, has made the style worse at a number of points. In my opinion, the overall style of the letter does not justify this: the Greek is good enough where it is not in doubt for us to prefer the stylistically superior reading where Kilpatrick rejects it. A second difference, one that is a consequence of the first, is that Kilpatrick's is longer by eight words.

Then, by way of contrast, we turn to what is generally regarded as the first fully critical edition, that of Lachmann.[10] When we have discounted sundry small orthographical matters, we have eighteen differences. The best way of comparing the editions is to focus on the materials available to the earlier editor. But I also note the papyrus readings.

Ref.	ECM	MS support	Lachmann	MS support
1.26	OM	01 02 03	δὲ	04 L:FV
	καρδίαν αὐτοῦ	044 min Byz	καρδίαν ἑαυτοῦ	03 04
2.3	ἐπιβλέψητε δὲ	03 04	καὶ ἐπιβλέψητε	P74V 01 02 L:V
6	οὐχ	01 03 04C2	οὐχὶ	02 04*V
14	τί τὸ ὄφελος	01 02 04C2	τί ὄφελος	03 04*
	λέγῃ τις	01 03	τις λέγῃ	02 04
16	τί τὸ ὄφελος	01 02 04C2	τί ὄφελος	03 04*
18	σοι δείξω	01 03	δείξω σοι	P74 02 04 L:V
	τὴν πίστιν	01 03 04	τὴν πίστιν μου	02 L:G
26	ἔργων	P20 P74 01 03	[τῶν] ἔργων	02 04
3.4	ὅπου ... βούλεται	01 03 only	ὅπου ἂν ... βούληται	02 04
15	ἀλλὰ	01 03 1893 only	ἀλλ'	02 04
4.9	μετατραπήτω	P100 03	μεταστραφήτω	01 02
14	ἀτμὶς γὰρ	03	ἀτμὶς	02 L:V
5.4	εἰσεληλύθασιν	01 02f1	εἰσεληλύθαν	03
7	ἕως	P74 02 03	ἕως ἂν	01
14	τοῦ κυρίου	01	κυρίου	02
16	εὔχεσθε	01	προσεύχεσθε	03

It is rather noticeable that Lachmann seems to be heavily dependent upon the combination 02 04. Where 04 is lacunose (from 4.2/30–32 onwards) he seems to have difficulty in making up his mind. Since 04 had only been made fully available (in Tischendorf's transcription) in 1843,[11] it seems that Lachmann was heavily influenced by this recent

[324]

---

10 K. Lachmann, *Novum Testamentum Graece et Latine*, Berlin, 1842–50.
11 The MS was first cited in Kuster's Mill (1710). See F.H.A. Scrivener, *A Plain Introduction to the Criticism of the New Testament for the Use of Biblical Students*, 2 vols., 4th ed., revd E. Miller; London, New York and Cambridge, 1894, 121f.

acquisition to knowledge. With eighteen differences, we see that Lachmann was still feeling his way towards a critical text.

Finally, there is a marked advance when we compare the new text with that of an English-speaking scholar whose contribution has been compared to that of Lachmann, the Cornishman Samuel Prideaux Tregelles.[12] There are fewest differences between this text and the *Editio Critica Maior*, only six:[13]

Ref.	ECM	Tregelles
2.3	ἐπιβλέψητε δὲ	καὶ ἐπιβλέψητε
4.4	ἐάν	ἄν
9	μετατραπήτω	μεταστραφήτω
5.4	ἀπεστερημένος	ἀφυστερημένος
	εἰσεληλύθασιν	εἰσεληλύθαν
20	αὐτοῦ	OM

Tregelles has his own system of • readings, by placing the variant in the left margin. These are not so much readings on which a decision cannot be made, as a provisional list of ones where further reflection is required. The system is very sophisticated, with the use of square brackets creating a system with at least four tiers:

text without any proviso
brackets around material in the text
square brackets around material in the margin.
unbracketed material in the margin

His explanations are as follows:

Words between brackets in the text are such as I judge to be of very doubtful authority . . .
A reading given in the margin without any mark, is an *alternative reading;* that is, one as to which the authorities are divided between what stands in the text and what is thus placed in the margin. These alternative readings may, in some cases, require a more detailed consideration; some additional ones may need to be specified, and more definite conclusions may at times be given.
Words in brackets in the margin imply that they are somewhat doubtful.
A reading bracketed in the text and marked 'om.' in the margin is exceedingly doubtful.
A possible or not improbable addition is given in brackets in the margin.[14]

---

12 S.P. Tregelles, *The Greek New Testament, edited from ancient authorities, with their various readings in full*, London,. 1857–79. Part III. Acts and Catholic Epistles, 1865.
13 One can hardly include 3.11 μήτι ECM] μή τι Tregelles.
14 Part III, i–ii.

The tradition of wise reticence where the editor is at a stand thus has a long history. Here follows a list of the readings where Tregelles was uncertain.

Ref.	Tregelles' Text	Tregelles' Margin
1.22	ἀκροαταὶ μόνον	μόνον ἀκροαταὶ
26	Εἴ τις	εἴ [δέ] τις[15]
2.3	καὶ ἐπιβλέψητε	ἐπιβλέψητε δὲ
14	τὸ	[τὸ]
	λέγῃ τις	τις λέγῃ
16	τὸ	[τὸ]
18	σοι δείξω	δείξω σοι
19	εἷς ἐστιν ὁ θεὸς	εἷς θεὸς ἐστιν
22	συνέργει	συνήργει
26	[τῶν] ἔργων	
3.3	αὐτοὺς ἡμῖν	ἡμῖν αὐτοὺς
4	ὅπου	ὅπου [ἂν]
8	δαμάσαι δύναται ἀνθρώπων	δύν. δαμ. ἀνθ.
4.14	τὸ τῆς αὔριον	[τὰ] τῆς αὔριον
	ποία [γὰρ]	
15	θελήσῃ	θέλῃ
5.14	[τοῦ] κυρίου	
16	εὔχεσθε	προσεύχεσθε
18	ἔδωκεν ὑετὸν	ὑετὸν ἔδωκεν
20	γινωσκέτω	γινώσκετε
	ψυχὴν	ψυχὴν [αὐτοῦ]

It is noteworthy that later editors tend to confirm Tregelles' provisional preference. Certainly, only at 2.3 and 5.14 does the *Editio Critica Maior* differ from it.

Let us look at the reasons for Tregelles' readings in a little more detail, by giving the *Editio Critica Maior* support for *its* readings, and Tregelles' for *his*:

Ref.		MS support
2.3	ECM ἐπιβλέψητε δὲ	03. 04. 025. 044. 30 minuscules. L:F. S:H
	Treg καὶ ἐπιβλέψητε	A ℵ 13.31 LK (e sil. Matt.) Vulg. Syr.Pst. (Memph.) Theb. Æth.
4.4	ECM ἐὰν	ℵ* B 01*f. 03. 025. 8 minuscules
	Treg ἂν	A ℵc. 13s. 31s. KsL.
4.9	ECM μετατραπήτω	P100. 03. 025. 26 minuscules. L596
	Treg μεταστραφήτω	Tregelles simply notes the reading of B
5.4	ECM ἀπεστερημένος	all witnesses except 01. 03* and those which are deficient or ambiguous

---

15 The brackets implies that such wording is 'somewhat doubtful' (p. ii).

	Treg ἀφυστερημένος	B* Rl.Mai ℵ.
	ECM εἰσεληλύθασιν	01. 02f1. 044. 59 minuscules. **Byz**. Cyr. Dam(f1). PsOec
	Treg εἰσεληλύθαν	BP.
5.20	ECM αὐτοῦ	all witnesses except L884 (omits), and those which are lacunose (also, 38 reads αὐτοῦ, and so the majuscules could read αὐτοῦ or αὑτοῦ).
	Treg OM	B. 31. KsL. *ff*.

It will be noted that Tregelles anticipated the *Editio Critica Maior* in nearly every place where the latter disagrees with Westcott and Hort. Only in the two readings at 5.4 do Tregelles and Westcott/Hort agree against the new edition.

With Tregelles, it is his preference for A which distinguishes him from the *Editio Critica Maior*. His preference for A against B in itself shows wisdom, for subsequent scholarship has continued to support the conclusion that A is indeed a better manuscript in this part of the New Testament.

Observations and Conclusions

1. If the impression has been given that there is any great dispute over most of the wording of James, it has been given accidentally. A total of 64 variants have been listed in one place or another. If one sets aside the Kilpatrick text, the number is only 41.

2. The differences between the editions consist for the most part in ones of word order, word formation, use of particles and conjunctions and articles, inclusion of pronouns. If any of them is of sufficient weight to cause extensive exegetical confusion, the fact has escaped my attention. Their interest, and it is not the less for that, is in the detailed study of James' style and, especially where conjunctions are concerned, the putting together of the epistle.

3. It is rather remarkable that in only one place are the five editions we have consulted unanimous against the *Editio Critica Maior*. Even if we except Kilpatrick, there is still only this one reading. It is εἰσεληλύθαν against εἰσεληλύθασιν at 5.4. This study would become unjustifiably long were it to study all those grammatical points where the editions differ. But this one is worth a glance.

An examination of the formation of the third person plural of the perfect indicative active in the Greek New Testament reveals the following places where there is no variation:[16]

Matthew 2.20	τεθνήκασιν
Matthew 12.47	ἑστήκασιν (ἑστήκεισαν D)
Mark 8.3	ἥκασιν ({ἤκουσιν pc)
Luke 8.20	ἑστήκασιν (εἱστήκεισαν 1342)
Luke 13.2	πεπόνθασιν
John 4.38	κεκοπιάκασιν (ἐκοπιάκασιν D)
John 15.24	ἑω(ο)ράκασιν
John 15.24	μεμ(ε)ισήκασιν
Acts 17.28	εἰρήκασι(ν)
Acts 26.4	ἴσασι(ν)
Romans 15.21	ἀκηκόασιν
Hebrews 12.8	γεγόνασιν
1 John 2.18	γεγόνασιν
1 John 4.1	ἐξεληλύθασιν
Revelation 8.2	ἑστήκασιν

Thus only the ending in -ασι(ν) is undisputed. Variation occurs at the following places:

1. Luke 9.36 ἑώ(ό)ρακαν P45C (ἑόρακεν P45*) 03 04C2 L X min pc
   ἑωράκασιν 01 02 Πc BYZ
   ἑωράκεισαν 443; ἑωράκησαν 472 1009; ἐθέασαν D

2. John 17.6 τετήρηκαν 03 05 W L
   τετηρήκασιν 02 04 A K Θ Π Ψ fam1 BYZ
   ἐτήρησαν 01 33

3. John 17.7 ἔγνωκαν pler
   ἐγνώκασιν S pc
   ἔγνων 01 pc

4. Acts 16.36 ἀπέστελκαν 01 02 03
   ἀπεστάλκασιν 05 08 014 020 025 pler

5. Romans 16.7 γέγοναν 01 02 03
   γεγόνασιν 04 020 025 pler

6. Colossians 2.1 ἑό(ώ)ρακαν 01* 02 03 04 06* 025
   ἑο(ω)ράκασι 01C 06C 018 020 cet

7. James 5.4 εἰσελήλυθασιν 01 02f1 044 Byz
   εἰσεληλύθαν 03 025 81 720 1175 1243 2492
   εἰσεληλύθεισαν 048V 235 1524 1850 2718
   ἐληλύθασιν 1505 2495

[328]

---

16 Of course I do not include οἴδασι(ν), which is unvaried (Lk 11.44; 23.34; Jn 10.4; 10.5; 15.21; 18.21; Jude 10).

8. Revelation 18.3   πέπ(τ)ωκαν 02 04 2031 al
                      πεπ(τ)ώκασιν 01 pc
                      also πέπ(τ)ωκε, πεπότικε, πέποκε etc
9. Revelation 19.3   εἴρηκαν 01 02 025 pc
                      εἰρήκασιν pler
10. Revelation 21.6   γέγοναν 02 min pc
                      γεγόνασιν min pc
                      γέγονε/ γέγονα etc pler

There is no reason why all New Testament authors should prefer one form to the other, and from this point of view the inconsistency of Alexandrinus outside the Gospels looks quite impressive. And in fact the Nestle-Aland[27] text follows A every time. See Westcott and Hort, who write that there are 'a few well attested examples of the curious substitution of –αν for –ασι in the 3 pl. of perfects (see Curtius *Gr.Verb.*[2] ii 187), a peculiarity called Alexandrian by Sextus Empiricus (*Adv.Gramm.* 213), but certainly of wider range'.[17] It could be argued that the ending –αν is more likely to have been eroded by the other than vice versa, and thus that it is original here. If anything, however, earlier editors may have understated the strength of –ασι in the tradition where there is variation. Here, the third reading, also attested fairly early, might appear to be a development from –ασι, leading to the conclusion that –ασι is original. One would then, of course, have to account for the introduction of the rarer ending in –αν, and this appears to be a very strong objection to the reading of the *Editio Critica Maior*. One would like to know the editors' explanation for their choice.

4. The example of Lachmann with Codex Ephraemi Rescriptus, Tischendorf with Sinaiticus, and Westcott and Hort with Vaticanus, illustrate how fatal too great a preoccupation with a single witness is to critical judgement, while Kilpatrick's mistaken application of his views to this letter shows the risks of applying a single principle to an entire *corpus* of texts. The fact that the Münster editors have been so careful in their use of the papyrus evidence speaks in their favour, while his consistency of view and breadth of appreciation of the material demonstrates Tregelles to be their precursor.

5. Another look at the places where the *Editio Critica Maior* and Tregelles differ gives credit to each. We have already seen that Tregelles is probably right at the second difference in 5.4. With regard to 4.4, Mayor observes that 'the use of ἐάν instead of ἄν with relatives

---

17   *The New Testament in the Original Greek*, Vol. 2, 173.

... is very common in N.T., especially after a vowel'.[18] Mayor points to the frequency with which the feature has also been removed from the manuscripts by editors of classical authors. The reading ἐάν is now well established.

The *Editio Critica Maior* is certainly right at 2.3 (the sequence γὰρ ... δὲ ... δὲ is found elsewhere in the letter: 1.13f). At 4.9 (ECM μετατραπήτω; Tregelles μεταστραφήτω), again the new text is preferable. The grounds for supporting it are that μετατρέπω (found nowhere else in early Christian literature) has been supplanted by the somewhat more familiar μεταστρέφω. A similar question arises with regard to the second divergence at 5.4. The reading is not without contemporary support.[19] Ἀφυστερημένος is the rarer word, and was subsequently emended by copyists to the more common word.

The final reading is one of the most interesting exegetically.[20] Tregelles may have been surprised by the repetition of the pronoun, although he accepted it in the similar circumstances at 5.14 (where the *Editio Critica Maior* is more confident than Nestle-Aland[27]). The pronoun should be read.

Of the six readings, I therefore find in favour of Tregelles three times (4.4 ἄν; 5.4 ἀφυστερημένος; εἰσεληλύθαν) and of the *Editio Critica Maior* three times (2.3 ἐπιβλέψητε δὲ; 4.9 μετατραπήτω; 5.20 αὐτοῦ). There are thus still a few places where the debate continues.

[330]

6. The fact that Tregelles comes out of this comparison with Lachmann, Tischendorf, Westcott and Hort and the *Editio Critica Maior* suggests that we need to reconsider the usual view of nineteenth-century textual criticism as a linear development culminating in *The New Testament in the Original Greek*. It may be that we have overlooked the significance and standard of Tregelles' achievement. For thoroughness of citation, the *Editio Critica Maior* may be the new Tischendorf, but so far as its text goes it deserves to be called the new Tregelles.

---

18   J.B. Mayor, *The Epistle of St. James. The Greek Text with Introduction Notes and Comments and Further Studies in the Epistle of St. James*, London, 1913, 139.
19   See Metzger, *Textual Commentary*[1], where Metzger records his own (minority) support for it.
20   It is preferred by Mayor on internal grounds (*op. cit.*, 183).

Notes

These comparisons were made against the original 1997 fascicle of the *Editio maior*. Users of any subsequent revisions should remember that the text may have changed.

The name Tregelles is a stumbling block to many, so a word of explanation may solve the problem. It is a Cornish name of three syllables, with the stress on the second syllable: Tre-*gel*-lis. There is a rhyme;

By Tre-, Pol- and Pen
You may know Cornishmen.

17 A Comparison between the *Text und Textwert* and the Claremont Profile Method Analyses of Manuscripts in the Gospel of Luke

The appearance of the Münster analysis of the Greek manuscripts containing Luke makes it possible to compare the Institut für Neutestamentliche Textforschung's (INTF) and the International Greek New Testament Project's (IGNTP) methods and results. The volumes compared are the INTF's two Lukan volumes in the *Text und Textwert* series[1] and Frederick Wisse's presentation of the IGNTP manuscript profiling.[2]

1. Introductory Comments

1. It is important to be aware that for *Text und Textwert* (*TuT*), the aim is to find a way of identifying those manuscripts which are Byzantine, and those which contain another form of text. The Claremont Profile Method (CPM), on the other hand, attempts to place a manuscript that *TuT* would describe as BYZ within a sub-group.

2. For INTF the text taken as point of reference is Nestle-Aland[27],[3] while for IGNTP it is the Textus Receptus (TR).[4] Both are used not as an authority but as a convenient tool.

3. The overlap of test passages between *TuT* and CPM is almost nil. The reason for this is that CPM selects blocks of text for analysis (in the case of Luke, chapters 1, 10 and 20), whereas *TuT* selects individual variants (Teststellen [TS]) from the whole text. There are 54 Teststellen

[109]

---

1 K. Aland†, B. Aland, K. Wachtel (eds., in association with Klaus Witte), *Text und Textwert der Griechischen Handschriften des Neuen Testaments. IV. Die Synoptischen Evangelien* (ANTT 26–31). 3. *Das Lukasevangelium. Band 3,1: Handschriftenliste und Vergleichende Beschreibung. Band 3,2: Resultate der Kollation und Hauptliste sowie Ergänzungen*, Berlin, 1999.
2 F. Wisse, *The Profile Method for Classifying and Evaluating Manuscript Evidence* (SD 44), Grand Rapids, 1982.
3 *Nestle-Aland*[27], Stuttgart, 1993.
4 *Novum Testamentum*, Oxford, 1873.

for Luke. This averages just over two per chapter, though they are not spread as evenly as that. In Luke, the first comes at 2.14, and the distribution thereafter is shown in Table 1:

Table 1: Chapter Distribution of Teststellen in Luke

Ch. no.	No. of TS	Ch. no.	No. of TS	Ch. no.	No. of TS	Ch. no.	No. of TS
1	0	7	1	13	2	19	3
2	3	8	2	14	1	20	1
3	0	9	5	15	2	21	2
4	2	10	3	16	3	22	2
5	2	11	2	17	1	23	4
6	4	12	3	18	2	24	4

There are therefore only four variants in common between the 196 of CPM and those in *TuT*.

10.21, CPM Reading 36 = TS 20 (N-A^{27} εν τω πνευματι τω αγιω)
10.22 CPM Reading 37 = TS 21 (inclusion/exclusion of και στραφεις προς τους μαθητας κατ᾿ ιδιαν ειπεν)
10.38, CPM Reading 59 = TS 22 (N-A^{27} αυτον)
20.27, CPM Reading 48 = TS 42 (N-A^{27} οι [αντι]λεγοντες)

The important question is whether CPM and *TuT* found similar results or not. In order to test this, I took the test case of Wisse's Group 1519. It is suitable, because it was a newly discovered group. That is, its existence is based on the CPM.

2. Group 1519 According to Wisse

Wisse found nineteen manuscripts to belong to the group in at least a part of Luke.[5] Nine are members in all three test chapters:

    32   269   871   1036   1321   1519   1566   2126   2437

Ten more were found to be members in chapter 20 only:

    5   558   844   1110   1211   1309   1416   1481   2132   2277

In chapters 1 and 10, these ten manuscripts stand close to K^x.[6] Among them, there were two pairs.[7] These pairs are 32/269 and 1309/2132. 1110

---

5 Wisse, *Profile Method*, 109.
6 The Kappa x group was named by von Soden. The 'x' indicates an unknown quantity: 'De diese zwischen K^I und K^r liegende Grösse bei erneuter Durcharbeitung des Materials also vielleicht noch aufgelöst werden kann, bezeichne ich sie mit K$^{x'}$.

and 2277 belong to K^x Cluster (Cl) 2592 in Luke 1 and 10. The full information for the group members is as follows:

Table 2: Profile Of Group 1519 Members According To CPM

MS	Ch 1	Ch 10	Ch 20	Comments
5	Mix[8]	Kmix[9]	1519	
32	1519	1519	1519	pair with 269
269	1519	1519	1519	pair with 32
558	K^r[10]	K^r	1519	
844	Mix	Kmix	1519	fragm in 1
871	1519	1519	1519	
1036	1519	NP[11]	1519	weak member
1110	K^x	K^x	1519	Cl 2592 in 1 and 10
1211	K^x	K^x	1519	surplus in 20[12]
1309	K^x	K^x	1519	pair with 2132
1321	1519	1519	1519	surplus in 1; fragm in 20
1416	Kmix	NP	1519	
1481	Kmix	K^x	1519	
1519	1519	1519	1519	
1566	1519	1519	1519	weak in 1
2126	1519	1519	1519	
2132	K^x	K^x	1519	pair with 1309
2277	K^x	K^x	1519	Cl 2592 in 1 and 10
2437	1519	1519	1519	surplus in 10}

H. von Soden, *Die Schriften des Neuen Testaments in ihrer ältesten erreichbarren Textgestalt hergestellt auf grund ihrer Textgeschichte*, Göttingen, 1902–13, 1, 2 (1911), 713. Wisse's definition is 'The dominant text from the ninth to the thirteenth century' (50). The term 'group' to define K^x certainly requires scrutiny.

Wisse's definition of clusters is: 'Clusters generally refer to groups of less than ten members. Many clusters are actually subgroups belonging to one of the main groups' (51). They are usually numbered after the Gregory-Aland number of the member manuscript with the lowest number (*ibid.*).

7   A pair of manuscripts is defined as being close enough for it to be possible that they form exemplar and copy (no attempt is possible on the basis of CPM to establish the direction of copying). Wisse, *Profile Method*, 49, n. 11.
8   Defined as 'Profiles which do not conform to any of the groups or clusters but which stand relatively close to K$^{x'}$ (51).
9   Defined as 'Profiles which do not conform to any of the groups or clusters and which diverge significantly from K$^{x'}$ (51).
10 Defined as 'A Byzantine recension of the twelfth century which is characterized by a distinct lectionary equipment and careful scribal control' (50).
11 Stands for No Profile (i.e. the manuscript was not profiled in this chapter).
12 'Most MSS will have some test readings which are not shared by the majority of the group to which they belong. These "surplus" readings tend to increase when a MS misses some of the primary readings of its group', Wisse, 41.

3. Group 1519 according to *TuT*

How does this group stand up in *TuT*? In the Hauptliste,[13] the answer is that it is not very evident. But, as we shall see, this is not as serious a problem as it first appears to be. These are the manuscripts listed as closest to 1519, in its 6 non-MT Teststellen,[14] with manuscripts in Wisse's Group 1519 in bold:

Table 3: Profile Of Group 1519 Members According To Hauptliste

MS	%[15]	no. of readings	CPM classification in Chapters 1/10/20 (+ notes)
36	66.7	4/6	NP (Commentary MS)
2100	66.7	2/3	NP (Commentary MS)
24	50.0	3/6	NP (Commentary MS)
1309	**50.0**	**3/6**	**Kˣ/Kˣ/1519 (pair with 2132)**
166	50.0	2/4	Def[16]/Λ/Λ[17] (Core member)
1814	50.0	1/2	NP (Commentary MS)
P75	40.0	2/5	NP (excluded as fragmentary)
496	40.0	2/5	1167/1167/1167[18]
527	40.0	2/5	Kˣ/Kˣ/Kˣ (corrected to conform with Π268[19])
948	40.0	2/5	Kmix/NP/Kˣ
2182	40.0	2/5	Kˣ/Kˣ/Kˣ

---

13 The Hauptliste is defined as follows: 'ermöglich die Hauptliste den Vergleich von Variationsprofilen oder Lesartenfolgen. Dabei werden nur die Teststellen einbezogen, an denen die jeweilige Ausgangshandschrift vom Mehrheitstext abweicht und keine Singulärlesart hat' (K. Aland†, B. Aland, K. Wachtel (eds, in association with Klaus Witte), *Text und Textwert der Griechischen Handschriften des Neuen Testaments. IV. Die Synoptischen Evangelien* (ANTT 26–31). 1. *Das Markusevangelium. Band 1,1: Handschriftenliste und Vergleichende Beschreibung*, Berlin, 1998 (cited below as *TuT, Markus*), 7*.

14 MT stands for Majority Text (i.e. the majority of witnesses in this passage). The figures in the following table differ from those published in *TuT* (Vol. 2, 297), because those were affected by a miscalculation. I am grateful to Dr Klaus Wachtel of INTF for spotting the discrepancy in an earlier draft of this paper and generously making the revised figures available to me. The corrections are also available online at http://purl.org/TC/downloads.

15 The percentage of agreements with the primary manuscript (1519) in the six readings (*TuT, Markus*, 8*).

16 Is deficient.

17 Group L is defined by Wisse, 102–3. Von Soden's Iʳ group, it is related to early forms of Kˣ.

18 Group 1167 'stands out from Kˣ mainly in Luke 20', Wisse, 108.

19 A cluster within the Π Group.

MS	%	no. of readings	CPM classification in Chapters 1/10/20 (+ notes)
01	33.3	2/6	B/B/B[20]
03	33.3	2/6	B/B/B
033	33.3	2/6	Mix/Mix/Def (fragmentary in 10; some relationship to Gr B)
15	33.3	2/6	K^x/NP/K^x (belongs to Cl 43; pair with 1163)
40	33.3	2/6	NP (Commentary MS)
98	33.3	2/6	K^x/K^x/Kmix (some relationship to M groups)[21]
169	33.3	2/6	K^x/NP/K^x (some relationship to Cl 1442)
186	33.3	2/6	NP (Commentary MS)
190	33.3	2/6	Cl 190/Cl 190/Cl 190[22]
213	33.3	2/6	Mix/Mix/Mix
240	33.3	2/6	NP (Commentary MS)
274	33.3	2/6	K^x/NP/K^x
475	33.3	2/6	K^x/Cl 475/Cl 475[23]
680	33.3	2/6	K^x/K^x/K^x (Cl 43)
863	33.3	2/6	NP (Commentary MS)
871	**33.3**	**2/6**	**1519/1519/1519**
892	33.3	2/6	B/B/B (core member)
951	33.3	2/6	1167/1167/1167
981	33.3	2/6	NP
1008	33.3	2/6	K^x/K^x/K^x
1163	33.3	2/6	K^x/K^x/K^x (Cl 43; pair with 15)
1166	33.3	2/6	Mix/K^x/K^x

[112]

Only 1309 and 871 are present in both lists. Given the closeness of Group 1519 to K^x pointed out by Wisse, and given the fact that this analysis covers such a narrow span of readings – a maximum of six! – and given that Wisse did not include commentary manuscripts (36 40 186 240 863 1814 2100 are all in this category) or fragmentary manuscripts (P75), the lack of connection between these two lists is not particularly surprising. It is at any rate worth noting that there are hints of consistency: three out of ten members of Cluster 43[24] and two (out of 22) of Group 1167[25] are present.

---

20 Wisse's name for Alexandrian witnesses. Mainly as a consequence of the exclusion of singular readings in his method, 05 is included in the group.
21 Von Soden's I$^{\Phi r}$, which Wisse found to be more diverse than had previously been thought.
22 A cluster consisting of 190 2472 2695 2724 (this only in chapters 1 and 10), closely related to Gr 1519 in ch. 20 (Wisse, 110).
23 Cl 375 consists of manuscripts 475 2609 2373 and 'appears' to be related to the M groups (Wisse, 110).
24 Cluster 43 is a cluster within K^x. The members are 15, 43, 680, 1163, 1350, 1364, 1592, 2195 (Luke 10), 2420 and 2539 (Wisse, 95).
25 Group 1167 'stands out from K^x mainly in Luke 20. Six of its members were classified A^k by von Soden' (Wisse, 108). Its members are 75, 116 (Luke 20), 225 (Luke 10 and 20), 245 (Luke 10 and 20), 431, 496, 546, 578 (Luke 20), 843, 896, 951,

[113]   When one turns to the Ergänzungsliste, rather more of Wisse's Group 1519 manuscripts are present – 32 269 558 1321 1481 1566 2132 2437.[26] Moreover, five of these are the manuscripts which Wisse found to be members in all three chapters.

The entry for 1519 in the Ergänzungsliste runs as follows (I mark the members of Wisse's Group 1519 in bold):[27]

> 54 Test., davon 48 mit Mehrheitstext, 0 mit Singulärlesart)
> •96% 23/24 2100¶ 21/22 2794 •94% 51/54 36 •93% 50/54 24 •92% 11/12 1112 •91% 49/54 2473¶ 39/54 **32** 2376¶ 10/21 739 •90% 46/51 261 948¶ 35/39 344¶ 27/30 777 1417 1662¶ 9/10 2748 2785 •89% 48/54 34 39 77 135 190 240 274 1008 1295 1347 1458 2176 **2437** 2458¶ 47/53 301 475 504 527 **1321 1566**¶41/46 2860¶ 33/37 531 •88% 45/41 2694¶44/50 711 1682 2301 2781¶ 43/49 584 1672 2683¶ 42/48 21¶ 36/41 011¶ 35/40 2175¶ 28/32 170¶ 22/25 2451 •87% 47/54 3 8 14 57 65 98 108 123 148 151 162 **269** 272 329 461 478 529 549 **558** 568 699 703 705 707 730 873 1019 1073 1078 1152 1191 1212 1214 1266 1294 1300 1341 1439 1444 1452 **1481** 1517 1535 1545 **2132** 2181 2224 2297 2563 2571 2622 2695 2727¶ 46/53 183 196 202 448 496 654 721 900 980 1021 2637¶ 45/52 78 161 669 971 981 1580 1677 2281¶ 40/46 998 1045¶ 33/38 2390¶ 27/31 2282 •86% 44/51 45 2101 2584 2811¶ 43/50 194 2442¶ 42/49 1643¶ 37/43 2524¶ 18/21 1683¶ 12/14 362 426 898 •85% 46/54 12 15 26 29 40 43 70 72 75 105 112 120 144 160 169 186 198 208 226 231 232 247 260 276 277 299 305

There is, therefore, a reasonably strong correlation between the two, in the sense that six of Wisse's nine manuscripts which always belong to the group appear in association with 1519 in *TuT*. The reason for this is clear – whereas the Hauptliste only shows agreement in the non-BYZ readings, the Ergänzungsliste includes Byzantine subvariants. The problem with this data is that we are entitled to wonder why manuscripts have appeared at the top of the Ergänzungsliste which are not placed in Group 1519 in CPM. Table 4 gives the answer for the first 17 manuscripts, those which have an agreement of 90 per cent and over with 1519, and might therefore be group members.

1015, 1167, 1242 (Luke 20), 1438, 1473, 1479 (Luke 20), 1511 (Luke 20), 1570, 2095 (Luke 20), 2220 and 2604.

26   'Die Ergänzungsliste tritt ergänzend zur Hauptliste hinzu. Sie liefert für die 160 Ausgangshandschriften der Hauptliste einen Vergleich, der auf der Grundlage aller jeweils gemeinsamen Teststellen, **einschließlich aller Mehrlesarten berechnet ist**. Geboten werden jeweils die 155 Vergleichhandschiften, die der Ausgangshandschrift am nächsten kommen' (Mark, 10*). 'Es sind ca. 10% der 1553 Handschriften, die am mindestens 10 Teststellen Text haben *und* an mindestens 3 Teststellen vom Mehrheitstext abweichen' (*ibid.*, n. 11).

27   Again, these figures are corrections to the published data kindly supplied by Dr Wachtel.

Table 4: *Manuscripts in the Ergänzungsliste for 1519 according to CPM*

2100	NP (Commentary MS)
2794	NP
36	NP (Commentary MS)
24	NP (Commentary MS)
870	NP (lacks the profiled chapters)
1112	NP (Commentary MS)
2472	Cl 190/Cl 190/Cl 190[28]
2376	K^x/K^x/K^x (Cl 202; fragmentary in chs 1 and 20)
739	NP (Commentary MS)
261	K^x/NP/K^x
948	Kmix/NP/K^x
344	K^x/NP/K^x (Cl Ω)
777	K^x/NP/K^x
1417	Kmix/NP/Def (pair with 1076); fragmentary in chs 1 and 10)
1662	K^x/K^x/Def (fragmentary in ch 1)
2748	NP (lacks chs 10 and 20)[29]
2785	NP (lacks chs 10 and 20)

The answer so far as the manuscripts at the very top are concerned is very simple: they were never profiled. It could be argued that the most secure way of pursuing this examination would be to profile the manuscripts which Wisse excluded on grounds other than deficiency. However, the purpose of this study is to compare the two published volumes, not to extend the data collected for a project which was completed several decades ago.

The link between Cluster 190 and Group 1519 seems to receive at least encouragement, with the presence of two of its four members. The pairing of 1309 and 2132 is confirmed by the groupings list in *TuT*.[30]

This concludes the first part of my investigation, in which I have examined the data as it is presented in the analyses of Wisse and the Münster team. In what follows, I shall demonstrate that there are other means of finding evidence in *TuT* to support the existence of Group 1519.

[114]

---

28 Note that 190 is present in the Hauptliste under 1519.
29 In a forthcoming article, I shall argue that this manuscript (Sofia, Nat. Lib. Cyril and Methodius 7) is a composite of two manuscripts. The first, Ff 1–91, contains Mt 12.44-Mk 8.10 (with Mt 24.50–26.38 replaced in the sixteenth century). The second, Ff 92–127, contains Mk 8.24-Lk 7.32. [See pp. 145-6 above]
30 *Lukas*, 33.

4. Profiling the INTF Data

It was stated at the outset that the aim of *TuT* is to distinguish non-Byzantine manuscripts from the mass. This is done by classifying readings into four types:
1. Byzantine (BYZ)
2. The text of Nestle-Aland[27] (NA[27])
3. A reading shared with other manuscripts that is neither 1: nor 2: (Sonderlesart, indicated below as SonderL)
4. Readings where NA[27] and BYZ agree are shown as 1/[31]
5. A singular reading (Singularlesart is indicated below as SingularL)

The raw data of readings is broken down in this form in the Verzeichnende Beschreibung section in *TuT*.[32] If we take the data referring to the members of Wisse's group in this section we get something like a general profile. The columns provide the number of each type of reading, with finally the statement BYZ where it is applicable.

Table 5: Profile of Wisse's group from data in the Verzeichnende Beschreibung section

MS no.	Reading 2:	Reading 1/2:	Reading 1:	SonderL	SingL	NES[33]	
5	2	8	41	3			BYZ
32		8	33	2		11	BYZ
269		8	45	1			BYZ
558		8	46				BYZ
844		8	43	3			BYZ
871	3	8	39	3	1	1	
1036		8	44	2			BYZ
1110		8	46				BYZ
1211	3	8	40	3			
1309	3	8	39	4	1		
1321	2	6	42	3		1	BYZ
1416	4	8	40	1			BYZ
1481	3	7	41	3			

---

31   Instead of 1/, I shall indicate these readings as 1/2. I place a colon after the indicators 1, 2 and 1/2 in my discussion where it will aid readers to recognise them. There are virtually no 1/2: variants in Group 1519:
    1309 has 1/G: at TS 38; 1519 has 1/K: at TS 40; 2277 has 1/C: at TS 43
32   Described in *Markus*, 4–6.
33   = Nicht erfasste Stellen – deficiencies of various kinds, including longer omissions.

1519	3	8	40	3		
1566	3	8	40	2		BYZ
2126	3	8	42	1		BYZ
2132	2	8	41	3		BYZ
2277		8	43	3		BYZ
2437	3	8	41	2	1	BYZ

This information is of value in discovering how many non-majority readings a manuscript shows. But it is of no use in comparing witnesses, because it does not tell us whether, for example, the three Sonderlesarten shown by 844 and 871 are the same three. To obtain the information we need, it is necessary to look at the 2: readings, the BYZ subvariants and the Sonderlesarten together, since they will provide all the readings which differ from the 1: readings. Although the 1: reading is not the same as the TR reading, it can perform exactly the same function of providing a base on which to build profiles. I take first the Sonderlesarten (see Table 6). Because there can be two or more different readings, the table is rather more complicated. This situation arises at Luke 12.14 (TS 25) and 13.19 (TS 28). I have set the variants side by side. The first line gives the chapter and verse reference; the second the TS number before the colon, and after it the variant; the third the number of manuscripts supporting that reading.[34] Below the rule, the left-hand column gives the Gregory-Aland number of the manuscript to which the lines applies. A + indicates that the manuscript has that reading. A blank indicates that the manuscript has another class of reading. The numbers in the bottom line indicate the number of manuscripts belonging to Wisse's Group 1519 which support each reading.

---

[34] The total number of manuscripts examined in the volumes on Luke is 1756.

[116]   Table 6: Sonderlesarten in the members of Wisse's Group 1519

Ref	4.4	6.38	9.55	9.56	10.21	12.14		13.19		15.21	16.14	18.11	22.43
TS	4:4	11:3	18:5	19:3	20:4	25:3	25:3B	28:5	28:6	28:6C	32:3	33:6	37:10	45:3
MSS	120	95	27	28	8	22	2	2	51	9	207	105	3	41
5		+			+				+					
32		+							+			NES		NES
269		+												
558														
844		+	+	+										
871		+			+				+					
1036	+								+					
1110														
1211	+								+					+
1309		+				+			+					+
1321		+							+	+				
1416									+					
1481		+							+				+	
1519		+								+				+
1566		+							+					
2126									+					
2132		+				+			+					
2277			+	+								+		
2437		+					+							
	1	13	2	1	2	1	1	1	12	1	1	1	1	3

[117]   Readings 11:3 and 28:6 appear to be group readings. The CPM definition of a group reading is that it requires 2/3 membership to be primary and 1/3–2/3 to be secondary. 11:3, with 13 out of 19 manuscripts supporting it, and 28:6, with 12, both qualify as primary readings. 28:6C in 1519 is therefore a corruption of the group reading. And note again that 1309 2132 share the same three readings, if we treat 25:3B as a corruption of 25:3.

To this we can add the 2: readings (that is, the Nestle-Aland against BYZ readings) of members of the group (see Table 7). A blank indicates that the manuscript has another class of reading.

Table 7: (Nestle-Aland) readings in Wisse's Group 1519 members

Ref	5.38	8.52	9.55		9.56	16.14	17.9	19.42		24.47(1)
TS2	7:2	14:2	18:2	18:2B	19:2	33:2	36:2	41:2	41:2B	53:2
MSS	18	187	433	13	451	53	24	16	1	8
5	+							+		
32							NES			NES
269										
558										
844										
871		+			+			+		
1036										
1110										
1211		+	+		+					
1309		+			+	+				
1321		+			+					
1416		+			+		+	+		
1481		+			+	+				
1519		+ (c)	+ (*)35	+						+
1566		+			+			+		
2126		+			+			+		
2132		+			+					
2277										
2437		+			+				+	
	1	1	10	1	11	2	1	5	1	1

TS 18 19 41 seem to be a fairly common denominator here. The first two are very common readings, and – one might suppose – would therefore contribute less towards helping establish a group identity. But CPM is based on the theory that, even when readings are commonly attested, there will be a distinctive profile that is as likely to include commonly attested 2: readings as much as any other kind. 41 contributes to the study of the group in another way. Here there are only 16 witnesses with the reading, and five of them are members of Group 1519. But at present it cannot even count as a secondary reading, although it would do were we to eliminate one or two members (as we shall).

[118]

---

35 This indicates a first hand reading (*) and a correction (c). It would be interesting to know whether this could be a correction by the first hand.

[119]

Finally, I looked at the Byzantine subvariants of all members of the group.[36] The results appear in Table 8. A Byzantine subvariant is a reading deemed by the compilers of *TuT* to be a variant of the BYZ reading.[37] I include those where the NA[27] and BYZ texts agree, showing them as 1/2.

Table 8: Byzantine and 1/2 subvariants in Wisse's group 1519 members

Ref.	9.54	9.55	10.22	18.24	19.25	19.42	21.6	23.16	23.45	24.19	24.42	
TS	17:1F	18:1ZA	21:1H	38:1/G	40:1/K	41:1N	43:1/C	47:1F	50:1C	51:1E	52:1B	52:1H
MSS	29	167	200	1	6	155	528	66	2	1	27	78
5								+				
32								NES	NES	NES	NES	NES
269		+						+				+
558		+						+				
844	+									+		
871								+	+			+
1036												
1110			+					+				
1211												
1309				+		+						
1321								+				
1416												
1481								+				
1519					+			+				
1566								+				
2126								+	+			
2132						+		+				
2277			+				+					
2437								+				
	1	2	2	1	1	2	1	13	1	1	1	2

47:1F seems a very strongly marked group reading.

---

36   These variants are indicated by a capital letter after the numeral 1.
37   Since the first reading is always the majority reading, I assume that the term subvariant is a numerical definition, rather than a statement of genealogical derivation.

If we take the 2: readings, the 1: subvariants and Sonderlesarten of the group together, we come up with a CPM-style profile of non-BYZ readings of 11 18 19 28 41 47. As a proportion of readings (six out of 54 Teststellen) this is very similar to the CPM (a profile of five out of 54 test readings in ch. 1; six out of 64 in ch. 10; 11 out of 78 in ch. 20).[38]

The full profile is 11:3 18:2 19:2 28:6 41:2 47:1F. How closely do the individual members conform to it? In Table 9, X indicates a primary group reading, • a secondary one. I have brought back in the subvariants.

Table 9: Profile Teststellen in the manuscripts of the group

Ref. TS No.	6.38 11:3 95	9.55 18:2 433	9.56 19:2 451	13.19 28:6 51	19.42 41:2 16	23.16 47:1F 66	Total	Wisse (all or 20 only)
5	X			X	•	X	4	20 only
32	X			X		NES	2	all
269	X					X	2	all
558						X	1	20 only
844	X						1	20 only
871	X	•	•	X	•	X	6	all
1036				X			1	all
1110						X	1	20 only
1211		•	•	X			3	20 only
1309	X	•	•	X			4	20 only
1321	X	•	•	X		X	4	all
1416		•	•	X	•		4	20 only
1481	X	•	•	X		X	5	20 only
1519	X	•c	•			X	3	all
1566	X	•	•	X	•	X	6	all
2126		•	•	X	•	X	5	all
2132	X	•	•	X		X	5	20 only
2277							0	20 only
2437	X	•	•			X	4	all
	12	10	11	12	5	13		

It is interesting to find two 'perfect members', 871 and 1566, and to note in the Hauptliste that the list of closest allies under 871 agrees, with

---

38 The Test Readings are listed by Wisse on 122–5.

1566 first, followed by 5, with 1309 1321 1416 1481 2126 2132 close behind.

There are two aberrancies, one due to the methodology of CPM, the other to that of *TuT*.

1. The manuscripts perceived by Wisse to be Group 1519 only in Chapter 20 often still show up as strong members. These are 5 1211 1309 1416 1481 2132. The most likely explanation for this is that I have used a different method from Wisse. CPM eliminated 'seven "Neutral" readings with negligible minuscule support apart from the "Neutrals" among them' in Chapter 1.[39] How many is negligible? Would a test reading like the *TuT* TS 41 disappear? That is, has a class of readings useful in identifying a group with surviving non-Byzantine readings been mistakenly removed? This is likely to be so.
2. The classification of some members of the group as BYZ by *TuT* does not necessarily help us. 871 and 1566 are both perfect members, yet 1566 is BYZ and 871 is not.

Table 9 masks some of the evidence, since it gives only the readings of the manuscripts in relation to the previously determined profile readings. It is necessary also to provide a full profile of each manuscript. This data is provided in Table 10. The first line gives the number of the Teststelle, the right- and left-hand columns the manuscript number, and the entry in the grid the precise reading of the manuscript. A blank means that it has the BYZ reading. It is not very clear from Wisse's study how much 'noise', or 'surplus' as he describes it, is permitted to group members.[40] 1566 has no divergences from the BYZ text apart from the group profile. 871 has three (20:4, 51:1E and 52:1H), and 1309 has four (25:3B, 33:2, 38:1G and 45:3). The example of 1309, which looks a pretty strong member, is an exception to Wisse's statement that weaker members will have more surplus.

5. Refining the Preliminary Results

Looking at the data above, it seems impossible for 2277 to be a member of the group, since it has does not share a single group reading. Doubt must also be cast on the claims to membership of 558 844 1036 1110.

---

39 Wisse, 39.
40 'How much divergence from the group profile is allowed [to the MS profile] is indicated in Chapter VI for each book' (Wisse, 43). I cannot find any data in Ch. VI which meet this description.

Table 10: Text und Textwert 'profiles' of individual manuscripts assigned by Wisse to Group 1519

Ref	4.4	5.38	6.38	8.52	9.54	9.55	9.56	10.21	10.22	12.14	13.19	15.21	16.14	17.9	18.11	18.24	19.25	19.42	21.6	22.43-4	23.16	23.45	24.19	24.42	24.47
T/S	4	7	11	14	17	18	19	20	21	25	28	32	33	36	37	38	40	41	43	45	47	50	51	52	53
5	2	3						4			6							2			1F	NES	NES	NES	NES
32		3									6			NES						NES	NES	NES	NES	NES	1H
269			3			1ZA															1F			1H	
558			3			1ZA															1F				
844		3			1F	5	3																	1B	
871		3				2	2	4															1E	1H	
1036											6														
1110									1H		6										1F				
1211				2																					
1309			3			2	2			3B	6		2							3	1F				
1321			3			2	2				6	3				1G		1N		3					
1416						2	2				6		2	2							1F				
1481		3				2	2				6				10			2			1F				
1519		3				*2B	2			6C			2				1K			3	1F				
1566		3	3			2	2				6							2			1F	1C			2
2126						2	2				6							2			1F				
2132			3			2	2			3	6							1N			1F				
2277									1H				6						1C		1F				
2437		3				2	2				5							2B			1F				

„Text und Textwert" and the Claremont Profile Methode 231

Wisse himself calls 1036 a 'weak member'.[41] The problem is that Wisse's study does not indicate how many group readings the individual manuscripts attest. It is of course possible that they belong to a strand of the tradition that follows Group 1519 in a block including Chapter 20 (though not apparently Chapter 19). However, on present evidence 558 844 1036 1110 2277 should be eliminated. 32 269 also seem very weak members. There is no received wisdom on the number of group readings a manuscript must have to be a group member. The best evidence available is the example of 477 and Group 1216. This is the group given as an example of a profile in Chapter 1.[42] There are thirteen primary and three secondary readings. Of these 477 has just three primary readings. It is described in the Profile Classification as belonging to the group as a weak member.[43] Of course, the profile is assisted by the fact that it is also a member in Chapters 10 and 20 (though weak in 10). The evidence with regard to 32 269 seems to be analogous in strength. It is as follows:

	CPM Ch.1	CPM Ch.10	CPM Ch.20	Teststellen
32	1519	1519	1519	1519 (weak)
269	1519	1519	1519	1519 (weak)

The question of strength of profile in a given manuscript, along with the question about noise (surplus), poses a significant problem for the CPM. It is an area which requires clarification.

Following the rules as they exist, the removal of 558 1036 1110 2277 brings the number of members down to 14. Five of the readings are now primary (18:2 and 19:2 have the support of two-thirds of the group members), and one is secondary (having the support of between one and two-thirds). The group profile becomes that shown in Table 11.

Table 11: Profile Teststellen in the manuscripts of the group

Ref. TS No.	6.38 11:3 95	9.55 18:2 433	9.56 19:2 451	13.19 28:6 51	19.42 41:2 16	23.16 47:1F 66	TOTAL	Wisse (all or 20 only)
5	X			X	•	X	4	20 only
32	X			X		NES	2	all
269	X					X	2	all
871	X	X	X	X	•	X	6	all

---

41 Wisse, 70.
42 Wisse, 44f.
43 Wisse, 61.

1211		X	X	X			3	20 only
1309	X	X	X	X			4	20 only
1321	X	X	X	X		X	5	all
1416		X	X	X	•		4	20 only
1481	X	X	X	X		X	5	20 only
1519	X	(Xc)	X			X	3	all
1566	X	X	X	X	•	X	6	all
2126		X	X	X	•	X	5	all
2132	X	X	X	X		X	5	20 only
2437	X	X	X			X	4	all
	11	(10)	11	11	5	10		

At this point in the study, it has been established that *TuT* supports the existence of Group 1519. Several weak members from Wisse's profiling have been eliminated. The group has two perfect members, 871 and 1566. 1519, after which the group is named, shows up less strongly. The data tell us that the distinguishing readings of the group consist of three 2: readings, two Sonderlesarten and one Byzantine subvariant.

It should be noted that in one respect it has not been possible to follow CPM. The method requires that a group profile must differ from other profiles by at least two readings per sampling chapter.[44] To ascertain that would require an undertaking far outside the bounds of this survey.

6. Looking for New Group Members

The next stage is to look for evidence among the Teststellen for other group members. Apart from the fact that CPM omitted rather a lot of manuscripts, this exercise is a necessary part of comparing the results of the two methods in screening witnesses. First, I looked in the Verzeichende Beschreibung at the non-BYZ readings in the other witnesses supporting the poorly attested TS 41:2. Would any of the other eleven manuscripts there share other group readings? I profiled them in the six distinctive readings of Group 1519. In Table 12 the 1: in the column for TS 47:1F means that the manuscript has the 1: reading. Since the status of primary and secondary readings may be affected by

---

44 Wisse, 41.

new additions, I revert in the following tables to using + to indicate the presence of a reading in a manuscript.

Table 12: Profile readings in manuscripts supporting Teststellen 41:2

Ref. TS No.	6.38 11:3 95	9.55 18:2 433	9.56 19:2 451	13.19 28:6 51	19.42 41:2 16	23.16 47:1F 66	Total
01		+	+		+	1	3
03		+	+		+		3
019		+	+		+		3
579					+		
892		+	+		+		3
968					+	1	1
1011				6B	+	1	1
1012					+	1	1
1048				+	+	1	2
1451					+	1	1
2328				+	+	1	2

It is pretty plain that none of these qualifies. As one would expect, several Alexandrian witnesses figure strongly in this list.

Another approach is to go back to the manuscripts listed as closest to 871 in the Hauptliste, now that we know it is a core member. The data has to be used rather indirectly because, unfortunately, the six readings taken as the basis of comparison are not the same six as the group profile: they are the non-BYZ readings, so that the subvariant 47:1F is not included, and the non-group reading 20:4 is. But the evidence is still informative. The closest witnesses (with manuscripts we know to be group members in bold) are

    83% (5/6)   **1566**
    66.7% (4/6)   5 186 **1309 1321 1416 1481 2126 2132**
    60% (3/5)   033 948 2182
    50% (3/6)   01 03 019 15 24 30 36 40 98 169 190 213 259 288 496 527 680 892 951 981 1163

Eliminating those which we already know to be group members, and those in the previous table, we get the following results when we profile them in the six group readings. This results can be found either from the Verzeichnende Beschreibung or from the Resultate der Kollation.

Table 13: Profile readings in manuscripts closest to 871 (Hauptliste)

Ref. TS No.	6.38 11:3 95	9.55 18:2 433	9.56 19:2 451	13.19 28:6 51	19.42 41:2 16	23.16 47:1F 66	Total	Wisse
186	+	+	+	+			4	-
033	+	+	+		NES	1	3	Mix/Mix/Def (fragmentary in 10)
948	+*	+	+	FF[45]		NES	3	Kmix/NP/Kˣ
2182	+	+	+	NES			3	Kˣ /Kˣ / Kˣ
15	+	+	+				3	Kˣ/NP/Kˣ(Cl 43; pair with 1163)
24	+	+	+	6C		+	4	-
30		+	+	+			3	Kˣ/NP/Kˣ
36	+	+	+	6C		+	4	-
40	+	+	+				3	-
98	+	+	+				3	Kˣ/Kˣ/Kmix (some relation to Mgroups)
169	+	+	+				3	Kˣ/NP/Kˣ (some relation to Cl 1442)
190	+	+	+			+	4	Cl 190/ Cl 190/ Cl 190
213	+	+	+				3	Mix/ Mix/ Mix
259		+	+	+			3	-
288		+	+	+			3	Kˣ/NP/Kˣ (Cl 17; pair with 30)
496	+	+	+				3	Gp 1167/ Gp 1167/ Gp 1167
527	+*	+*	+*				3	Kˣ / Kˣ / Kˣ(Corr to Π268)
680	+	+	+				3	Kˣ/ Kˣ / Kˣ (Cl 43)
951	+	+	+				3	Gp 1167
981	+	+	+				3	-
1163	+	+	+				3	Kˣ/ Kˣ / Kˣ (Cl 43; pair with 15)

186 has the same readings as 1211 1309. 24 36 190 are also strong candidates, since they show the distinctive 47:1F reading. These four witnesses also have either very little surplus or none at all. It is worth noting that the variant 28:6C is also read in 1519. Manuscripts with only the first three readings are weaker candidates, and may belong to a group or groups whose profile(s) share these readings.[46]

The Ergänzungsliste suggests only one more candidate for inclusion in the group. These are the witnesses with more than two readings:

---

[45] = Filmfehler.
[46] A note for the curious on some of the other witnesses here: the three corrections to 527 bring it into line with the 1: readings; the pairing of 15/1163 is strengthened by the fact that they are identical in all Lukan Teststellen; that of 30/288 is not so strong: they differ in three Teststellen, 30 being non-BYZ on each occasion.

Table 14: Profile readings in manuscripts closest to 871 (Ergänzungsliste)

Ref. TS No.	6.38 11:3 95	9.55 18:2 433	9.56 19:2 451	13.19 28:6 51	19.42 41:2 16	23.16 47:1F 66	Total	Wisse
34		+	+			+	3	-
39		+	+			+	3	-
77	+			+		+	3	-
135		+	+			+	3	$K^x/K^x/K^x$
948	+*	+	+	FF			3	Kmix/NP/K^x
1358		+	+			+	3	K^x/K^y/Kmix (related to Cl 202)
2458	+			+		+	3	-
2812	+	+		+		+	4	-
301		+	+			+	2	$K^x/K^x/K^x$
261		+	+			+	3	K^x/NP/K^x
1357		+*	+*	+			3	Mix/NP/K^x

I stopped at 87 per cent. Although two manuscripts are interesting in having the three non–2: readings of the group – 77 2458 – there is only one manuscript that could belong, and that is 2812.

We thus have five possible manuscripts for inclusion: 24 36 186 190 2812. The strongest are 36 186, which have the same profile as 5 2132. Since Wisse did not collate either of these two manuscripts, we may presume that their absence from his Group 1519 is fortuitous. Let us add these two to the group. The result then looks like Table 15.

There is now a decision to be made. There are 18 members of the group. This means that 41:2 should not be allowed as a part of the profile after all, since it is attested by less than one third of the group members. On the other hand, two members of the group are pretty weak – 32 269. If they are deemed not to belong to it, reading 41:2 could almost survive as a secondary reading, with the support of five out of the sixteen members, including the core members 871 1566.

Table 15: Profile of all group members

Ref. TS No.	6.38 11:3 95	9.55 18:2 433	9.56 19:2 451	13.19 28:6 51	19.42 41:2 16	23.16 47:1F 66	Total	Wisse (all or 20 only)
5	+			+	+	+	4	20 only
24	+	+	+	6C		+	4	-
32	+			+		NES	2	all
36	+	+	+	6C		+	4 (5)	-
186	+	+	+	+			4	-
269	+					+	2	all
871	+	+	+	+	+	+	6	all
1211		+	+	+			3	20 only
1309	+	+	+	+			4	20 only
1321	+	+	+	+		+	4	all
1416		+	+	+	+		4	20 only
1481	+	+	+	+		+	5	20 only
1519	+	2B*	+	6C		+	3	all
1566	+	+	+	+	+	+	6	all
2126		+	+	+	+	+	5	all
2132	+	+	+	+		+	5	20 only
2437	+	+	+		2B	+	(5)	all
2812	+	+		+		+	4	all
	16	14	14	13	5	13		

The reading has a good case in its favour. It is read by 871 and 1566, two core members (and 1566 has no surplus), another witness (2437) supports a subvariant of it, and it is a very rare reading. As we have seen, outside the group it is found only in 01 03 019 579 892 968 1011 1012 1048 1451 2328. Perhaps one needs the flexibility to retain readings like this as part of the profile, indicating them in a third way. On the other hand, to remove it would produce three more manuscripts with a 'perfect profile', 1321, 1481, and 2132, and none with fewer than 60 per cent of the group readings. The profile would look like Table 16:

Table 16: Profile of group without TS 41:2

Ref. TS No.	6.38 11:3 95	9.55 18:2 433	9.56 19:2 451	13.19 28:6 51	23.16 47:1F 66	Total	Wisse (all or 20 only)
5	X			X	X	3	20 only
24	X	X	X	6C	X	4	-
36	X	X	X	6C	X	4 (5)	-
186	X	X	X	X		4	-
871	X	X	X	X	X	5	all
1211		X	X	X		3	20 only
1309	X	X	X	X		4	20 only
1321	X	X	X	X	X	5	all
1416		X	X	X		3	20 only
1481	X	X	X	X	X	5	20 only
1519	X	(2B*)	X^c X	6C	X	3	all
1566	X	X	X	X	X	5	all
2126		X	X	X	X	4	all
2132	X	X	X	X	X	5	20 only
2437	X	X	X		X	4	all
2812	X	X		X	X	4	all
	14	14	13	12	12		

The choice between a significant and weak reading and a few weak members would be in favour of the reading. But it may be an unnecessary choice. Readings need to be studied more seriously than as a statistic, and here we have one distinctive enough to warrant serious attention, something of the kind that in traditional philology is an indication of genealogical association between witnesses. I propose therefore to retain the reading with the symbol of a dagger, drawing attention to the fact that it is significant but not a secondary reading, and to retain 32 269 as very weak family members.[47] The final profile is therefore as shown in Table 17:

---

47 See Wisse: 'it is better to establish the group profile on the basis of the core members and to leave it unchanged when weak members are added' (42). This almost meets the present case, except that the reading does not qualify as secondary.

Table 17: Final profile of Group 1519 members

Ref. TS No.	6.38 11:3 95	9.55 18:2 433	9.56 19:2 451	13.19 28:6 51	19.42 41:2 16	23.16 47:1F 66
5	X			X	†	X
24	X	X	X	6C		X
32	X			X		NES
36	X	X	X	6C		X
186	X	X	X	X		
269	X					X
871	X	X	X	X	†	X
1211		X	X	X		
1309	X	X	X	X		
1321	X	X	X	X		X
1416		X	X	X	†	
1481	X	X	X	X		X
1519	X	2B*	X	6C		X
1566	X	X	X	X	†	X
2126		X	X	X	†	X
2132	X	X	X	X		X
2437	X	X	X		2B	X
2812	X	X		X		X

7. Group 1519 in Mark and Matthew

We would expect Group 1519 to show up best from *TuT* in Mark, where there are 196 test readings. So I had a look at that, and had the immediate impression that Group 1519 had melted into air, into thin air. To be more precise, it has melted into the Byzantine mainstream, that is, into K^x. I omit detailing the preliminary stages of gathering this information, which were the same as those for the Lukan profile. In Table 18 at the end of each profile, I give the number of readings in full, followed by the number of primary readings in brackets.

Table 18: Group 1519 in Mark

Ref. TS No.	1.14(1) 11:3 35	1.16 13:3 175	3.32 55:3 476	5.41 70:2 269	6.14 (2) 76:3 134	10.35 143:3 528	13.28 169:9 139	14.65 178:1B 619	
5	•	X	•	•	X		X	•	7 (3)
24	NES	NES	NES				X		1
32	•	X	•				X		4 (2)
36	•	X	•				X		4 (2)
186	•		•						2
269	•	X	•				X	•	5 (2)
871	•	X	•	•	X	•	X	•	8 (3)
1211		X			X		X		3 (3)
1309		X			X	•	X	•	5 (3)
1321		X	•		X		X		4 (3)
1416				•	X	•		•	4 (1)
1481		X		•	X		X		4 (3)
1519	•	X	•				X		4 (2)
1566		X		•	X		X	•	5 (3)
2126		X			X	•	X	•	5 (3)
2132					X	•	X	•	4 (2)
2437			•	•	X	•	X	•*	6 (2)
2812	•	corr[48]	•				X		3 (1)
	8/17	12/17	10/17	6	11	6	16	9	

Three primary readings out of 196 are hardly very many on which to build evidence for a group, and almost all of these readings are quite highly attested, while some of them are very common indeed. On the other hand, the same manuscripts are stronger members of the group here as in Luke. 871 is again a perfect member (with a slight surplus of 2: readings, 63:1F and 148:4). And, positively, the manuscripts which looked very weak in Luke (32 and 269) come in quite strongly. Perhaps the problem is that it is a group too near to a much stronger one, probably K^x, as Wisse suggested.

Again, in Matthew the evidence is not strong (Table 19).

---

[48] The first hand has the 1: reading.

Table 19: Group 1519 in Matthew

Ref. TS No.	4.10 9:2 180	6.6 18:2 29	11.8 32:2 590	17.20(1) 53:1N 162	27.49 63:3 18	
5		•		X	•	3 (1)
24	•			X	NES	2 (1)
32	NES	NES		X		1 (1)
36	•			X		2 (1)
186		•				1
269				X		1 (1)
871	•	•		X	•	4 (1)
1211			•			1
1309			•			1
1321	•	•	•	X		4 (1)
1416		NES	•	X	3B	3 (1)
1481				X		1 (1)
1519				X		1 (1)
1566	NES	NES	NES	X	•	2 (1)
2126	•	•	•	X	•	5 (1)
2132				X		1
2437	NES	NES		X	3C	2 (1)
2812	•			X		2 (1)
	6	4	6	15	4	

My table treats 18:2 as a secondary reading, on the grounds that four witnesses are deficient, and 63:3 by treating the subvariants as part of the total. Just one primary reading is very weak, especially since this one is quite well attested. Again, however, much the same manuscripts remain at the core of the group. 2126 is perfect, with slight surplus (17:3 and 31:5), and so is 1566 where it is extant. There are 64 Teststellen in this Gospel. The frequency of group readings is therefore greater than in Mark.

The evidence of the study so far therefore confirms that Group 1519 does exist, though less strongly in Matthew. The best provisional solution for some of the problems of definition that have been encountered is that it is a closer to a stronger group. Any process of correction to a stronger text is likely to have been more thoroughly executed in Matthew than in later books.

8. The Relationship between 871 and 1566

The relationship between this pair, the core members of the group, seemed well worth pursuing further. I therefore looked at their whole profiles in the Verzeichnende Beschreibung in each Gospel. Fits, in Luke:

[130]
A. LESART 2:		
871 18, 19, 41		3
1566 18, 19, 41		3
B. LESART 12:		
871 16, 23, 32, 37, 38, 40, 42, 43		8
1566 16, 23, 32, 37, 38, 40, 42, 43		8
C. LESART 1:		
871 1–10, 12–15, 17, 21, 22, 24–27, 30, 31, 33–36, 39, 44–46, 48–50, 53, 54		39
1566 1–10, 12–15, 17, 20, 21, 22, 24–27, 30, 31, 33–36, 39, 44–46, 48–50, 51, 52, 53, 54		40
SUBVARIANTEN:		
871 1F:47, 1E:51, 1H:52		
1566 1F:47		
D. SINGULÄRLESARTEN		
871 51:1E		
1566 -		

[131]
E. SONDERLESARTEN		
871 11:3, 20:4, 28:6		3
1566 11:3, 28:6		2
I. NICHT ERFASSTE STELLEN		
871 29		1
1566 29		1

They differ in three readings only: 20, 51 and 52. The reading at 51 is a small orthographical oddity in 871, and that at 52 is also a slight difference within the BYZ reading. The difference at 20 (Luke 10.21, Variant 36 in CPM) is interesting. Here 1566 (actually the older manuscript) has the BYZ reading. Trying to relate the information to Wisse (123) is rather difficult. According to Wisse, the test reading is ο Ιησους τω πνευματι. But this cannot be right, for he records Group 13 for this, whereas according to *TuT* it reads ο ιησους εν τω πνευματι. In any case, the two manuscripts are closely related. The 'Nicht erfasste Stelle' is where they, in common with 42 other witnesses, omit by hom. a block including the Teststelle. In fact, to call 1566 the manuscript with the BYZ reading is not using the language of CPM. In CPM there are only groups, no BYZ as such. Looking at the witnesses which agree with 871 at TS 20, we find that they are from the following groups, using the Profile Classification in Wisse:

MS	CPM classification in Chs 1 10 and 20
5	Mix/Kmix/1519
497	K˟/NP/K˟
1166	Mix/K˟/K˟
1233*	Π171/ Π171/ Π171
1542*	Mix/K˟/K˟
1579	1216/1216/1216 (core member; pair with 1243)
2144	K˟/K˟/K˟ (fragm in 1)

This is hard to interpret. But I suggest that 1566 has one group reading, and 871 another.

Turning to Matthew, we find the problem that 1566 is lacunose. It is only available for 22 Teststellen: 28, and 44–64. 871 is classified as BYZ. Here are the details, where both are present.

```
A. LESART 2:
871      -                                    -
1566     -                                    -
B. LESART 12:
871      28, 51                               2
1566     28, 51                               2
C. LESART 1:
871      44–50, 52, 54–62, 64                 18
1566     44–50, 52, 54–62, 64                 18
SUBVARIANTEN:
871      1N:53
1566     1N:53
E. SONDERLESARTEN
871      63:3                                 1
1566     63:3                                 1
I. NICHT ERFASSTE STELLEN
871
1566     1–27, 29–39                          42
```

[132]

This gives them a perfect match.

Going finally to Mark, they continue very close to one another. For 12: and 1:, I note only where they differ.

```
A. LESART 2:
871      70                                   1
1566     11, 70                               2
B. LESART 12:
871                                           71
1566     +55, +143                            73
C. LESART 1:
871      +154                                 117
1566     +148                                 117
```

```
SUBVARIANTEN:
871      1B:178, 1F:63                                    2
1566     1B:178                                           1
D. SINGULÄRLESARTEN
871      -                                                0
1566     -                                                0
E. SONDERLESARTEN
871      11:3, 13:3, 55:3, 76:3, 143:3, 148:4,   169:9    7
1566           13:3,       76:3,           154:4, 169:9   4
```

There are six differences in all in the 196 Markan Teststellen. This compares reasonably with 1 and 1584, two closely related members of Family 1, which differ in three places. Six out of 196 is a lesser proportion than the three out of 54 in Luke.

It seems, therefore, that there is a close relationship between these two manuscripts.

9. The Full Manuscript Profiles and the Question of Surplus

We now return to the Gospel of Luke. In Table 10, I gave the manuscript profiles of the members that had been assigned to the group at that stage. It is now necessary to do this for the final membership. The information is provided in Table 20 (see p. 245). Bold type indicates a group reading.

The only manuscripts without surplus are

24 (if we count 28:6C with 28:6)
32 (but it is not complete)
1566

For the rest, the degree of surplus is

5	2	1416	1
36	1 (excluding 28:6C)	1481	2
186	3	1519	4 (excluding 28:6C)
269	2	2126	1
871	3	2132	2
1211	3	2437	2
1309	5	2812	3
1321	1		

1566 is therefore the group's only perfect member. It remains unclear whether the high degree of surplus in 1309 is a significant problem in allocating it to the group.

„Text und Textwert" and the Claremont Profile Methode   245

Table 20: Text und Textwert 'Profiles' of the 18 Manuscripts Finally Assigned To Group 1519

Ref.	4.4	6.38 / 5.38		9.54 / 8.52		9.56 / 9.55		10.22 / 10.21		13.19 / 12.14		15.21 / 14.17		17.9 / 16.14		18.24 / 18.11		19.42 / 19.25		21.11 / 21.6		22.43-4	23.16 / 23.45		24.19 / 24.42		24.47	
T/S	4	7	11	14	17	18	19	20	21	25	28	30	32	33	36	37	38	40	41	43	44	45	47	50	51	52	53
5	2		3				4				6								2				1F				
24			3			2	2				6C												1F				
32			3								6				NES							NES	NES	NES	NES	NES	
36			3						1H		6C												1F				
186			3			2	2				6				7								1F				
269			3			2	2				6												1F			1H	
871			3			1ZA					6								2				1F		1E	1H	
1211	4			2		2	2			3B	6																
1309			3			2	2				6			2			1G					3	1F				
1321			3			2	2				6		3						1N			3	1F				
1416			3			2	2				6				2				2								
1481			3			2	2				6			2		10											
1519			3			2B*	2				6C							1K				3	1F		2		
1566			3			2	2				6								2				1F				
2126						2	2				6								2				1F	1C			
2132			3			2	2			3	6								1N				1F				
2437			3			2	2				5								2B				1F				
2812			3			2					6	4									1Q		1F			1H	

10. Conclusions

What have we learned from this study?
1. The most obvious point is that the *TuT* data can be used to gather evidence according to methods chosen by the user.
2. The habit in CPM of generally only giving one variation from the TR at any given place seems, in comparison with the Teststellen, a very blunt instrument to use. The only instance of more than one variant in the profile of Group 1519 is at 10.58, where TR reads ουν. It is curious that CPM, while allegedly more specifically designed to elucidate the history of the Byzantine groups, shows less of the actual textual history than *TuT*, which not only includes all the subvariants, but reconstructs their development by its sequence and subvariants.
3. One of the significant questions is whether it is better to analyse the variants in blocks of text (CPM) or in individual examples taken throughout the text (*TuT*). There is a disadvantage with the execution of each project, since CPM was ill advised to use Luke 1, while *TuT* should have spread the variants more evenly through the book.

It has often been stated that one of the demands on the selection of test passages is that they should be sufficient to detect block mixture, or even what Colwell used to call box-car mixture, in a witness. That is, it should pick up witnesses which are Byzantine in one part of a Gospel and not in the rest, or even witnesses which switch from one to the other more than once. It may be that the rather thin spread in the second half of Matthew could make it less likely for a text change to show up.

This is a problem for *TuT*, at least in Matthew and Luke, because there are not enough variants. I checked this with 118 205 209, three members of Family 1 which are BYZ between Mt 10.35 and 21.45.[49] The incidence of Teststellen in Matthew is shown in Table 21.

---

49 See most recently A.S. Anderson, 'Codex 1582 and Family 1 of the Gospels. The Gospel of Matthew', University of Birmingham Ph.D. thesis, 1999. [Now published as *The Textual Tradition of the Gospels. Family 1 in Matthew* (NTTS 32), Leiden and Boston, 2004]

Table 21: Chapter distribution of Teststellen in Matthew [131]

Ch. no.	No. of TS	Ch. no.	No. of TS	Ch. no.	No. of TS	Ch. no.	No. of TS
1	4	8	3	15	2	22	0
2	1	9	3	16	2	23	1
3	3	10	2	17	3	24	2
4	2	11	5	18	1	25	1
5	6	12	3	19	1	26	0
6	5	13	4	20	1	27	2
7	1	14	4	21	1	28	1

Thus the incidence of 2: readings (17–20, 27, 41, 59) and Sonderlesarten (24 25 26 30 58) in 118 give no indication of this change, especially since the 2: reading at 41 is actually in the BYZ block. The same seems true of 205 209. So far as I have been able to ascertain, it is not possible to ascertain the block mixture of these manuscripts from *TuT*. There are 64 Teststellen in Matthew, of which 46 come in chapters 1–14 and 18 in chapters 15–28. If one were to assume that texts were most carefully corrected in the early folios, then the TS would be more heavily weighted where the evidence may be most scanty. If one were further to posit that correction was most frequently towards the majority reading, there could be a tendency towards over emphasising the majority tendency in individual witnesses. It should, however, be emphasised that this suggestion needs testing.

It should be recognised that CPM also contains a hit or miss risk, since a manuscript might simply be a different group in Luke 11–19, or 2–9 and 11–19. The profile would not reveal this. In fact, any sampling method has a chance element in it. The BYZ section of 118 205 209 showed up when they were collated for the whole of Matthew. Sampling has to hit a balance between the best size of net and the time available for fishing.

4. The fact that some members of Group 1519 are statistically BYZ in *TuT*, while others are not, leads me to suspect that this statistic is not one of the most helpful elements in the series. But of course the method accepts that the 10 per cent limit is arbitrary. It is important that the user be alert to this fact.
5. It is frustrating that one cannot find out from Wisse how much a manuscript conforms to the profile of its group. Without the profile for each manuscript, one is too much in the hands of the profiler. [136]

By contrast, *TuT* provides all the information that has been collected. It is clear that scientific work should make all the evidence available for verification.

6. The claim by Wisse that finding more manuscripts will not affect a group's profile seems improbable. It may be suspected that the Byzantine situation is so complicated, that the more manuscripts are added, the less defined each group becomes. Or at any rate, with Group 1519 it could be that what this study has shown is that as the core becomes better defined, the periphery gets more and blurred and confused with other groups. That would mean that the more manuscripts were profiled, the more there would emerge something like a spectrum, with colours shading into each other. In that case, the designation BYZ might in the end be more appropriate. The present survey is too limited in scope to do more than raise this question.

7. The definition of a group is obviously important. The fact that Wisse can call his 'B' a group and say that it is over-represented in the apparatus suggests that he regards it as quite an elastic (or perhaps one should say broad) term.[50] Behind this approach lies a problem of Colwell's critique of genealogy.[51] Is the treating of variants as numerical sets, each with the same weight, an adequate treatment of the data? For example, the Profile evidence for 871 1566 invites the genealogical questions. This is why the poorly attested reading 41:2 remains, in my view, significant to Group 1519. This difference in approach will affect the process subsequent to profiling, the representation of a group in an apparatus. To a full adherent of CPM, the preferred way would be to pick the manuscript with the best profile. In my opinion, it would be to reconstruct the text of the archetype and cite that in the apparatus. This of course is not always fully possible, and indeed it has been strongly suggested to me that only manuscripts should be cited in an apparatus, with attempts to reconstruct archetypal texts made in separate studies.[52]

8. Part of the essential theory of CPM is that there is no such thing as the Byzantine text. All manuscripts belong to one of 16 categories: B and then all the other groups in sequence. Obviously B is not a BYZ sub-group, but neither are any of the other 15 categories. The

---

50 His Group B even includes 05, since all singular readings are eliminated. Singularity is very likely to be more common in the oldest manuscripts.

51 See my study (not all of which is my current thinking) 'The Development of Textual Criticism since B.H. Streeter', *NTS* 24 (1977), 149–62. [Chapter 13 above]

52 By Klaus Wachtel, in an e-mail of 3 May 2002.

closest to BYZ is the largest of these, K^x (734 out of the 1385 manuscripts profiled in Wisse's study belong in whole or in part to it).

BYZ in *TuT* is a statistical convenience, and stands for the majority reading. But this is saved from the purely mechanical by the care with which variants are identified as either subvariants of the 1: or 2: reading or as Sonderlesarten.

Even 1/2: readings, which could be dismissed as useless in distinguishing between older and BYZ readings, are significant. Their value is that they are older readings. That is, the internal analysis of the reading in its relationship to the history of the text is treated as part of the profiling. Compared to this, CPM might be seen as a method that ignores the textual history (although Wisse does say that 'Care must be taken to judge the value of each reading for the definition of a group',[53] he does not offer any criteria). Textual history should pay attention to the whole shape of a text, its agreements and differences.

9. There follows from this a point which this writer has always been afraid of expressing, because it seems so obvious as to be absurd. What do we mean by, for example, 'the Byzantine text'? Where there is no difference between the manuscripts and no need to conjecture error, the text is Alexandrian *and* Byzantine *and* every other text-type. It follows that a reading is not Byzantine just because it is in Byzantine manuscripts. That is why the difference between 2: + 1/2: readings in *TuT* is so important. Where (a) Byzantine manuscript(s) agree(s) with the text of NA[27], agreements of 1 1582, or 01 03 with BYZ do not necessarily constitute a BYZ reading. Nor do they necessarily constitute an Alexandrian reading, of course, except in the historical sense that the BYZ reading is later than the Alexandrian reading. This could be expressed in another way, by pointing to the distinction between the 'majority' and the 'Byzantine' text. One may say that all Byzantine readings are attested by the majority of manuscripts, but not all majority readings are Byzantine.[54]

While differences from a norm are a convenient way of defining agreement, the actual agreement between two manuscripts will be all the places where they agree (to be tautologous). Obvious indeed, but it would be a mistake to forget it. The significance of the

---

53 Wisse, 43.
54 This point is suggested by Dr Wachtel, in the same e-mail (note 3 above).

question 'what is the Byzantine text?' is that divergencies from the TR do not necessarily constitute all that is distinctive about a manuscript. That is why it was helpful to look at the whole profile of 871 and 1566. Places where they do *not* depart from the 'Byzantine' text are as important as those where they do. At present, the restrictions of the printed book make it rather hard to gather all this information, and to find closely related witnesses. An electronic database would make it much easier to gather all the necessary data for more complex analysis. It would be very helpful to be able to process the *TuT* data by computer in order to find pairings and small groups.

10. What would happen if one treated Wisse's K^x as BYZ, and reported its majority reading as the 1: or 1/2: reading? This begs the question whether this is what it is every time. 'Due to the overwhelming numbers, any attempt to represent the Byzantine minuscules by a single siglum will result in the obliteration by K^x of all other Byzantine groups'.[55]

11. It is evident that CPM in Luke used far too few manuscripts. The number excluded (468 out of the 1853 in the *Liste* in 1969) represents 25 per cent of the whole. In addition, the abbreviation NP (No Profile) for Chapter 10 shows up very often. In all, I count 425 manuscripts, just under a third of those profiled, of which this is true. Just over two-thirds therefore of the 1385 manuscripts classified by Wisse were profiled in all three chapters. In fact, this means that we only have the full three-chapter profile of 960 out of 1853 manuscripts in the *Liste* at that time, that is, just over half.

12. Further problems with CPM include the formation of group profiles on the basis of a sample, and the ignoring of all singular readings. This may have seemed reasonable at the time, but the more scientific way is to collate all manuscripts in full in the test chapters, and compile the profiles on that basis. This is more feasible now that many tasks can be done by computer.[56]

13. The only sure way to check whether the evidence on Group 1519 is reliable would be to make a full examination of the manuscripts concerned, their known history, codicological and palaeographical comparisons, and full textual analyses. This would provide an independent assessment of the CPM and *TuT* methods. As a very

---

55 Wisse, 94.
56 The IGNTP profiling of manuscripts of John is following this principle.

unsatisfactory beginning to that, I offer here an indication of the dates of the member manuscripts.

Cent.	MSS
X	24 36 2812
XI	186 269 1211 1309 1321 1519 1566 (XI/XII) 2132 2437 (XI/XII)
XII	32 1416 1481 2126
XIII	5 871

This crude information might illuminate the pattern of readings shared and disputed by the group members. It is interesting enough to note that the core members are not the oldest.

14. Where the numbers of readings creating a profile are quite small, error in collation could make a rather significant difference in the allocation of a witness to a group.

New Testament textual scholars are slowly advancing towards a fuller knowledge of the history of the text than has ever been possible before. Both the methods surveyed here make a significant contribution towards this goal.

18 The Quest of the Critical Edition

'When, at some future day,
(so begins Albert Schweitzer's *The Quest of the Historical Jesus*)
> our period of civilisation shall lie, closed and completed, before the eyes of later generations, German theology will stand out as a great, a unique phenomenon in the mental and spiritual life of our time ...
> And the greatest achievement of German theology is the critical investigation of the life of Jesus. What it has accomplished here has laid down the conditions and determined the course of the religious thinking of the future.'[1]

It might be said that, having come to praise Caesar, Schweitzer proceeds to bury him, for he goes on to demonstrate the shortcomings, and the inevitable failure, of the Quest of the Historical Jesus, how each writer 'created him in accordance with his own character' and, finally and devastatingly, himself presents a Jesus who believed that in his own actions he was bringing the world order to an end, a Jesus who indeed (although not as he intended) 'destroyed the world into which he was born', who 'leads to battle against our thought a host of dead ideas, a ghostly army upon which death has no power, and himself destroys again the truth and goodness which His Spirit creates in us, so that it cannot rule the world'.[2] What Schweitzer so convincingly claimed was the historical futility of trying to speak about the historical Jesus, and the religious futility of trying to live with a first-century millenarian prophet. Given the huge impact of Schweitzer's work on twentieth-century thought, it is perhaps surprising that so much endeavour has been continued to be given to the attempt to present a reconstruction of Jesus as a historical figure. Since 1906, when Schweitzer brought the Quest to an end, we have had the New Quest of the fifties and sixties, followed by the Third Quest of the eighties and nineties. More today than ever before, there is a desire to uncover the historical, the ancient and the authentic. The study of the Gospels, in particular of their sources and of the relationship between them, has

---

1 A. Schweitzer, *Von Reimarus zu Wrede. Eine Geschichte der Leben-Jesu-Forschung*, Tübingen, 1906. Quotations from the English translation by W. Montgomery, London, 1910. This quotation from p. 1.
2 Schweitzer, 2.

continued unabated. In recent years, it has even led to a critical edition, presented in quasi-text critical language, of the putative common source of Matthew and Luke known as Q.

Schweitzer sets out in his memorable opening the conviction that critical historical investigation is the greatest achievement possible in theology. Whether all theologians would accept this is a moot point. But it is true that the overwhelming majority would accept that the thoughtful study of the Bible is an essential part of the theologian's work. It is very curious, therefore, to discover that, in spite of all this intense historical activity, in spite of the place of the Bible in theology, relatively little attention has been paid to the study of the text of the New Testament. The theologian may be content with almost anything in whatever language is convenient, and professional New Testament scholars are content to assume that the standard hand-edition is adequate for their purposes. Incredibly, the critical edition of Q uses this text without even referring to variant readings in the *apparatus*. And this disregard is in spite of the fact that, in the past century, and especially between 1930 and 1970, our knowledge of the text was dramatically altered by the discovery of third-, and even second-century papyri. The number of New Testament textual critics is small, so that progress is slow: we have still fully to assimilate this new material. Moreover, in addition to having to reappraise earlier histories of the text in the light of the papyrus finds, scholarship has been faced with two further momentous challenges: the dramatic developments in textual theory of recent decades, and the advent of the electronic text. Both these phenomena have led us to abandon many of our preconceptions, so that we have left behind a great deal of what we believed we knew about our texts. And yet, and yet, the world of New Testament scholarship and the world of theology seem to be sailing across the ocean under full sail and on their own course, oblivious to all other shipping, and even unaware that their own decks may not be as secure as they seem.

The situation is very similar in the textual criticism of the Hebrew Bible.[3] There are scrolls from Qumran, pre-dating the first century of the common era, in which for the first time we find readings in Hebrew manuscripts which support variants in the Septuagint. Where scholars

---

3   On the textual criticism of the Hebrew Bible, see Emanuel Tov, *Textual Criticism of the Hebrew Bible*, Minneapolis, 1992. On the Septuagint, see R.W. Klein, *Textual Criticism of the Old Testament. The Septuagint after Qumran*, Philadelphia, 1974; Emanuel Tov, *The Text-critical Use of the Septuagint in Biblical Research* (Jerusalem Biblical Studies 8), 2nd edn., Jerusalem, 1997.

had always supposed the Septuagint to be a free rendering, or to have formed its own variants, it is now arguable that it represents a form of the Hebrew text which had been lost until the discovery of the scrolls. The critical edition of these writings currently being produced, the so-called *Biblia Hebraica Quinta*, follows its predecessors in presenting a diplomatic edition of the famed Leningrad Codex, even in its errors, even where the evidence of the ancient versions and Qumran manuscripts demonstrate that one could do better.[4] It is reasonable to produce a critical edition of the Massoretic Text, which is a very carefully produced text, containing the fruit of intensive study and which, moreover, has shaped a thousand years of reading and living and it is arguable that a representation of the Leningrad Codex is a good way in which to do this. What is surprising is that there is so little ambition on the part of textual critics to reconstruct older forms of the Hebrew text. Scholars are as tied to the Massoretic Text as once critics of the Greek Testament were to the Textus Receptus. Hebrew textual criticism still awaits its Lachmann.

It should by now be plain that the textual criticism of the New Testament has been deeply influenced by many other factors. I would like to speak about several of these factors, and suggest how the Quest of the Critical Edition is affected by them. Because the quest is not an axiom of life. Whatever it is, it is a product of a number of intellectual and technological developments.

1. The *User* of the Critical Edition

The situation in which textual criticism of the New Testament is currently placed is as follows. For the most part, it has been practised in Europe. Indeed, so rich are the resources and tradition, that it is easy to see it as a western preserve. The power of western European scholarship has been such that many manuscripts that were produced in Greek and Coptic and Syriac-speaking and other regions have been brought into our libraries. The reference works, the technical aids and the critical editions that have poured forth over several centuries can for the most part be found only in European and North American libraries. But, although the weight of scholarship may lie in these

---

4   For information on the *Biblia Hebraica Quinta*, see http://www.unifr.ch/bif/Chapters/bh5.html. Comments by Professor David Clines on a draft fascicle are available at http://www.shef.ac.uk/uni/academic/A-C/biblst/DJACcurrres/BHQNotes.html.

regions, it is also the case that students all over the world are learning Koine Greek and studying the New Testament text. What are the textual aspirations of these readers, the range of whose languages make Luke's list of native tongues present on the day of Pentecost into a mere side-show? Is textual criticism nothing to them? Are these increasingly significant groups of users going to be content with what we are able to give them, or will they have demands of their own? Pragmatically, New Testament textual critics may have to acknowledge that the size of their European clientele is dwindling. Globally, however, the number of people interested in the texts in question is at least no smaller than it was a century ago.

That is promising. But it is also true to say that the worldwide interest in the text is not currently matched by a worldwide interest in textual criticism. There are exceptions, of course. For years the only journal devoted to New Testament textual criticism was one written in Japanese.[5] One of the most interesting questions is whether, and if so how, we can change this situation. We are not helped by the fact that those teachers and scholars in Asia, Africa and South America who have studied in Europe are unlikely to have learned the importance of textual criticism as the foundation of studying the text.[6] A vital task before us is to stimulate a worldwide interest in the importance, problems and tasks of textual study. In all honesty, we should attempt to do this without attempting to dictate the directions, methodologies and responses to which scholars from different backgrounds and with different presuppositions may be led. This is because the important thing is to introduce people to the significance and fascination of the problem and the questions. They will not be open to that if we claim to know all the possible answers. And we should be alert also to the dangers of textual globalisation and of intellectual neo-imperialism. But the task is of the utmost importance. There is at present the potential for textual study to take stimulating new directions and to be reborn. There is also a possibility that it may wither on the vine in the face of new kinds of fundamentalism. In the current world climate, textual criticism is as important as it has ever been as a bulwark against all fundamentalism.

---

5   Toshio Hirunuma (ed.), *Studia Textus Novi Testamenti*. The last issue to have reached me is No. 334 (March 1999). The series began in 1966.
6   For a survey of the topic, see E.A. Nida, 'The New Testament Greek Text in the Third World', E.J. Epp and G.D. Fee (eds.), *New Testament Textual Criticism, Its Significance for Exegesis. Essays in Honour of Bruce M. Metzger*, Oxford, 1981, 375–80.

With regard to the creation of new users, there is hope in the potential of the electronic text. This may make the primary materials available to those who for good reasons are unable to access the manuscripts and printed books which are essential to our work. The study of the manuscripts is essential to New Testament textual criticism. To many people, access to the manuscripts is almost impossible, and the acquisition of microfilm a daunting task. Online digital images are a solution to their problem.

It is sometimes said that the European Union has the potential to look either inwards or outwards. As we launch a new textual initiative, we need to ask ourselves what aspirations our society might have towards a relationship with the rest of the globe.

I add here an animadversion on *editors*. I believe that some long-standing projects have difficulty in finding adequately trained editors. This could be a cause for regret, except that it should be remembered that new *users* become new *editors*. What third-world Lachmann (to take that name again) still unborn awaits the New Testament? One thing is certain: that it will not be another Lachmann. As the nature of critical editions changes, new gifts will come to the fore. Although some parts of editing (and the degree of mechanical – and, to many people, tedious – labour) may remain the same, some of what goes to make a good editor will be different. Certainly, nobody any longer wants a key to all mythologies.

2. The *Goal* of the Critical Edition

What is the purpose of the Quest? According to Schweitzer, the significance of the quest of the historical Jesus was that it provided an opportunity to rid ourselves of the Christ of faith, 'to strip from Him the robes of splendour with which He had been apparelled, and clothe Him once more with the coarse garments in which He had walked in Galilee'.[7] Many an editor has had a similar ambition to restore a text as it lay before its first readers. In the field of New Testament editing, the two ambitions have sometimes been as one. Some of those scholars of the eighteenth and nineteenth centuries who fought to rid us of the Textus Receptus had a similar ambition to sweep away the accretions of dogmatic construction. At its most extreme, this is represented today by those scholars who believe that the text of the Gospels as it survives

---

7   Schweitzer, *op. cit.*, 5.

is the product of second-century thought. According to the American scholar W.L. Petersen, there is evidence in some witnesses to the text of Matthew that this Gospel once existed in a form which would have been much more congenial to first-century Jewish Christianity.[8] These traces are so slight as to demonstrate the total success of later orthodoxy in ridding the text of tenets which it found distasteful. Another view is presented by the French researcher C.-B. Amphoux, who believes that the four-Gospel format is a pious fiction, and that the Gospels were put together out of a chaotic tradition as late as the first part of the second century.[9]

To others, the quest is based on a belief that is contrary, yet based on a similar presupposition: that we can recover primitive forms of the text which, by their close approximation to the autographs, have a higher claim than later forms to be read and heeded, that is, to be treated with the utmost respect both historically and theologically. It is undeniable that New Testament textual criticism has been strongly driven by the demands of the majority of users of the text. The idea that there can be no such thing as an authoritative autograph has not, at least until recently, occurred to many users of the New Testament. There is instead a belief in a 'final form' of the text (this final form they usually identify with the self-styled 'working text' of Nestle-Aland[27]).[10]

I think that these approaches have, in their different ways, both contributed to a remarkable phenomenon in the study of the New Testament text. I mean the almost total lack of interest in the possibility of theological motivation in the creation of variant readings. Exploration of this subject scarcely began before the middle of the last century, and only received its first full-scale treatment in 1993. In *The Orthodox Corruption of Scripture*, Bart Ehrman produced compelling evidence of textual variation that arose as a result of theological debate in early Christianity.[11] Specifically, he adduced variants that plausibly

---

8 He has argued this most explicitly in several as yet unpublished papers. But see his articles 'Constructing the Matrix of Judaic Christianity from Texts', in S. Mimoumi (ed.), *Le Judéo-Christianisme dans tous ses états* (Lectio Divina, sine numero), Paris, 2001, 126–44; 'The Parable of the Lost Sheep in the Gospel of Thomas and the Synoptics', *NovT* 23 (1981), 128–47.

9 See, for example, 'Schéma d'Histoire du Texte du Nouveau Testament, *New Testament Textual Research Update* 3/3 (May/June, 1995), 41–6. English summary 47–51. See also D.C. Parker, 'Professor Amphoux's History of the New Testament Text: A Response', *New Testament Textual Research Update* 4/3 (May/June, 1996), 41–45.

10 *Nestle-Aland[27]*, 45*. It was suggested in discussion after the paper by Hans Gabler that the original German 'Arbeitstext' (2*) has perhaps a somewhat different sense.

11 B.D. Ehrman, *The Orthodox Corruption of Scripture*, Oxford, 1993.

arose out of 'orthodox' conviction that wordings which supported 'heretical' views must be misleading. 'Orthodox' scribes and readers believed that the authors of the New Testament writings could not have intended what they appeared to write, and so 'corrected', rewrote the text. I refer to this work because I believe it to be significant for our quest in two ways. The first is that in it for the first time we see fully that the study of the New Testament text and its variants can provide a theological and social as well as a textual history. The second is that the editorial task – as we well know – is to provide the proper materials for a study of that textual history, and not just the original form – but it should also be to provide the materials for the theological and social history. Here, of course, palaeography and codicology have a no less important part to play. I wonder how far our interest as textual critics in the more technical aspects of our craft blinds us to the variants that other people might find most interesting?

3. The *Use* of the Critical Edition

Here, most obviously, the demands of users have affected textual criticism. It has generally been assumed that translations for use in public worship and private reading and devotion will be based on the best available editions. As a matter of fact, the reality has always been more complicated, with a good dose of conservatism holding back the translators. For example, obscurities in the Hebrew Bible are often resolved in Christian translations by recourse to the Septuagint (which in its extant representatives is unlikely to be free from Christian interpretation). There are those today who would advocate a separation between the critical and the ecclesiastical text. For example, David Trobisch has argued that there was a 'first edition' of the Christian, Greek, Bible in the late second century, and that Christianity should re-adopt that, with an Old Testament based on the Greek and not the Hebrew text.[12] Similarly, Amphoux believes that the traditional Bible should be read in church, although to the scholar it is a text that cannot make a claim on the allegiance.[13] And a similar, very specific issue, has led to an interesting development in my own view of the task of editing the Greek text. To eastern orthodoxy, the assumption of western scholarship that the editor's task is to restore the oldest

[39]

---

12   D. Trobisch, *The First Edition of the New Testament*, Oxford, 2000, final chapter.
13   I report a conversation between us.

recoverable form of text, has never been axiomatic. And in particular, it has found the result unsatisfactory. The Byzantine text is to the western critical scholar the final development of the New Testament text, at the end of its history and as far as possible from anything authentic. To the Orthodox it is the form in which they receive the apostolic tradition, the familiar and hallowed words that are recited in worship and read in private. To them modern translations based on a modern critical text are unwelcome and are variants without a context. As a result, they challenged the United Bible Societies to produce a critical edition of the Byzantine text. A prototype of this project has been begun in Birmingham, an edition of the text of John. For the users, it is hoped that they will be provided for the first time with a scientifically produced form of the text, showing the readings of the main groups of witnesses and the historical development of the text. For the scholars producing it, there are some important challenges and gains. The challenges include the technical difficulties of reconstructing the text and deciding how to present it. The gains include a fresh perspective on the evidence, and a deeper historical understanding. Above all it offers the interest of an alternative to the traditional task of textual criticism.

The matter of usage is certainly one that is changing, quite simply because we can do different things with our new texts (as well as not being able to do some of the things we used to).

[40]

4. The Medium

I should at this stage refer briefly to the question of the *medium*. I do not want to go over familiar ground here, but I would like to make one comment. It is that we invent things, not by chance but because we need them. Printing was 'invented' because mass production seemed a good idea, was necessary to someone's thinking. Computers have been invented, specifically invented in textual work, because we wanted them. To get the best out of them, we need to keep reminding ourselves of this, and of two questions: what have they got to offer that quill pens and typewriters lacked? and what do they lack that the pens and hot metal possessed?

Ulrich Schmid, a member of our Principio Project research team, has an observation that helps us to grasp this point, and Valerie Edden has capped it. Early Christianity devised the codex because it was more convenient than the roll. In order to be able to study the codices they produced more easily, we invented a new kind of roll, the microfilm. And going a stage further, modern scholarship, presented with an exciting new development, has now invented the vertical scroll on the computer screen. We have to agree that the electronic text is wonderful, but the electronic scroll is a step back into the past. The codex facilitated the comparison of parallel passages in the Gospels. Hypertext is an arguably less convenient way of doing the same thing.

5. The Nature of Quests

In one form or another, the quest of the critical text is as old as the texts with which it deals. It is arguable that P75, one of the most significant of the papyri to which I referred earlier, is a late second-century product of thoughtful textual criticism. It presents a careful, 'controlled' text.[14] Certainly, within a generation, Origen with his remarkable Hexapla was producing a major critical edition, of the Greek versions of the Hebrew Scriptures.[15] It is noteworthy, to revert briefly to an earlier theme, that he was motivated not solely by philology. The need for a reliable text to be used in controversy with the Jews, as well as with pagan writers, was at least as important a motivation.

And the quest is, it goes without saying, an unending one. This is the case both technically and in terms of result. If you have been editing the Acta Sanctorum, having begun at January 1 in 1643, what do you do when you get to December 31 in the twenty-first century? The answer is, you begin again at the beginning, because the technology, the critical theory, the materials available, and the user requirements, have all changed dramatically in the interim. The same will certainly happen to the brilliant technical achievements of our new computer age. We are in the exciting position of being pioneers, so that at least we can hope that future generations will hail our audacity. But we must also accept that our efforts will quite quickly be overtaken.

[41]

However, there are yet stronger reasons why the quest is unending. One is the endless human restlessness, our sense that it is much more pleasant to travel than to arrive. Another is that in each generation we need the stimulating presence of those who are recasting our texts, and thereby asking awkward questions and stirring up fresh research. And,

---

14 Martini, *Il problema del codice B*.
15 For the Hexapla, see footnote 3. See also S. Jellicoe, *The Septuagint and Modern Study*, Oxford, 1968.

finally, there is the strangest point of all. There is in the editing of texts a curious paradox. All along, we have believed that we were trying to edit an ever-older and more reliable form of the text. Yet all that we have succeeded in doing is creating fresh forms of an old text, by our habit of editing eclectically, with a reading from here and a reading from there. We shake the kaleidoscope, and a new pattern emerges.

I have spoken about the quest of the critical edition, not about the critical edition itself. And I have spoken on the whole about ways in which the quest is subject to outside influence. But it is also true that textual criticism has had an influence on the reading and usage of the New Testament. As a matter of fact, that influence is probably weaker than it should have been, not least because treating it as a discrete discipline rather than as an aspect of the whole is bound to have that affect. For the future, we can be rather more optimistic about our influence, since the decisions we are making right now will be especially significant in moulding how the texts will be read and used by generations to come.

Context

This is the published version of a paper read to a gathering of textual scholars in Leicester. The colloquium was attended by textual scholars and editors of all kinds. It therefore assumes an audience with no particular expertise in New Testament philology, but a great deal of knowledge about text-critical theory and a combined experience of editing many of the western world's most influential texts.

III. TEXTUAL CRITICISM AND THEOLOGY

19 Scripture is Tradition

At a point in New Testament studies where some of the older orthodoxies seem to be in danger of finding themselves turned into heresies, and in a climate where it is tempting to dismiss textual criticism as a thing of the past and a phenomenon of western theology and culture, I would like to examine the wider implications both of the practice of textual criticism, and of some recent text-critical findings.[1] These implications make themselves felt in questions of methodology, and even more strongly in historical and theological matters. An account of the reasons why textual criticism should continue to be practised shows that the discipline provides, not an escape from those realities of life presented by the text, but a challenge to the unhistorical biblicism of much theology, whether radical or conservative in character.

It is never the case that a text written in the past has its future assured. All the writings of antiquity that have come down to us have endured the tribulations of the saints. They have been at risk from fire, from water, and, if not the sword, at least the penknife. And for the surviving copies, these risks continue. The task of each generation in preserving them has been wearisome and fraught. What has survived is a bundle of fragments.

But, despite this, it might still be claimed that the text of the New Testament is well established. Is there any substantial disagreement? Do we not have Nestle-Aland?[2] The answer to the first question is that there *are* substantial disagreements. Most pressingly, The Trinitarian Bible Society, and many fundamentalist groups in the USA and elsewhere, maintain the inerrancy of the Textus Receptus, a bad text created haphazardly by the sixteenth century out of the imperfectly understood materials it had to hand. And among those who accept the need for something better than that hopeless anachronism, there is by no means full agreement. The seven major editions from Tischendorf's last (1872) to the twenty-fifth of Nestle-Aland (1963) (the others are

---

1 I refer particularly to my book *Codex Bezae*, to be published by Cambridge University Press in 1991.
2 *Nestle-Aland*[26].

Westcott and Hort, von Soden, Vogels, Merk, and Bover)[3] agree in the wording of 62.9 per cent of the verses of the New Testament. (Note: this is *not* the same as saying that they agree in 62.9 per cent of the wording of the New Testament.) The proportion ranges from 45.1 per cent in Mark to 81.4 per cent in 2 Timothy. This represents *something* of a consensus, but it should be realised that, especially in the last half-century, there has been a steady change in thinking which means that the twenty-sixth edition of Nestle-Aland is different from its predecessor in over five hundred places. The task of evaluating new evidence – and the significance of papyrus copies found in the half-century has been considerable – continues, and we have no knowledge of what may still be found.

[12] Apart from this, to say that there is a consensus is simply to acknowledge that there is a dominant interpretation of the mass of evidence which confronts us. The correct text is not self-evident, and a future generation might establish a quite different text, one which abolished most of our current assumptions. Indeed, were we to include the editions of Luke and Acts by Blass,[4] and of Acts by Clark[5] with the statistics of the seven major editions that we have just examined, the proportion of agreement in those books would be very dramatically reduced. There is a mass of material to be considered: in Nestle-Aland's twenty-fifth edition, 10.3 variants per page in Mark down to 2.5 in Philippians. The International Greek New Testament's apparatus of Luke[6] provides, I reckon, upwards of 30,000 variants for that Gospel, so that we have, for example, 81 in the Lord's Prayer. There is certainly no reason to suppose that the volume of material for the apparatus to the Fourth Gospel will be any smaller. Something more than personal preference and a theology which is on the side of the angels is necessary if we are to have a text that can be taken seriously by the churches as a representative of the first centuries rather than the present. This is supplied by the textual critic in the form of a reconstruction of the history of the text.

---

3   For bibliographical references, see Aland and Aland, *Text*[1], Chapter 1. The statistical information is derived from Tables 1 and 2 (29f).

4   F. Blass (ed.), *Euangelium secundum Lucam . . . secundum formam quae videtur romanam*, Leipzig, 1897; *Acta Apostolorum . . . secundum formam quae videtur romanam*, Leipzig, 1896.

5   A.C. Clark (ed.), *The Acts of the Apostles*, Oxford, 1933.

6   *The New Testament in Greek. The Gospel according to St Luke*, edited by the American and British Committees of the International Greek New Testament Project, 2 vols., Oxford, 1984–7.

It is important to realise that we do not possess the Greek New Testament. What we have is a mass of manuscripts, of which only about three hundred date from before 800 AD. A mere thirty-four of these are older than 400, of which only four were at any time complete. All these differ, and all at one time or another *had* authority as the known text. The reconstruction of the history of the text is the relating of these known points in such a way that we can see how readings entered the text. The tradition flows on[7] – and the manuscripts are just points in it. A history of the text is a means of evaluating the 30,000 variants in Luke. A major task in the reconstruction of this history is the examination of individual manuscripts to discover *why* each one takes the form that it does. It is an examination, both of the text and of the physical characteristics of the manuscripts. This includes trying to see why a manuscript is *visually* as it is, and to reconstruct the appearance of its ancestors. The initial aim, therefore, is not to establish the original wording of the New Testament, but to assess our materials and to give a history. What is left after that will be the material for establishing a better text.

The basis for the history of the text that is about to be offered is the study of a particular New Testament manuscript, one that represents a remarkably free form of text. This manuscript, Codex Bezae, now consists of the Gospels and Acts, in parallel Greek and Latin columns. It was copied in about the year 400. One of the most significant features of its text of the Gospels is extensive harmonisation (in all there are over 1200 examples; a harmonisation is the alteration of the wording of one Gospel to agree with that of one or more of the other three). Other characteristics are the introduction of material about Jesus from elsewhere, and a tendency to rewrite or to alter the text, frequently in a more colloquial style. An example of the former is an addition after Lk 6.4, where Jesus sees a man working on the sabbath and says to him, 'If you know what you are doing, you are blessed; if you do not, then you are accursed and a transgressor of the law'. In Acts, the text is considerably longer than that generally known, and contains extensive rewritings of passages, to the extent that we have what could be described as a separate version of Acts.[8] This text is even willing to change the content of the apostolic decree of Acts 15. It omits the reference to what is strangled, adding 'and that whatsoever they would not should be done to them ye do not to others' (Acts 15.20). This free

[13]

---

7   The image is used by Zuntz, *The Text of the Epistles*, particularly 265.
8   It has been translated by J.M. Wilson, *The Acts of the Apostles Translated from the Codex Bezae*, London, 1924 (1923).

version developed by stages, which can be at least partially reconstructed. Of these books, then, the text of Acts was the most freely treated, that of Matthew the most secure. The text of Mark was the most harmonised, that of John the least, and that of Luke the most freely recast of the Gospels. It should be noted that we are concerned only with the Gospels and Acts. The other books and collections of the New Testament all have their own histories.

Although it has sometimes been claimed that the free text form of Codex Bezae is of a late date – the work of the manuscript's scribe, or of 'an outstanding early theologian of the third/fourth century'[9] – there is substantial evidence that it is as old as the second century. This period has long been known to have been one of great significance for the text of the Gospels. It has even been argued that almost all significant deliberate variations in copying were first made before the year 200. There are a number of reasons for the importance of this period.

The first of these is that there occurred a change in attitudes to the oral tradition. Papias, early in the century, is actually cited by Eusebius as preferring oral to written traditions about Jesus: 'I supposed that things out of books did not profit me so much as the utterances of a voice *which liveth and abideth*'.[10] In such a context, it is unlikely that written texts can have been free from alterations or additions from trusted oral sources. For example, may not a saying received at one remove from an eyewitness have been more highly estimated than the version of Luke, whose authorities were, as he himself confesses, other written accounts?

Secondly, there was in the middle of the second century a considerable discussion about the fourfold witness of the Gospels. Marcion, who claimed the authority of Paul for maintaining that there could only be one Gospel, produced his own highly distinctive version of Luke as the only admissible account. Slightly later, Tatian produced his Diatessaron, a harmony in which the materials from all of our Gospels were combined into a single account. Debate continues as to the effect that Marcion or Tatian and their several opponents may have had on the text. One effect of this period is undeniable: the process of harmonisation, which is so major a feature of the Gospel of Mark in Codex Bezae.

Thirdly, it may be that only in the course of the second century did the Gospels and Acts achieve literary status. While Luke and Acts may

---

9   Aland/Aland, *Text*[1] 69.
10 Eusebius, *History of the Church* 3.39. See J. Stevenson, *A New Eusebius*, revised edition, London, 1987, 47.

have been properly published as a two-volume work on two separate rolls, it has been argued that Mark was originally written in a notebook – a codex – for private circulation and not for publication.[11] There need have been no reason why such a book could not have been altered or enlarged. It seems that the non-literary status of Mark may have been extended, by association, to the other Gospels, including Luke's second volume. Certainly, the most distinctive physical characteristic of early Christian texts is that (with three exceptions) all copies of New Testament writings are written on codices, while Jewish and Greek literary texts continued to be copied onto rolls.

Fourthly, the process of selecting four Gospels can lead us to forget that in the second century there existed material about Jesus which was preserved in other places and, even if freely treated thereafter, found its way into other documents. The *Gospel of Thomas* from Nag Hammadi has a *form* that is not dissimilar to that of the hypothetical document Q. This is in itself significant, apart from any sayings that may be shown by analysis to have a claim to authenticity, or to represent a *form* independent of that in any of our four Gospels.

This evidence, when we examine it in the particular form in which it is found in Codex Bezae, shows us that the text, including sayings of Jesus, could be treated very freely, so that the wording is expanded, shortened, or altered on many occasions.

It seems that from at least about the year 200, a textual criticism that had been learned from producing improved texts of the Greek classics was practised upon the New Testament text. From this point on, a literary status will thereby have been granted to the text, in a way that became increasingly normative. As to the possibility that such a criticism may have been undertaken earlier, and as to its success or the quality of the texts available to it – these are important matters that await further study. What I hope to have established is the existence, in the second century and later, of a free text form.

What is most striking is the similarity between this free text and the ways in which the teaching of Jesus was transmitted *before* our Gospels were written. There are a historical and a theological point to be drawn from this.

---

11   C.H. Roberts, 'The Codex', *PBA* 40 (1954), 169–204. See, more recently, C.H. Roberts and T.C. Skeat, *The Birth of the Codex*, Oxford, 1983. They abandon the earlier emphasis on Mark, suggesting instead that the papyrus codex originated at Antioch before the year 100, on the analogy of notebooks in which the oral law was recorded (see 58–61).

The historical fact is that this free text form is proof that at least some people in the early church altered the received sayings of Jesus. It is not possible to dismiss as sheer conjecture claims that there were earlier forms of sayings in the oral stage. Apart from the different forms of sayings in the various Gospels, which it is sometimes argued are not variant forms of a single base text, the free text form *proves* that to change sayings of Jesus was an option for at least some people in the early church.

The theological point begins with the recognition that modern debate has generally been about whether the earliest Christians were *able* to hand down the teaching of Jesus unchanged. The existence of the free text form shows that the real question is whether they *chose* to. This text indicates that to at least some early Christians, it was more important to hand on the spirit of Jesus' teaching than to remember the letter. It is of considerable importance that the existence of this way of thinking be remembered today, if the character of early Christianity and of the way in which Jesus' teaching was preserved are not to be distorted in polemic. For example, debate on a given contemporary issue often focuses on the precise wording of a saying of Jesus. Any attempt to produce an alternative view founded on broad principles is then regarded as open to attack as unhistorical. Once it is recognised that the material about Jesus was preserved in an interpretative rather than an exact fashion, then a view based on a precise interpretation of the wording may be shown to be an attempt to absolutize a particular post-Jesus interpretation, which itself requires scrutiny. It has also to be asked whether such an attitude to the sayings of Jesus is not consonant with the radical character of much of Jesus' own attitude to tradition.

These are the broader implications of my study of a single manuscript. We now apply them to the role of textual criticism in current theological scholarship, in the three areas with which I began.

1. Methodology. We have to begin with a critical foundation for analysis, as for that of any other ancient text. This critical method has been practised in New Testament studies since at least the third century. It is not a product of modern western culture, and is in a sense integral to the character of the documents.

2. The historical perspective. This should be clear from our discussion of the handling of the sayings of Jesus in the text. To repeat, there is a continuum between the transmission of the oral period and the copying of the written documents. That is to say, the task of analysing the traditions about Jesus is conducted by the analogous disciplines of textual criticism and Gospel criticism. The one studies the

manuscript traditions to establish the text of the Gospels, the other analyses traditions within the Gospels. If the latter is to be true to the character of the tradition, then its practitioners should avoid behaving as though the Nestle text provided them with copies of the evangelists' autographs, and realise that all textual critics can soberly hope to give them is a version of one of the available early texts. Thus Lachmann and Westcott and Hort gave us the text of the fourth century.[12] Nestle-Aland sets out to give us a pre-Constantinian Alexandrian text based on some of the papyri. Behind this third/fourth-century text lies an earlier period of more than a century in which the tradition about Jesus was handled in a particular way, irrespective of whether the type of transmission was oral or written.

A further dimension is provided by the study of extra-canonical Gospels – for example, the *Gospel of Thomas* – and of other materials. We are no longer in a period when the New Testament provides the *only* witness to first-century Judaeo-Christian thought. Instead, we have a more extensive body of documents, of which a few were later adopted by the church as consonant with or foundational for, depending on how you see it, the *regula fidei*. [16]

3. Some theological implications. I have already made the most important one, with regard to the freedom with which the tradition could be handled. There are several others.

The first is that the question of *sola scriptura* has to be approached rather differently once we appreciate that what we call the New Testament, and what we call the Gospels, are a fairly late reaction by the church to certain events. This is to say that in the beginning there were traditions about Jesus. Then there were Gospels, a part of these streams of tradition. Later still, there were deemed to be four Gospels, and the question of the accuracy of the traditions became subordinate to the claim for the authority of the writings. Yet, even then, the character of all manuscript copying meant that there was a continuing interplay between the Scripture – the text copied – and the tradition – the person engaged in the process of copying in and for the church. That is, we have a double interaction of Scripture and tradition in the copying; the one arising out of the fluidity of the early period, the other out of the inevitably provisional character of all manuscript copies. Finally, there came printed texts. Here we have a claim for authority made on behalf of texts that, instead of being provisional (unique

---

12 For bibliographical references, see Aland and Aland, *Text*[1], Chapter 1.

attempts to copy a text in the knowledge that the result will be imperfect), can be reproduced exactly thousands or millions of times.

This leads to the second point, one which is necessary if we are to understand the character of a manuscript as opposed to a printed tradition. There is a sense in which there is no such thing as the New Testament. What is available to us is a number of reconstructions of some or all of the documents classified as belonging to the New Testament – some of these reconstructions are manuscripts, say P75 or Codex Vaticanus; others are printed texts like Nestle-Aland. Textual criticism makes it clear that the text is in a sense inaccessible to us. The fact that the recovery of the original text is a task that remains beyond all of us sets a question mark against any claim that we can in any sense 'possess' the text – literally or metaphorically.

To draw these final points together: the traditions about Jesus flow through the early church. The writing of Gospels by their evangelists represent some fixed points in the continuum, ones which are not directly available to us. The copyings of these texts represent further points, of which a few have survived. To a greater or lesser extent, they make the Gospels available to us. Then there are printed texts, the most recent and most persuasively authentic forms of the tradition. All are the traditions conveying the traditions about Jesus.

In no sense can it be said that the Gospels may be regarded as independent of the traditions. They convey part of the early tradition, and are transmitted to us only by tradition. In fact, Scripture is tradition.

Explanation

This began life as a paper read to the termly joint meeting held by the staff of Queen's and Oscott colleges in Birmingham. It took place in the Common Room at Oscott in 1990, and was the piece of writing which led on from the last chapter of *Codex Bezae* and set me on the road towards *The Living Text of the Gospels*. In fact a small part of it was reworked there. The title came out of the meeting. During the discussion, David McLoughlin, then of Oscott, observed 'What you're saying is that Scripture *is* tradition'. So it is his title.

20 The Early Tradition of Jesus' Sayings on Divorce

The nature of marriage, the problem of divorce, and the possibility of remarriage, have been pressing theological and pastoral concerns in the modern churches. Inevitably, the sayings of Jesus have been claimed as support in what has been said and done. Tragically, discussion of these sayings has been marked by ignorance and dishonesty in discussion of the historical questions, and consequently by theological confusion and nonsense. Generally, debate has centred on the meaning of a single authoritative text. It is the purpose of this article to demonstrate that such a text does not exist today, and never has existed, and that therefore the theological arguments are castles in the air. I shall first analyse the sayings concerned, and then examine a number of church reports in the light of my findings.[1]

Study of the sayings about divorce in the Gospels has almost invariably followed a standard pattern. First, the text of each evangelist is described, using a modern printed Greek or English text. Then the differences between them are discussed, and certain of these shown to be secondary. Finally, one form or another is declared authentic, and by implication authoritative. But there are two massive problems with this approach: the first is that there are also variations within the manuscript traditions of each passages. Sometimes the differences between the manuscripts of one passage are greater than those between our printed Gospels. The problem is not simply one of explaining the differences between Matthew, Mark and Luke. As we shall see, we are in fact discussing a score of different forms of words of Jesus. The second problem is that in general practice an equivalence has been assumed in the meaning of words such as 'divorce' and 'adultery' between our culture and those of early Christianity. A study of the manuscripts shows this set of presuppositions to be gravely mistaken.

In listing the variations, I shall provide my own English translation of each variant form of the text, in a way that attempts to bring out

---

[1] I have discussed the challenge of textual criticism to theology, in particular by drawing attention to the freedom of the early versions of the text, in 'Scripture is Tradition', *Theology* 94 (January/February 1991), 11–17. [See Chapter 19]

smaller variations which do not affect the sense. The principal evidence for each variation is also given,[2] followed by the major English versions that support it.[3]

---

[2] The symbols used indicate the following manuscripts and versions:

א – Codex Sinaiticus, copied towards the middle of the fourth century, gives for the most part an Alexandrian text, though it has a number of readings found in free texts like D.

B – Codex Vaticanus, the principal representative of the Alexandrian text, copied at the same time or slightly before א.

Byz – the Byzantine text, the Greek 'Authorized Version' from the sixth century onwards.

cet (*ceteri*) – the other ancient witnesses.

C – Codex Ephraemi Rescriptus, a fifth-century manuscript. It has an Alexandrian text, with a considerable number of Byzantine readings. It is not extant at Mt 5.32 or Lk 16.18. C* indicates the original scribe, in readings where the text was later corrected. C³ was a corrector of the ninth century.

D – the Greek column of Codex Bezae, the best known 'free text', copied in about the year 400, at Beirut. Lower-case d indicates the parallel (though not always identical) Latin version.

f^1 – Family 1, a group of minuscule manuscripts copied at various dates in the twelfth to fourteenth centuries. Their text is largely Caesarean in Mark.

f^{13} – Family 13, a family of a dozen medieval manuscripts that, like f^1, contains Caesarean features.

L – an eighth-century manuscript which often supports the Alexandrian text.

mae – a fourth- or fifth-century Coptic text of Matthew (the Codex Scheide) in the Middle Egyptian dialect.

N – a sixth-century manuscript which preserves a number of Caesarean readings in its mainly Byzantine text-type.

P25 – a fourth-century papyrus manuscript containing a few fragments of Matthew's Gospel.

pc (*pauci*) – a few witnesses.

sy – the Syriac versional tradition. sy (s) is the fourth-century Sinaitic Syriac manuscript, representing the oldest known (*c.* 200?) Syriac version; sy (p) is the Peshitta version, produced early in the sixth century.

W – the Washington Codex, also known as the Freer Gospels, written in the late fourth or early fifth century. The most recent survey of its text of Mark has rejected the earlier theory that it is Caesarean, concluding that it was 'a MS prepared for popular reading, for religious edification, and for easy comprehension . . . such readings show that some scribes exercised noticeable freedom in making their text intelligible for readers', L.W. Hurtado, *Text-critical Methodology and the Pre-Caesarean Text: Codex W in the Gospel of Mark* (SD 41), Grand Rapids, 1981.

Θ – the Koridethi codex, of the ninth century. Its text is Caesarean in Mark, Byzantine in the other Gospels.

078 – a sixth-century fragment with a distinctive text.

For further details, I refer the reader to Metzger, *Text of the New Testament*[3]; and to Aland and Aland, *Text*[2].

The passages are Mt 5.27–32 and 19.3–9; Mk 10.2–12; Lk 16.18. One could also include Jn 7.53–8.11 and 1 Cor 7.12–16. The textual variation in the latter passage is less remarkable and, since the problems of Paul's letters are of a different character, we will set the passage aside for the present. The story of the woman taken in adultery is one of the best-known examples of expansion to the Gospel text, and would merit a discussion on its own. It did not become part of the Fourth Gospel until the second century; in f^{13} it is placed after Lk 21.38.

We begin with a passage which is unique to Matthew.

Matthew 5.27–32

There are two major variations within it. The first is that D, along with a few other witnesses (including sy (s)), omits the whole of verse 30. This may be an accidental copying error, in which the scribe's eye jumped from the end of verse 29 (which he made more like the end of verse 30) to the end of verse 30. The versional support for the reading shows it to be probably third century, perhaps even older. The other alteration is to verse 32. This is found in three forms:

1. (D and three early Latin witnesses)
Whoever divorces his wife, except for the cause of *porneia*, makes her an adulteress. (d accidentally omits the last four words).

2. (B)
Everyone divorcing his wife, except for the cause of *porneia*, makes her an adulteress, and the person marrying a divorced woman commits adultery.

3. (ℵ W N.-A.[26] Greeven AV RSV JB NJB)
Everyone divorcing his wife, except for the cause of *porneia*, makes her an adulteress, and whoever should marry a divorced woman commits adultery.

---

[3] I cite the following, *Authorized Version* (= AV); *Revised Standard Version*, London, 1946 and 1952 (= RSV); *The New English Bible*, Oxford and Cambridge, 1970 (= NEB); *The Jerusalem Bible*, London, 1974 (= JB); *Good News Bible*, London, 1976 (= GNB); *New International Version*, London, 1979 (=NIV); *The New Jerusalem Bible*, London, 1985 (= NJB); *New Revised Standard Version*, New York and Oxford, 1989 (= NRSV); *The Revised English Bible*, Oxford and Cambridge, 1989 (=REB). In addition, I give the reading of Nestle-Aland[26] (= N.-A.[26]), whose text is identical with UBS[3]; and of H. Greeven, *Synopse der drei Ersten Evangelien*, Tübingen, 1981 (= Greeven). This last authority provides an excellently constructed text, the chief alternative to Nestle-Aland.

4. (NEB NIV NRSV REB)
Whoever divorces his wife, except for the cause of *porneia*, makes her an adulteress, and whoever should marry a divorced woman (her REB) commits adultery.

5. (GNB)
If a man divorces his wife, even though she has not been unfaithful, then he is guilty of making her commit adultery if she marries again; and the man who marries her commits adultery also.

The form of the rendering in GNB is so free that we suggest it to demonstrate that variant readings are still coming into existence. The second, third and fourth forms do not differ significantly from each other (the beginning 'whoever divorces' is a harmonisation of Matthew to Mark 10 that does not affect the sense). Our interest is therefore in comparing two forms of the text. In the first, D keeps the concern of the logion clearly focused on divorce, without including any discussion on the further vexed question of remarriage. This is at least an old text. It seems to have been the form known to Origen.[4] It makes much simpler and better sense than the longer form. For the logion's concern is essentially with 'hardness of heart'. And it is the cruelty of putting off the wife that Jesus is criticising – divorce makes the wife into an adulteress, one guilty of *porneia*, even though she is not. The second part in the longer text could appear to return to preoccupation with the man as the centre of attention – don't marry a divorced woman. But it could also be aimed at protecting a rejected wife from further ignominy, by establishing her right to remain single: her loyalty to her husband has not, from her side, been broken. From her point of view, it is as though she were married still, and this is to be respected. She is not disposable property. We can see that this is consonant with the practice recommended by Paul (1 Cor 7.10–11) and elsewhere in the early church.

The text of the Good News Bible highlights for us that there continue to be widely divergent presuppositions about the content of the key words in this passage. What constitutes the adultery: the divorcing or the remarrying?

Mark 10.2–12

This longer unit is fairly uniformly transmitted in our witnesses until we get to the last two verses. Here we have the following forms:

---

4 *Commentarii in Matthaeum* XVI.16–24, Patrologia Graeca 13, col. 1224–1249.

1. (W)
If a woman divorces her husband and marry another, she commits adultery; and if a man divorces his wife, he commits adultery.

2. (f¹ sy (s))
If a woman divorces her husband and marries another, she commits adultery; and if a man divorces his wife and marries another, he commits adultery.

3. (ℵ B C N.-A.[26] RSV NEB NIV NRSV REB)
Whoever divorces his wife and marries another commits adultery against her; and if she, divorcing her husband marries another, she commits adultery.

[375]

4. (D; f with minor variations)
Whoever divorces his wife and marries another commits adultery against her; and if a woman goes out from her husband and marries another, she commits adultery.

5. (A Byz AV)
Whoever divorces his wife and marries another commits adultery against her; and if a woman divorces her husband and be married to another, she commits adultery.

6. (Greeven JB GNB NJB)
Whoever divorces his wife and marries another commits adultery against her (GNB 'his wife'); and if a woman divorces her husband and marries another, she commits adultery.

The double prohibition that is distinctive to all the forms of the Markan version presupposes that a woman *could* divorce her husband. This was possible in the pagan world, but not in Judaism. It is generally argued that the clause referring to the woman divorcing a man is therefore a formulation by the Roman community.

We note that the text of No. 6 is not attested by any surviving manuscript. It combines elements from Nos. 3 (active 'marry' instead of passive 'be married') and 5 ('a woman' instead of 'she'). Such reconstruction is a perfectly respectable pursuit – as long as one knows what one is doing.

No. 5 has the mark of ecclesiastical sanction. The potentially confusing 'she' has been replaced with the clear 'a woman', and we have a simple prohibition of remarriage (not divorce, but remarriage) applied to both sexes.

The form in W (No. 1) is unusual. Its oldest witness the Sinaitic Syriac, it seems to take the behaviour of women as the more serious matter for concern. There is also a difference in the act that 'constitutes' adultery. For a woman it is remarriage, for a man it is the prior step of divorce. This text may represent a reinterpretation of the tradition in the light of concern over the status of single, formerly married women in the Christian community. The concern with hardness of heart in Matthew 5 is here replaced by a certain anxiety about those of uncertain status.[5] The second prohibition has also the effect of protecting a wife. This is the least 'rigorist' form of the text.

No. 4 may reflect a situation where formal divorce is not possible for a woman. She can only 'go out' from her husband.

Matthew 19.3–9

This, the parallel passage to Mark, is textually extremely complex in its final verse.

1. (ℵ C³ L N.-A.²⁶ RSV NIV JB NJB NRSV)
Whoever divorces his wife, except for *porneia*, and marries another commits adultery.

2. (D NEB GNB REB)
= 1, but reads 'except for the cause of *porneia*' instead of 'except for *porneia*'.

3. (N pc)
Whoever divorces his wife, except for *porneia*, makes her an adulteress; and the person marrying a divorced woman commits adultery.

4. (f¹ Lvt (ff¹) bo and B, with a minor difference in the second 'marrying')
= 3, but reads 'except for the cause of *porneia*' instead of 'except for *porneia*'.

5. (W Θ 078 and, with a minor difference in the second 'marrying', Byz sy Greeven AV)
Whoever divorces his wife, except for *porneia*, and marries another commits adultery; and whoever marries a divorced woman commits adultery.

6. (C*)
Whoever divorces his wife, except for *porneia*, and marries another makes her an adulteress; and whoever marries a divorced woman commits adultery.

7. (P25)
Whoever divorces his wife, except for *porneia*, and marries another commits adultery; and likewise also he who marries a divorced woman commits adultery.

8. (mae)
= 7, but reads 'except for the cause of *porneia*' instead of 'except for *porneia*'.

As we look at these, we have to remember the tendency to harmonize, both within a Gospel and between Gospels. Thus we must be prepared

---

5   Peter Brown's *The Body and Society. Men, Women and Sexual Renunciation in Early Christianity*, London, 1989, tells the story.

for the influence of both Mt 5.32 and Mk 10.11–12. And we immediately find that in Nos. 2, 4, and 8 'except for the cause of' from Mt 5.32 has displaced 'except for'.

Nos. 3, 4 and 6 give the D text of Mt 5.32 for the first clause, though only 4 has the exact wording 'except for the cause of'. Here, they seem to assume a situation where a man cannot commit adultery in the sense of stepping over a personal boundary. It is the second wife who is in an adulterous state (assuming that 'her' refers to the second and not to the first wife; this may be a very large assumption, affecting our understanding of Mark 10 as well). These, No. 5, and No. 7 all add the extension of adultery to a man who marries a divorced woman. The wording is a mixture of the second cluase forms in Matthew 5 and Luke 16.

Almost all these Matthaean forms put it differently from Mark. There, adultery is described as divorcing one's spouse and remarrying. Here it consists in marrying a divorced person. Exceptions to this are Nos. 1 and 2. Both of these present, in the form of their statement, the same words as form 3 of Mark without the words 'against her', except for the 'Matthaean exception' which, in the case of No. 2, is derived from Matthew 5. Here we have a conflict of interests. Source criticism has generally maintained that Matthew here takes over Mark, adding the exception clause. Textual criticism is aware of the tendency to harmonise the text. And D is especially prone to this – less so in Matthew than elsewhere, it is true. But prone nonetheless. ℵ, it is also known, has a more mixed text than B, preserving a number of readings that are typical of D. Here, ℵ D agree, except that D has a secondary harmonisation to Matthew 5.

If Matthew is to be expected to show consistency, then we may propose that the most Matthaean form of the saying must be one clause, addressing the divorce of a wife rather than the remarriage. Such a saying can be found enshrined in Nos. 3 and 4:

> Whoever divorces his wife, except for *porneia*, makes her an adulteress.

This saying, identical in form to the D version of Mt 5.32, and in principle to all versions of that saying, was later changed in three ways. The first was by the addition at least partly taken from Lk 16.18 that is found in forms 3 and 4:

> and whoever marries a divorced woman commits adultery.

The second was by harmonization to Mark, found in Nos. 1 and 2, introducing the reference to remarriage in the first clause and making the adultery the man's:

[377]

Whoever divorces his wife, except for *porneia*, and marries another commits adultery.

The third text conflates these two options, giving us the harmonisation to Mark *and* the additions from Luke 16; this is forms 5, 7 and 8:

Whoever divorces his wife, except for *porneia*, and marries another commits adultery; and whoever marries a divorced woman commits adultery.

There are a few other combinations; some forms harmonise the exception clause to Matthew 5. Form 6 gives us the double harmonisation (Mark 19 and Luke 16), but keeps the wording 'makes her an adulteress' found in Nos. 2 and 3.

These various developments can all be dated fairly early. Indeed, they may reflect the claim that all significant variants had come into being by the end of the second century.

A different solution was proposed by Jean Duplacy.[6] In his view, the original text of the first half of the verse was 'Whoever divorces his wife, except for *porneia*, and marries another commits adultery'. He states that it cannot be decided whether or not there was a second part to the verse (as in Nos. 5–8), although a mechanical explanation for the shorter form is feasible: that the clause could have dropped out by homoioteleuton.

Luke 16.18

The text is here found in one form, with only slight variations:

1. (Nearly all witnesses and all English versions cited)
Whoever divorces his wife and marries another commits adultery, and whoever marries a woman divorced from her husband commits adultery.

2. (D, a few medieval manuscripts, sy (s p) and some other early versions)
The words 'from her husband' are absent. The fact that they are not found in the addition to Mt 19.9 in text forms 5, 6 and 7 suggests that it was not part of the second-century text.

3. (One fourth-century Latin manuscript, one Latin Vulgate manuscript, and four medieval Greek manuscripts)
Whoever divorces his wife and marries another commits adultery.

The emphasis in this text is again on the adultery of the man.

---

6 'Note sur les variantes et le texte original de *Matthieu* 19,9', *Études de critique textuelle du Nouveau Testament* (BETL 78), ed. J. Delobel, Leuven, 1987, 387–412.

The complexity of text, particularly in Matthew 19, provides a valuable insight into the tradition. The first point is that 'hard sayings' were hard from the beginning. It is certainly not the case that they are made hard by an over-sophistication on the part of modern society. Passages which were the focus of contentious issues were particularly prone to change.

Further, the differences in emphasis, not between Matthew 5, Mark 10, Matthew 19, and Luke 16, but between different versions of those Gospels, show the oral period and the first centuries of the written period to have been a continuum of re-interpretation. Even after the development of 'standard', 'ecclesiastical' texts – such as the Greek Byzantine text and the Syriac Peshitta – variant forms survived.

[379]

This question of emphasis and interpretation is, in Matthew's context for the saying in chapter 5, said to stem from Jesus' own interpretation of the tradition. For the saying at Mt 5.27–8 about the nature of adultery changes the content and nature of the language being used. The question can no longer be 'Who is guilty?' It is now 'Who is innocent?'

It seems that the early Church took *porneia* to mean 'adultery'. This is the important point so far as our understanding of the manuscript tradition is concerned. The point is that, if one gives 'except for the cause of *porneia*' a meaning such as 'even though she has not been unfaithful' (GNB) or 'for any cause other than unchastity' (REB) or 'except for the case of an illicit marriage' (NJB), then the link with verse 28 is lost, and the absurdity of the paradox sinks in the legal verbiage. A clear account of the reasons why *porneia* should be translated as 'adultery' is provided by the latest major commentary.[7] We are left with a saying that condemns the cruel and arbitrary dismissal of a faithful wife. We can see that such a saying is devoid of the casuistry and problematical exceptions of the modern versions. We can also see that the problem addressed is the opposite of the use to which the passage is often put. It is employed to hinder divorced people who wish to remarry. It was intended to protect vulnerable people who wished not to be divorced.

Let us return to the variations in the manuscript tradition; in particular, to the difficulty of establishing a fixed point in the tradition that has any unique 'authority'. We have seen that to compare the Gospels with a view to establishing the priority of one form is to

---

7   W.D. Davies and D.C. Allison, *A Critical and Exegetical Commentary on the Gospel According to Saint Matthew* (The International Critical Commentary), Edinburgh, 1988, Vol. 1, 528–32.

presuppose that each Gospel has a definitive form. There is no evidence that either the evangelists or their successors believed such a form to exist. The recovery of a definitive 'original' text that is consequently 'authoritative' cannot be presumed to be an attainable target. The concept of such a text, essentially the 'ecclesiastical text' of a modern printed book, is present to modern minds, but was foreign to those of the early Christians.

Many church reports have struggled with the questions raised by these passages.[8] On the whole, their examinations seem to have presupposed that each saying exists only in one text form. They could have advanced their studies considerably by looking at the bottom of the page and reading the *apparatus criticus*. They would have discovered that they were grasping at shadows. What we have is a collection of interpretative rewritings of a tradition. It would be unscientific to claim, on the basis of these few passages, that there was no such thing as a Gospel in the sense of a recension, an attempt to produce a fixed form. But any writer who crystallises a point in a changing tradition (which he thereby also changes) must accept that his writing may also be liable to alteration by somebody else. And once this is acknowledged, then the concept of a Gospel that is fixed in shape, authoritative, and final as a piece of literature, has to be abandoned. The invitation to pay heed to the words of Jesus is then freed from the demand to accept the authority of the text. And the freedom with which the early churches altered the tradition to make sense of their own difficulties and conflicts is another invitation – to find the living word of Jesus that spoke to the tradition and that continues to speak.

The 1971 Anglican report to General Synod by the Root Commission, *Marriage Divorce and the Church*,[9] contains an appendix by Bishop Hugh Montefiore, 'Jesus on Divorce and Remarriage'. The text used by Montefiore is that of the Authorized Version. On Mark 10, he notes: 'Other scholars prefer the alternative rendering "if she be divorced from her husband"; but the principle of *difficilior lectio potior* (the more difficult reading is to be preferred) seems to apply here, and

---

8   The reports to be discussed all come from the last twenty years. I here note briefly *The Church and the Law of Nullity of Marriage*, London, 1955. It uses the text of the Revised Version. G.D. Kilpatrick briefly discussed a few of the textual problems in Appendix 7 (61–3). He suggested only one emendation that concerns us: at Mk 10.12, 'go out from her husband' instead of 'divorcing her husband'. Otherwise, rather surprisingly, he accepted the text of the Revised Version.

9   London, 1971.

for this reason this alternative reading is to be resisted' (82). This makes very little sense. Montefiore is using the AV's 'put away', which is its version of *apoluse*. 'Divorce' is the equivalent in the modern versions. It may be that he is intending to speak of a variant reading in which the wife is divorced by her husband (passive) rather than divorcing him (active). Unfortunately, I can find no trace of such a variant. It seems extraordinary that such a report, published in the second half of the twentieth century, should lean on that broken reed, the Textus Receptus, and should show such total unawareness of the textual problems.

The work between 1967 and 1975 of the Anglican–Roman Catholic International Commission on the Theology of Marriage and its Application to Mixed Marriages appeared in the latter year.[10] The consultants stated that 'We agree ... on the priority of Mark's version in this pericope' (15). Unfortunately, they do not tell us which version of Mark's version they discussed.

The Church in Wales produced a report in 1976.[11] It cites the passages from Mark and Luke in full, from the RSV. The Matthaean passages are also cited in full, and from the RSV except that it replaces 'unchastity' with 'fornication (*porneia*)'.

In 1978 there appeared another Church of England report, called *Marriage and the Church's Task* (the Lichfield Report).[12] Appendix Four is entitled 'The New Testament Evidence'. It shows an ignorance that there is any dispute at all about the text, or indeed that there are any variants, equal to that of the 1971 report. The text that is accepted is the RSV. We can therefore see that the Greek text followed in Matthew 5 and Luke 16 is that adopted in the 1971 report. But in Mark 10 and Matthew 19, it is a quite different text that is treated as authoritative! The authors no doubt believed themselves to be discussing the same texts ('Mark 10' and 'Matthew 19'). In fact, they were not.

The 1989 Methodist Conference debated the report *A Christian Understanding of Family Life, the Single Person and Marriage*.[13] This report contains no explicit citation of any of our four passages, though we note that 'the saying in Mark 10.11f may well be Jesus' original

---

10 *Anglican–Roman Catholic Marriage*, Church Information Office and Catholic Information Office, 1975.
11 *Marriage and Divorce*, The Governing Body of the Church in Wales, 1976.
12 The Report by the General Synod Marriage Commission, CIO Publishing, 1978.
    The relevant section is reprinted in *Marriage and the Doctrine of the Church of England. Study Extracts from the Reports of two recent Marriage Commissions*, Central Board of Finance of the Church of England, n.d., 81–106.
13 DSR Bookshop, 1989.

teaching' (23). We also note that it accepts the authenticity of the story of the woman caught in adultery: 'he clearly opposed the infliction of the death penalty' (30).

Enough has been said to show that the material from the Gospels has been repeatedly used in a manner that is inappropriate to the character of the material. The quest for a law in the teaching of Jesus cannot be pursued in the face of the evidence that, for those early Christians who passed the tradition to us, there was no law, but an idea to be explored, a tradition whose meaning had to be kept alive by reflection and re-interpretation. The task demanded of us is a similar one. In one respect we are well placed today. We are better able to see the variant forms and to compare them: who before in the history of theological thought has had access to the text of dozens of early manuscripts?

The story of the woman taken in adultery poses a particular problem for those who believe that they are discussing a single authoritative text, a problem that they generally ignore. For this passage is demonstrably spurious to that text. Read in the lectionaries of most denominations, it attests an early tradition about Jesus received into several places in the Gospels at a later date. It is not part of the putative authoritative and original text. They cannot have it both ways. The similarly placed logion in Codex Bezae (Lk 6.4) must be levelled against them: 'If you know what you are doing, then you are blessed; if you do not know, then you are accursed and a transgressor of the law'.

To conclude with a suggestion: that those who write on these texts for the purpose of guiding the churches should begin with the textual variation, and seek to understand the place of each form in the history of the early Christian community from which we receive it. There will be a gain ecumenically – we shall all be working with the same material, rather than with the divergent forms of our favourite versions. And there will be a theological gain: we will find that there is no single letter of 'Scripture' to absolutise. Instead there will be the invitation to explore and to honour the traditions. Textual criticism is often seen as the most recondite of pursuits. The study of these passages show it to be indispensable if we are to deal in realities rather than in pious fictions.

Note

Because quite a lot of this article was reproduced in *The Living Text of the Gospels*, it was an uncertain candidate for inclusion here. I kept it because the purpose and tone are quite different. The last section was not used, and is worth reprinting as a study of how writings such as reports engage (or fail to engage) with biblical texts. The setting is the Church of England, but the moral of the tale applies widely.

21 Through a Screen Darkly: Digital Texts and the New Testament

The use of computers in textual work may seem a neutral and merely convenient way of avoiding the traditional drudgery of either writing everything out by hand or typing it. But it is in fact changing for ever the relationship between the scholar, the text which the scholar is studying, and the text which the scholar is creating.[1]

Traditional Text-Editing [396]

The traditional method of recording and presenting variation between witnesses was by showing lists of readings. In the recording this took the form of a collation of each witness against a base text. In the presentation, it took the form of an *apparatus criticus,* in which a more-or-less complete list of these divergences was turned into a list of divergences from the critically selected text. This method had the advantage of brevity. For example, the collations of Wake manuscripts made by John Walker for Bentley are very simple. He used a printed New Testament, listed the manuscripts to be collated in the end papers with an upper-case letter for each, and recorded the variants in the margins, using the letter indicators to show which manuscript(s)

---

1 Important work on computers in textual editing include: P.L. Shillingsburg, *Scholarly Editing in the Computer Age. Theory and Practice,* Ann Arbor, 1996. George Bornstein and Theresa Tinkle (eds.), *The Iconic Page in Manuscript, Print and Digital Culture,* Ann Arbor, 1998. For earlier stages in the use of computers in New Testament textual research see Robert A. Kraft, 'The Use of Computers in New Testament Textual Criticism', in Ehrman and Holmes, *Contemporary Research,* 268–82. For work by the present writer, see *The Living Text of the Gospels,* 182–202; 'Manuscripts of the Gospels in the Electronic Age', *Restoration Quarterly* 42 (2000), 221–9; 'The Text of the New Testament and Computers: the International Greek New Testament Project', *Literary and Linguistic Computing* 15 (2000), 27–41. This instalment also contains important articles by Klaus Wachtel, 'Editing the Greek New Testament on the Threshold of the Twenty-First Century' (43–50) and Gerd Mink 'Editing and Genealogical Studies: the New Testament' (51–6).

supported the reading.² The critical apparatus has taken the same form, although the more sophisticated have also recorded the agreement of witnesses with the base text.³ It had several disadvantages. One is that it is very difficult to re-arrange the variations from the initial base text into variations from the critical text. This problem led some editors of very large editions to desist from producing a critical text.⁴ But a much more interesting problem is that it led scholars into abandoning a proper concern with the manuscripts themselves as complete forms of the text, in favour of an obsession with the points of variation between them. Such obsession has taken the form, especially in our own day, of hugely detailed statistical analyses of manuscript relationships, in which we have not only a focus on points of variation, but also a total disregard for the fact that points of variation are not necessarily comparable. In fact, sensible use of mathematical analysis does have a part to play as one of various tools in the hands of the textual scholar. But it must be used alongside the other tools, such as codicological and palaeographical evidence, historical information, proper philological scholarship, and common sense. And we must not allow the fact that the differences between witnesses are the easiest way to come at comparing them to distort our judgement.

Electronic Transcriptions

Electronic transcription leads in a quite different direction from traditional collation. The International Greek New Testament Project (IGNTP) and the Institut für Neutestamentliche Textforschung, Münster (INTF) have been developing a set of shared methods and standards in making digital transcriptions. For the former organisation, its developments have been focused in a discrete project. A description

---

2   Examples of Walker's work include Cambridge, Trinity College B.17.44, 45 and Oxford, Christ Church, MS Wake Gr. 35.
3   For example, C. Tischendorf, *Novum Testamentum Graece . . . editio octava critica maior*, Leipzig, 1872. Most recently, *Editio Critica Maior. IV Die Katholischen Briefe*. Teil 1. *Text*. Teil 2 .1. Lieferung *Der Jakobusbrief*, Stuttgart, 1997, 2. Lieferung *Die Petrusbriefe*, 2000.
4   For example, the editions of Matthew and Mark by Legg, which used the Westcott and Hort text, and their successor, the International Greek New Testament Project's thesaurus of readings in Luke: Legg, *Mark* and *Matthew*. *The New Testament in Greek; The Gospel According to St Luke, Part One, Chapters 1–12*, Oxford University Press, 1984, *Part Two,Chapters 13–24*, Oxford University Press, 1987.

of this will be the entry into the discussion of the significance of scholarly digital editing for New Testament studies.

The Principio Project was established to study the Greek manuscript tradition of John's Gospel. It has a duration of three years (2000–2003), and the team has four members.[5] Our main tasks include the preparation of a volume presenting transcriptions of all the fragmentary majuscule manuscripts with an apparatus that will include them and all the other majuscules, and an analysis of the whole manuscript tradition, which includes producing a Claremont Profile Method analysis of all witnesses in chapter 18 and comparing the results with those produced from 153 Teststellen in chs. 1–10 selected and analysed by the INTF.[6] In order to make the transcriptions, the project is using Collate, the software produced by Peter Robinson.[7] Once the transcriptions have been made, Collate will automatically produce a collation of them, a ready-made apparatus needing only to be adjusted to the user's precise requirements. The transcription can be translated comparatively easily into XML, HTML and SGML, thus making possible further use of the transcriptions. The transcription is made by taking a base text, altering it at each place as you compare it with your facsimile or microfilm, and saving it under the manuscript number. But the process is essentially different from producing a collation. The task is to produce an electronic equivalent to the manuscript itself. And this bends the mind in strange new directions. In transcribing Codex Sinaiticus, I found myself seeking new ways of indicating just what I found. It goes without saying that every letter is recorded, so that each itacism is faithfully reproduced. So of course are all corrections and annotations, so are superlines for *nu* at line ends, *nomina sacra*, abbreviations indicated by brackets around the supplied letters, running titles, quire signatures, modern folio numbers. I soon found after making the transcription on the basis of paper collations that the most accurate way to check it was to divide the text into the folios, columns and lines of the manuscript, and from there to go through it letter by letter. But then I began to worry about other things. Should I indicate which letters were written smaller at the end of a line? How should I indicate punctuation, paragraphing, the Eusebian apparatus and the running titles? These are all worth recording, and in

[398]

---

5 David Parker, Bill Elliott, Bruce Morrill, Ulrich Schmid. Rachel Kevern also contributed to the early stages of this project.
6 For the associated Byzantine Text Project, see below.
7 For an introduction to the output of which Collate is capable, see the Canterbury Tales Project homepage: http://www.canterburytalesprojects.org.

such a way that the software would be able to distinguish between the text and the paraphernalia.

At the end of this process it was clear that the activity on which I was engaged was quite different in character from collating. I was trying to decide what features in the manuscript I could and should represent in my transcription, and then finding ways of doing so. And I was thinking not only about the possibilities immediately available to me, but also about possibilities which might be available to scholars at a future date, if only I had the forethought to set out my material in such a way that they could capture it for their own ends.

But then, I thought: what I am trying to do is not to capture the manuscript, but to examine its surface and contents in a new way, as a whole and not for its variants. The transcription is secondary to the examination. What I really need is a way of turning the facsimile, the image of the manuscript itself, into an electronic text, so that if I want to search through the occurrences of a word, I can go from place to place *in the manuscript*; so that if from the *apparatus criticus* I want to see how a reading is on the page, I will be taken to that very place. The reason why this would be superior is that a manuscript page is able to contain a huge amount of information, much more than a printed page, since the scribe has freedom to vary every single stroke, to place material anywhere on the page, and to use many different colours, to convey a particular significance. There is so much information that it is probably impossible to capture all of it in transcription. Incidentally, the point highlights a way that may today be appreciated more keenly in which the manuscript page is superior to the printed format. The draughtsmanship and, indeed, artistic ability of the scribe permits a degree of control over the presentation beyond even the most advanced typography. In some ways computer keying is even more mechanical. The contrast between scribal artistry and the tedium of typing in front of a screen has, in the opinion of the French scholar Gasparri, led to a resurgence of interest in manuscripts as the modern world looks nostalgically back to a more creative era.[8] This intoxicating possibility

---

8   Françoise Gasparri, *Introduction à l'histoire de l'écriture* (Reference Works for the Study of Mediaeval Civilization), Turnhout, 1994, 5: 'L'univers uniforme, banalisé, de l'informatique, le monde automatisé de l'ordinateur, la monotonie des boutons, tous égaux, de même matière, synthétique, sur lesquels les doigts tapent à longeur de journée, où aucune surprise ne les attend, le champ monochrome de l'écran, qui arrache les yeux et vide l'esprit, donnent à l'humanité la nostalgie de la main entière qui écrit, serrant entre ses doigts le support d'une plume qui glisse sur le papier, créant à travers courbes, boucles et traits de fuite un plaisir à la fois sensuel et esthétique, la nostalgie aussi de la page que l'on peut toucher, éclairer à sa guise, qui

will revolutionise the study of the text, because editions will not be distillations of certain kinds of evidence, but will be an interaction, not with the actual witnesses, but at least with digital representations of the witnesses. The technology is probably available already. But in the foreseeable future, what will be made will be separate digital images and transcriptions.

The Effect of Electronic Transcriptions on the Understanding and Use of Texts

[400]

There are a number of significant consequences of this development. The first is conceptual, and it is from this that the paper's title is derived: 'Through a Screen Darkly'. The title attempts to reflect the ambiguity that I at least experience in working with a computer. When I hold a codex in my hand, I know where the text is physically. But with a computer, which generates its text as electronic magnetism, as screen image and as printed copy, I am totally baffled. What am I really looking at when I gaze at the screen? I literally have no idea. Certainly it is pretending to look something like a page of text, but it equally certainly is *not* a page of text. It is an image of some kind on a screen.

While I was first struggling with these ideas, I was struck by a passage I came across in Italo Calvino's novel *If on a Winter's Night a Traveller*. A novelist is reflecting in his diary on the difficulties of writing:

> Today I will begin by copying the first sentences of a famous novel, to see if the charge of energy contained in that start is communicated to my hand, which, once it has received the right push, should run on its own.
>
> *On an exceptionally hot evening early in July, a young man came out of the garret in which he lodged in S. Place, and walked slowly, as though in hesitation, towards K. Bridge.*

And so on until:

> I stop before I succumb to the temptation to copy out all of *Crime and Punishment*. For an instant I seem to understand the meaning and fascination of a now inconceivable vocation: that of the copyist. The copyist lived simultaneously in two temporal dimensions, that of reading and that of writing; he could write without the anguish of having the void open

---

se couvre peu à peu de caractères assemblés, tous différents, liés entre eux, jamais de la même manière, dans un originalité unique au monde, en autant de variétés qu'il y a d'hommes écrivant sur la terre'.

before his pen; read without the anguish of having his own act become concrete in some material object.[9]

There are two things to give us pause for thought here. The first is the perception of the scribal world with which we deal as a borderline between imitation and creativity. It is a matter with which scholars have had some difficulty, often attributing to the scribe changes which may more plausibly have been introduced into exemplars by thoughtful (and not so thoughtful) readers. That is a topic for exploration another time. The second is the opportunity to recognise the way in which the textual critic, and today especially the scholar working with a computer, behaves in a very similar way to a copyist. Both are slavishly reproducing the text of the manuscript, and yet recreating it as something new.

In peering through the darkling screen at the version of a manuscript which I have created, I find myself face to face with a new version of the old text, one in which the traces of the archetype, the temporal dimensions of the scribe, and the alterations of the correctors appear in a new way in the new text which I have made. In fact, I find myself realising for the first time in its fullness the strange ambiguity of textual scholarship. For textual critics, under the guise of reconstructing original texts, are really creating new ones. Technically, one could say that this is due to eclecticism, to fusing together readings from manuscripts and thus forming new hybrids. From a historian's point of view, what one is doing is readjusting the textual gene pool. The image used elsewhere of a pool is more often that of a reservoir, in the thinking for example of Günther Zuntz and G.D. Kilpatrick.[10] But the concept of a gene pool indicates that the variations between manuscripts can be taken as a clue to the fact that individuals, while possessed of distinctive characteristics, have a set of characteristics that associate them with other individuals, and have a set of attributes largely determined by heredity but to some small extent contributing to evolution. There is a deeper parallel between the study of manuscripts and that of genetics than an image, which will be discussed later in this article. Turning back to the creation of new texts out of a store of readings and speaking about it theologically, it might be described as the eschatological dimension to textual thought.

---

9 Italo Calvino, *If on a Winter's Night a Traveller*, tr. William Weaver, London, 1992, 177–8.

10 Zuntz, *The Text of the Epistles*. For Kilpatrick's theories, see G.D. Kilpatrick, *The Principles and Practice of New Testament Textual Criticism. Collected Essays*, edited by J.K. Elliott (BETL 96), Leuven, 1990. [for which see also Chapter 15]

One may express this dimension in the following way. That the biblical text, rather than corrupted and needing to be restored (this traditional text-critical language has interesting parallels to the language of fall and redemption), is constantly under development, one might even say of becoming the text. In this light, the quest for the original text may be seen as a complete misunderstanding of what editors were really doing.

The progression of form (reaching in our day the creation of electronic texts), with which I began, could also be viewed through the Pauline lens, if I may put it like that, with which my title is associated. That is, the forms in which the text is found are only approximations to what we are looking for. I do not mean that the texts we are creating are necessarily superior to earlier creations. It is more significant that they are the texts which we need to create. They supersede their predecessors, and will in turn be superseded.

Electronic Editions and New Testament Studies

Why these thoughts in a journal of New Testament studies? Because the scholars who create the editions of the New Testament on which others rely are beginning to produce new kinds of editions. It is not clear that there is yet any general awareness among scholars of the New Testament about the current revolution in textual editing. Without such awareness, and without a debate about its significance, New Testament scholars will be poorly equipped to understand the new generation of editions that are beginning to emerge, or even to make full use of them. The current revolution is as significant as that brought about by the Complutensian Polyglot and Erasmus' *Novum Instrumentum*. It is to be hoped that it will be received with less confusion.

What issues demand particular consideration? Perhaps the most important point is that the era of a critically reconstructed text with an *apparatus criticus* as it has been known is over. Editions will pay greater attention to individual witnesses, providing transcriptions and images of them. The emphasis will therefore be less on a theoretically reconstructed 'original' or 'best available' text, and much more on the significance of the many forms in which the text has existed and continues to exist. Students of the New Testament will need to consider how their work will be affected if they study their text as it survives in a number of real witnesses, rather than in a reconstructed single text to which they have granted authority. *Wirkungsgeschichte* has so far gone quite a short way. It will need to take into account not only the views of many writers at different times, but also the physical and textual realities of the text which they were interpreting.

What editions of the text may be taken as examples of these new developments? Apart from the Principio Project, which has already been described, I select two.

The first of these is the Byzantine Text Project. This was conceived in response to a serious question from the Greek Orthodox delegates at a gathering organised by the United Bible Societies. The question concerned the fact that new translations being made into Greek were based on the critical text presented by Nestle-Aland[27] and the fourth edition of the United Bible Societies' *The Greek New Testament*. The text of the New Testament in continuing use among them and accepted as the traditional text of the community is the Byzantine text, known most widely through the Antoniades edition of 1904. The 'western' critical text is perceived as alien. At the same time, it is recognised that the available editions of the Byzantine text are not scientifically produced. The question was whether the UBS would sponsor a proper edition of the Byzantine text which could then be used as the basis for translation work. Since one of the planks of general perception of the Byzantine text is that it is a 'bad text' which nineteenth-century scholarship consigned to history, this invitation presents a considerable challenge to textual criticism as it is practised in western Europe, North America and elsewhere. It also presents a considerable technical challenge, since the production of such an edition demands the study of most of the extant manuscripts.[11]

However, the production of electronic transcriptions of manuscripts and the use of databases to analyse them means that research carried out on the whole of the manuscript tradition for the production of a critical edition can also serve to produce a critical edition of a part of the tradition, in this case the Byzantine text.

Two movements are at work here. The first is the recognition that texts are not inherently good or bad. The Byzantine text is certainly late, and certainly contains features lacking in the oldest copies, but it also happens to have been extremely successful, and to have existed as the honoured text of the Orthodox for well over a thousand years. The second movement is a fundamental change in the processes of making

---

11 For this reason, the project is based at the University of Birmingham, where Dr Rod Mullen, the Director, is able to work with data generated by the Principio Project.

a critical edition. The focus is, as I have said, on the transcription of witnesses as the creation of a collection of data that can be used to produce editions of many different kinds. In the Collate program, one can select any of the transcriptions as a base text from which the apparatus of variants is created, and one can choose from a menu the preferred form of apparatus – for example, with each witness in full on a separate line, or in a more traditional format listing either agreements and disagreements, or disagreements only.

The second example makes the second point even clearer. It is the digital Nestle-Aland[28], currently in preparation.[12] In parallel to a print volume, this will be a digital edition with the following features: transcriptions of approximately twenty of the most ancient and significant Greek manuscripts (the consistently cited witnesses of both the first and the second order), and an interactive *apparatus criticus* in which the kind of information visible will be partly controlled by the user. The transcriptions will be accessible from individual variants in the apparatus, and will be displayed if requested in the page layout of the manuscript. Several features of this call for particular comment. One is that the focus is totally on the apparatus and the transcriptions. There is no intention of revising the text significantly from the twenty-seventh edition. The text functions as a peg on which to hang the other kinds of information. The other is the degree to which the user can manipulate the presentation. An interesting aspect of this is that the apparatus will show the readings selected by the editors, and will have 'regularised' certain features of the individual manuscripts. Regularisation is a feature of Collate that instructs the program to treat two words spelled differently as identical. For example, at 1 Jn 1.1 some manuscripts read ὑμῶν and not ἡμῶν. This is a common variation, generally resulting from the identical pronunciation of the two words. By regularising ὑμῶν to ἡμῶν, the editors make a decision – a perfectly reasonable one – to exclude it. In a print edition, the general user would be none the wiser. In the digital edition, the transcription of the verse will be available, and the user will be able to scrutinise the editorial decisions.[13]

The editorial process is thus moving away from the creation of an authoritative text to a more diffuse process, in which the raw materials of the editor – the manuscripts – are given a higher priority and made

[404]

---

12 Details are available on the Institut homepage, at http://nestlealand.uni-muenster.de/.
13 Elsewhere, as appropriate, the variant is shown in Nestle-Aland[27] and will continue to be present – for example, at Col 2.13, where it appears twice.

available to the user. The result, I suggest, will be a weakening of the status of standard editions, and with that a change in the way in which users of texts perceive their tasks. I have already indicated how Bible translation may be more open to recognising the claims of long-used texts to be respected and to be, if one may put it like that, restored. There will be similar changes in the task of exegesis. It is comparatively easy at present for the commentator to treat the most widely available text as 'virtually John'. This is because a single coherent form of text has been chiselled out of the available materials, and the variation from it reduced to a heap of fragments lying at its feet. A commentator who tried to write a commentary based on an individual manuscript, and then looked at another manuscript might be surprised to discover how much of the commentary needed changing.

It is even more remarkable that the major Q Project reconstructs its putative document from a printed text. The project even cloaks this by using quasi-text-critical language to describe the relationship between the real and supposed documents with which it deals.[14] It would be interesting to see how well these conclusions stood up if the editors were to recognise that their textual base is no more than a provisional working printed text of the late twentieth century. I have argued elsewhere that this approach treats as two-dimensional a relationship which is in fact *three*-dimensional – in addition to the differences between Matthew, Mark and Luke familiar to us from the printed text, there were differences between copies of each Gospel so that, to name but one complication, it is highly unlikely to have been the case that the form of Mark known to Matthew was identical to that known to Luke.[15] To vary the metaphor, our modern printed versions of the three synoptists are still photographs reconstructed from a motion picture.

Electronic Transcriptions and the Future of Textual Criticism

Another matter worth pondering is that more text-critical materials will become available and will be more accurate (and perhaps more widely used), because it is no longer necessary for every researcher to begin from scratch making fresh collations or transcriptions. In the Principio

---

14 See M.S. Goodacre, *The Case Against Q: Studies in Markan Priority and the Synoptic Problem*, Harrisburg, PA, 2002, 8–9.

15 Parker, *The Living Text of the Gospels*, 103–23.

Project, we have developed a modular approach to making our transcriptions. To explain this, the procedure of transcribing needs to be explained.

Of course the prime concern is accuracy, and our rule is to produce two separate transcriptions of each witness. They are then compared with each other by Collate, and one of the two is made the basis for a corrected version. Further transcriptions would act as an extra check, but with a law of diminishing returns.

The transcription is not made by starting from scratch, but by beginning with a base text and modifying it to match the witness. Generally speaking, the task has two parts. One consists in making the text of the file conform to that of the first hand and its correctors. This is a letter-by-letter correspondence, in which the text appears 'warts and all'. The second part consists in indicating as much else of the surface of the page as is thought necessary or feasible.

[406]

The following is a transcription of part of the first column of the first page of John in Codex Sinaiticus.

```
|F 48r|
|C 1|
{-qs- oθ}
|L A|<B 4> <K 0> <V 0> κατα ιωαννην
|L 1|<K 1> <V 1> {-ep- ā}{-ec- γ}εν αρχη ην ο λογοσ
|L 2|και ο λογοσ ην
|L 3|προσ τον θεον και
|L 4|θσ̄ ην ο λογοσ <V 2> ου=
|L 5|τοσ ην εν αρχη
|L 6|προσ τον θν̄ <V 3> πᾱ=
|L 7|τα δι αυτου εγενε=
|L 8|το και χωρισ αυτου
|L 9|εγενετο [app][*]ουδεν[/*][Cca]ουδε εν[/Cca][/app] [lit]ουδ[i-Cca]ε[i]ν[/lit]
|L 10|ο γεγονεν· <V 4> εν αυ=
|L 11|τω ζωη εστιν·
|L 12|και η ζωη ην το
|L 13|φωσ των ανθρω=
|L 14|πων· <V 5> και το φωσ
|L 15|εν τη σκοτια φαι=
|L 16|νει και η σκοτι=
|L 17|α αυτο ου κατε=
|L 18|λαβεν·
|L 19|<V 6> {-ep- β}{-ec- γ} εγενετο ανθρω=
|L 20|ποσ απεσταλμε=
|L 21|νοσ παρα θυ [app][*]ην[/*][S1]OM[/S1][Cca]OM[/Cca][/app] [lit][st-S1][od-Cca]ην[/od][/st][/lit] ο=
|L 22|νομα αυτω ϊω=
|L 23|αννησ <V 7> ουτοσ
```

Beginning at the top, the following features appear with appropriate tagging:

Folio number
Column number
The quire signature
Line A, representing the superscription, with the book-chapter-verse number 4–0–0
Line 1, chapter and verse number 1–1, followed by the two numbers of the Eusebian Apparatus
The beginning of the text

The whole process follows rules laid down by Collate, themselves based on practice adopted by the Text Encoding Initiative, and developed for New Testament manuscripts by the INTF and IGNTP.

If we move down a few lines, we find the first correction in line 9. At every place it is necessary to give the first hand reading, followed by the correction. The correction is tagged in order to convey both textual and physical information. The first part is:

[app][*]ουδεν[/*][Cca]ουδε εν[/Cca][/app]

Within the 'app' tag, which indicates to the program that the two readings refer to the same piece of text, is the reading of the first hand, tagged with an *, and that of a corrector, Cca.[16] After comes the physical information:

[lit]ουδ[i-Cca]ε[/i]ν[/lit]

[lit] indicates what is 'literally' there, an epsilon added interlineally (tagged as i) by Corrector Cca. Further down, in line 21, there is a piece of interpretation of the physical evidence which indicates that the word ην was deleted by two correctors, S1 and Cca, the first striking the letters through – [st] – and the second placing a dot above them – od:

[app][*]ην[/*][S1]OM[/S1][Cca]OM[/Cca][/app] [lit][st-S1][od-Cca]ην[/od][/st][/lit]

We have reached a certain level of detail. Later, it would be possible for us or others to revise the transcriptions, adding further information. Any errors that are found will also be removed. I have taken the example of a transcription in which we have tried to achieve a very high standard of detail. There are not currently the resources available to do this for every important manuscript of the Gospel of John, let alone for the whole New Testament. But all the Principio Project transcriptions of papyrus and majuscule manuscripts of John contain a

---

16 The 'names' of the correctors are those given by Milne and Skeat, *Scribes and Correctors of the Codex Sinaiticus*.

precise replication of the text of the first hand of the manuscript and of all correctors (without the physical information) and folio, column and line breaks. The same will be true of the transcriptions in the digital Nestle-Aland. From the coding given, it will be possible to make a transcription in which the textual material will appear on the screen as it does on the page, with the line breaks and columns of the manuscript, and the corrections in the place in which they are made. It will also be possible to make searches of a kinds not previously available, for example all corrections made in a particular way.

[408]

Electronic Editing and the Reading and Readership of the New Testament

A reasonable question is to ask – why all this effort? There are several ways of answering this question. There is the desire to explore as fully as possible the new opportunities and challenges presented by the electronic transcription. One is able to find new outlets to the interest that there is in paying careful attention to the detail of a manuscript, and to make decisions not previously available to scholars as to what is significant.[17] We do not know what evidence as yet uncovered may cast valuable light on the development of the New Testament texts, nor what use the ingenuity of scholars may find for our evidence. The inclusion of punctuation, for example, leaves open the possibility that by studying it scholars will be able to make new discoveries about the use and reading of texts by their first users, and perhaps even about the relationship between witnesses.

There are also important questions regarding the accessibility of the data out of which we build up the editions of the New Testament which are essential to all teaching and research on the documents. At present a copy of the Greek New Testament contains a text and an

---

17 A particularly interesting example of a new discovery, generated not it is true by electronic transcribing, but at any rate by fresh contemporary insights into a textual problem, is Philip Payne's discovery of the so-called 'bar-umlaut' feature in Codex Vaticanus, apparently marking passages known to the makers of the manuscript to contain textual problems. He first spotted it in the margin against 1 Cor 14.34–5. See P.B. Payne, 'Fuldensis, Sigla for Variants in Vaticanus, and 1 Cor 14.34–5', *NTS* 41 (1995), 240–62; this was challenged by C. Niccum, 'The Voice of the Manuscripts on the Silence of Women: The External Evidence for 1 Cor 14.34–5', *NTS* 43 (1997), 242–55. Payne successfully vindicated his case: Philip B. Payne and Paul Canart, 'The Originality of Text-Critical Symbols in Codex Vaticanus', *NovT* 42 (2000), 105–13 (also available at http://rosetta.reltech.org/TC/TC-links-main.html).

apparatus. Why? Let me suggest an unusual answer, that the *apparatus* exists only because in the past it was so much harder to find out what the manuscripts and other witnesses to the text read that the majority of scholars were dependent on the few who travelled to libraries and gathered the information on their behalf. Today, with the digital imaging of ever-increasing numbers of manuscripts of the New Testament, and the making of electronic transcriptions, the primary data is becoming virtually available to every New Testament scholar. The apparatus may serve as a rough guide for the user, or as a filter and organiser of the information, but in an edition such as the digital Nestle-Aland[28], the user will also have access to highly informative versions of the primary material.

Through these changes the study of the primary material will be democratised. It will no longer be available only to people with access to large research libraries containing expensive facsimiles, editions, microform collections and manuscripts, but to anybody with a browser. We are at the beginning of a revolution, not only in textual criticism, but in New Testament studies, and indeed in the role of scholars, who will no longer be the only people with reasonable practical access to the materials.

Digitisation will alter the nature of editions in other ways as well. The custom of citing versions in support of Greek readings will be reduced to a system of hints, and be replaced instead by a link to the text of the version. Patristic citations, similarly, rather than being taken out of context and manipulated by editors, will be referenced by a link to electronic editions such as CETEDOC.

Finally, the material that is in electronic format can be analysed in sophisticated ways. Concordances based on manuscript transcriptions rather than on printed texts will contain far more information about words and forms in the historical development of the language and in scribal practice than has been possible hitherto.

The Application of Genetic Models to the Study of Manuscripts

We are already seeing exciting results in the application of mathematical models from evolutionary biology to manuscript traditions.[18] This was scarcely feasible in the past, when manuscript relations were worked out by visual comparison of lists of variant readings. But today manuscripts and their groupings are analysed by means of databases. The *Text und Textwert* volumes produced by the Münster Institut are database products. The Principio Project is analysing the manuscript groupings of John's Gospel by exporting the manuscript transcriptions into a database. Different models may then be used to determine the relationships. Apart from the technical advantages, there are also appearing new concepts of manuscript relationships. The approaches of the Stemma group are of significance for a number of reasons. Textual criticism has for long used models and language that seem to have parallels with the natural sciences. We talk, for example, about genealogy, family trees and stemmata. This often rather imprecise language has become somewhat old-fashioned. But from the Stemma project, whose membership contains both textual scholars and biologists, some more precise parallels have emerged between the way in which the development of cells and the development of manuscript traditions may be described. In both we have the appearance of the same form in two or more places independently, the mutation back to an earlier form, the problem of contamination (crossover between different branches), and the same general phenomenon of types having marked similarities with and differences from other types. In fact it is hard to find a problem in the analysis of manuscript relationships which is not encountered in a different guise by a geneticist. It is in the models to describe the phenomena used by the geneticists that the second point of interest lies. These models, when applied to a group of manuscripts, attempt to describe the relationship between them but make absolutely no attempt to prioritise one group or individual over another. The model is simply an expression of relationships. This is in stark contrast to traditional genealogical and stemmatological analysis of manuscripts, which is based upon a quest for an archetype called X or a sub-archetype called *y*. It provides, yet again, an approach to the witnesses to the New Testament or to any other text which seeks to interpret the phenomena that are available while paying no attention to phenomena which may have existed (in this case, forms of the text which one could be tempted to attempt to reconstruct) but do so no longer. Thirdly, the methodologies employed take into account similarities as much as

[410]

---

18 In the work of the Stemma Project. See e.g. Christopher Howe, Adrian C. Barbrook, Matthew Spencer, Peter Robinson, Barbara Bordalejo and Linne R. Mooney, 'Manuscript Evolution', *Trends in Genetics* 17 (2001), 147–52.

differences between witnesses as a means towards describing their relationship. This represents a radical change from the emphasis mentioned at the beginning of this paper on the differences between manuscripts. After all, the observation of similarities *and* differences between species is essential to the evolutionary biologist, while the methods in grouping New Testament manuscripts have become fixated with difference.

Consequences of a New Technology

Further developments may even affect how we view the concept of 'the New Testament'. Recent research has demonstrated how the emergence of the larger collections of early Christian writings was dependent upon the available technology. For example, the Pauline *corpus* could not have fitted on a roll, and must therefore have been first collected only when the codex had been invented.[19] This will have been a single-quire codex, and larger collections of material, bringing the Gospels and Paul together, will have been possible only after the invention of the multiple-quire codex. The potential of this to include whole libraries seems to have been recognised in the fourth century, when large-format multi-volume productions such as Codex Sinaiticus included not only the Septuagint and the New Testament as listed, for example, in Athanasius' Festal Letter, but other writings such as Hermas. The potential of the CD and the web is for much larger collections of literature used or created by early Christians, in which such categories as 'canonical' or 'uncanonical', or 'orthodox' and 'Gnostic' cease to have any role in the formation of the collection. It will be interesting to see whether, or perhaps one should say when, these changes will begin to affect the New Testament as used in the churches.

The digital editing currently in progress is experimental. At present there are ways in which digital texts still mirror printed codices (and in the act of scrolling, the roll) rather closely, just as the earliest printed texts look remarkably like contemporary manuscripts. In time the similarity will become fainter. It is reasonable to expect that, once the wider circle of New Testament scholars have begun to use it, they will be asking for modifications and developments of what is being done.

---

19 It is even possible that the concept of a Pauline *corpus* contributed to the development and popularisation of the codex. See H.Y. Gamble, *Books and Readers in the Early Church. A History of Early Christian Texts*, New Haven, 1995.

There will then be a challenge to textual scholars to look at what they have done. For the present, the challenge is to all users of the Greek New Testament to respond to the new forms and concepts of texts which are appearing.

Addendum

For John Walker, see my account in *The Oxford Dictionary of National Biography*, Oxford, 2005 (also available at http://www.oxforddnb.com/view/article/28495?docPos=6).

22 Jesus in Textual Criticism

This may be the first article on Jesus in textual criticism ever to be written. And so the first question is one of scope. The area to be explored should be the presentation of Jesus in the Gospels rather than the Christology of the early Church. As a matter of fact, the distinction is rather an artificial one, since the texts are received only through the medium of early Christian interpretation of Jesus as the Christ. This interpretation may be searched for in two ways. The first is through an examination of the physical evidence of the manuscripts. The second is in the text contained by the manuscripts. After that, it will be necessary to explore the relationship between textual criticism and Christology. Finally, the significance of textual theory for the study of Jesus will be discussed.

The Physical Presentation

The most obvious source is illuminations. Much could be said, especially with regard to Byzantine miniatures. The reader is referred to the sections discussing the portrayal of Jesus in art and in icons. But it is worthwhile for this discussion to draw attention to one interesting feature of the sixth-century Rossano Gospels. The miniature of the story of the Good Samaritan depicts the Samaritan as Christ. This feature, described as unique by K. Weitzmann, provides a full theological interpretation of the passage.[1] Its significance will become more fully apparent in a moment. Instead, I wish to discuss certain features of scribal practice.

The *Nomina Sacra*

Nomina sacra (sacred names) is a term used by palaeographers to describe the practice in Greek and Latin Christian (and especially New

---

1 K. Weitzmann, *Late Antique and Early Christian Book Illumination*, New York, 1977.

Testament) manuscripts of writing certain words in an abbreviated form, with a horizontal line above them. In the earliest manuscripts, four are used: *Theos* (God), *Kurios* (Lord), *Iesous* (Jesus) and *Christos* (Christ). By and large, three evidently refer to Jesus. One of them, *Kurios*, has considerable significance, for it is found in the New Testament writers referring to God, to Jesus as Lord, and as a polite form of address to Jesus ('Lord' in the AV, often 'Sir' in modern versions), and to various figures in parables. By treating all three forms as *nomina sacra*, the written texts place every reference to Jesus as *Kurios* on the same theological level as references to God. Moreover, in the visual distinctiveness of the phenomenon, the presence of Jesus stands out on the page. And stands out in the company of God. It is a strong visual claim for his status as within the story and yet above the story. This pre-eminence was lost when the canon of names was extended to include, not only *Huios* (Son), *Pneuma* (Spirit), and *stauros* (cross), but also *anthropos* (man), *ouranos* (heaven), *Israel*, *Dauid* and the like.

The presentation of the *nomina sacra* in purple manuscripts can be especially dramatic. These manuscripts use silver ink (even gold, as in the example of one magnificent ninth-century purple minuscule manuscript now in St Petersburg, no. 565 in the list of Greek New Testament manuscripts), to be more easily read and more impressive. It looked splendid, and was certainly not neutral. The practice angered Jerome, who said that the church would find Christ naked and hungry at the gate, not in the glitter.

The use of *nomina sacra* can have some other interesting theological results. At Heb 4.8, the Israelite leader Joshua, Iesous in Greek, is given in the *nomen sacrum* form in the famous fourth-century manuscript Codex Sinaiticus. It is hard not to suspect a typological intent, one which most modern interpreters would say was lacking from the author's thought. More significant still is the use of *nomina sacra* in Matthaean and Lukan parables featuring lords, for example, in those featuring the lord of the vineyard (Mt 20.8); the lord of the house (Lk 14.21, 22); and the lord who distributed the talents (Mt 25.19, 20ff//Lk 19.15ff). These examples do not necessarily occur in all manuscripts.

At one time I thought of these cases as due to the force of scribal habit, but I begin to suspect that they may be interpretative, especially since there are also 'lords' found written out in full. There may be an analogy between the *nomina sacra* and the practice in many Syriac manuscripts of adding 'our Lord' where the name Jesus appears. Whatever the scribal motivation, the effect on the *reader* is to make these parables involving lords into stories in which there is a straight correspondence between the boss and the Christian *Kurios*. What about the *listener*? Was there any way in which a *nomen sacrum* (at least those in the original four) was marked by a response, a bowing of the head perhaps? It is perhaps noteworthy that in the temple service for Yom Kippur, at the point at which the high priest pronounced the divine name, those present bowed down.[2]

Just as the space within which Jesus was worshipped changed with the Church's fortunes, from private room to grand basilica to Byzantine splendour or Gothic magnificence, so the copies of the Gospels changed. They began as simple papyrus codices. They became, at least on occasion, sumptuous parchment volumes with the Peace of Constantine.[3] And in the Byzantine period they acquired a neat and convenient format, with a range of useful guides for the reader, illuminations of the evangelists, and a consistent and safe text form.

Textual Variation

This huge field may be divided into smaller groups:

1. Passages whose inclusion or removal add to or diminish information about Jesus in the Gospels. The larger examples are Jn 7.53–8.11, Lk 22.43–44, Lk 23.34, Mk 16.9–20 and Luke 6.4 D. Curiously enough, the first three of these belong among the most significant defining moments of history's perception of Jesus: a deeper justice towards a woman; his agony before death, receiving divine comfort; the prayer for his enemies' forgiveness.

It is hard to see this as coincidence. It is more likely to be evidence of the way in which early Christianity responded to the Gospel stories and to the arguments about faith and practice which they implicitly contained or were seen to contain. At least the majority of these stories appear to have originated by the middle of the second century.

2. The history of harmonisation. Down to the modern critical era, the Gospels were extensively harmonised. In early Christianity, the existence of four divergent accounts of Jesus was rather embarrassing, since their differences were used as evidence by detractors of Christianity. On the whole, the tendency was to treat the four versions

---

[2] For a view of the role of the *nomima sacra* in the development of Christian book culture, see D. Trobisch, *The First Edition of the New Testament*, New York, 2000.

[3] For other matters relating to book format and presentation, see H.Y. Gamble, *Books and Readers in the Early Church. A History of Early Christian Texts*, New Haven and London, 1995.

as a single account. In the middle of the second century, Tatian produced his Diatessaron, a harmony of the four Gospels into a single narrative. This was to prove enormously influential, both directly and through the many other harmonies in many tongues of the Middle Ages. In fact, it is fair to say that most people have been most familiar with a composite image of Jesus. For example, the birth narratives of Matthew and Luke and the prologue of John are taken as a sequence of complementary readings at most Christmas carol services. Until the introduction of the Common Lectionary in 1999, in England it has been only in the practice of reading the entire Passion narrative of a single evangelist in Holy Week that the coherence of the separate writers has been maintained in the lectionary. For nearly two centuries, however, critical scholarship has moved in a different direction. Since the editions of Karl Lachmann (1831 and 1842–50) and Westcott and Hort (1881), harmonisation has been to a considerable extent removed from the text, with the obvious corollary that the number of differences between the portrayals of Jesus in the four Gospels has increased significantly. The rule of thumb for editing the text is that the reading which is different from that of the other Gospels is more likely to be authentic. Thus, a small number of manuscripts preserve a different version of the Lord's Prayer in Lk 11.2–4 from Mt 6.9–13, while the vast majority have very similar texts in both places. Only since 1881 has the distinctive Lukan form gained currency as the form found in most editions and translations.

The same Karl Lachmann separately produced convincing evidence for Markan priority. This led to the recognition that Mark was not (as had always previously been supposed) simply an abbreviated version of Matthew, but an independent voice. The hitherto unknown greater degree of variation from the other Gospels that was being found in manuscripts of Mark could be interpreted within this framework. In fact, the study of the distinctiveness of each Gospel has been an important contribution of modern scholarship. Within it, textual criticism has contributed in two ways: first with the raw materials, in the form of rediscovery of the variations which, though often slight individually, have together made up the distinctive profile of each Gospel. Second, textual scholarship has more recently demonstrated how textual variation continued to arise from early Christian responses to the traditions about Jesus, so that the kinds of factors which led Matthew to revise Mark and led Luke probably to revise both of them also led later readers and copyists to modify the text further.

3. The third area spills over into Christology. It used to be claimed that textual variation did not influence any significant element of Christian belief, including beliefs about the person of Jesus. A single example shows how far this is from the case. At the baptism story in Lk 3.22, according to a manuscript copied in about 400 and some Latin witnesses, the words from heaven are 'You are my Son, today I have begotten you'. In all other witnesses it is found in the form 'You are my beloved Son, in you I am well pleased'. There is a strong case for arguing that the former version was older, but was displaced under orthodox influence because it played into the hands of the adoptianists.[4]

In fact, it is difficult to separate theologically motivated variation from other kinds of variants, since the evangelists were writing under the influence of theological questions, and the texts were preserved in highly charged theological environments. Another example is the question whether Jesus was angry or compassionate at the plight of the leper (Mk 1.41). The anger, if it was original, could have been removed on either theological or moral grounds.

Other passages which show signs of alteration on Christological grounds are:

Mk 1.1: insertion of title 'Son of God' again avoids adoptianism at 1.11; Jesus was already God's Son.

Mk 15.34: 'forsaken' changed to 'reviled' in order to avoid separationism (that is, making a gap between Father and Son).

Lk 2.43: removal of reference to 'his parents'; Jesus had no human father.

Jn 1.18: 'God' rather than 'Son' seems to show a more advanced Christology.

Outside the Gospels, one of the most interesting readings is found in Heb 2.9, where the author originally wrote 'apart from God', a reading surviving only in two Greek manuscripts. Because of the use to which this idea, paralleled elsewhere in the book, was put by separationists, it was changed to the anodyne 'by the grace of God', a usage of the word 'grace' atypical of the writing.

---

4   This case is made most forcibly by B.D. Ehrman, *The Orthodox Corruption of Scripture*, New York, 1993. For an older approach, see C.S.C. Williams, *Alterations to the Text of the Synoptic Gospels and Acts*, Oxford, 1951.

Textual Theory

Although it is sometimes assumed that the role of textual criticism is to recover the original text of a writing, there has never been agreement on this among practitioners in either the practice or the theory. With regard to the Gospels, it is generally agreed that it is not possible to recover a form of their texts older than the late second century, though it is arguable that the task of the editor of Paul is to reconstruct the oldest recoverable text of the collection of letters, not of the separate writings. On the theory there is especially fierce debate today. Textual scholars have interest in witnesses and text forms of all periods, and it is important to realise that all these witnesses and texts represent Jesus as he has been understood and portrayed at a particular time and in a certain place. This is true of every witness that we have, just as it is true of the original writings. The contribution of textual criticism is not to provide a window in time to an authentic original Jesus. It is not even to provide a window to four authentic portrayals of Jesus in four Gospels. It is to provide a window to an almost innumerable number of Jesuses in different manuscripts, and thus in different communities and theologies.[5]

Conclusion

Textual criticism's contribution to the study of Jesus lies in the following areas:

1. The study of the Greek manuscripts and manuscripts of the versions (especially Syriac, Latin and Coptic, as well as Gothic, Old Slavonic, Armenian, Ethiopic and Georgian), showing how the narratives about Jesus were graphically presented in the early centuries and what impact those presentations had on views about him.

2. The study of variation between the witnesses, showing the sum of different interpretations of the Gospels and the relationship between them, and the theological and other reasons which gave rise to them.

3. The study of the history of the text, including the social and theological locations within which views of Jesus changed and developed, demonstrates that the oldest Gospels do not exist in a time capsule. The truth is very different. They have survived only through the medium of Christian interpretation of them.

---

5   Parker, *The Living Text of the Gospels.*

23 Et Incarnatus Est*

While the Christian tradition in some of its language takes very seriously the idea that God's revelation in Jesus Christ took place on a historical stage, it too often treats the inevitable historical problems as negative, overlooking their positive value.

One reason for this is a problem that has its origin in the difference in world-view between late antiquity and the contemporary western world. It seems that the theologian, even in using the imagery and language of another age, has no choice but to treat it as though it were of the same character as the scientific or pseudo-scientific language of our own world. In actual fact, the theologian is faced with a choice that has only become possible in recent centuries. For example, even five hundred years ago Europeans did not need to choose between Genesis 1 as a poetic depiction of the divine creativity and as a scientific account of the origins of life. Of course, given the gulf between the cosmological and psychological discourse of our present age and that of antiquity, we cannot even begin to determine the way in which our ancestors of other times thought that they were using it. Although they 'believed it to be true', they cannot have used it in the same way that we do, because they were not setting it against the language of the modern world. Nor can we be using it in the same way as they did, because we *have to* make claims with the language that they did not. Moreover, we can see that they had a choice which we do not. For while our choice is almost certainly between a Judaeo-Christian story and a scientific account, the makers of those stories were presenting them as alternatives to other similar stories. For example, one might see Genesis 1 as an alternative to a Babylonian creation myth. More to the point of what is to follow, the story of the woman giving birth of Rev 12.1–6 may be read as a narrative presented as superior to similar stories, such as the Greeks told of the birth of Apollo or the Egyptians of the birth of Horus. In a world where dryads haunted every copse

---

* Parts of this paper were first presented to Professor Christopher Rowland's postgraduate seminar in Oxford in May 2000, and all of it was read to the Open End discussion group in Birmingham in July 2000. I am grateful to members of both groups for their comments.

and there was a nymph by every pool, the biblical stories may be seen as a presentation of divine immanence which, while very distinctive, assumes a great deal in common with them. Today, the great god Pan is dead and the biblical narratives survive.

From this problem of world-view stems the problem which is to be discussed here. It is the problem of another gulf, that between theological and historical observations. The gulf arises because it is often assumed that when a historical observation places a question mark against a theological statement, the theological statement has to be persisted in, even absolutely in the face of the historical observation. Too often, the task of finding truth in the biblical text is seen as requiring either that the reader's eyes be closed to the historical problems or, more subtly, that a reconceptualising of the faith be found which finds a way around the historical obstacle. Theology sometimes seems to require faith in events in space and time, yet to refuse to allow to these events the usual scrutiny required of rational behaviour.[1] The consequence of this is to preserve a certain traditional manner of speaking about matters of faith, while in fact indulging in docetism: docetism, because to persist in the statement is to make a decision about the language which robs it of any historical content. This paper offers the contention that, if one accepts a faith which proclaims the significance of certain historical events, one has to regard the historical problems as innate to that which is believed, and not as a challenge to some sort of blind faith. Faith without historical reason is as valueless as hope without love. Instead, we may begin with the recognition of the value of historical research. This research is of value for two reasons: first, because in its rigour it will provide a control over the interpretation and possible meanings of texts; second, because it is conducted by our contemporaries and recent ancestors, and so will inevitably provide a commentary, even if it is *sotto voce* or even silent, on the theological questions which address today.

An example is provided by my theory of the nature of the Gospels. In *The Living Text of the Gospels*, I attempted to develop a theory of the history of the text of the Gospels that also provided a starting point for understanding them, both historically and from a theological point of view. Here I set out some salient points from that study, as a starting point for further investigation.

---

1 In the word 'theology' I include all Christian reflection on the tradition, and do not intend to restrict it to 'academic' activity.

The concept of a 'living text' is, among other things, a denial that there is such a thing as a recoverable, theologically authoritative set of Gospel texts. The implication is not that there is also such a thing as a dead text, but that the text is living, living because it continues to change. Moreover, the barrier between text and interpretation and Gospels[2] and tradition is simply removed, for the reason that the manifold forms of text that are available to us all represent the interpretation of the text, the tradition of the scripture. The distinction between scriptural authority and ecclesial obedience is abandoned. This is an attempt to replace a theological *a priori* with a view based on historical observation, that is the examination of the manuscript variation and the resultant theory of a free text. Rather than presenting a view of the Gospels as divinely inspired or infallible or anything else which then applies the theory to the texts, I began with a study of the textual data, then developed a theory which would account for it, and then moved on to a theological exploration. That is, I have attempted to build a theological argument with a verifiable historical basis.

There are various ways in which the arguments which I have already set out, particularly in the final chapter of my book, could be further explored. Here an analogy will be developed, between the nature of the manuscript tradition and the nature of the incarnation. It is integral to the concept of God becoming a human being that historical problems will arise. One might say that exposure to historiographical difficulties is included in the *kenosis*. It follows that there is required a theological response which finds the incarnate God in what is actually there, in the historical reality as it is credible to us, and not in a short-circuited interpretation which simply ignores the problems. What follows is an attempt to provide such a response. It is something of a truism that a theologian's view of the Bible will reflect that theologian's Christology. This attempts to work in both directions. There are two areas of historical work which will be explored. One is the study of the manuscript tradition, the other is the study of the Gospel of Mark.

[333]

---

2 In fact, it should be stressed that I am only discussing the Gospels, not the whole New Testament, or the Bible. For each collection of writings was transmitted under its own set of circumstances.

1. Textual criticism

I have observed elsewhere that 'the individual text must be taken seriously as a physical object', that 'it is necessary to study a text in conjunction with its material representatives'.[3] A similar approach is followed in *The Living Text of the Gospels*, where I attempt to show 'the importance of the physical characteristics of the copies of a text for the way in which it is understood'.[4] In particular in the present argument, is the insistence that texts exist only as manuscripts.[5]

The incarnation provides a precise analogy to the Gospels which exist only as manuscripts, as ink and papyrus. God is not behind or beyond the Word made flesh, but the Word made flesh is God. In the same way, the text of the Gospels is not beyond the manuscripts. It is not the surviving manuscripts that are meant here, though for us perhaps it might as well be, but all those manuscripts, lost or extant, in which the Gospels have ever existed. Text-critical docetism is quite out of order. The Gospels exist, we might say, as *real* ink and papyrus.

The main analogy can be carried further. Just as in the incarnation the Word accepts the contingencies of human history such as growth and change, decay and death, confusion, misunderstanding and conflict, so the Gospels cannot escape the realities of scribal error, orthodox corruption, damage by accident or intent, total destruction, false emendation, and so on. The concept of a perfect original text is false, in that the text only exists as imperfect copies.

When one continues the comparison, a difference emerges. How may one compare the uniqueness of the Word made flesh with the multiplicity of manuscript copies of the proclaimed word made text? One possible approach would be to view incarnation as a general way in which God is present to humanity. The deficiency of that approach in the present argument is that there will be nothing specific to be said about the manuscript tradition of the Gospels which could not be said about any text. But in fact, in their particular nature as a free text, the Gospels do have a specific tradition. Indeed, each manuscript tradition is unique. The analogy is perhaps only to be sustained in the main point.

Even the history of the relationship between the written text and Christology bears out the essential historical point. The belief that the single authoritative word of Scripture matches the word made flesh is an

---

3 Parker, *Codex Bezae*, 2, 2f.
4 Parker, *The Living Text of the Gospels*, 184.
5 *Ibid.*, 188.

idea most fully and imaginatively conceived by the reformers of the sixteenth century. But it was in that very period that the new technology of the printing press gave rise to a new attitude to texts. The role of the new learning and the power of the press in the Reformation are clearly observable. Did not a bishop of the late fifteenth century protest that printing with movable type would sweep away all his familiar landmarks? It is no criticism of a quite understandable enthusiasm, to say that the reformers made the error of attributing to a manuscript tradition the characteristics of the printed book. This idea must have been particularly attractive, because it seemed possible to make a pretty theological analogy between the one incarnate word and the one authoritative Scripture. We may say in passing, that it is because of this confusion that the reformers' idea of the nature of Scripture, set out as liberating, became increasingly a straitjacket.

Today, our new experience of the electronic text allows us to recognise the normalisation of the experience of the printed text for what it was – an anachronism. Perhaps we stand on the verge of new ideas about the relationship between Christology and the written text. Meanwhile, we have a new opportunity to make theological use of the analogy between the incarnation and the text. Although the analogy was presented as between the incarnation and the text, it will be seen that it will work just as well in the opposite direction and, indeed, that it is in that opposite direction that the rhetoric of the argument places it. For, starting with the physical reality of the manuscript tradition, it then develops a textual analogy to the *kenosis* of the incarnation. The heart of the analogy lies in the fact that the historical problems which, it has already been observed, theology so often finds problematical may be seen as belonging within the consequences of *kenosis*.

[335]

And, appropriately enough, the historical investigation of the New Testament enables us to find a theology which manages to begin with history as well as with the doctrine, holding them together with the concept of *kenosis*.

2. The Gospel of Mark

From the earliest surviving writers on the subject down to the modern period, Mark was treated as a summary of Matthew, with the consequence that its unique features were completely overlooked. It was even studied little enough, and the oldest commentaries post-date those on the other Gospels by a very long time. The oldest is by the fifth-century Victor of Antioch, who compiled comments by earlier writers on Matthew, Mark and Luke into the appropriate Markan parallel. Bede's commentary is mostly derived from Jerome on Matthew. In fact the first independent commentary is that of Theophylact in the second half of the eleventh century. It is thus fair to say that Mark's individual voice was unheard in the formative years of Christian thought. It was only in the nineteenth century that the theory of Matthaean priority was overthrown, and succeeded by the recognition that Mark is the oldest of the four canonical Gospels; and not only the oldest, but also a source for both Matthew and Luke.[6] Even then, the Markan framework of Jesus' career (in fact Matthew's framework) was treated as a reliable historical source. However, the theory of Markan priority had cleared the way, and it was not long before William Wrede managed to demonstrate that the oldest Gospel was a careful theological construct, based on the idea that Jesus' messiahship was purposely hidden, an artifice that also skilfully concealed the actual historical truth, that Jesus was never called Messiah in his lifetime.[7] In modern times also, the demonstration that Mark ends at 16.8 has rid the text of an accretion that distorted its whole meaning. The consequence is that modern theology has a new source at its disposal, the radical and disturbingly modern Gospel of Mark. While the tradition has often treated a Matthaean–Lukan combination (with Johannine additions) as normative, Mark offers at the very root of the tradition a version of the story that has Jesus made Son of God at his baptism (no birth story!), that rejects the idea of Jesus as a wonder-worker[8] and instead presents him as a suffering servant, and that knows no tradition of resurrection appearances – not only that, but also ends with a final enigma (how can we know the story, since the women told nobody?).

This version of the story has certain elements in common with Pauline theology. In particular, the *kenosis* of the figure of Phil 2.6–11 is developed.

The theory that the sequence of miracles of the first chapters of Mark is a rejection of Jesus as a wonder-worker, a *theios aner*, allows

---

6   First stated by Lachmann in 1835.
7   W. Wrede, *The Messianic Secret*, 1901.
8   T.H. Weeden, 'The Heresy that necessitated Mark's Gospel', ZNW 59 (1968), 145–58. Reprinted in W.R. Telford (ed.), *The Interpretation of Mark*, London, 1983, also 2nd edition. Of course, there is plenty of room for debate about many of the details of the story, and here I have only sketched in the merest outlines some of the elements which I consider significant. But, however one looks at it, there is plenty of material for theology to work with.

one to develop this idea further. A whole series of other motifs in the story bear a similar function. Even the miracles sometimes have difficulties, such as the two-stage healing of the blind man, and the disciples' difficulty with the possessed boy. The parables are told not so as to clarify but so as to conceal the message. The paradox of the Transfiguration is not that Jesus is once transformed, but that he is generally untransformed (a point highlighted by the violent struggle with evil that at once ensues). The declaration of Jesus' messiahship carries within it the declaration of the way of suffering and death. Jesus' divine sonship is proclaimed at the moment of that death.

[337]

The point is that the Markan theology is able to express the view that God is present to the world in Jesus, with only limited or even sometimes ironic reference to the language of what we could call the miraculous, and that the high Christological points are found at the darkest moments of the story. We may note also the wonderful unification of literary construction and theological purpose in Mark's writing, found especially in the use of the concept of hiddenness to justify a historical anachronism in his story. The same subtlety may be observed in the conclusion, where it is sufficient for the story to end at 16.8. The proclamation of the resurrection to the women does not need any further validation. The story is complete in itself.

We find in Markan theology a dramatic and compelling early Christian account of Jesus. How radical it would have been to its first readers and hearers is demonstrated by the fact that to them only the Messianic Secret would have been abnormal – the miracle stories would have been accepted quite naturally (in fact, reactions would have been the opposite of our own). Mark has given twentieth-century theology an authentic, in that it is so primitive, and radical alternative to a tradition coated in two thousand years of whitewash. In a rather unexpected way, it also short-circuits the traditional view of the linear and unbroken development of Christian belief. For the discovery of Mark's independence has led to the discovery of an untapped primitive Christology. Moreover, this discovery has cast the views of other early Christian writers in a new light – one can see, for example, how Matthew and Luke rejected many of Mark's interpretations, and how other writers, such as Paul, stand in relation to him (there is no evidence that Paul accepted a tradition of Jesus as a miracle-worker); and then one can also look in a new way at how the sub-apostolic and later traditions developed. In short, historical criticism has made available a document which provides theology with a fresh opportunity to reflect on the tradition, and with a new range of possibilities. It is a tradition which has lain as hidden as the women's encounter at the tomb, as mysterious as the parables – spoken openly, yet secret and untold.

One may set this paper in the context of contemporary debate, by referring to a sequence of contributions to *The Scottish Journal of Theology*. The pair of articles by Christopher Seitz[9] and Francis Watson[10] I set aside as not within my immediate theme here, but the reader will note similarities of themes. The subject of Nicholas Peter Harvey[11] is very different from mine, but two of his initial comments are parallel to two of my themes: 'the touchstone is observation of what goes on in peoples' lives [which I may gloss for my purposes with "and consequently what kinds of manuscripts they produced"] ... People sometimes ask: "Where does God come in?" The question is based on a misunderstanding, for what is happening is, if anywhere, the place of God [to be glossed with "i.e., incarnation"]'.[12]

I begin with Iain Torrance's study, 'Gadamer, Polanyi and Ways of Being Closed'.[13] Beginning with Gadamer's analysis of playing and Polanyi's of skills, he draws some interesting analogies between them: 'Gadamer is looking for a model which will allow for the autonomy of the text from its author ... And Gadamer argues that there is no access to the text outside of this relationship of "performing" it: "It is to move out of the actual experience of a piece of literature if one investigates the origins of the plot on which it is based ..." Now, on this understanding, the closedness or autonomy of the text is bestowed from the side of the audience'.[14] 'We begin to see here the structure of Polanyi's account of the autonomy of the text. It is autonomous because it has been blocked off, but here the closedness is from the side of the author, so that others are free to enter into that integration'.[15] Both these theories of authorial intention and textual autonomy provide a way of understanding the nature of the manuscript tradition of the Gospels. They may even be used together, if we say that the fact that the texts survive for us only as they were 're-written' by or for successive users

---

9   'Christological Interpretation of Texts and Trinitarian Claims to Truth: An Engagement with Francis Watson's *Text and Truth*', *SJT* 52 (1999), 209–26.
10 'The Old Testament as Christian Scripture: A Response to Professor Seitz', *idem*, 227–32.
11 'Christian Morality?', *idem*, 106–16.
12 *Ibid.*, 106.
13 *SJT* 46 (1993), 497–505.
14 499f.
15 503.

(and in formats which the authors could not have conceived of) may be seen as closedness from the side of the author, in that we have only a sequence of performances of it. But the closedness is not due at this point directly to the nature of the activity of being an author, as is the theories of both Gadamer and Polanyi, but to the ways in which the users chose to and were able to respond to the author's text. Again, the character of a text and our responses to it are inseparable from the physical restraints and possibilities which surround its creation and copying. This fact is unifying both for the analysis of Gadamer and Polanyi and for the present response to it, because it is particularly interesting with regard to the question of classic texts and of genre, to which the article then turns: 'The Gospels are particular integrations of particular power which are honoured by a particular tradition. Does this mean that they are definitive? No, but the Christian tradition may take them as such. We may *choose* to see them as classics. Thus, I suggest that a "gospel" is not so much a different "genre". That would be a closing from the side of the reader. Instead there is a choosing to give classical status to certain pieces'.[16] The question of classical status and genre is raised in the textual history in many ways, including the range of differences between utilitarian papyrus notebooks and magnificent parchment codices de luxe.[17] It is raised (as has been noted more than once before) also in a particular way by the different endings of Mark. The latest and longest ending gives to the whole story a distance from everything else in life and hence a closedness that places it very firmly in the category of 'classic'. It is also an ending which, with its pastiche of phrases from the other canonical Gospels, is quite clear what material is needed to make a Gospel complete. It might be said that the different forms of Mark belong to different genres, and to different views of what a Gospel should set out to achieve. More broadly, it may be stated that the range of physical manifestations in which the Gospels have been produced testifies to their existence as a

[339]

[340]

---

16 505.
17 To illustrate the point almost at random, I happened at the same time as writing this across a quatrain found at the end of the four Gospels in a group of thirteenth-century Greek manuscripts, which accords the texts status in a particular way by drawing on Jn 7.37–8:
These Four Gospels by the disciples of the Word
Pour out the stream of ever-flowing words.
Therefore, thirsty one, do not hesitate to drink,
But water your soul, and give your mind refreshment.
See E.C. Colwell, *The Four Gospels of Karahissar*, Vol. 1, *History and Text*, Chicago, 1936, 29.

number of separate genres. It is thus true that the concept of genre is unhelpful in understanding the value of the Gospels in the church and moreover that even in choosing to accord them classic status we are not confining ourselves to a single view of them, for that classical status may and has been presented in many different ways.

I turn next to an exchange between Christopher Rowland and Francis Watson.[18] Watson believes that 'the obsession with reconstructing the world behind the text has led to a neglect of the text itself in its final form ... The concept of the "final form" itself presupposes the historical knowledge which, within its limitations, textual criticism has made available'.[19] The claim that there is a final form, which matters so much to canonical approaches, is one that has to be challenged. It is only very recently that I have actually noticed that my observations with regard to the history of the Gospels stand so diametrically opposed to this claim. To put it very simply, I do not believe that there is such a final form. There are three problems with the concept. The first is that the text exists in a variety of forms, and that the prioritising of one at the expense of the others is in his terms an arbitrary act, since it cannot be on theological grounds; unless one selects a doctrinally acceptable version, but once that is done the independence of the text against the theologian has been cancelled. The second is that the concept 'final form' presupposes the normative status of the printed text he happens to know, that is, the eclectic, commonly available printed text. So far as the manuscript tradition is concerned, the final form actually is the Byzantine text-type. But, since the printed text has gone through a constant process of modification, it has to be said that the final form has yet to appear. The third problem is that the final form presupposes a canon which I believe to be conceived according to the norm of our western printed Bibles and New Testaments. It is something of a surprise to discover that there are no Bibles surviving from antiquity which contain only all of 'our' canonical books. They all have either more or less in them. From the Byzantine period, there are not more than a couple of dozen.[20] The point is that the canonical texts scarcely existed within one covering. For the overwhelming majority of people who worked with New Testament texts, they knew books of the

---

18 'An Open Letter to Francis Watson on *Text, Church and World*, from Professor Christopher Rowland and a Response by Dr Francis Watson', *SJT* 48 (1995), 507–22.

19 *Ibid.*, 519.

20 This is an approximation. I am still in the process of gathering information. [Further information now available in D.C. Parker, *An Introduction to the New Testament Manuscripts and their Texts*, Cambridge, 2008, Chapter 1.8.]

four Gospels (the greatest number of manuscripts), or some other part such as Paul's letters or Acts and the Catholic Epistles. Only with the invention of the printed book did the complete Greek Testament become normal.

In another paper in the sequence, John Webster[21] writes of 'the Bible' in a quite undifferentiated way. He writes that 'At its simplest, my proposal is that the Christian activity of reading the Bible is most properly (that is, Christianly) understood as a spiritual affair, and accordingly a matter for theological description. That is to say, a Christian description of the Christian reading of the Bible will be the kind of description which talks of God and therefore talks of all other realities *sub specie divinitatis*.'[22] What is strange is that in what follows, the Bible is written about, and claims are made about it, almost with no reference whatsoever to its actual character and contents. The interpretation seems to be driven by a set of *a priori* decisions. Would one not expect to find an attempt to engage with the biblical text itself, as a test of the decisions, given that the Bible is spoken of as having an authority that is 'real and functional'? Part of the purpose of Webster's argument is to reject the idea that a kind of blanket hermeneutics, applicable to every text, should be used in biblical interpretation. This is in harmony with the arguments that I am advancing, but on very different grounds. In my view, the reason is that these are different texts with different histories. The way that you interpret the text should begin with the actual text that you are interpreting. And part of beginning with the text that you are interpreting is including its text history, because we have the text only as it has actually been copied and received. The texts are three-dimensional.

[342]

I note that in neither of these last contributions is there anything other than an assumption that the printed text is normative. Yet the printed text has been around for only a quarter of the history of the earliest Christian writings, and with the speed of present change it is unlikely that it will be possible to hold the line for very long. I venture to predict that the electronic text will very soon be leading us to unlearn what we thought we knew about texts. For example, it will be, indeed it already is, possible to read texts three-dimensionally. It is a matter of time before both the blanket hermeneutics and the specifically Christian interpretations will be in need of revising. For already the textual critics are producing the kinds of texts that they are

---

21 'Hermeneutics in Modern Theology: Some Doctrinal Reflections', *SJT* 51 (1998), 307–41.
22 *Ibid.*, 307.

able to make and want to create, and the users will find that the forgotten lower critics are calling the tune. Assuredly, theology will be at the mercy of historical vicissitudes.

There have been two arguments here presented, each of them attempting to use historical evidence as a foundation for theological enquiry. The one is based on an examination of the physical evidences of the Gospels, and attempts to find an analogy between the manuscript tradition and the event, belief in which led to the tradition's continuing existence. The other attempts to find the idea on which that analogy is based (the *kenosis*) in the fruit of a century and a half of historical investigation of the Gospels. If the first person to write a narrative about Jesus found the literary means and the theological framework in the primitive view of the self-emptying of Christ, then there is a historical sense (given the dependence of the other Gospels on Mark),[23] in which the development of the doctrine of the incarnation depends on that concept of the *kenosis*. In that case, the miraculous elements of the tradition emerge, paradoxically, out of a theology which insists on their impossibility. That is to say, the theology has nothing to lose by beginning with the history.

---

23 This is true in the literary sense for Matthew and Luke. Even if John is independent (as he is in my view), there is still a fascinatingly Johannine character to the Markan theology – or is it just that we have not yet fully liberated him from what we already knew?

24 Textual Criticism and Theology[1]

A title with these two components seems an impossibility, as difficult as dealings between Athens and Jerusalem. Textual Criticism you expect to be the minutiae of dry scholars producing keys to all mythologies, while Theology, the queen of the sciences deigns not even to notice this most mundane of disciplines. Not that it was always thus. Origen, after all, was both the first and one of the greatest of all textual scholars of the Christian Bible and a figure of colossal significance in the development of Christian theology, and he certainly had no difficulty in practising both at once. One well-known passage in which he does so is in his commentary on Jn 1.28, where he proposes that the place where John baptised cannot have been Bethany, because the home town of Lazarus and his sisters is in the wrong place. Instead, he suggests, it must be Bethabara which, moreover, since it means 'house of preparation' is a far more fitting place than Bethany, meaning 'house of obedience'.[2] In a few words he combines geography, textual evidence and interpretation. While modern scholarship can easily deride Origen for being a bad textual critic in our own terms, we would also do well to recognise how much more sophisticated he was than we are in recognising that variant readings are not theologically neutral. They carry meanings, if you like they are 'political', and we need to be as cunning as serpents in dealing with them or, as Codex Sinaiticus has it, as cunning as *the* serpent. It is of course anachronistic to apply the terms 'textual criticism' and 'theology' to Origen's activity, since these disciplines as we think of them did not exist. And it is arguably because of the way we do think of them that we cannot very easily relate the two. This has arisen as the result of various events in the past half millennium or so. I single out four. Two of them refer to textual criticism, two to theology.

---

1 This paper was presented at the Postgraduate Seminar in the Department of Theology, University of Nottingham and subsequently at a day event to mark Frances Young's retirement from the University of Birmingham in September, 2005. I am grateful to the participants for the discussion at each event. I am also grateful to Peter Harvey, who decided to edit it for me and made many improvements.
2 *Commentary on John*, Sources Chrétiennes 157, 286.

I will begin by describing them, then indicate reasons why I consider them to be inadequate, describe alternative approaches, and finally offer a view of the relationship between textual criticism and theology.

1. The first is the opinion that the only goal of textual criticism is the restoration of the original text. According to this view, texts have been corrupted in the process of transmission, and require a process of cleansing, in which the errors and accretions and losses are either corrected, removed or rectified, until the text as it left its author's hand is made available to the lucky reader. As it happens, the history of the printed Greek New Testament plays rather well for this point of view. Made by Erasmus from a mixed bunch of late Byzantine manuscripts, patchily altered over the following century and then set in stone for another two hundred, it was only the determination of first Lachmann, then Tischendorf, Tregelles, and finally Westcott and Hort in 1881 that a purified text, based upon the best ancient sources, became available. The touchstone of this process is the ridiculous business of the Johannine comma, the presence in a few manuscripts, most of them Latin, of the addition at 1 Jn 5.8 of a blatantly secondary trinitarian formula. To be honest, it was a problem that should not cause a novice a moment's hesitation in divining the most likely explanation of the way the text changed.

2. At quite an early stage in the development of a challenge to the so-called Received Text, the textual critics found themselves in an unpleasant situation, and from the early eighteenth century were at pains to stress that textual variation was not theologically motivated, and indeed that no article of faith was affected by any variant reading. The cause of this was the debate caused by John Mill's *Novum Testamentum Graece* of 1707. Although Mill printed the commonly received text, he placed beneath it an apparatus said to contain 30,000 variant readings from manuscripts, versions and patristic citations. Hitherto, nobody had had any idea that there were so many differences between copies of the sacred text. And it caused a furore on two fronts. Daniel Whitby, in the 1710 version of his *Paraphrase and Commentary on the New Testament*, wrote that he was grieved and vexed 'that I have found so much in Mill's Prolegomena which seems plainly to render the standard of faith insecure, or at best to give others too good a handle for doubting'.[3] The 'free-thinker' Anthony Collins took up the

---

3   D. Whitby, *Examen variantium lectionum Joannis Millii, S.T.P. in Novum Testamentum*, London, 1710, cited by A. Fox, *John Mill and Richard Bentley. A Study of the Textual Criticism of the New Testament 1675–1729*, Oxford, 1954, 106.

matter in 1713 with his *Discourse of Free-thinking*, in which he refers to the Anglican clergy 'owning and labouring to prove the Text of the Scripture to be precarious'.[4] The message is clear: that textual criticism brings down the wrath of non-practitioners on the critic, for they at once provide stumbling blocks for the faithful and ammunition for the impious. Even in 1881, Westcott and Hort claimed that there was not a single theologically motivated variant reading in the New Testament.

3. Theology, and by this I mean what I was brought up to think of as dogmatic theology, principally of the Protestant variety, has generally accepted a concept of a linear development of orthodoxy, responsible for all surviving texts.[5] This opinion has to hold the view that the works within the New Testament canon of twenty-seven books are both the product of orthodox thought and have been preserved within orthodoxy. The unspoken corollary of this is that the manuscripts in which these works were preserved were also the product of orthodoxy. It follows that the possibility of finding divergent, 'heretical', opinions expressed within these manuscripts, let alone the works they contain, does not appear to have been considered by theologians. This is due to an emphasis on the Bible as divine revelation which does not consider the means by which the Bible has been preserved as in any way significant. It is therefore possible, on the assumption of the linear development of orthodoxy, for the theologian to assume what is in her received text to have a single source, the pens of the evangelists and apostles.

4. Rather closely connected to this is my fourth observation, that much theological formulation with regard to the Bible as revelation, as the Word of God and so forth, takes the form of a set of assertions which resolutely ignore the reality of the origin, nature and historical development of the Bible, and with that of the realities of textual

[585]

---

4   A. Collins, *Discourse of Free-Thinking*, London, 1713, 87, cited by Fox, 108.
5   I am aware that this assessment runs counter to a general view of the difference between Protestant and Catholic thought as traditionally polarised, as well as another part of reformed theology as it emerged in the Renaissance period. This is the view that pure forms of Christian thought became debased after a while, so that it was necessary to purify the Church of these later accretions, including various doctrines not held by either the New Testament writers or, more broadly, the fathers down to Augustine. There was evidently a significant parallel between this view and the humanist return to textual fountainheads, including the Greek New Testament. But for this school of thought, the same general principle holds good, that first- or fifth- or sixteenth- or twenty-first-century orthodoxy are all the same, receiving and passing on the truth.

criticism. In fact, as *a priori* statements, they might as well be made about the telephone directory.

As a result of these things, textual critics have gone their own very cautious way, happy to have their work viewed as the lower criticism, the process of restoring the text, their editions then to be handed over to the higher critics to develop their historical theories and the theologians to wave from their lecterns and pulpits. At the same time, the higher critics have been complacent with regard to the true nature and value of the critical edition, while the theologians have been patronising in regard to textual critics – when they mention them. We find Kierkegaard in *For Self-examination* referring to John Mill's edition. Speaking of the mirror of God's Word, he speaks of the 'limitless horizons of prolixity', among which he includes Mill's 30,000 variant readings.[6] 'If thou art a learned man, then take care lest with all thy erudite reading (which is not reading God's Word) thou forgettest perchance to read God's Word'.[7] We find Barth writing that 'If we have a particular interest in antiquities, we read [the Bible] at our own risk, at the risk of failing to serve even our own interest and missing the real nature and character of the writings'.[8] Both these warnings, which we may take as addressed to textual critics as much as to any other erudite readers and students of antiquities, set up a regrettable antithesis, between reading as historians and reading in order to be taught. Is the textual critic forced to read manuscripts only critically and without other benefits? Must we leave our textual knowledge behind when we put on our theological reading glasses? How can we? When we know that the text which is presented to us as the source of revelation is an eclectic text, produced by our fellows from a set of manuscripts of many different origins and characters, must we not insist that what we know is listened to and understood by those who claim such theological high ground? I could go on, but I will begin to anticipate my conclusion. Instead, I will return to the four points which I have set out, and both show why there is good reason to reject the view they represent, and offer an alternative approach to each.

---

6   S. Kierkegaard, *For Self-Examination*, London, 1941, 50.
7   *Ibid.*, 54f.
8   K. Barth, *Church Dogmatics*, Volume 1, Part 2, Edinburgh, 1956, 493.

1. The Restoration of the Original Text as the Goal of Textual Criticism

This concept assumes that the restoration of an original text is both appropriate and possible. Both assumptions are dubious. With regard to appropriateness, it is not the case that all texts were intended by their originators to remain in the earliest form in which they produced them. There are many possible situations, apart from the particular writing processes of individual works. I single out two, that an originator produced a form of text which he intended to be changed by its users, and that the receivers of a text felt themselves at liberty to change it. With regard to the New Testament, its constituent parts must be treated separately in this regard. The largest section, the Gospels, developed in both situations. It is a reasonable argument that Matthew, having produced a thoroughly revised and expanded version of Mark, would not have been surprised to know that Luke took both Mark and Matthew and made a very different version. And, as I have argued extensively in various places, the wealth of textual variation in our manuscripts of the Gospels is proof enough that the early Christian users of the Gospels treated them as *living texts*, which were re-worded, expanded or reduced, to bring out what these users believed to be the true meaning of the text.

With regard to the Pauline *corpus*, it has been well argued by Günther Zuntz, in his seminal work *The Text of the Epistles*, that the goal of the textual critic is to restore, not the text of Paul's letters as sent by him to their several destinations, but the text of the collected edition, which he dates to about 100 CE.[9] This collected edition, Zuntz argued, shows clear signs of editorial activity on the part of the compilers. We might explore similarly the process by which the Catholic Epistles came to be gathered together. The Acts of the Apostles is a book which was so thoroughly revised and expanded in the course of the second and third centuries that it is customary to refer to two editions of Acts, the 'old uncial' and the 'western'. It is only with the Apocalypse, which has a unique and in many ways more 'normal' textual history, that we can begin to wonder whether the process of restoring the original text is an appropriate methodology.

In short, the attempt to produce an original form of a living text is worse than trying to shoot a moving target, it is turning a movie into a

[586]

---

9   Zuntz, *The Text of the Epistles*.

single snapshot, it is taking a single part of a complex entity and claiming it to be the whole.

But, even if it were appropriate, it is even more damaging to the claim when we discover that the restoration of the original text has yet to be achieved, and is unlikely ever to be achieved. It cannot be emphasised too strongly that the Nestle-Aland[27], on which so many scholars and theologians rely, without reference to the critical apparatus, as '*the* New Testament', is described by its editors as representing a 'working text', and in no way as something believed by its editors to represent the autograph text.[10] At present, the central question is the degree to which we can recover forms of the text older than the end of the second century. This is the approximate date of our oldest extensive manuscripts, and also seems to represent the point at which the text of the Gospels began to be produced in reasonably carefully controlled forms. Before that lies a period for which we have no manuscript attestation, and in which we know the greatest amount of change and variation to have arisen: the perplexing forms of text we find in writers such as Justin and Clement of Alexandria, Tatian's Diatessaron, Marcion's Gospel, and the appearance of passages such as Jn 7.53–8.11. At present, the best editors can hope to do is, where the manuscripts are available, to recreate forms of text that were current in the period 200–300 CE. It is worth recalling that our oldest complete, indeed even extensive, manuscript of Mark dates from the second quarter of the fourth century.

The theological problem posed by the continuing absence of an original text is that it is hard to see how the view can be sustained that there is a text which can be described as received by the church from the witnesses to it, in a way formulated so powerfully and clearly by Barth. The texts that are available to us we receive from the hands of the scribes who produced our oldest extant manuscripts, in the third and fourth centuries. The division between inspired Word, received by the church, and church tradition, is given the lie by the brutal facts of our manuscript tradition, both in the living quality of the productions themselves, and in the historical accidents of manuscript survival.

If, then, the goal of textual criticism is not, and in the case of the New Testament cannot be, the restoration of the original text, what is it? It is in fact the thing which textual critics have always done, it is the reconstruction of the development of the text, the demonstration that one reading arose as the result of either a particular understanding of a

---

10   *Nestle-Aland*[27], 45*.

theological matter, or as a misunderstanding or emendation of another reading, and so forth. The abandonment of the quest for an original text does not de-historicise textual criticism. We still find textual forms that are older than other ones, and seek to describe sequences of development. What one does not do is to regard the later developments as irrelevant. If the text was a living and developing one, then the later forms of the text are significant, since they are interpretations of the text by a user or group of users. If the quest for an original form is set aside, the oldest recoverable form has of course great significance. But there is no obvious reason theologically why that particular form of the text should be given a greater authority than a later one.

2. The Claim that Textual Variation is not Theologically Motivated

Until the middle of the last century, textual critics provided any number of explanations for variant readings: they could be due to grammatical problems, interpretative problems, palaeographical errors, and sheer chance in the process of copying. In fact, accident was given a high place among the causes of variation. What a variant could not be was theologically motivated. The first scholars to mount a challenge to this were members of the Chicago School, and among them especially Kenneth Clark.[11] Subsequently, the work of Eldon Epp, arguing that the text of Acts in Codex Bezae showed an anti-Judaic bias, was the most significant among a number of studies of the formation of the western text of Acts.[12] In 1993, Bart Ehrman's book *The Orthodox Corruption of Scripture* provided the first sustained thesis arguing that many variations in the text are alterations made as a result of theological

[587]

---

11 K.W. Clark, 'Textual Criticism and Doctrine', *Studia Paulina, Festschrift Johannis de Zwaan*, ed. W.C. van Unnik and J.N. Sevenster, Leiden, 1953, reprinted in *The Gentile Bias and other essays*, ed. J.L. Sharpe (NovT Suppl 54), Leiden, 1980, 90–103; 'The Theological Relevance of Textual Criticism in Current Criticism of the Greek New Testament', *JBL* 85 (1966), 1–16, reprinted in *The Gentile Bias and other essays*, ed. J.L. Sharpe (NovT Suppl 54), Leiden, 1980, 104–19. For a thorough account of the Chicago School and subsequent developments, see E.J. Epp, 'The Multivalence of the Term "Original Text" in New Testament Textual Criticism', *HTR* 92 (1999), 254–81, reprinted in *Perspectives on New Testament Textual Criticism. Collected Essays, 1962–2004* (NovT Suppl 116), Brill, 2005, 551–93, with Added Notes (592–3).
12 E.J. Epp, *The Theological Tendency of Codex Bezae Cantabrigiensis in Acts* (SNTSMS 3), Cambridge, 1966.

controversies in the early Church.[13] Time and again, he takes texts which were debated by both sides in such controversies, and argues that older readings which were used by one side, that which came to be called 'heretical', to bolster their point of view, were revised by their opponents – the 'orthodox' – to bring out what they knew to be their true meaning. A classic example is Lk 3.22: 'Thou art my Son, this day have I begotten thee'. This verse was used by adoptianists to argue in support of their view. We find also the text 'Thou art my beloved Son, in whom I am well-pleased', borrowed from Mk 1.11, which provides an 'orthodox' form of the verse.

My argument of course is cumulative. Both these forms of text survive because of their use in theological debate within the church. Thus, we do not have a text received by the church, but one produced within the church.

3. The Concept of a Linear Development of Orthodoxy

Bart Ehrman makes extensive use in his monograph of Walter Bauer's *Orthodoxy and Heresy in Earliest Christianity*. This view offers a challenge to what I describe as the linear development of orthodoxy, by stressing that what we know as orthodoxy was only able to emerge once certain groups had the political power to outlaw groups with other points of view. In the first couple of centuries what we see are groups with various points of view, none of them able to do much more than condemn the views of others. Some of these groups held views which were later claimed by other groups which successfully promulgated themselves as orthodox and claimed to be their heirs. In counter-argument to Ehrman, some have suggested that the textual development happened the other way, and that it was 'heretics' who introduced variations, altering the text to suit their own interests. While it is possible that one might make alternative suggestions to some of his examples, and find others to support the alternative, the cumulative effect of his study is hard to gainsay. Rather than getting locked into an either/or debate, we would be wiser to recognise pragmatically that the central issue is that theological debate led to textual variation. Textual variation was introduced by both heretical and orthodox groups. In terms of the textual tradition, we can say that the forms of text known to us, and on which our critical editions are based, contain readings

---

13   B.D. Ehrman, *The Orthodox Corruption of Scripture*, Oxford, 1993.

introduced by tradents of the text. What we lose is the possibility of finding a pure tradition, a text transmitted through 'orthodox' groups. This reality is highlighted when we consider our almost total ignorance about the origins of some of our oldest manuscripts. In what circles were they created and used? Do they represent a broad spectrum of ancient textual forms? The fact that they almost all were found in Egypt, and the majority of these at Oxyrhynchus, suggests that they may not.

4. Making Theological Statements about the Text without Reference to the Nature of the Text and the Way in which it Has Been Received, and Ignoring the Realities of Textual Criticism

The different textual histories of the sections of the New Testament, which I described earlier, are not incidental to these books. The books survive for us only in certain physical forms, and as a result of a sequence of decisions by editors, copyists and readers. Whatever, therefore, we have to say about these books must reflect these realities. To make theological statements about the character of the New Testament or the Bible, simply short cutting the most basic text-critical data, and indeed dismissing it as the pedantry of antiquarians or as a dead end for theology, which must return to a point of view held before these data were known and adequately understood, is in my view dishonest obfuscation. Any theological *a priori*, which says this or that about the New Testament, but with no reference to what the New Testament *is*, is an arbitrary attempt to impose dogma on reality.

There is a second matter, which is plainly a problem for ecclesiastical legislators, but also for theologians seeking a source for theological claims, and that is the lack of an authoritative text. There cannot be an authoritative text when the text has survived for us as a number of competing and equal forms. I have taken a number of examples of this in the past, including the striking instance of the multiple and contradictory forms of Jesus' sayings on marriage and divorce.

I promised that I would set out an alternative approach. It has to be one that recognises the nature of the living text, that accepts the role of theological modification in the development of the text, that acknowledges the text as a result of the pluralism of early Christianity,

[588]

and that has as its starting point the realities of the textual tradition and the manuscripts of early Christianity.

At the heart of my frustration with a theology of the Bible that ignores all this is the fact that it seems to me to sit so awkwardly with the concept of the incarnation. Given a faith in a God become human, how can one have a Word of God which consistently defies the nature of human existence?[14] There are always good reasons, of course, along the lines of the necessity for corroboration of the truth. But why is it necessary to have a reliable guarantee of the apostolic faith, or of the text produced by the evangelists? Whether it is necessary or not to have a reliable guarantee of the apostolic faith, theology has to get used to the fact that none is available.

We have become accustomed to questions such as the degree to which the early church reformed and created sayings and acts of Jesus, so that the concept of the Gospels as kerygmatic narratives has even been a helpful and reassuring one for theology. What we have not had is the recognition that we do not even directly possess first-century kerygmatic narratives. What is at our disposal are versions of these kerygmatic narratives, if you like multiple kerygmatic narratives, copied a century and more after the evangelists lived and worked.

To return to Barth. I am rather taken with one detail, his liking for the descriptions of the New Testament texts as 'witnesses'.[15] This word 'witnesses' is used also by textual critics to describe evidence in support of a reading. It can mean Greek manuscripts, manuscripts of a version, or citations in an early Christian writer. These witnesses to the text are all that we have. Any 'authoritative' text is formed by selecting readings from this reservoir or bank of variant readings. If we set aside the citations, which are of a different nature, we have a collection of witnesses, the manuscripts. And although traditionally textual criticism has focused on variant readings, so that the individual witnesses lose their individuality and become carriers of nuggets of significant data, it is also possible to follow a different approach and to develop a textual criticism which pays attention to the significance of the witnesses as they are. It is noteworthy that, although users of the text such as theologians work with a single critical text, some of the most useful tools are ones which present multiple text forms, such as Rope's edition of Acts with two parallel texts, the old uncial and the western, or Reuben Swanson's edition with multiple parallel lines, the Beuron

---

14 For more on this theme, see D.C. Parker, 'Et Incarnatus Est', *SJT* 54 (2001), 330–43.
15 A major theme in *Church Dogmatics* Volume 1, Part 1.

Vetus Latina and Kiraz' Syriac Gospels, each with a different line for each text type.[16] In these instances, the attempt to recreate a single Urtext is abandoned, in favour of a presentation which at least attempts to do justice to the way in which the material came into being and was transmitted.

Today, we can go even further and say that the kind of electronic editions which we are now creating pay even less attention to an Urtext. Indeed, the base text even in the Münster *Editio Critica Maior* functions mostly as a series of pegs on which to hang a critical apparatus.[17] Instead of revolving around a critical text like a traditional print volume, the electronic edition consists of a set of transcriptions of the witnesses, held together by a series of links and tools for analysis, each capable of holding centre stage with a presentation of the surface of the page, images and analytical tools.

[598]

These artefacts are, if you like, witnesses to the witness of which Barth was writing. What we do not have is direct access to the witness in the way which he envisaged. It would be tempting to say that instead, we have witnesses to the witness. But even that presupposes that the witness is at least theoretically accessible. I am rejecting even that possibility. *All* that we have are the witnesses to the text, and it is in them, in their physical reality, that we will find what there is to find. The first piece which I wrote on this theme had the title 'Scripture is Tradition'. What I have offered here is a further exploration of the simple point with which my thinking on this topic began twenty years ago, that all study of the New Testament text has to begin with the manuscripts, and having begun with them, cannot progress beyond them.

---

16   J.H. Ropes, *The Text of Acts* (*The Beginnings of Christianity, Part I The Acts of the Apostles*, Vol. 3), London, 1926; R.J. Swanson, *New Testament Greek Manuscripts. Variant Readings Arranged in Horizontal Lines against Codex Vaticanus*, 4 vols. (one for each Gospel), Sheffield and Pasadena, 1995, followed by Acts (1998), Galatians (1999), Romans (2001) and 1 Corinthians (2003); *Vetus Latina. Die Reste der altlateinischen Bibel*, Freiburg, 1949– ; G.A. Kiraz, *Comparative Edition of the Syriac Gospels. Aligning the Sinaiticus, Curetonianus, Peshitta and Harklean Versions*, 4 vols., Piscataway, 2004.
17   *Editio Critica Maior* IV. *Die Katholischen Briefe*.

25 Calvin's Biblical Text

Discussion about the character of Calvin's biblical text generally revolves around two main questions: is he working with a Greek or a Latin text? and what is the base text which he is using? Before proposing a somewhat different approach to the issue, several preliminary remarks are necessary.

With regard to the debate as to whether this is a commentary on a Greek or a Latin text, the answer is not as obvious as might be supposed. On the one hand, the fact that there are few words of Greek in the entire work might encourage one to conclude that it is exegesis of a Latin version of Paul. This is not a commentary on the Greek text in the way of a Zahn or of Sanday and Headlam. On the other, the fact that Calvin is at some pains to reject existing translations and to make his own interpretation of the Greek clear suggests that his Latin version is a tool to bring out the sense of Paul's Greek.

With regard to the question of Calvin's base text, the search is partly determined by one's answer to the first main question. For example, has he modified an existing Latin translation where he considers it deficient, or has he translated from a Greek edition, no doubt imitating existing Latin versions where he was content with them? It is also possible that the truth lies somewhere between these two extremes. It must be added that the various Greek New Testaments available to Calvin in 1540, 1551, and again in 1556 do not show a large number of dramatic differences between their texts of Romans, and even fewer which would show up in a Latin translation.

The approach taken to these problems here is to begin by collecting and observing information, and then to ask what light it casts on Calvin's way of working. It turns out that the study of the biblical citations casts light on more than Calvin's biblical text.

An analysis of the text indicates two important sets of data: the one is a significant degree of variation between the lemmata (the quotation of the verses about to be discussed, at the beginning of a new section) and the running texts (citations within the exposition); the other is a considerable number of changes between the three editions of the commentary, mainly ones introduced in the third. The two problems must be taken together, but the different parts of each set of data are significant at different stages of the investigation. The matter must be approached by beginning with an analysis of the situation in the first edition of the commentary.

The First Edition

The first task is to discriminate between different categories of difference between lemma and running text. First, there are differences which are due to Calvin's working the reference into the grammar of his own sentence, as for example at 1.18, where *omnem impietatem et iniustitiam hominum* in the lemma becomes 'Deinde, *Omnis hominum impietas*, per hypallagen . . .' Or again, 3.13, where *Sepulchrum apertum guttur eorum* becomes 'Contra autem subiicitur, *guttur eorum sepulchrum esse apertum*'. The number of such places is dependent on the selection of words for printing in different type – there are many allusions and Pauline phrases in the commentary which are not selected, although they are found in the lemma.[1] These places, once noted, are not worthy of further comment at this point. Second, in some places the exposition text is evidently an abbreviated form of the text. Sometimes this is indicated by a few words and '*etc*'. Elsewhere words such as particles, pronouns and the auxiliary verb are dropped. For example, *enim* is omitted seven times in the running text where it is found in the lemma (1.16; 6.14; 7.5, 14, 22; 13.4, 8). A third tiny category consists of typographical errors in the lemma: at 14.22 it reads *indicat* instead of *iudicat*, and at 15.20 *amittens* instead of *annitens*. At 14.20 the phrase *malum est homini* in the lemma becomes *malum est ei*, probably by a recollection of Lk 17.1 (*vae autem illi* Vulgate). On several other occasions a similar sounding word to the lemma appears in the Running Text: 15.7, *gloriam/gratiam*[2] and 15.29, *scio/spero*. We may also note the interesting reading at 4.16, where *ei* is read as *enim* in the Running Text.[3] There may be another error at 6.22, where the lemma has *sanctificationem* and the Running Text *sanctificatione*. The accusative ending may have become corrupted, perhaps because it had been indicated with a superline. A fourth rather

---

1 But since the selection is found in the printed editions, one is justified in treating them as belonging in a separate category.
2 See XVII above, where we refer to instances of this confusion in the commentary as well as the text.
3 This mistake is also made by four Vulgate manuscripts cited in Wordsworth and White's apparatus. It is a good example of unrelated witnesses independently introducing a common error.

large category is of places where the running text has the same words as the lemma, but in a different order. Generally, any versions which agree with either (see below), support the lemma. There are nineteen of these readings.[4] Once all these groups have been eliminated, we are left with 165 places where the lemmata and the running texts differ. This is rather a lot, about ten per chapter, though in fact they are bunched, with 40 in the first two chapters and 61 between Chapters 6 and 11. Although a number are probably still to be ascribed to the features of adaptation and abbreviation by which we have eliminated many, we are left with readings where the two texts stand as separate translations. For example, at 1.6 we have *inter quas* in the lemma and *in quibus* in the Running Text. As a matter of fact, this number could be further reduced, since some of the differences seem to be due to carelessness. This must be the explanation at 1.10, where *Dei* in the lemma is replaced by *Domini* in the Running Text. But a genuine difference in translation emerges at 1.32, between *iudicium* and *iustitiam*. The explanation here seems to be that Calvin has created his own translation in the lemma, but when he comes to the passage he reverts to the Vulgate text. Although this is the text also of Faber and Erasmus, there are plenty of places where the running text follows the Vulgate against the lemma: certainly 12, and arguably 16, times in Chapter One:

[XXXIV]

verse	lemma	Running Text
6	inter quas	in quibus
10	per voluntatem	in voluntate
11	ad vos confirmandos	ad conf. vos
13	impeditus	prohibitum (prohibitus *Vg*)
15	Itaque	Ita
16	deinde	et
17	Nam iustitia	Iustitia enim
19	cognoscitur de Deo	notum est Dei
20	Siquidem invisibilia	Invisibilia enim
21	Quoniam	Quia
	Non tanquam Deo	Non ut Deum
	gloriam dederunt	glorificaverunt (sicut *Vg*)
22	Quum se putarent	Quum enim putarent (enim *Vg*)
25	transmutarunt	transmutaverunt (mutaverunt *Vg*)
26	inquam	OM (agreement only in this)
	ignominiosas	ignominiae
32	iudicium	iustitiam

Overall, the rest of the commentary remains consistent to this. We may see the evidence from the following table. The evidence is based on the

---

4 1.7, 16; 2.11, 13, 21; 5.2, 9; 6.10, 27; 9.10; 11.22; 12.18, 19; 13.1, 4; 14.4, 18; 15.30, 32.

hypothesis outlined above, so that we discount places where the Vulgate agrees with Erasmus (=E) and/or Faber (=F) in the lemma, and places where Erasmus and/or Faber agree with the Vulgate in the running text. However, this might be an error of method, and so we [XXXV] place in brackets the corrected figure, that is the number of readings where Calvin's text stands with either only the Vulgate or only one or both of the other two:[5]

Ch	Total	L=Vg[6]	L=E	L=F	L=E/F	RT=Vg	RT=E	RT=F	RT=E/F
1	21	0	1	1	0	14 (3)	1	1	0
2	19	2	7	1	3 (2)	9 (3)	1	0	0
3	11	2	2	3 (1)	1 (0)	4 (1)	1	0	0
4	8	0	2	0	0	1 (0)	1	0	0
5	3	2	1	1 (0)	1 (0)	1 (0)	1	0	0
6	9	0	3	1	0	7 (0)	0	0	0
7	11	3	2 (1)	0	2 (0)	5 (2)	0	0	0
8	18	4	4	1 (0)	2 (0)	4 (1)	3	2	0
9	10	2	3	1 (0)	1 (0)	5 (0)	1	0	0
10	7	3	1	0	0	3 (0)	1	0	1
11	15	3	1	1	3 (1)	9 (2)	2	0	0
12	5	0	0	0	0	1 (0)	1	0	0
13	5	0	2	0	0	0	0	0	0
14	13	2	1	1 (0)	1 (0)	4 (1)	2	0	0
15	6	1	1	1 (0)	0	1	0	0	1
16	4	0	0	0	0	1	1	0	0
Total	165	24	31 (30)	12 (5)	14 (3)	69 (15)	16	3	2

Overall, the three lemma columns of Erasmus and Faber total 57 (45), and the three running text columns 21. There is thus a clear tendency of the lemma to follow the modern versions, and the running text the Vulgate. Moreover, only exceptionally do we find a lemma following the Vulgate *against* the versions of Erasmus and Faber: 8.7 *nec*; 10.18 and 19 *numquid*; 10.20 *ac*; 11.19 *ergo*. The very small number of places in

---

5 We define agreement with another translation as agreement in that part of a phrase in which the Lemma and Running Text differ, and not necessarily as agreement in the whole phrase.

6 It is necessary to define what we mean by Vulgate: there are three places where Calvin's lemmata and running texts differ where there is also a difference between the Vulgate texts printed by Erasmus and by Faber:
2.6 Erasmus Vg *reddit*, Faber Vg *reddet*
2.9 Erasmus Vg *Iudaei*, Faber Vg *Iudaeo*
3.6 Erasmus Vg *hunc mundum*; Faber Vg *mundum*
In both 2.6 and 2.9, Calvin's running text has Faber's reading. In the second, none of the other witnesses we have examined reads *Iudaeo*. On the other hand, at 3.6 Calvin's running text follows *Erasmus'* Vulgate text with *hunc mundum*, again against our other witnesses. It thus seems that Calvin used both these editions.

the running text where *only* the Vulgate supports a reading appears anomalous, but is readily explained: the edition of Faber is really very close to the Vulgate, so it frequently shows up in its company. The evidence as it is set out so far permits a clear conclusion: that Calvin made his own translation for the lemmata, but tended without thinking about it to revert to the Vulgate in the running texts. However, the exceptions cast doubt on this. A collation against Erasmus' Latin text of his third edition (=E) and Faber's translation (=F) yields the following results in Chapter One:

[XXXVI]

Verse	Lemma	Running text
10	rogans =F	postulans
11	donum spirituale =E	charismata spiritualia
27	decebat	decuit
28	ad facienda	ut facerent =E
	decerunt	decent =F

There is no evidence of a consistent working method here. The questions to be asked are: which version came first? and, how do they relate to other versions? Since at verse 27 both versions are independent, while it is the running text that is independent in verses 10 and 11, and the lemma in 28, the answer must be that on this evidence we do not know. But it may be that the explanation is to be found in the composition of the commentary. Two possibilities arise.

The first is that Calvin in writing the commentary worked only with the running text, and that the lemmata were added after, either by Calvin or by the printer. The alternative, that the running text was added later, is not possible, so firmly is it woven into Calvin's own prose. Indeed, it is often difficult to decide how much of the text should be shown typographically to belong to Paul, especially where the commentator has changed cases and tenses in order to bring the biblical text into his own sentence. If the lemmata were a later addition, then the text for exposition will be the running text not the lemma.

This is sometimes the case. For example, at 1.10, in *A* the lemma read *rogans si quo*, and the running text *Postulans si quo modo*, with the comment

> Quare ut habeas plenum sensum, lege haec verba perinde acsi interposita 'etiam', *Postulans etiam si quo modo, etc.*

The true text for exposition is found in the running text, and the lemma's *rogo* is not found. Moreover, this is the first that we have heard of *etiam*. But the words *Postulans etiam si quo modo, etc.* are intended as a paraphrase, not as the text. It would be misleading to print them in a different type.

[XXXVII] If this is the correct explanation, we would expect the lemma fairly consistently to provide a printed text. Unfortunately, the situation is not so simple. For example, at 1.10 neither *rogans* nor *postulans* is to be found in Erasmus or the Vulgate: the former prefers *orans*, the latter *obsecrans*.

The second possibility is that the lemmata and not the running texts form the basis of the commentary. And there is evidence to support this hypothesis also. For example, at 9.33 the lemma runs *Et omnis qui crediderit in eum, non pudefiet*. The running text has *Et omnis qui crediderit, non confundetur*. In the comment we read

> Quod autem pro Festinare, seu praecipitare, Pudefieri posuit, id habuit a Septuaginta. Certum quidem est, illic Dominum voluisse spem suorum confirmare. Ubi autem Dominus bene sperare nos iubet, ex eo sequitur, non posse nos pudefieri.

It is *pudefiet* and not *confundetur* that Calvin has had in mind.[7] The same may be seen at 9.23, with the lemma *Ut notas quoque faceret*, and the running text *Ut etiam notas faceret divitias*, followed by the commentary

> Ego quoniam in istis duabus particulis καὶ ἵνα, non dubitabam esse ὕστερον πρότερον; quo melius cohaeret hoc membrum cum superiore, verti *Ut notas quoque faceret*.

The same tendency can be found as early as 1.13, where the *impeditus* of the lemma is echoed several times in the exposition, while the running text has *prohibitum*.

There are also various other kinds of confusion. At 2.8 the lemma is *excandescentia, ira, tribulatio*. To this the running text adds *et Anxietas*, which is one noun too many. This is then taken up again with the running text *Excandescentia et ira*, on which he comments

> Sic vertere coegit me verborum proprietas. Graecis enim id significat θυμός, quod Latinis excandescentiam notare docet Cicero ... In aliis sequor Erasmum.

Erasmus, however, reads *indignatio, et ira, afflictio et anxietas* in all his editions. It is as though Calvin had forgotten how he had translated it.

It will be clear, therefore, only that the evidence is not clear. There are two general conclusions to be made at this point. First, that Calvin did [XXXVIII] not work particularly consistently. Second, that in his running text he tended to revert to the familiar Vulgate. We shall reserve fuller conclusions until after the other editions have been described.

---

7   See page XVII, in our examination of the development of the commentary.

The Second Edition

We turn now to the second set of data: the changes in the second and third editions of the commentary. The number of changes introduced into the biblical citations in *B* is very small. There are eleven of them, and they may be listed in short space:

Verse	Lemma	Running Text
1.10	si quo *A*; si quo modo *B*	si quo modo
2.16	occultum *A*; occulta *B*	occulta
3.27	glorificatio *A*; gloriatio *B*	gloriatio
4.16	ei quod	enim qui *A*; ei qui *B*
6.22	sanctificationem	sanctificatione *A*; sanctificationem *B*
7.7	cognovi	cognoscebam *A*; cognovi *B*
8.26	non enim quid	Nam id quod *A*; Non enim quid *B*
9.10	et	OM *A*; et *B*
10.8	Scriptura *A*; OM *B*	OM section *A*
14.22	indicat *A*; iudicat *B*	iudicat
15.20	amittens *A*; annitens *B*	annitens
15.29	Scio	Spero *A*; Scio *B*
16.11	ex Narcissi familiaribus	ex Narcissi familiaribus *A*; Narcissi *B*

Some are the removal of errors in *A*: 4.16; 6.22; 14.22; 15.20, 29. Most remove differences between the lemma and running text: 1.10; 2.16 (perhaps another error in *A*); 3.27; 7.7; 8.26; 9.10. Different is 16.11, where some rather drastic abbreviation occurs. At 10.8, there is a change to the text of the lemma, which will be discussed in the section on Calvin's Greek text. With these exceptions, the list has the look of a silent correction of some rather obvious *errata*.

The Third Edition

The degree of correction in this final stage is extensive. The main points are as follows:
(1) There are 127 places in which *C* changes *B*.
(2) The changes in *C* are usually made by altering the running text, not the lemma. The figures are: change to the lemma, 14; change to the running text, 103; change to both, 10. The few changes to the lemmata after Chapter 8 all have the effect of introducing a difference.
(3) There are few changes in the initial chapters. The figures are interesting:

[XXXIX]

Ch.	Changes	Ch.	Changes
1	1	9	3
2	1	10	8
3	1	11	20
4	4	12	8
5	8	13	9
6	8	14	11
7	12	15	9
8	20	16	4

(4) Most of the changes (just over one hundred in fact) have the effect of removing a difference between the lemma and the running text, and only a few of introducing one.

It is not possible to compare these figures directly against those provided in the discussion of the first edition, because a significant proportion of the changes introduced by C alter differences which for the purposes of that part of the study we had discounted. However, we may gauge the degree to which C has affected the genuine differences of translation between the lemma and running text, by looking to see what it has done with the 165 differences which we listed as significant.

Chapter	Total	Changed in C
1	21	0
2	19	1
3	11	1
4	8	3
5	3	2
6	9	6
7	11	10
8	18	15
9	10	2
10	7	6
11	15	15
12	5	4
13	5	4
14	13	10
15	6	6
16	4	3
Total	165	78

[XL] Setting aside the first four chapters, we find that C has eliminated 73 out of 104 readings. That is to say, three-quarters of the more noteworthy differences have been removed. This represents a remarkably thorough change to the character of the relationship between the lemmata and the running text.

Turning back to the minor differences between lemma and running text in A which C removes, we find that in all, there are twenty-nine readings where C has removed one of these minor differences, of which eleven are insertion of a missing word, five adjustment of the word order, and the rest tightening up of adaptations and allusions. For example, the *enim* missing from the running text in A is introduced into it in C at 7.14, 22; 13.8. Remarkably, at 4.16 it changes *ei* back to the corrupt *enim*. *Homini* replaces *ei* at 14.20. Since there are probably about just over 100 of these minor differences (depending on how much one assigns to the running text), the revision may be seen to have been less interested in these than in the genuine differences of translation, for he has removed less than a third as compared to about one half. This provides transcriptional support for our distinction between the two types of differences.

The places where a change has been made to both the lemma and the running text of a verse are also instructive:

verse	lemma	Running Text
4.25	traditus *A B*; + fuit *C*	mortuus est *A B*; traditus fuit *C*
8.23	ipsi quoque qui primitias *A B* ipsi quoque qui primordia *C*	Nos ipsi qui primordia *A B* Ipsi qui primordia *C*
25	videmus *A B*; conspicimus *C*	videmus *A B*; conspicimus *C*
37	superiores evadimus *A B*; supervincimus *C*	superiores evadimus *A B*; supervincimus *C*
11.22	Ecce *A B*; Vide *C*	running text *OM A B*; Vide *C*
13.9	scortaberis *A B*; moechaberis *C*	scortaberis *A B*; moechaberis *C*
10	non male facit *A B*; malum non infert *C*	non malefacit *A B*; malum non infert *C*
11	Et cum illud *A B*; Hoc etiam *C* ²Hoc etiam	¹Hoc etiam *C*; *OM* running text *A B*
12	praecessit *A B*; progressa est *C*	praecessit *A B*; progressa est *C*
16.25	revelationem scilicet mysterii *A B*; Revelationem praeconium scilicet Iesu Christi secundum revelationem mysterii *C*	Praedicationem Iesu Christi ... arcani *A B*; Praeconium Iesus Christi . . . Revelationem mysterii *C*

[XLI]

In five of these (4.25; 8.23; 11.22; 13.11; 16.25) C has removed a difference between the lemma and the running text. In the other five it has changed both the lemma and the running text. There is no particular tendency to favour one existing version over another. 4.25 *traditus fuit*, 13.12 *progressa est*, and 16.25 *praeconium* are all Erasmus renderings. But 11.22 *Vide* is from the Vulgate.

It is no easier to find any trend in the other changes. Since most are to the running text, and we saw that the running text in A is closer to the Vulgate and the lemma to Erasmus, it is inevitable that this tendency will be exaggerated in C. But it is more likely to be due to a change of attitude to style of the commentary, than to a change in preference for either version, for otherwise we would expect changes to lemma readings which follow the Vulgate.

The Greek Text

Before seeking to draw this material together, there is one other type of evidence to be examined, and that is the question of the text which Calvin used. It has already been seen that Calvin may have used the Latin Vulgate printed by Erasmus – and what could be more convenient than those three columns, one Greek and two Latin – and perhaps that of Faber? But what other evidence is there for different Greek texts?

It was argued in *Calvin's New Testament Commentaries* that Calvin produced his commentary from a Greek text, namely that edited by Colinaeus and published in 1534.[8] The evidence there advanced was that, in Chapters 1–5, Calvin's translation can always be retroverted into Colinaeus' Greek, and that there are a number of passages where it follows that text against all other editions. Perhaps most striking is 3.19, where Calvin's lemma is *sub Lege* and Colinaeus reads ὑπὸ τοῦ νόμου. However, this conclusion has been challenged.[9] In order to attempt to answer the question more fully, the text of Erasmus' fourth edition of 1527 has been collated with Colinaeus in Chapters Six to Sixteen.[10] The reason for the use of Erasmus 1527 text is the way in which the presence of the two Latin versions of Erasmus and Jerome may contribute to the variety in Calvin's own renderings. The study leads to the following results.[11]

---

8   T.H.L. Parker. *Calvin's New Testament Commentaries*, 2nd ed., Edinburgh, 1993, Chapter Six (123–157).

9   B. Girardin, *Rhétorique et theologique. Calvin. Le commentaire de l'Épître aux Romains* (Théologique Historique 54), Paris, 1979, 365–68.

10 The collation of Chapters 1–5 may be found in T.H.L. Parker, *Calvin's New Testament Commentaries*, 137–40.

11 There are a few typographical errors, which we have ignored (including προσευξόμεθα in Erasmus at 8.26 and ἐφ' in Erasmus at 15.24). The punctuation in Erasmus at 8.35 is also to be regarded as a mistake. It concerns a question mark. Erasmus' Greek text reads θλίψις ἤ, and Colinaeus has θλίψις; ἤ. Calvin's Lemma

Verse	Erasmus] Colinaeus	
1.24	διὸ καὶ] διὸ	*Calvin* Propterea
29	πορνεία, πονηρία] πονηρία, πορνεία	*Calvin* nequitia, libidine
2.26	λογισθήσεται;] λογισθήσεται,	*Calvin* censebitur:
3.19	ἐν τοῦ νόμου] ὑπὸ τοῦ νόμου	*Calvin A B* sub; *Calvin C* in
31	ἱστῶμεν] συνιστάνομεν	*Calvin* stabilimus
4.1	ἀβραὰμ τὸν πατέρα ἡμῶν εὑρηκέναι] εὑρηκέναι ἀβραὰμ τὸν πατέρα ἡμῶν	*Calvin* invenisse Abraham patrem nostrum
5.11	καυχώμενοι] καυχώμεθα	*Calvin* gloriamur
19	καθεστάθημεν] καθεστάθησαν	*Calvin* constituti sunt
21	OM] τοῦ κυρίου ἡμῶν	*Calvin* Dominum nostrum
6.11	ἑαυτοὺς, νεκροὺς μὲν εἶναι] ἑαυτοὺς εἶναι, νεκροὺς μὲν *Calvin* vosmet esse mortuos quidem	
8.11	διὰ τὸ ἐνοικοῦν αὐτοῦ πνεῦμα] διὰ τοῦ ἐνοικοῦντος αὐτοῦ πνεύματος *Calvin A B* propter Spiritum suum in vobis habitantem; *Calvin C^{mg}* + vel, eius *after* suum	
12	ἐσμὲν] ἐσμὲν,	*Calvin* sumus,
28	ἀγαθὸν,] ἀγαθὸν.	*Calvin* bonum:
32	χαρίσεται.] χαρίσηται;	*Calvin* omnia?
35	θλίψις ἢ] θλίψις; ἢ	*Calvin* tribulatio? an
9.11	γεννηθέντων] + αὐτῶν	*Calvin* nati essent
10.8	OM] ἡ γραφή	*Calvin A* Scriptura; *Calvin B C* OM [XLIII]
11.28	μὲν] + οὖν	*Calvin A B* OM; *Calvin C* quidem
14.2	ὃς] ὁ δὲ	*Calvin A B C* qui autem.[12]
14. 22	πίστιν ἔχεις,] πίστιν ἔχεις;	*Calvin* fidem habes?
16.20	OM] ἀμήν	*Calvin A* OM (OM also preceding phrase); *Calvin B* Amen (OM preceding phrase); *Calvin C* Amen (adds preceding phrase)
27	ᾧ] αὐτῷ	*Calvin* OM

At first glance, the majority of the evidence suggests reliance on Colinaeus. In the punctuation, one may note the readings at 8.12, 28, 32, 35; 14.22; in word order, 6.11; in wording, 10.8 and 14.2. The readings at

---

and Running Text both read *tribulatio? an.* But Erasmus' Latin version is *num afflictio? num*, and there is a question mark in the Greek after στενοχωρία. It seems fairly certain that Erasmus' text is a misprint. There are also various differences with regard to the use of the comma, which we have only retained where a difference in sense is apparent. The difference between ἀποθνήσκομεν and ἀποθνήσκωμεν at 14.8 does not show up in translation, so has also been set aside.

12 Although the text reads *qui autem*, the comment in *A B* makes clear that he is following Colinaeus: *In hac versione secutus sum lectionem codicis mei, ubi non repetitur secundo loco relativum, sed articulus praepositivus, eius loco, habetur: quae mihi etiam melius quadrare videbatur.* This is omitted in *C*, and replaced with a stricture of Erasmus. But the wording in *C*, with its reference to a single relative pronoun (plainly at the beginning of the verse), suggests that he has seen no reason to change his view on the correct reading: *et pro articulo relativo improprie posuit, Alius quidem credit.*

8.11 and 11.28 are indeterminate.[13] At 16.20 the fact that the whole phrase is absent in *A* removes the evidence. Only at 8.11 and 16.27 does it seem that Calvin may have used a model other than Colinaeus. In 16.27, he seems to follow a third form of the text, that which omits any word between Χριστοῦ and ἡ. Finally, the text of 8.11 clearly follows the text adopted by Erasmus. As one would expect, throughout the commentary Calvin translates διά with the genitive by *per*. There are no other occurrences of διά with the accusative.

However, at least one of these readings would need to be unique to Colinaeus, before it could be proved that this was Calvin's text.[14] A comparison with the Vulgate columns of Erasmus' fourth edition reveals the following information, in the places where Calvin agrees with Colinaeus. The differences which do not show up in translation,[15] and 16.20, are ignored.

Verse	Colinaeus	Calvin] Vulgate
1.29	πονηρίᾳ, πορνείᾳ	nequitia, libidine] malitia, fornicatio
2.26	λογισθήσεται,	censebitur:] reputabit?
3.19	ὑπὸ νόμον	A B sub Lege; C in Lege] in Lege
4.1	εὑρηκέναι ἀβραὰμ τὸν πατέρα ἡμῶν	invenisse Abraham patrem nostrum] invenisse Abraam patrem nostrum
5.21	τοῦ κυρίου ἡμῶν	Dominum nostrum] Dominum nostrum
6.11	ἑαυτοὺς εἶναι, νεκροὺς μὲν	vosmet esse mortuos quidem] vos mortuos quidem esse peccato
8.11	διὰ τοῦ ἐνοικοῦντος αὐτοῦ πνεύματος	propter Spiritum suum in vobis habitantem] propter inhabitantem spiritus eius in vobis
12	ἐσμὲν,	sumus,] sumus
28	ἀγαθὸν.	bonum:] bonum
32	χαρίσηται;	omnia?] donavit?
35	θλίψις; ἤ	tribulatio? an] Tribulatio, an
10.8	ἡ γραφή	A Scriptura; B C OM] Scriptura
14.2	ὁ δὲ	qui autem] qui autem
14.22	πίστιν ἔχεις;	fidem habes?] fidem quam habes

Many of these readings are in common with the Vulgate. But some are not: 2.26; 3.19; 6.11; 8.12, 28, 35; 14.22. All of these are translational, except for 3.19 and 6.11. The former is the most striking evidence in

---

13 At 11.28 *quidem* is found in Erasmus for μέν without οὖν.
14 Reuss listed the distinctive readings of editions in a thousand test passages (E. Reuss, *Bibliotheca Novi Testamenti Graeci*, Strasbourg, 1872, 46–8). Unfortunately, none of the 52 readings which he lists as unique to Colinaeus is in a Romans test passage.
15 This includes 1.24: the Vulgate reads *Propter quod*. Erasmus has *quapropter*, indicating that καί does not need a word to itself.

favour of Calvin having used Colinaeus, for the reading is almost unique to him. It must have been a conjectural emendation. Erasmus and (so far as we know) every other edition, then and ever since, reads ἐν τῷ νόμῳ. The only reasonable argument against Calvin's dependence on Colinaeus is the possibility that Calvin has independently assimilated the text to 6.14, 15. He would not be the only writer to have done so. For this is the best explanation of the fact that Oecumenius also reads ὑπὸ τοῦ νόμου at 3.19. If Calvin nowhere else followed Colinaeus, one would need to adopt this explanation. But the cumulative force of the evidence is that, where Colinaeus differs from Erasmus, Calvin follows the former.

The argument from unique readings is, however, two-edged. Since we know that Calvin used a Greek text, we would need to be able to show that a rival also had a unique reading shared by Calvin. As has been seen already, the only reading where Calvin follows Erasmus against Colinaeus is at 8.11. But here he may equally be following the Vulgate, which reads *propter inhabitantem spiritum eius*.

The evidence presented so far in this section has been derived from a reconstruction of the Greek text underlying Calvin's Latin lemmata. By comparing Greek texts with Calvin, one is able to ignore readings such as Calvin's frequent omissions of words, which do not have any bearing on this problem. There is a danger with this method, that it may lead one to overlook the degree of freedom which Calvin exercised, so that often his text is *sui generis*.[16] The best way forward from this is to look for evidence in the commentary itself. Here, we may note particularly 14.2. *A B* read

[XLV]

> In hac versione secutus sum lectionem codicis mei, ubi non repetitur secundo loco relativum, sed articulus prapositivus, eius loco, habetur: quae mihi etiam melius quadrare videbatur.

This is especially striking, for Calvin must be referring to a Greek text: Latin has no article. Erasmus reads ὅς δὲ ἀσθενῶν. There are a number of Greek editions with ὁ δὲ ἀσθενῶν, including Colinaeus. It is thus likely that *codex meus* means Colinaeus. It is interesting that the focus of Calvin's comment on this variant changes in *C* from his own choice of Greek reading to the shortcomings of Erasmus' version:

> In diversa lectione quid sequutus fuerit Erasmus, non video. Mutilam enim sententiam reddidit, quum plena sit in verbis Pauli: et pro articulo relativo improprie posuit, Alius quidem credit.

---

16 Perhaps it should be noted here that the reading κατεργαζεῖν in the commentary on 3.3 in *A*, corrected to καταργεῖν is not a variant but an error.

The commentary on 2.17 contains a discussion of a variant reading: ἴδε / εἰ δὲ. Calvin follows the former, with all Erasmus' editions, Colinaeus, and Stephanus. The Vulgate reads *Si autem*, Faber has *Vide, tu*, and Erasmus *Ecce tu*. Calvin adds nothing new to the matter – he draws on Erasmus' *Annotationes* for information on the variation in the Greek witnesses.

Thus, of these two pieces of evidence, the former supports the case for Calvin's use of Colinaeus. The latter is inconclusive.

Another possible type of evidence consists in the differences between the lemmata and running texts; but it must be reported that the differences are almost all versional, and cannot be traced to different Greek texts. There are only four significant readings.

At 1.10 Calvin has the lemma *per voluntatem Dei* and the running text *in voluntate Domini*. This looks promising, but detailed scrutiny reveals that there is absolutely no other attestation of *Domini*, which must simply be an approximation on Calvin's part.

4.14 (*Si enim ii* and *Si enim*) is also an error. At 9.23, however, we do have a variant: Calvin's lemma has *ut notas quoque faceret*, and his running text *ut etiam notas faceret*. *Quoque* and *etiam* both reflect the Greek (of both Erasmus and Colinaeus) καὶ ἵνα γνωρίσῃ, the first two words of which Calvin helpfully happens explicitly to cite. *Et* is found in a few Vulgate witnesses, and καί is omitted in a few Greek, but this is primarily a difference between the Greek and Latin traditions. In fact Faber already had *et ut notas faceret*, in which he is followed by Erasmus. Calvin's versions are both derived from the Greek.

At 10.8, there is a change to the text of the lemma in the second edition. *A* reads *Scriptura*, with Colinaeus and the Vulgate. The word is removed in *B*, producing a text in agreement with Erasmus. The running text in *A* reads *Sed prope est verbum*, which is an abbreviation of the whole phrase *Sed quid dicit Scriptura? Prope est verbum*. *B* changes this, with an insertion of a new piece of commentary, so that the running text is divided in two: *Sed quid dicit?* and *Prope est verbum*. The removal of *Scriptura* is most likely to be an adjustment of the lemma to this new running text. Whether the lemma in *A* is based on Colinaeus or on the Vulgate is uncertain; it is clearer that the *B* lemma is based on Erasmus' text.

There is another variant at 14.14. Here the lemma has *Domino Iesu*, and the running text *Christo Iesu* in *A B*, corrected to *Domino Iesu* in *C*. Χριστῷ is read by a few Greek manuscripts, although κυρίῳ is read by Erasmus and Colinaeus. The reading of the Vulgate is *Domino*. The Greek manuscripts cited by Tischendorf are unlikely to have had any influence on the sixteenth-century text, though they do include the celebrated Leicester Codex (MS 69 in the Gregory-Aland cataloguing system). It must therefore be concluded that this also is a casual error.

No very clear picture emerges from these passages. The fact that there are so few differences between the Greek versions available to Calvin, the degree of freedom with which he produced his translation, and the variations between the lemmata and the running texts conspire against the attempt to trace his steps. But certain provisional conclusions may be reached.

That Calvin is writing in a humanist's world where the Greek text receives proper attention is absolutely evident. To be more precise, we have cumulative evidence that Calvin knew Colinaeus. But we also have several other pieces of evidence which suggest a more complicated picture. At 16.27 Calvin follows neither Erasmus nor Colinaeus nor the Vulgate. At 8.11 he may follow either Erasmus or the Vulgate, and certainly not Colinaeus. The process of 'Vulgatisation', in which a textual tradition becomes harmonised to the standard and best known text is a well-attested phenomenon, and we may expect a degree of it in Calvin.

It is rarely in textual study of this kind that all the evidence points unequivocally to a single conclusion. One cannot expect any collection of citations to agree completely with a single text, particularly when those two texts are in different languages. And so we must accept here a measure of uncertainty. It is certainly safe to conclude that he knew both the Erasmus and the Colinaeus texts. The textual evidence points towards his using the latter as a basis for his text. The likelihood and some of the circumstantial evidence (that is, the knowledge of Erasmus' *Latin* text and use of the Vulgate) point towards his using the former.

Conclusion

The evidence from the analysis of the data suggests the following. In the first composition of the commentary, Calvin printed what almost amount to two separate Latin versions of the text. The lemma version of this is somewhat closer to Erasmus, the running text to the Vulgate. In addition, the running text tends to be abbreviated and allusive. But it may also be that he sometimes (as one would expect) had second thoughts, and abandoned his original translation in the running text, but did not correct the lemma. This would explain the places where the running text agrees neither with the lemma nor with any other version.

It would of course give a mistaken impression if one implied that there were no links between the lemma and the commentary. We gave evidence of places where Calvin in fact commentates on it and not on the running text. Elsewhere, where there is no difference between the two, we may find him explaining his translation, as at 3.9 over the word *constituimus*. We have carefully considered what seem to be the two best possible explanations for this.

The first is that he did so at least partly intentionally, in order by several versions to bring out the sense of a Greek word or phrase. That is to say, he regarded his Latin lemmata and running text only as vehicles to get across the sense of the Greek, so that *rogans* and *postulans* (1.10) are both imperfect representations of δεόμενος, yet by their combined use convey more of its range of meaning than either could alone. Thus also at 9.23 he provides two versions of the Greek καὶ ἵνα. But not all of the differences are genuine variations in translation. Moreover, the evidence of the third edition casts doubt on this hypothesis. The removal of so many differences makes their existence seem more like an oversight corrected fifteen years after the event.

We turn therefore to the second possibility, that the differences in the first edition arose out of the way in which Calvin worked. We discussed in the first section the evidence that the commentary may have begun as lectures. If for a moment we grant this premiss, then the differences [XLVIII] between lemmata and running text may be explained as follows: Calvin began his lecture by making an extemporary translation of the Greek text (there is contemporary testimony that this was always his custom in lecturing on the Old Testament[17] and we may, by analogy, assume the same for the New). If he used a copy of one of Erasmus' editions, then the number of agreements with Erasmus' Latin text may be readily explained by a suitable phrase in that adjacent column catching both his eye and his fancy. He then, in the course of his exposition, refers to the biblical text partly as he remembers his recent ad hoc version. But where he forgets it, he cites either from the familiar Vulgate, or by making up new renderings. Something similar may be seen from some of the Old Testament lectures, which were subsequently published: 'The translation was almost extemporary, and might vary every time he quoted a verse.'[18]

---

17 This is stated by Crispin, in G. Baum *et al.*, eds., *Ioannis Calvini Opera quae supersunt omnia*, Brunwick, 1862ff, Vol. 40, 23–4. See T.H.L. Parker, *Calvin's Old Testament Commentaries*, Edinburgh, 1986, 20.

18 T.H.L. Parker, *Calvin's Old Testament Commentaries*, 37, n. 72.

This hypothesis best explains the data:
1. The existence of differences between the lemmata and running text.
2. The higher number of Erasmian readings in the lemmata than in the running text.
3. The higher number of Vulgate readings in the running text than in the lemmata.
4. The occurrence of renderings unique to Calvin both in the lemmata and in the running text.
5. The tendency of the running text to be a curtailed form of the text. In speaking one would easily repeat only the salient words of a phrase.
6. The variations in word order in the running text, which might reflect the rhythms and euphony of a trained rhetorician.
7. At 2.8, his confusion with remembering what he had said.

One may add that, on this reconstruction, the degree of *agreement* between the lemmata and running text bears testimony to the excellence of Calvin's memory and his ability to hold a sequence of thought in his head.
This explanation does not totally rule out the possibility that some of the differences between lemma and running text were intentional.

The birth of the commentary in the lecture hall therefore provides an explanation for the data. But there are two difficulties with the hypothesis. The first is that it requires the commentary to have been written up from notes taken by a member of the audience. Only from 1549, when we know Raguenier began his work as an amanuensis, is there direct evidence for such work. Hitherto, as one of us has pointed out, there has been no certain evidence as to whether any of the New Testament commentaries are transcripts of lectures.[19] But on this evidence, the issue now stands open.

[XLIX]

The second difficulty is that it requires particular care on the part of the student stenographer, and that seems unlikely. It might have been easier to have noted the passage, and to have added a printed text later. However, it should also be noted that the lemmata of *A* are by no means complete. For example, the second half of 7.2 is missing. Such omissions might suggest a failure to transcribe all that Calvin had said. A comparison with the Isaiah sermons is instructive. These contain the lemmata in full, and the translation is demonstrably Calvin's own. That overlaps between consecutive sermons are translated differently also

---

19 T.H.L. Parker, *Calvin's New Testament Commentaries*, 28.

indicates that these are the translations made in the pulpit, and not later insertions.[20]

There is thus also evidence, some historical and some of probability, against this suggestion. A study of the relationship between the lemmata and running texts in the other New Testament commentaries (and especially those on the Pauline corpus) is necessary before it will be possible to resolve the issue. Meanwhile, the evidence encourages us to believe that this commentary indeed began as lectures, and that notes, perhaps by a student, formed the basis for the published text. We know that this happened with Melanchthon.[21] But the comparison is only partial, for his lectures were published without his knowledge. This published text was made through the agency of Calvin himself.

Is it possible to suggest that the lemmata represent a partial transcription, corrected by Calvin in a process of preparing the edition for the press? Might the somewhat contradictory textual evidence be due to the fact that he used Erasmus' text in the lecture hall, but for some reason supplemented deficiencies in the transcription of the lemmata from Colinaeus? For this to be the case, there would have to be no places in the running texts which followed Colinaeus against Erasmus. And there are no such places. Everywhere, the running text omits the relevant words of text.[22] There are therefore no places where the running text supports Colinaeus against the Erasmus text. The only place where the lemma supports Erasmus against Colinaeus (8.11) may be due to classroom use of Erasmus, and the places where it supports Colinaeus against Erasmus may be the result of subsequent supplementation of the lemma texts. The reading at 16.27, where it supports neither, could be due to a third text being used.

In the second edition, Calvin (or an amanuensis, or the printer) did no more than correct a few evident errors and discrepancies.

In the third edition, it seems that either Calvin or an editor noticed, somewhere in the second half of Chapter Four, that there were many differences between lemma and running text, and made an effort to eliminate the worst of them, managing to get rid of rather more than two-thirds. This move towards consistency may be seen as the commentary's final transition from lecture notes to literary work. The restoration of previously omitted passages such as 7.2b also testifies to a

---

20 *Sermons sue le livre d'Esaïe, Supplementa Calviniana* III, XX-XXV.
21 See Philip Melanchthon, *Paul's Letter to the Colossians*, trans. by D.C. Parker, Sheffield, 1989, 27, 111, n. 2.
22 The question mark at 8.35 is an apparent exception, but it is a typographical error in Erasmus.

greater desire for accuracy. This is further substantiated by what was noted in an earlier section, that Erasmus is explicitly cited only six times in the first edition, and in a further twenty-two places in the third. That Calvin was thinking seriously about these issues in 1556 is attested by such a passage as 8.6, where he revised the earlier editions, prefixing his remarks with

> Erasmus, 'affectum': vetus interpres, 'prudentiam' posuit.

To return to the two questions central to much debate on Calvin's text. It turns out that the answers are both more complicated and simpler than one might have expected. Simple, in that it is clear that Calvin is working with a Greek text as his base. Complex, in that it is a base text which, except for the occasional discussion of a Greek word or phrase, comes to us through an extempore translation and a rather loose recollection of that translation, the whole transmitted by notes taken in the audience. One is reminded of the story of J. Armitage Robinson in Wells Cathedral, speaking aloud from memory the lessons in the Authorized Version while reading his Greek Testament. The audience and reader of the commentary, especially of the first version, will have received it as a rather sophisticated set of Latin renderings of the Greek, that is, as Calvin's interpretation of it.

One final point remains to be established. *B* shows no interest in removing differences between the lemmata and running text. Yet *C* represents a thorough revision in this respect. Was the reviser Calvin, or an assistant, or the printer? There is little evidence in this regard, except that we have noted places where Calvin introduced new comments on the different Latin versions into the 1556 text. This indicates that he continued to be interested in these questions and that, even if he delegated the tedious task of correcting discrepancies to an assistant, the motivation to do so came from him. [LI]

Indexes

1. Index of Manuscripts

Note: references in support for variant readings are not normally included.

1. Greek New Testament manuscripts by Gregory-Aland number

Note: manuscripts itemised in lists in Chapter 4 are not included.

P4	See P64
P11	38
P14	38
P17	66
P25	274 n. 2
P27	66
P33	44
P35	44
P38	46
P45	46, 47, 125
P46	47, 159
P47	47, 73, 75-91
P52	58-9
P55	121-38 *passim*
P59	121-38 *passim*
P60	121-38 *passim*
P63	121-38 *passim*
P64	55-63
P66	48, 199
P67	See P64
P69	41 n. 35, 49
P72	47
P75	48, 49 n. 81, 125, 200, 261, 272
P76	121-38 *passim*
P80	121-38 *passim*
P85	80, n. 19
P95	125
P115	73-91
01 (ℵ)	15-16, 34, 36, 38, 47, 48, 49, 50, 71, 73, 75-91, 108, 156-8, 205, 214, 234, 249, 274 n. 2, 279, 289, 297-9, 302, 306, 323
02 (A)	37, 47, 48, 50, 75-91, 156 n. 30, 165, 209-10, 212, 214
03 (B)	36-7, 47, 48, 49 n. 81, 66, 71, 75 n. 9, 90 n. 47, 132, 153, 156-8, 159, 200, 204, 207, 214, 234, 249, 272, 274 n. 2, 279, 299 n. 17
04 (C)	38, 47, 48, 50, 74, 75-91, 209-10, 214, 274 n. 2
05 (D)	5-18, 37, 44, 49, 50, 51-2, 65-72, 103-12, 121, 124, 156-8, 167-95, esp. 184-94, 221 n. 20, 248 n. 50, 267-8, 269, 274 n. 2, 275, 276, 279, 284, 329
06	37, 51
D^{abs1}	37, 51
D^{abs2}	51
07	37-8
08	37, 38, 51

010	44, 51	13	155-6. See also Family 1 in Index 3.
012	38, 51		
016	38	15	235
017	37, 113	19	29 n. 14
019 (L)	37, 234, 274 n. 2	24	217-51
021	38	28	155-6
022 (N)	118 n. 16, 136, 274 n. 2	30	235
023	118 n. 16	32	217-51
026	115	34	236
032 (W)	37, 38, 44, 47, 52, 274 n. 2, 277	36	217-51
033	29 n. 14, 234-5	38	97
037	44	39	236
038 (Θ)	38-9, 44, 47, 155-6, 274 n. 2	40	235
040	66, 113-9	60	96 n. 9
041	50, 156	69	189, 349
042	44, 113-9 *passim*, 305	77	236
043	118 n. 16	90	29 n. 14
055	39	98	235
070	39	118	246-7
078	274 n. 2	135	236
093	67	157	187 n. 28
0107	115-6	169	235
0162	42	186	217-51
0171	41	190	235, 236
0189	41, 46	205	246-7
0210	121-38 *passim*	209	246-7
0212	39, 40, 138	213	235
0220	40	259	235
0229	44	269	217-51
0230	51	288	235
0232	44	461	56
0234	39	496	235
0235	39	527	220, 222, 235
0237	39	558	217-51
0246	67	565	47, 155-6, 306
0302	121-38 *passim*	574	97, 319 n. 17
0308	80, n. 19	579	234
		628	78, n. 15
1	155-6, 246 n. 49, 249. See also Family 1 in Index 3.	680	235
		700	155-6
5	217-51	792	96

1. Index of Manuscripts

844	217-51	2250	148
871	217-51	2277	217-51
892	234	2314	143, 144
948	235, 236	2315	144
951	235	2316	144
968	234	2317	144
981	235	2318	143, 144
1006	96	2323	96
1011	234	2327	97
1012	234	2328	234
1036	217-51	2329	75-91, esp. 90-1
1048	234	2400	97
1064	96	2437	217-51
1110	217-51	2458	236
1163	235	2462	146
1211	217-51	2463	146
1309	217-51	2472	142, 143
1321	217-51	2476	144
1328	96	2477	144
1358	236	2554	142, 143
1416	217-51	2555	142, 143
1451	234	2643	96
1481	217-51	2656	96
1505	97	2748	145-6, 223
1519	217-51	2760	144
1551	96	2761	144
1566	217-51	2767	142, 143
1582	246 n. 49, 249	2773	146
1611	75-91	2774	146
1685	96	2775	146, 147
1739	47, 159, 165	2794	96
1783	148	2811	94
1784	147-8	2812	236
1854	75-91	2856	147
1957	75 n. 9, 90 n. 47	2863	96-8
2126	217-51	2864	98
2127	97	2865	99-100
2132	217-51	2868	144
2182	235		
2214	148	*l*184	186 n. 27
2249	148	*l*299	66, 113

*l*311	66	*Dublin, Chester Beatty Library*	
*l*1354	66	XI	41
*l*1575	66		
*l*1737	144, 145	*Dublin, Trinity College*	
*l*1738	144	52	176-7
*l*1840	94		
*l*1883	145	*Fulda, Landesbibliothek*	
*l*2146	142	Bonifatianus 1 (Codex Fuldensis)	
*l*2403	145		299 n. 17
*l*2415	93-4, 95-6	*Harvard, Houghton Library*	
		MS typ. 243	94 n. 7
		MS typ. 491, folios 220-end	
			101

2. Old Latin manuscripts (by Beuron number and letter)

London, British Museum
Add. 31919   36
Egerton 609   176

all	167-95 *passim*
1 (e)	49, 172-3
2 (k)	172-3
4 (b)	49, 172
5 (d)	5-18, 174 (see also Index 1.1, 05)
11 (l)	174, 185
13 (q)	185
14 (r¹)	172

Lyons, Bibliothèque Municipale
431   68, 106
484   105 n. 8

Manchester, John Rylands University Library
P. Herm. Rees 5   42

Milan, Biblioteca Ambrosiana
C.39.inf (Codex Mediolanensis)
            19-23

Oxford, Bodleian Library
Auct. T 4.21   36

3. Of all other manuscripts

Oxford, Christ Church
Wake Gr. 35   288 n. 2

Bucharest, Romanian Academy
353   144

Oxford, Sackler Library
P. Oxy. 34.2699   42

Cambridge, Trinity College
B.17.44, 45   288 n. 2

Paris, Bibliothèque Nationale
Coislin. 1   38, 39
Copt. 156   123

Cava, archivio della Badia
Codex Cavensis 8

Dead Sea Scrolls
4QLXXLev$^{a, b}$ 61-2
7Q6$_1$ 61
8Hev12gr   62

Patmos, Monastery of St John
Cod. 171   117

1. Index of Manuscripts

Rome, Biblioteca Vallicelliana
B.vi   6

St Gall, Stiftsbibliothek
908   68, 121

St Petersburg, National Library of Russia
B19ᴬ (Leningrad Codex)
                    255

Sofia, National Library Cyril and Methodius
sine numero   145

Turin, Biblioteca Nazionale
G.VII.15 (Codex Bobbiensis)
                    25-32, 41

van Haelst 1124   123

Vatican, Biblioteca Apostolica
Gr. 13   96-7
Gr. 2061   36

Vienna, Österreichische Nationalbibliothek
MS Med. gr. 1   115
Papyrus G. 1384   115
Papyrus G. 2312   138

Wolfenbüttel, Herzog August Bibliothek
75a Helmst.   116

Zürich, Zentralbibliothek
Cod. RP 1   117

2. Index of Biblical Citations

Includes Teststellen mentioned between pages 230 and 248.

1 Maccabees
5.20   15-16

Psalms
2.9   77

Matthew
2.1   179
2.20   213
4.10   241
5.4-10   177
5.19   173
5.27-32   273-84
6.6   241
6.9-13   308
6.22   173
6.33   179
7.20   178
9.14   243
9.38   192
10.23   41
11.8   241
11.23   7
12.12   178
12.28   178
12.47   213
13.23   8
13.28   186
15.36   27-8
16.10   8
16.15   188
16.16   189
17.15   243
17.20   241, 243
17.25   109
17.26   178
18.4   173
18.26   182, 183, 186, 193
18.31   182, 183
19.3-9   273-84
19.3   7, 37 n. 12
19.6   178
19.25   178
19.27   178
20.8   306
21.36   175, 191
22.18   7
22.21   188
22.25   188
23.3   173
23.31   178
23.35   7
24.3   188
24.15   182
24.44   192
24.45   178
25.3   175, 182, 183, 186
25.11   9
25.19   306
25.20   180, 306
25.27   188
26.15   6
26.24   174, 191
26.63   174, 179, 187
27.17   179, 182
27.39   7
27.49   241, 243
28.19   175, 187, 189

2. Index of Biblical Citations

Mark

1.1	309
1.11	309, 330
1.14	240, 243, 244
1.16	240, 244
1.41	309
2.28	178
3.11	191
3.32	240, 243, 244
4.41	244
5.41	240, 243
6,14	240, 244
6.28	7
6,33	152
8.3	213
8.5	8
8.26	152
8.29	188
9.38	152
9.49	152
10.2-12	273-84
10.8	178
10.9	191
10.35	240, 243, 244
10.47	243, 244
12.4	191
12.6	175, 191, 243, 244
12.17	188
12.20	182, 183, 188
12.27	175
12.37	188
12.61	191
13.4	188
13.23	179, 180
13.28	240, 244
13.33	187
14.61	174, 187
14.65	240, 244
15.14	179
15.16	179
15.34	109
16.9-20	307

Luke

1	217-51 *passim*
1.3	7
1.66	178
2.19	12
2.43	109
2.51	12
3.7	182
3.10	187
3.22	309, 330
4.4	226, 231, 245
4.12	7
4.7	175
5.7	187
5.38	227, 231, 245
6.1-11	69-71
6.4	267, 284, 307
6.38	226, 229, 231-9, 242, 245
7.31	179
8.20	213
8.52	226, 231, 245
9.3	242
9.10	152
9.20	188
9.36	213
9.54	228, 231, 245
9.55	226, 227, 228, 229, 231-9, 242, 245
9.56	227, 229, 231-9, 242, 245
10	217-51 *passim*
10.2	192
10.4	179
10.21	218, 226, 230, 231, 242, 245
10.22	218, 228, 231, 245
10.25	7
10.38	8, 218
10.58	246
11.2-4	194, 308
11.14	242

11.16	7	20.25	188
11.36	173	20.27	218, 242
11.44	213 n. 16	20.29	188
11.48	178	20.44	173, 188
11.50	7	21.6	228, 231, 242, 245
11.51	7	21.7	188
11.54	152	21.11	245
12.14	225, 226, 230, 231, 245	21.36	182
12.16	9	21.38	275
12.18	152	22.43-4	226, 230, 231, 245, 307
12.20	182, 187	22.61	41 n. 36
12.40	192, 193	23.16	228, 229, 231-9, 242, 245
12.42	178	23.34	213 n. 16, 307
13.2	213	23.45	228, 231, 245
13.6	192	24.19	228, 230, 231, 242, 245
13.18	182, 192, 193	24.42	228, 230, 231, 242, 245
13.19	225, 226, 229, 231-9, 242, 244, 245	24.47	227, 231, 245
14.17	245	24.53	152
14.21-2	306	*John*	
15.21	226, 231, 242, 245	1.18	309
15.28	182	1.26	132
16.14	226, 227, 230, 231, 245	1.28	323
16.18	273-84	1.31	132
17.1	336	1.32	132
17.9	227, 231, 245	1.35	130, 132
17.22	182, 188	1.36	126, 132
18.11	226, 231, 242, 245	1.37	132
18.24	228, 230, 231, 242, 245	1.38	132
18.26	179, 192, 193	2.15	132, 133
19.12	173, 182, 188, 193	2.18	182
19.13	180	3.14	131, 136
19.15ff	306	3.15	136
19.16	180, 192, 193	3.16	131, 136-2
19.23	174, 188	3.17	136
19.25	228, 231, 242, 245	3.18	126
19.42	227, 228, 229, 230, 231-9, 242, 245, 248	3.25	182, 183
20	217-51 *passim*	3.31	7
20.1	8	3.34	136
20.15	191	4.6	182
		4.9	131-2, 136

2. Index of Biblical Citations

4.10	131, 136	9.25	174, 180, 182, 183
4.12	127, 136	9.26	174
4.25	180	9.30	173, 180, 189, 193
4.33	182, 183, 192	9.41	174, 189
4.38	213	10.4	213 n. 16
4.52	182	10.5	213 n. 16
5.10	177	10.29	137
5.44	131, 136	10.39	174, 189, 190
6.1	131, 136	11.31	172
6.2	136	11.32	172
6.3	174, 182	11.38	12 n. 10
6.10	174, 182, 183	11.40	130, 132
6.14	175	11.41	7, 133, 190
6.19	175, 192	11.42	126
6.24	174	11.43	133
6.30	173	11.44	126, 130, 133
6.35	182, 183	11.46	133
6.41	131, 136, 192, 193	11.47	126, 130
6.42	126	11.48	126
6.59	180	11.49	130
6.61	182, 183	11.51	126, 133
6.62	192	11.52	133
6.67	182, 188, 193	11.55	174, 190
6.68	182, 183, 188	11.56	174, 190
7.6	192	12.2	174, 190
7.15	174	12.4	174
7.23	189	12.9	182, 183, 184, 193
7.27	180	12.19	182
7.30	190	12.28	193
7.37-8	319 n. 17	12.29	182, 184, 193
7.47	174	12.34	190
7.53-8.11	158, 275, 284, 307, 328	12.35	130, 190
8.5	182, 189	12.44	183, 190
8.6	180	12.50	173, 175
8.7	180	13.1-18.36	19-23
8.9	8	13.8	95
8.59	175, 189	13.23	180
9.11	174	13.24	174
9.12	174, 177	13.26	174
9.18	189	13.27	174, 190
9.20	174	13.30	183

15.21	213 n. 16	18.33	134, 135
15.24	213	18.34	131, 134
15.26	180, 181	18.36	127, 131, 134
16.13	180	18.37	134
16.29	133	18.39	127, 134
16.33	126, 133, 135	18.40	134, 174
17.1	130, 133	19.1	179
17.5	193	19.2	134, 135
17.6	213	19.5	134
17.7	213	19.6	127
17.8	126	19.7	127, 131
17.9	133, 135	19.10	127, 131, 132, 134
17.11	127	19.11	134
17.12	134	19.12	127, 131-2, 134, 135
17.21	127	19.13	135
17.22	127, 134	19.14	131
17.23	127	19.15	135, 183
17.24	1344	19.16	135, 175
17.25	133	19.17	135
18.1-40	98	19.20	135
18.1	127	19.23	131-2
18.2	126	19.25	127, 135, 135
18.4	127, 134, 135, 183	19.26	183
18.5	134	19.29	183
18.7	127	19.38	175
18.10	127, 134	20.7	7
18.12	127	20.12	7
18.13	134	20.17	183
18.14	134, 135	20.19	175, 183
18.15	127, 130, 131-2	20.20	183
18.17	133	20.26	190
18.18	134	21.6	175
18.19	187	21.7	175
18.21	213 n. 16	21.15	126
18.22	126, 133	21.17	130
18.24	127, 134, 183, 184	21.18	133
18.25	127, 134, 135	21.19	130
18.26	130	21.20	126, 133
18.28	130, 131-2	21.23	133, 174
18.31	130, 131-2		
18.32	127, 130-1		

2. Index of Biblical Citations

Acts
1.5	16	7.32	12, 17
1.11	8, 14	7.46	12
1.14	7, 14	7.54	13
1.22	7, 14	7.56	200
2.4	13, 14	8.30-40	100
2.6	8, 14	9.17	157
2.15	8, 14	9.40	157
2.19	7, 14	10.9	10
2.30	16	10.11	8
2.40	13, 14	10.34	12
2.42-3.4	103-12	10.43	7
2.45	107, 110	11.5	7, 8
2.46	11, 14, 107, 110-1	11.11	10
3.7	7, 14	11.22	10
3.8	7, 14	11.23	12
3.16	13, 14	11.30	8, 158
3.24	9, 14	12.6	12
4.3	12, 14	12.10	17, 157, 158
4.6	7, 9, 13, 14	12.11	12, n. 10
4.11	7, 14	12.16	10
4.15	9, 14	12.25	158
4.17	13	13.1-3	158
4,33	157	13.2	10
5.4	6	13.6	7
5.5	9, 11	13.7	10
5.9	7	13.8	10
5.13	9	13.10	10
5.15	16	13.12	10
5.17	9	13.19	8
5.18	16	13.31	7
5.24	9	13.34	13
5.27	9	13.42	10
5.36	9	13.43	10
5.38	9	13.47	7
6.1	16	13.50	10
6.8	152, 154, 157	14.2	17
7.9	13	14.10	157
7.10	9	14.12	10
7.15	13	14.19	13
7.20	12	14.20	10
		14.23	8

15.2	8	21.21	11
15.4	8	24.7	158
15.12	10	26.4	213
15.17	11, 17	28.16	157, 158
15.19	12		
15.20	267	*Romans*	
15.22	8	1.6	337
15.29	12	1.7	337 n. 4
15.36	10	1.10	337, 339, 340, 341, 348, 350
16.4	8, 157	1.11	337, 339
16.6	13	1.13	337, 340
16.12	7	1.15	337
16.19	11	1.16	336, 337
16.20	11	1.17	337
16.30	187	1.18	336
16.36	213	1.19	337
17.5	13	1.20	337
17.11	11	1.21	337
17.12	12	1.22	337
17.19	6	1.24	345
17.28	213	1.25	337
18.4	157	1.26	337
18.8	157	1.27	339
18.12	10	1.28	339
18.22	13	1.29	345, 346
18.23	8	1.32	337
18.26-7	17	2.6	338 n. 6
19.8	11	2.8	340
19.9	157, 158	2.9	338 n. 6
19.19	12	2.11	337 n. 4
19.37	11	2.13	337 n. 4
19.38	10	2.16	341
20.4	7, 158	2.17	348
20.5	6	2.21	337 n. 4
20.6	8	2.26	345, 346
20.11	7	3.3	347 n. 16
20.15	157, 158	3.6	338 n. 6
20.23	6, 13	3.9	350
21.16	157, 158	3.13	336
21.18	8	3.19	344, 345, 346-7
21.20	13	3.27	341

2. Index of Biblical Citations

3.31	345	11.22	337 n. 4, 343
4.1	345, 346	11.28	345, 346
4.14	348	12.18	337 n. 4
4.16	336, 341, 343	12.19	337 n. 4
4.25	343	13.1	337 n. 4
5.2	337 n. 4	13.4	336, 337 n. 4
5.9	337 n. 4	13.8	336, 343
5.11	345	13.9	343
5.19	345	13.10	343
5.21	345, 346	13.11	343
6.10	337 n. 4	13.12	343
6.11	345, 346	14.2	345, 346, 347
6.14	336, 347	14.4	337 n. 4, 348-9
6.15	347	14.8	345 n. 11
6.22	336, 341	14.18	337 n. 4
6.27	337 n. 4	14.20	336, 343
7.2	351, 352-3	14.22	336, 341, 345, 346
7.5	336	15.7	336
7.7	341	15.20	336, 341
7.14	336, 343	15.21	213
7.22	336, 343	15.24	344 n. 11
8.6	353	15.29	336, 341
8.7	338	15.30	337 n. 4
8.11	345, 346, 347, 349, 352	15.32	337 n. 4
8.12	345, 346	16.7	213
8.23	343	16.11	341
8.25	343	16.20	345, 346
8.26	341, 344 n. 11	16.25	343
8.28	345, 346	16.27	345, 346, 349, 352
8.32	345, 346		
8.35	344 n. 11, 345, 346, 352	*1 Corinthians*	
8.37	343	7.8	181
9.10	337 n. 4, 341	7.10-11	276
9.11	345	7.12-16	275
9.23	340, 348, 350	8.8	159
9.33	340	14.34-5	299 n. 17
10.8	341, 345, 346, 348		
10.18	338	*2 Corinthians*	
10.19	338	8.11	181
10.20	338		
11.19	338		

Philippians
2.6-11   316

Colossians
2.1   213
2.13   295 n. 13

1 Timothy
3.16   37 n. 12

Hebrews
2.9   309
4.8   306
12.8   213

James
1.13f   215
1.18   206
1.20   203, 205, 206, 208 n. 9
1.22   203, 205, 211
1.25   208
1.26   206, 208, 209, 211
1.27   205
2.3   203, 205, 206, 208, 208 n. 9, 209, 210, 211, 215
2.4   206
2.6   205, 208, 209
2.10   208
2.13   208
2.14   207, 209, 211
2.16   207, 209, 211
2.18   208, 209, 211
2.19   203, 204, 206, 207, 211
2.22   205, 211
2.26   206, 208, 209, 211
3.3   211
3.4   203, 205, 206, 209, 211
3.6   205
3.8   203, 205, 206, 208, 211
3.11   210 n. 13
3.12   208
3.14   205, 207 n. 7
3.15   203, 206, 209
3.17   207 n. 7, 208
4.2   205, 208
4.4   205, 208, 210, 211, 214-5
4.7   208
4.8   207, 208
4.9   205, 206, 209, 210, 211, 215
4.12   203, 204, 206, 208
4.13   208
4.14   204, 205, 206, 207, 208 n. 9, 209, 211
4.15   206, 208, 211
5.4   205, 207, 208, 209, 210, 211-2, 212, 213, 214, 215
5.5   208
5.7   209
5.9   205, 208
5.10   204, 205, 206, 207 n. 7
5.11   206, 208
5.13   208
5.14   205, 209, 211, 215
5.16   206, 208, 209, 211
5.18   204, 205, 206, 208 n. 9, 211
5.20   206, 207, 208, 210, 211, 212, 215

1 Peter
4.1   173 n. 12

1 John
1.1   295
2.18   213
4.1   213
5.8   324

Jude
10   213 n. 16

Revelation
2.14   82

2.23	79	11.19	79, 87
2.27	77, 78, 87	12.1-6	311
4.5	79	12.3	88, 89
6.4	89	12.4	78, 89, 91
7.11	89	12.9	88
8.2	213	12.10	88
8.5	79, 86, 89	13.3	87
8.6	86	13.7	87, 88, 90
8.12	78	13.8	83, 88
9.3	85, 86, 91	13.13	78
9.5	85, 86	13.18	84, 86, 91, 92
9.11	85, 86	14.2	87, 88, 91
9.19	78	14.5	88
9.20	82, 83	14.6	79, 83, 87, 88, 91
10.2	82 n. 23	14.7	80
10.7	88	14.18	89
10.8	85, 91	14.20	79, 87
10.9	85, 86	16.18	79
10.10	85, 86, 91	18.3	214
11.3	85, 86	19.3	214
11.9	87	21.6	214
11.11	82	22	165
11.12	82-3		
11.15	85, 86		
11.18	82		

3. Index of Names and Subjects

Acts, text of   5-18, 46, 52, 65, 71, 72, 107-11, 152, 156-8, 166, 185, 195, 199-200, 266, 267-8, 327, 329
Ado of Lyons   68
Aland, B.   IX, X, 39 n. 23, 40 n. 30, 41, 42, 140 n. 5, 217, 220 n. 13, 266 n. 3, 271 n. 12, 274 n. 2
Aland, K.   IX, X, XII, 35 n. 6, 39 n. 23, 40 n. 30, 41, 42, 49, 162-3, 167, 178 n. 14, 183, 192, 199, 204 n. 2, 217, 220 n. 13, 266 n. 3, 271 n. 12, 274 n. 2
Alexandrian Majuscule   44
Alexandrian School, the   15
Alexandrian text-type   45, 47, 48, 49, 159-60, 163, 164, 165, 200, 221 n. 20, 234, 249, 271
Allen, H.M.   37 n. 16
Allen, P.S.   37 n. 16
Allison, D.C.   281 n. 7
Amphoux, C.-B.   XII, 48, 103 nn,. 106 nn., 107 n. 15, 112 nn., 142 n. 9, 258, 259
Anderson, A.S.   246
Antioch   269 n. 11
Antoniades, B.   294
Apocalypse, the   47, 73-92, 96, 143, 327
Apollonius Rhodius   42
Apparatus criticus   184, 194, 248, 266, 295, 299-300, 328, 333
– electronic   53, 289, 290, 295
– history   37, 105, 161-3, 164, 287-8, 293, 324
– theory of   151
Aristophanes   198

Armenian manuscripts   121
– version, the   46, 310
Assimilation of readings   5-18 *passim*, 175, 178-94 *passim*
Athanasius   302
Atticisms   197-201
Augustine of Hippo   173 n. 12, 176, 325 n. 5
Auwers, J.-M.   112 n. 28
Ayuso, T.   46

Baarda, T.   107 n. 15, 121 n. 4
Bachmann, H.   39, 167
Bakker, A.H.A.   25 n. 1
Bammel, E.   71
Barbour, R.   97 n. 10
Barbrook, A.C.   141 n. 8, 301 n. 18
Barth, K.   326, 332-3
Bartoletti, V.   41 n. 31
Bauer, W.   330-1
Baum, G.   350 n. 17
b-d uncial   104
Bede   316
Bédier, J.   152-3, 166
Beis, N.   90 n. 47
Bekker, I.   151
Bell, H.I.   151
Benduhn-Mertz, A.   204 n. 2
Bentley, R.   105, 160, 163, 164-6, 287
Berytus (Beirut)   67, 68, 104, 106
Bethge, H.-M.   39 n. 24
Bèze, T. de   68-9, 105, 179
Bible, complete   320
Bible translations and textual criticism   273-84, 294, 296
Biblia Hebraica Quinta   255

Biblical majuscule   42-3, 42-3, 61, 104, 114-6
Bieler, L.   30 n. 18, 105 n. 8, 106 n. 10
Bilingual manuscripts   17-18, 33-4, 36, 39, 44, 51, 66-7, 104, 112, 121, 191
Birdsall, J.N.   41, 46 n. 60, 47, 68 n. 1, 104 n. 3, 106 n. 10, 114
Black, M.   XI, XII
Blaj, C.   139 n. 1
Blake, R.P.   155-6
Blass, F.   185, 192, 266
Bobbio   36
Bombasius, P.   37
Book technology and the New Testament   261, 287-303, esp. 302-3, 307, 319
Bordalejo, B.   141 n. 8, 301 n. 18
Bornstein, G.   287 n. 1
Bover, J.M.   163-4, 266
Brock, S.P.   181 n. 19
Brown, P.   278 n. 5
Bucharest, manuscripts in   139, 142-4
Buck, H.M., Jr   94
Burchard, C.   121 n. 3
Burkitt, F.C.   25 n. 1, 109, 156, 181 n. 18
Byzantine text, the   45, 50, 159-60, 164, 200, 217-51 *passim*, 260, 274 n. 2, 281, 294, 320, 324
Byzantine Text Project, the   259-60, 289 n. 6, 294-5

Cabrol, F.   40 n. 25
Cadbury, H.J.   46 n. 61
Caesarean text-type   45, 46-7, 49, 151, 156, 164, 199
Cairo, Old   40
Cairo Genizah, the   36
Callahan, A.D.   104 n. 3
Calvin, J.   335-53
Calvino, I.   291-2
Canart, P.   299 n. 17
Cândea, V.   143 n. 12
Canterbury Tales Project, the   141, 289 n. 7
Capitalis   51
Carataşu, M.   143 n. 12
Carolingian Greek manuscripts   44
Casey, R.P.   113 n. 1
Casson, L.   122 n. 8, 127 n. 15
Catena manuscripts   66, 113-9 *passim*
Catholic Letters   327
Cavalieri, P.F. de   97 n. 10
Cavallo, G.   IX, 33 n. 2, 40 n. 27, 41, 43, 44, 50 n. 83, 61, 107 n. 14, 115-8
CETEDOC   300
Champlin, R.   50
Chapa, J.   73, n. 1
Charles, R.H.   90 n. 52
Charlier, C.   105 n. 8
Chicago School, the   329
Cicero   12, 157
Cipolla, C.   25-32 *passim*
Claremont Profile Method, the   140, 154-5, 217-51, 289
Clark, A.C.   16, 46, 51, 156-8, 266
Clark, K.W.   329
Clement of Alexandria   47, 328
Clines, D.   255 n. 4
Coakley, J.F.   94 n. 6
Cockerill, D.   67
Codex format, the   260-61, 268-9, 302
Colinaeus, S.   344-352
Collate Program, the   141, 289, 295, 297, 298
Collins, A.   324-5

Colwell, E.C.   49, 97, 153-5, 166, 246, 248, 319 n. 17
Comfort, P.W.   60
Complutensian Polyglot, the   293
Coptic versions, the   47, 121, 255, 274 n. 2
Crisci, E.   115 n. 6, 116-8
Crisp. S.   139 n. 1, n. 3
Crispin, J.   350 n. 17
Critical editing and editions of the New Testament   37-8, 151, 161-4, 183-4, 203-16, 252-61, 288, 293-6, 326, 328, 330, 332. See also editions under name of editor.
– electronic editing   257, 260-61, 287-302
Crum, W.E.   186 n. 26
Curtius, G.   214
Cyprian   177, 179 ɔ. 15

Dain, A.   15
Dating manuscripts   42, 55-63, 100, 113-19, 143
Davies, W.D.   281 n. 7
Dead Sea Scrolls   56, 61-2
Debrunner, A.   192
Delobel, J.   49 n. 78, 280 n. 6
Devreesse, R.   35 n. 7
Diatessaron, the   39, 40, 194, 268, 308, 328
Dictation   5-18 *passim*, esp. 15-16
Digital imaging   257, 291, 300
Diobouniotis, K.   90
Dmitri, I.   139 n. 1
Dumitrescu, G.   139 n. 1
Duplacy, J.   48, 49, 52, 162, 280
Dura Europos   40
Džurova, A.   139 n. 1, 148 n. 27

Eclecticism   292

– thoroughgoing   197-201
Eco, U.   103
Edden, V.   260-61
Editio critica maior, the   162-3, 203-16, 288 n. 3, 333
Egypt   68, 116, 118
Ehrman, B.D.   X, 258-9, 287 n. 1, 309 n. 4, 329-31
Elliott, J.K.   38 n. 19, 39 n. 21, n. 22, 96 n. 9, 142 n. 9, 181 n. 19, 184 n. 22, 197, 292 n. 10
Elliott, W.J.   121 n. 5, 122 n. 8, 123, 128 n. 16, 130 n. 19, 139 n. 2, 139 n. 3, 289 n. 5
English versions   273-85
Epicurus   198
Epp, E.J.   41, 51-2, 256 n. 6, 329
Erasmus   37, 293, 324, 337-40, 344-353
Eusebius of Caesarea   268
Euthaliana, the   45
Extra-canonical texts   271

Faber, J.   337-40, 344, 348
Family 1   155, 274 n. 2
Family 13   47, 147, 155, 156, 274 n. 2
Family Θ   151, 156
Family Π   156
Fee, G.D.   48, 256 n. 6
Feissel, D.   40 n. 25
Findlay, J.A.   191 n. 30, 193-4
Fink, R.O.   40 n. 26
Fischer, B.   18, 167, 175, 176, 179 n. 16
Fleck, F.F.   25-32 *passim*
Florea, P.M.   143 n. 12
Florus of Lyons   68, 105-6
Foakes Jackson, F.J.   46 n. 61
Follieri, E.   97 n. 10
Fox, A.   324 n. 3, 325 n. 4

Freer manuscripts   38
Free text forms   47-8, 72, 256-7, 265-72, 276, 313, 314
Funk, R.W.   192 n. 33

Gabler, H.W.   258 n. 9
Gadamer, H.G.   318-20
Gamble, H.Y.   302 n. 19, 307 n. 3
Gasparri, F.   290
Geden, A.S.   167
Geerlings, J.   50
Genealogical method   49, 151-6, 160, 238, 248, 300-2
Genetic research and New Testament textual research   300-2
Geneva   68
Georgian manuscripts   36, 44, 121
– version   46, 310
Getov, D.   146 n. 23
Gillian, J.F.   40 n. 26
Girardin, B.   344 n. 9
Glaue, P.   191 n. 31
Gonis, N.   73, n. 1
Goodacre, M.   296 n. 14
Gospels, the   46-7, 48-9, 58-9, 69-72, 93, 95-8, 139-48 *passim*, 156, 158, 167-95, 252-3, 257-8, 265-72, 296, 302, 318-20
– orders of   28-9
Gospel of Thomas, The   269, 271
Greenlee, J.H.   113 n. 2
Greeven, H.   68 n. 1, 104 n. 3
Gregory, C.R.   36 n. 11, n. 12, 38, 97 n. 14, 113
Grenfell, B.P.   43, 59, 61
Griesbach, J.J.   156, 160, 200
Group 1519   217-51
Gryson, R.   41 n. 36, 92
Grunewald, W.   50 n. 85
Guineau, B.   105 n. 8

Harlfinger, D.   147 n. 24
Harmonies of the Gospels   308. See also Diatessaron
Harmonisation of texts   79, 85, 88, 349
– in the Gospels   178-94 *passim*, 267, 268, 276, 278-9, 280, 307-8
Harris, J.R.   6, 107 n. 13, 121
Harvey, N.P.   318
Hatch, W.H.P.   35 n. 8, 40, 44 n. 54, 113-9 *passim*
Hebrew Bible, textual criticism of   256-7, 259, 261
Hellenica Oxyrhynchia   198
Herculaneum papyri   56, 61
Hermeneiai   68, 107, 121-38
Hettich, E.L.   122 n. 8, 127 n. 15
Hexapla, the   261
Hilhorst, A.   107 n. 15
Hirunuma, T.   256 n. 5
Hippolytus   90
Hofer, F.   95
Hofer, P.   94, 99
Hoffmann, P.   99 n. 15
Holmes, M.W.   X, 52, 112, 287 n. 1
Holtz, L.   105 n. 8, 106 n. 10
Hort, F.J.A.   XII, 49, 89 n. 44, 151-6, 158, 160, 161, 163, 164, 198, 199, 200, 204, 206-8, 212, 214, 215, 266, 271, 288 n. 4, 308, 324, 325
Hoskier, H.C.   76, 78 n. 15, n. 16, 90, 187 n. 28
Housman, A.E.   151, 165, 195, 197, 198, 201
Howe, C.   141 n. 8, 301 n. 18
Hunger, H.   97 n. 10
Hunt, A.S.   43, 59, 61
Hurtado, L.W.   46-7, 52

Illumination in manuscripts 305
Inscriptions 40
Institut für neutestamentliche Textforschung 114, 140, 141, 162-3, 203, 217-51, 288, 289, 295 n. 12, 298
Institut Vetus Latina, Beuron 162, 332-3, 333 n. 16
International Greek New Testament Project, the 106, 118, 121, 123, 124, 129 n. 18, 130, 134 n. 20, 139-42, 154-5, 162, 163, 164, 217-51, 266, 288, 288 n. 4, 298
Italy 50, 147

Jalabert, L. 40 n. 25
James, Letter of 203-16
Janeras, S. 41 n. 35, 49
Jellicoe, J. 261 n. 15
Jeremias, J. 71
Jerome 33, 176, 195, 344
Jerusalem 68
Jesus 252-3, 257-8, 305-10
– sayings, text of 273-85, 331
John Chrysostom 116
John, Gospel of 19-23, 48-9, 58-9, 68, 71, 98, 121-38, 139-40, 144, 147, 260, 268, 288-91
Jude, Letter of 47-8
Jülicher, A. X, 6, 20, 25 n. 1, 167
Justin Martyr 328

Karahissar style, the 97
Karavidopoulos, J. XI
Kenyon, F.G. 46 n. 66, 75 n. 9, 151, 157, 159
Kevern, R. 139 n. 3, 289 n. 5
Kieffer, R. 48
Kierkegaard, S. 326

Kilpatrick, G.D. 161, 163, 178 n. 14, 197-201, 208-9, 212, 214, 282 n. 8, 292
Kipling, T, 69
Kiraz, G. 333
Klein, R.W. 254 n. 3
Klijn, A.F.J. 107 n. 15, 121 n. 4
Knox, B.M.W. 16
Koester, H. 40 n. 29
Kosinitza 147
Kraeling, C.H. 40 n. 26
Kraft, R.A. 287 n. 1
Küster, L. 38, 209 n. 11
K^x Group 217-51 *passim*

Lachmann, K. 25 n. 1, 151, 153, 160, 163, 200, 209-10, 214, 215, 271, 308, 316 n. 6, 324
Lagrange, M.-J. 41
Lake, A.K. 113 n. 1
Lake, H. 75 n. 9
Lake, K. 46 n. 61, 49, 75 n. 9, 97 n. 10, 113, 155-6
Lake, S. 50, 97 n. 10, 113 n. 1, 156. See also New, S.
Latin versions 5-18 *passim*, 41, 49, 51, 72, 112, 167-95, 333, 335-53
Leclercq, H. 40 n. 25
Lectionary manuscripts 33, 35, 36, 39, 66, 93, 94, 113, 130, 131, 145, 148, 163
– annotations in manuscripts 22, 107
Legg, S.C.E. X, 161-2, 163, 167, 183, 186, 288 n. 4
Liber commicus, the 47
Lietzmann, H. 47, 97 n. 10
Living text 312-3, 327, 331
Liste, the X, 38
Lord's Prayer, text of 194, 266, 308

Lowe, E.A. X, 15, 19, 25 n. 1, 26, 30, 36 n. 10, 105 n. 8, 106 n. 10
Lucan 152
Lucretius 153
Luke, Gospel of 48, 69-72, 111, 217-51, 246, 266, 268, 316, 327
Lupieri, E. 30-1
Luttikhuizen, G.P. 107 n. 15
Lyon, R.W. 50
Lyons 68, 69, 105-6

Mabillon, J. 33
Macaulay, C. 113
MacKenzie, R.S. 5-18
Macrobius 12, n. 11
Maehler, H. 33 n. 2, 41, 43, 44, 115 n. 6, 116-8
Maggs Bros. 94
Mai, A. 90 n. 47
Majuscule 33-4, 42-4, 57, 62, 66, 114-8
Manilius 151
Manson, T.W. 161-2
Manuscripts as bearers of the text 314
Marcion 268, 328
Mark, Gospel of 46-7, 71, 111, 121, 239-40, 266, 268, 315-8, 327, 328
– endings 316, 317, 319
Markan Priority 308, 316
Martini, C.M. XI, XII, 37 n. 13, 48, 200, 261 n. 14
Massoretic Text 254
Matthew, Gospel of 55-63, 71, 111, 240-1, 246-7, 258, 268, 315, 327
Matzkow, W. X
Mayor, J.B. 214-5
Mayvaert, P. 33 n. 1
McGurk, P. 30 n. 16

McLoughlin, D. 272
McReynolds, P.R. 154 n. 20
Mees, M. 52
Melanchthon, P. 352 n. 21
Menander 198
Merk, A. 163-4, 266
Messianic Secret, the 316
Metzger, B.M. XI, XII, 34, 35 n. 6, 45, 107 n. 15, 121, 122 nn., 124 n. 14, 152 n. 8, 161 n. 51, 164, 175 n. 13, 181 n. 19, 186 n. 26, 256 n. 6, 274 n. 2
Mill, J. 37, 69, 209 n. 11, 324, 326
Miller, E. 37 n. 17, 209 n. 11
Milne, H.J.M. XI, 16, 37 n. 12, 50, 298 n. 16
Mimoumi, S. 258 n. 8
Mink, G. X, 204 n. 2, 287 n. 1
Mondesert, C. 40 n. 25
Mondrain, B. 99 n. 15
de Montfaucon, B. 55
Montefiore, H. 282
Montgomery, W. 252 n. 1
Mooney, L.R. 141 n. 8, 301 n. 18
Morrill, M.B. 139 n. 3, 140 n. 7, 289 n. 5
Mosin, V.A. 147 n. 25
Moulton, W.F. 167
Mullen, R.L. 139 n. 3, 294 n. 11
Multiple readings method, the 154, 163
Muñoz, A. 115 n. 7, 118 n. 16
Mussies, G. 89 n. 44

Neutral text-type 46
Nestle, Eb. 110, 163
Nestle Er. 163
Nestle-Aland editions 82 n. 23, 86, 88, 91, 129 n. 18, 163, 184, 201, 203, 204, 214, 215, 217, 258, 265, 266, 271, 295, 299, 300, 328

Neutral text   156
New, S.   46, 156; see also Lake, S.
Niccum, C.   299 n. 17
Nida, E.A.   256 n. 6
Nomina sacra, the   45, 125-6, 185, 305-7
Norsa, M.   41 n. 31

O'Callaghan, J.   45 n. 57
O'Driscoll, C.   139 n. 1
Oecumenius   347
Old Latin Gospels, the   167-95. See also Latin versions
Oliver, J.   93 n. 1, 95
Oral traditions   270-1
Origen   15, 47, 90, 164, 261, 276, 323
Origenian scholia on Revelation   90
Original text, concept of   281-2, 284, 310, 324, 327-9
Orthodoxy, development of   330-1
Orthography   5-18 *passim*, 126-8
Ostraka   39
Outtier, B.   107 n. 15, 121 n. 3
Ovid   165
Oxyrhynchus   331

Paap, A.H.R.E.   45 n. 57
Palaeography   55-63
Palestine
– manuscripts from   118
Papias   268
Papyrology   55-63
Papyrus manuscripts   254, 271
– and the majuscules   45-50
Parker, D.C.   XII, 18, 37 n. 14, 45 n. 57, 49 n. 81, 51 n. 92, 52 nn., 68 n. 1, 103-12 passim, 114, 121 n. 5, 122 n. 8, 123, 124 n. 13, 128 n. 16, 130 n. 19, 139 n. 2, 140 n. 6, 142 n. 9, 140 n. 7, 139 n. 3, 258 n. 9, 265 n. 1, 273 n. 1, 287 n. 1, 289 n. 5, 296 n. 15, 310 n. 5, 312, 320 n. 20, 332 n. 14, 352 n. 21
Parker, T.H.L.   344 n. 10, 350 nn., 351 n. 19
Parvis, M.M.   154
Pasini, C.   20, n. 4
Patristic citations   300
Pauline letters   47, 158-60, 166, 266, 275, 302, 317, 327
Payne, P.   299 n. 17
Pelekasis, D.   93
Perfect, 3rd person plural forms   213-3
Petersen, W.L.   40 n. 29, 41 n. 35
Petrine epistles, text of   47-8
Phillips, C.A.   46 n. 66
Philoxenian version, the   47
Pickering, S.R.   138
Pietersen, W.L.   258
Plato   198
Plumley, J.M.   186 n. 26
Pluperfect, form of in Greek   89
Pocock, N.   113 n. 4
Polanyi, M.   318-20
Principio Project, the   139-43, 288-91, 294, 296-9, 301
Printed texts   260-61, 282, 315, 320, 321
Prosper of Aquitaine   36
Pulieva, D.   139 n. 1

Q source of the Gospels   254, 269, 296
Quantitative Relationship analysis   48
Quentin, H.   155
Quire signatures in Latin manuscripts   28
Qumran   254-5

3. Index of Names and Subjects

Raguenier, D.   351
Rand, E.K.   155
Reuss, E.   161, 346 n. 14
Revelation, Book of   47, 73-92
Rhodes, E.F.   IX
Rhône valley   68
Rice, G.E.   52
Richard, M.   147 n. 24
Roberts, C.H.   15, 40, 45 n. 57, 61, 269 n. 11
Robinson, J.A.   353
Robinson, P.M.R.   141, 289, 301 n. 18
Roca-Puig, R.   124, 124 n. 14
Roll format, the   260-61, 268-9, 302
Romans   335-53
Ropes, J.H.   41, 46, 332, 333 n. 16
Rowland, C.   311 n., 320
Ruling in Latin manuscripts   25-32 *passim*
Rustic capital   51
Rutgers, L.V.   121 n. 2

Salonius, A.H.   41 n. 37
Sanday, W.   25-32 *passim*
Sanders, H.A.   46
Schlossnikel R.F.   51
Schmid, J.   47, 73-92
Schmid, U.B.   130 n. 19, 139 n. 3, 260, 289 n. 5
Schmitz F.-J.   39 n. 24
Schrage, W.   68 n. 1, 104 n. 3
Schubart, W.   43
Schweitzer, A.   252-3, 257
Scrivener, F.H.(A.)   37 n. 17, n. 18, 69, 107 n. 13, 113, 186 n. 27, 191 n. 30, 204 n. 2, 209 n. 11
Second-century text, the   328
Seitz, C.   318
Septuagint, the   254-5, 259, 302
Sevenster, J.N.   329 n. 11

Sextus Empiricus   214
Sharpe, J.L.   329 n. 11
Shillingsburg, P.   287 n. 1
Sicily   106
Sidon   106
Singular readings   16, 186
Sirletto, G.   68
Skeat, T.C.   XI, 15, 16, 37 n. 12, n. 15, 50, 151, 269 n. 11, 298 n. 16
Slaby, W.A.   167
Sloping pointed majuscule   44
Smith, A.M.   94
Snodgrass, K.   158
Sofia, manuscripts in   139, 145-8
Sokoloff, M.   35 n. 8
Souter, A.   12
Sparks, I.A.   154 n. 20
Spencer, M.   141 n. 8, 301 n. 18
Stegmüller, O.   123
Stemma Group, the   301
Stephanus, R.   37, 105, 204, 348
Stevenson, J.   268 n. 10
Stojanov, M.   145
Stone, R.C.   13, 167
Streeter, B.H.   152, 155, 156, 157, 161, 164
Stuttgart Vulgate, the   20-3
Swanson, R.J.   332, 333 n. 16
Syria   68
– manuscripts from   107, 118
Syriac versions of the Bible   72, 112, 181, 254, 274 n. 2, 275, 277, 281, 306, 333

Talismans   39
Tănăsoiu, C.   139 n. 1, 143 n. 12
Tatian   39, 40, 268, 308, 328
Telford, W.R.   316 n. 8
Ten Orators, the   198
Terence   165

Text Encoding Initiative, the 298
text-types, theory of 199
Textual criticism 151-66, 197-201, 265-72
– globally 254-6
– in Orthodoxy 259-60
Textual history 103, 199, 246, 257-9, 267, 319, 331
Text und Textwert 204, 217-51, 289, 301
Textus Receptus, the 161, 164, 199, 217, 254, 257, 265, 324
Theologically motivated variation 53, 258-9, 309, 325, 329-30
Theophylact of Achrida 148, 316
Thiede, C.P. 55-63
Thiele, W. 168 n. 11, 173 n. 12, 178 n. 14
Thomas of Harkel 46
Thucydides 198
Tinkle, T. 287 n. 1
Tischendorf, C. 25-32 *passim*, 35 n. 8, 36 n. 12, 38, 50, 69, 75, 82 n. 23, 113 n. 3, 163, 167, 183, 203, 205, 214, 215, 265, 288 n. 3, 324, 348
Torrance, I.R. 318-20
Tov, E. 62 n. 9, 254 n. 3
Traljic, S.M. 147 n. 25
Transcription 38, 50, 141, 288-92, 333
Traube, L. 45, 185 n. 25
Tregelles, S.P. 113, 114 n. 5, 119, 160, 210-2, 214-5, 216, 324
Trent, Council of 68
Treu, K. 41, 123
Trinitarian Bible Society text 265
Trobisch, D. 259, 307 n. 2
Tugearu, L. 143 nn.
Turner, C.H. 25 n. 1, 198
Turner, E.G. 16, 42, 43, 124 n. 12

Tyndale, W. 177

Uncial 33
United Bible Societies 114, 164, 165, 183-4, 259-60, 294
Upright pointed majuscule 114, 116-8

Vaganay, L. 153, 154, 166
van Unnik, W.C. 329 n. 11
van der Horst, P.W. 121, 124 n. 14
van der Woude, A.S. 107 n. 15
Vatican paragraph sections 66
Versions of the New Testament 300, 310. See also individual versions
Vezin, J. 105 n. 8
Victor of Antioch 316
Vikan, G. 93 n. 4
Villa, F. 20, n. 4
Vitelli, G. 41 n. 31
Vogels, H.J. 194, 199, 266
von Dobschütz, E. 35 n. 8, 38
von Harnack, A. 90
von Soden, H. 25 n. 1, n. 2, 78 n. 15, 218 n. 6, 220 n. 17, 221 n. 21, 266
Vulgate, the 167-95, 335-53 *passim*
– orthography of 5-18 *passim*
Vulgatisation 349

Wachtel, K. X, 140 n. 5, 217, 220 n. 13, n. 14, 222 n. 27, 248 n. 52, 249 n. 54, 287 n. 1
Walker, J. 288
Walther, O.K. 51 n. 91
Walton, B. 37
Watson, F. 318, 320
Webster, J. 321
Weeden, T.H. 316 n. 8
Weiss, B. 163

Weitzmann, K.   95, 305
Weitzman, M.P.   34
Welles, C.B.   40 n. 26
Welte, M.   93 n. 3
Westcott, B.F.   XII, 89 n. 44, 151-6, 160, 161, 163, 164, 198, 199, 200, 204, 206-8, 212, 214, 215, 266, 271, 288 n. 4, 308, 324, 325
Western Non-Interpolations   158
Western text-type   45, 46, 47, 156, 156-8, 159-60, 164, 166, 199
Wettstein, J.J.   37 n. 16, 38, 69, 82 n. 23
Whitby, D.   324
White, H.J.   6, 20, 25-32 *passim*, 167, 177, 336 n. 3
Wikgren, A.   XI, XII
Willard, L.C.   45
Williams, C.S.C.   309 n. 4
Willis, J.   5-18 *passim*
Wilson, J.M.   108 n. 17, 267 n. 8

Wilson, N.   97 n. 11
Wisse, F.   140 n. 4, 154 n. 20, 217-51
Witte, K.   140 n. 5, 204 n. 2, 217, 220 n. 13
Wolf, F.A.   151
Wordsworth, J.   6, 20, 25-32 *passim*, 167, 177, 336 n. 3
Wrede, W.   316

Yahalom, J.   35 n. 8
Yoder, J.D.   167
Young, F.   323 n. 1
Young, R.   181

Zacagni, L.A.   45
Zante   113, 118
Zoumboulakis, B.   95
Zuntz, G.   XII, 47, 158-61, 165-6, 267 n. 7, 292, 327

www.ingramcontent.com/pod-product-compliance
Lightning Source LLC
Chambersburg PA
CBHW050850160426
43194CB00011B/2093